WILBERFORCE

William Wilberforce

From the unfinished portrait by Sir Thomas Lawrence P.R.A.
in the National Portrait Gallery

WILBERFORCE

by

SIR REGINALD COUPLAND

K.C.M.G., C.I.E., HON. D.LITT. (Durham)

FELLOW OF ALL SOULS COLLEGE
BEIT PROFESSOR OF COLONIAL HISTORY
IN THE UNIVERSITY OF OXFORD

Second Edition

Collins

FOURTEEN ST. JAMES'S PLACE · LONDON

1945

First Edition, 1923.
New Edition, 1945.

C 6127557-3

306305

B/wil

COPYRIGHT
PRINTED IN GREAT BRITAIN
COLLINS CLEAR-TYPE PRESS : LONDON AND GLASGOW

Contents

Frontispiece

WILLIAM WILBERFORCE
From the unfinished portrait by Sir Thomas Lawrence

I

Youth

ON March 25, 1784, a great public meeting was held in the Castle Yard at York. More than most English counties, Yorkshire was interested in politics, and politics at that moment were more than usually interesting. The crisis was approaching in the strange parliamentary battle between the Fox-North Coalition which George III, by the least unwise of his constitutional adventures, had thrown out of office in the previous December and the young, untried Prime Minister whom he had appointed in its place. Public opinion had long been hardened to the cynicism of eighteenth-century political life. Every one knew that the making and unmaking of Governments were dictated by personal interests, by the concert or conflict of individual ambitions, by the intrigues of the great families, by the King's masterfulness or caprice, by anything rather than the welfare of the nation. But there was something novel and refreshing, something almost suggestive of a new political era, in Pitt's appointment. He was, of course, absurdly young—he was only twenty-four—but he was Chatham's son; and like Chatham, he was not closely tied to the old oligarchy of great families, and like Chatham, he had not gone into politics to make money for himself or for his friends. Three years of political apprenticeship, moreover, had proved him the possessor of great parliamentary gifts—a cool head and, for his age, an astonishing self-assurance; a skill and weight in argument that made him already a match for any veteran in the House of Commons; and an eloquence, not indeed as inspired, as overwhelming as his father's—colder, stiffer, prosier—but fluent and logical and convincing. He was obviously an interesting, an attractive figure, this new young man, so capable and with such hereditary claims. At the start the electors were willing enough to support him, within the limits of good electoral business; and in a few weeks' time he had made himself positively popular. It was not only that his bold and lonely stand against almost all the experience, prestige, and debating power in the House had appealed to English instincts. Fox had made one of the worst blunders of his career. He had denounced Pitt's maintenance of office against the will of the Commons and at the same time done all he could to prevent him taking the verdict of those of whom the Commons were but the representatives. To all his enemies' assaults, therefore, to their repeated votes of censure, to their address to the King for the removal of Ministers, to the rejection of his first big Government measure, Pitt could make a confident reply. His constitutional position might indeed be irregular: Fox might even threaten him with impeachment; but, with increasing certainty as those stormy weeks went by, he could assert that, if the House were against him, the people were on his side. At last the time was ripe, and the machine was ready, for this assertion to be tested. On March 24 Parliament was dissolved. The subsequent election was not conducted, as has often been supposed, on a new and purer system. The "influence" of the King and of the Whig nobles flowed along its well-known channels; and the great commercial houses made a special effort at corruption. But corruption, as a Tory chronicler admitted, "for once became almost unnecessary." The electors returned Pitt to power with a great majority; and save for one brief interval, he stayed there for the rest of his life.

It was on the day after the dissolution and before the news of it had reached the North that some thousands of the electors of Yorkshire—yeomen, clothiers, squires, county magnates—had poured into York to hear the issue of the hour publicly debated, according to custom, by the rival spokesmen of the Coalition and of the King's young Minister. It was a bleak wintry day. A gale of wind, with occasional storms of hail, swept through the Yard. Yet from ten in the morning till late in the afternoon the huge crowd stood patiently listening to the oratorical contest. At last, however, even those sturdy Yorkshiremen had begun to weary of the verbiage and the weather when suddenly their attention was recaptured. The young Member for Hull had climbed on to the speakers' table— a figure so youthful and slightly built that it seemed, said an observer, as if it would be unable to make head against the violence of the storm. But Wilberforce kept his feet; and, whereas several previous speakers had been hardly audible in the uproar, his exceptionally musical and well-pitched voice penetrated to the farthest fringes of the crowd. "He spoke like an angel," said one of its members: and, though the speech lasted over an hour, from the first sentence to the last the young orator held the whole meeting in chains. It chanced that Boswell was there, and Dr. Johnson's biographer was a well-schooled critic. "I saw," he reported to Dundas, "what seemed a mere shrimp mount upon the table; but, as I listened, he grew, and grew, until the shrimp became a whale."

In the course of the speech a note was handed to the speaker. It had just arrived by a special messenger who had started on horseback from London two days before. "Dear Wilberforce," it ran, "Parliament will be prorogued to-day and dissolved to-morrow. . . . I send you a copy of the speech which will be made in a few hours from the Throne. . . . You must take care to keep all our friends together, and *to tear the enemy to pieces.* . . . Ever faithfully yours, W. Pitt." A less skilful speaker might have been disconcerted by this interruption, but not Wilberforce. In half a minute he had mastered the contents of the note, and in the next he was telling his audience the great news that Pitt had appealed to the people. It was a dramatic stroke, and the speech ended in a clamour of applause. It had not been merely the best speech of the day : it had won the hearts of the Yorkshire freeholders. "We'll have this little man for our county member," they shouted: and, true enough, despite the seeming futility of a young man quite unconnected with the great local families disputing one of the seats for the county with the nominees of the Cavendishes and Fitzwilliams and Carlisles, Wilberforce and his colleague, Duncombe, obtained such a "vast majority" at the show of hands at the election that the magnates accepted their defeat without asking for a poll. And the price of the victory was the small one—for those days—of less than £5000. "I can never enough congratulate you on such glorious success," wrote Pitt.

2

Born in the same year, 1759, Pitt and Wilberforce had become acquainted as undergraduates at Cambridge, but no more than acquainted. In University standing Pitt, who had come into residence at the precocious age of fourteen, was three years Wilberforce's senior. They were at different colleges—Pitt at Pembroke, Wilberforce at St. John's—and they were not thrown together by

similar pursuits. Pitt was a not unworthy member of a college
which he described as "a sober staid college, and nothing but solid
study there." He solidly studied Thucydides and Polybius and the
ancient orators commended to him by his father, and ranged beyond
them over the whole field of Greek and Roman literature; he translated obscure classics and wrote classical verses with equal facility;
and he studied mathematics and astronomy and Shakespeare and
civil law. But Wilberforce, at any rate in his first years when he
overlapped with Pitt, was making a different use of Cambridge. He
had no Chatham to supervise his training: he had lost his father
when he was eight years old. He had more money to spend than
Pitt; for his father, a successful merchant in the Baltic trade at
Hull, had left his family well provided for, and his father's elder
brother, who had a house in London and a villa at Wimbledon, had
promised to make nephew William his heir. And he was unfortunate in the atmosphere he found awaiting him at St. John's.
Years afterwards, when his views of life were far more serious, he
spoke rather bitterly of his first companions. "On the very first
night of my arrival I was introduced to as licentious a set of men
as can well be conceived. They were in the habit of drinking hard,
and their conversation was in perfect accordance with their principles. Though often mingling in their parties, I never relished their
society—indeed I was often horror-struck at their conduct, and felt
miserable." At the end of the year he drifted away from this set, and
thenceforward he was taken up by the fellows of his college. But
his afterthoughts of those dons were scarcely kindlier. "Their object
seemed to be to make and keep me idle. If I occasionally appeared
studious, they would say to me, 'Why in the world should a man
of great fortune trouble himself with fagging?' I was a good
classic, and acquitted myself well in some of our examinations; but
I greatly neglected mathematical lectures and was often told that,
being so quick of apprehension, it was needless for me to toil." In
the Universities, as in the Church, there were plenty of men in those
days who did no justice to their vocation; and, though something
perhaps should be discounted from the stern judgments of the older
Wilberforce, it is to be feared that some of the dons at St. John's did
their best to spoil the wealthy and attractive young man. They
frequently invited him to play cards with them: they petted him
and praised his gifts: they even declared, in his hearing, that men
who "were fagging hard and constantly attended lectures" were

"mere saps, but that he did everything by real talent." So he had little inducement and no natural desire to shut himself up in his rooms and work. Indeed he hated being alone. If he could not play cards, at least he must talk. And there were usually plenty of undergraduates ready to come and talk, and eat "the great Yorkshire pie" which was always to be found in his rooms. As a last resort he could rout out the man who lived next door, a studious man, a "mere sap" indeed, called Gisborne. Often after a hard day's work, when he was raking out his fire at ten o'clock, bent on early sleep and a good start next day, Gisborne would hear Wilberforce's "melodious voice calling aloud to me to come and sit with him before I went to bed." "It was a dangerous thing to do," he adds, "for his amusing conversation was sure to keep me up so late that I was behindhand the next morning."

It was not Cambridge, then, but London and politics that brought Wilberforce and Pitt together. Wilberforce had soon determined not to bury himself in the family business at Hull. The obvious career, he thought, for an English gentleman of parts and leisure lay in the House of Commons; and it was easy enough for him, with his wealth and his local position, to get there. His family had been originally settled in the township of Wilberfoss, eight miles east of York. In the seventeenth century it had moved to Beverley, where a William Wilberfoss was mayor at the time of the Civil War, and later to Hull. The great-grandson of the mayor of Beverley, another William and the first to spell his surname, Wilberforce, was twice mayor of Hull; and in his old age he would tell his little grandson, the William of this narrative, great stories of his past—how the Duke of Marlborough, no less, had invited him to come out to Flanders and witness an approaching battle from a neighbouring hill, an offer which the prudent merchant had declined; and how in 1745 the news had come to Hull that the young Pretender was in England and the north country up in arms, and how the mayor had set his townsfolk to strengthen the defences of the arsenal. Our William's father, too, had been a highly respected citizen of Hull; and with such a local tradition—and with a little expenditure of money—the present representative of the family, young as he was, might make a confident bid for the votes of the Hull electors. So, early in 1780, before indeed he had come of age, Wilberforce made his preliminary canvass, shook hands with Johnny Bell, the butcher, and all the rest, and then drove off to London to lay siege to the affections of the three hundred free-men of Hull who lived on Thames-side. Great suppers were held at sundry public-houses in Wapping; and amid the candles and the beer Wilberforce would get on his feet and beguile his simple, seafaring guests with his Yorkshire patriotism and a voice so beautiful that it was soon to win him the title of "the nightingale of the House of Commons."

A useful training this for politics; still better the long nights spent in the gallery at Westminster, listening to the historic debates on the American War, to North's cool and capable defence of the King's disastrous policy, to Burke's eloquence and Fox's passion. It was all intensely interesting, intensely attractive. Night after night he haunted the gallery, and night after night he found Pitt there. For Pitt, too, was serving his apprenticeship in politics. On taking his degree in 1776 he had gone into chambers at Lincoln's Inn and was now about to be called to the Bar. But this was nothing but a step to Parliament; and like Wilberforce, but without his local or financial advantages, he was already thinking of a seat. It was in the gallery of the House of Commons, then, that the Cambridge acquaintance began to ripen into intimacy. They were not senior or junior now, in different colleges and cliques, but fellow apprentices, almost exactly of an age, bent on the same career. And, almost inevitably, their politics were the same. If Wilberforce had sat up there alone, it is probable enough that his very youth and his vivacious, adventurous spirits would have enlisted him on the Opposition side against North's placid majority and a policy already darkened with the shadows of humiliation and defeat by Saratoga and the French alliance. But with Chatham's son beside him, burning with detestation of the whole American war and of his father's enemies who made it, never forgetting the dreadful day when he had listened to his father's last faltering protest in the Lords, run to his side when he fell back fainting in his seat, and helped to carry him away—with the younger Pitt beside him, it was impossible for Wilberforce to be anything but an opponent of the Government and the war. He was included, therefore, with other young politicians who were already looking to Pitt as their leader, with Eliot and Bankes and Pepper Arden and Grenville and some twenty others, in the new and small and exceedingly select political club which established itself, in the course of 1780, in the premises of a certain Goosetree in Pall Mall

—"a society of young Ministers," George Selwyn sarcastically called it, "who are to fight under Pitt's banner."

Suppers and long talks at Goosetree's, when the House was up, brought Pitt and Wilberforce still closer to each other. They were sufficiently alike and sufficiently unlike to make the best of friends. Both had been so delicate from early childhood as to cause continual anxiety to their parents. Even the American colonists had scarcely worried Chatham more than the fear lest his precocious William, fortified though he was with poisonous quantities of port, should overstrain himself. And Wilberforce had been so tiny, so feeble, with weak eyesight inherited from his mother and a quite inadequate digestion, that he seriously thanked God, in after days, that he had not come into the world "in less civilised times, when it would have been thought impossible to rear so delicate a child." Pitt was taller than Wilberforce: but he was not so very much bigger or broader; and if nobody called him a "shrimp," it was chiefly because he held himself stiffly erect while Wilberforce had early acquired the rounded shoulders and the bent, peering posture of the short-sighted man. And they were alike in other things than physique—in their intellectual eagerness and subtlety, their love of literature as well as politics, their passion for talk and the ready wit that irradiated it, and in a natural refinement which kept them from the uglier pastimes of young London. Yet they were very different. Pitt's was the cooler temper. He was earnest rather than ardent, resolute rather than enthusiastic. No sparks—and no smoke either—rose from that clear, steady fire. But Wilberforce was impulsive and emotional, easily exalted, easily depressed. He could show at need, indeed, a courage and a patience no less stubborn than Pitt's; he was never a weak man; but there was something of gentleness and sweetness in his character, something of almost womanly grace and sensibility, which gave him a charm denied to Pitt. Both of them could still be frivolous; but Pitt was shy and reserved with strangers—almost superciliously aloof, he seemed to some; he kept his laughter for children and his intimates; while Wilberforce, who could laugh—and cry—more easily, was almost as voluble and sportive in the coldest company as with his friends. All in all, they were a wonderful pair of young men, so attractive, so gifted, with such historic lives ahead of them; and for two or three years, at any rate, they were more closely drawn to one another than to any one else. If it was never quite the same afterwards as in those first years in the gallery of the House and at Goosetree's, still, for Wilberforce at any rate, if not in the same degree for Pitt, their friendship remained to the end one of the things that most mattered in their lives.

3

In the early autumn of 1780 Wilberforce returned to Hull to celebrate his coming of age on August 24. It was a great day in the town and for the local candidate for its seat. All and sundry were invited to attend the feast, and an ox was roasted whole in one of Wilberforce's fields. As his biographers put it, "the election opportunely followed." Despite the opposition of the Rockingham "interest," of Sir George Savile and of the King's Government, the result was almost a foregone conclusion. Wilberforce belonged to Hull like his fathers before him, he was personally very popular indeed—and he spent between eight and nine thousand pounds. He received 1126 votes: his two opponents exactly the same number between them.

At the same election Pitt stood for Cambridge University, a seat he hankered after, partly because it was honourable and independent and partly because it was cheap. He was defeated; but, before the year was up, Sir James Lowther, monarch of Cumberland, made him a present of the borough of Appleby. And so, in January, 1781, the alliance which had been struck up in the gallery was transferred to the floor of the House. Of the two, Pitt quickly took the lead. Within a few weeks he had proved his heredity with a maiden speech on financial reform, which Burke declared to be not a chip merely, but the old block itself, which Lord North described as the best speech he had ever heard, and which prompted Fox to "put up" the orator forthwith for Brooks's. In the following May he made an even abler speech on the audit of public accounts. This "famous speech," wrote Wilberforce to a friend at Hull, "did not convince me, and I staid in with the old fat fellow" (Lord North to wit). But in the same letter he described Pitt as "a ready-made orator." "I doubt not but that I shall, one day or other, see him the first man in the country." The day soon came. In June Pitt delivered a violent attack on the American War, and in December he drove home the fatal news of Yorktown and demanded immediate peace. Six months later, at the age of twenty-three, he was appointed Chancellor of the Exchequer in Shelburne's Government. A year and a half more, and he was Prime Minister. With so swift a rocket Wilberforce, for all his talents, could scarcely keep pace. But at every stage of the advance he was at Pitt's back; his vote and his voice almost, if not (as has been seen) quite, always at Pitt's service. His maiden speech, on May 17, was a brief attack on the revenue laws, introducing a petition of protest from Hull ; his second speech a light essay in criticism of the Government's failure to increase the navy, with a note on Hull's capacity for building ships. Thus for a year, it seems, he watched and waited; but in 1782 he let himself go. Speaking on General Conway's motion for putting an end to the war, he told Ministers that they were more like furious lunatics than prudent statesmen and had conducted the war in "a cruel, bloody and impracticable manner." It is probable that at this period he spoke more often, it is certain that he spoke better, than the few and brief reports in Hansard suggest. At any rate he had made his mark by the time the North Ministry collapsed; and when Rockingham was in office, so strong was the rumour about town that Wilberforce was shortly to be included in the Government, with a seat in the Upper House, that several tradesmen requested his custom for the supply of peer's robes. If such a plan was really in Rockingham's mind—and certainly he made himself very agreeable to the eloquent upstart who had beaten his own nominee at Hull —he did not live long enough to execute it; and Shelburne, his successor, was satisfied with securing the abler of the two young allies. But Pitt could still count on Wilberforce's support; and it was at Pitt's request that he seconded the Address on the Preliminaries of Peace. Already there was talk of the impending Coalition; and, the rumour having been confirmed by Bankes whom he met on his way to the House, Wilberforce took occasion in his speech to denounce what he regarded as an infamous intrigue. And when it materialised, when the Coalition was in power and Pitt left in the cold, he made a series of fiery and not ineffective attacks on Fox and North. The report of his speech on Fox's ill-fated India Bill may be quoted in full. "Mr. Wilberforce answered Mr. Burke, and with humour and ability compared the seven Commissioners and eight Directors to seven physicians and eight apothecaries come to put the patient to death *secundum artem*. After laughing with this idea he became more serious and said he wished that in the end, if the present Bill passed, we might not see the Government of Great Britain set up in India instead of that of India in Great Britain." A few days later he made a more personal assault on Fox. Once the country had believed in him, he said, but now that he had joined hands with North, he had lost its trust; and then, with that silvery resonant voice, he declaimed Satan's famous greeting to Beelzebub in Hell: "But O how fall'n, how chang'd, from him who in the happy Realms of Light . . ."

Wilberforce, in fact, was thoroughly enjoying himself. He had found his feet in the House. He had proved himself too clever and too eloquent to be snubbed or ridiculed. He could be as offensive as he liked, in the best parliamentary manner, to any one on the Government bench. And soon it was still more pleasantly exciting. For, presently, he was on the Government bench himself, not indeed a Minister, but almost the only ready and attractive speaker—for Dundas was neither—whom the young Prime Minister could call to his aid in his unequal battle with the ousted Coalition. He had naturally been one of the inner circle about Pitt throughout the crisis that brought him into power. "Lord Temple resigned," notes his diary for November 22: "No dissolution declared. Drove about for Pitt"; and for the 23rd, "Morning Pitt's . . . Pitt nobly firm." "We had a great meeting that night," he afterwards recalled, "of all Pitt's friends in Downing St. . . . I remember well the great penetration showed by Lord Mahon. 'What am I to do,' said Pitt, 'if they stop the supplies?' 'They will not stop them,' said Mahon, 'it is the very thing they will not venture to do.'" Anxiously the little clique awaited the meeting of Parliament in January: and on the very first day Wilberforce's gloves were off and his heart on his sleeve. "My right honourable friend," he said, "did not look up to ease and emolument solely, as the right honourable gentleman opposite to him did, when he came into office. He is another sort of patriot. He considered the good of his country and the salvation of the constitution as matters of infinitely greater moment than his own personal interests." "Mr. Wilberforce," adds Hansard, dryly, "pursued his panegyric for some minutes in terms of great eloquence." A fortnight later he roundly asserted that there was nothing unconstitutional in the circumstances of the Coalition's dismissal and Pitt's appointment. Were all those noble lords who voted against the India Bill to be charged with servile obedience to the royal wishes? And what had it to do, in any case, with the appointment of the present Government? "If the India Bill had passed the Lords with as great a majority as it did the Commons, I should still have thanked the Crown for dismissing the late Ministers." But Wilberforce could do better than that. His speech in the debate on March 1 on the Address for the removal of Ministers was in a quieter and more rational vein—a capable exposition of the only valid constitutional defence that could be made for George III and Pitt. Wisely treating the dismissal of Fox and North as past history, he concentrated on the present facts. It was clear, he argued, from the stream of addresses daily flowing in from all parts of the country, that the Government and not the majority of the House of Commons possessed the confidence of the people; and the policy of the Coalition was to make the Government's position impossible, to force the King to change it, without considering the people's will. He confessed that, not long ago, he had voted with Fox, "whose abilities every one with discernment must admire," when he was trying to reduce the undue influence of the Crown by abolishing certain places and pensions. But the Constitution might just as easily be undone by the undue influence of a corrupt majority of the House of Commons. A despotic faction in the Commons, unsupported by the people, could not only destroy the just preroga- tive of the crown but subvert the very pillars of our freedom : and were not many tyrants worse than one ?

A few weeks later came the General Election of 1784; and when Wilberforce took his seat for the new session, he had become, as one of the members for Yorkshire, a very important person in the House, second only in importance to Ministers and the Opposition chiefs. But it was no longer quite such an exciting game. He attended very regularly: he was immensely interested in the daily ebb and flow of party conflict: but to fight for Pitt in a minority had been far more thrilling than it was to stand at ease among his safe majority. Nor was there much to rouse his youthful ardour in the quiet measures, mainly financial, by which Pitt began his great work of nursing England back to strength after the crushing losses of the American War. His vote, of course, was still always at Pitt's command; but for the next two years he seems to have taken an active part only in two questions—Reform and Ireland. With Reform the member for Yorkshire was necessarily concerned. For Yorkshire was the cradle of the movement. Christopher Wyvill was as deep-rooted a Yorkshireman as Wilberforce himself; and the

W. B

meeting and petition he organised in 1779 and his foundation of
the Yorkshire Association in 1780 had been the first steps in the
mobilisation of public opinion for its fifty-years' campaign. Naturally, therefore, Wilberforce, as he reminded Fox, had supported
Burke's measures of "economical reform"; and he had voted with
the minority for Pitt's first proposal for "parliamentary reform"
in 1782. And now that Pitt was in office and faced with the hazardous
duty of pressing his Reform ideas on a following by no means
unitedly or eagerly in favour of them, Wilberforce was one of the
few on whose assistance he could safely count. Thus, when Wyvill
and his colleagues grew impatient and when Alderman Sawbridge,
in the summer of 1784, tried to draw Pitt on with a motion of his
own, Wilberforce, speaking "as a hearty and zealous well-wisher to
a parliamentary reform," seconded Pitt's plea for a few months'
more delay. By mid-winter Pitt was ready to move, and he wrote
off to Wilberforce, who was spending Christmas with his family at
Nice, to warn him that his presence would be needed. "I have some
remorse," he says, "in the immediate occasion of my writing to
you just now, which, however, all things considered, I am bound
to overcome. Be it known to you, then, that, as much as I wish you
to bask on under an Italian sun, I am perhaps likely to be the instrument of snatching you from your present paradise and hurrying
you back to ' the rank vapours of this sin-worn mould.'" He intends,
he goes on, to fix a day early in February for the introduction of
his Bill. "I would not for a thousand reasons have you absent,
though I hate that you should come before your time; and if any
particular circumstances make a week or ten days a matter of real
importance to you, I think I could postpone it as long as that.
Only let me hear from you positively before the meeting of Parliament." Although other things than politics, as will be seen, were
now already beginning to occupy Wilberforce's mind, he at once
responded to this summons; but he was obstructed by snow-drifts
and dangerous roads in the hills of Burgundy, and he only arrived
in London on February 22. He was in plenty of time. Parliament
had been sitting since January 25, but it was not till April 18 that
Pitt moved for leave to introduce his Bill. His plan, though it
completely satisfied Wyvill, was by no means revolutionary. It
merely provided for the establishment of a public fund for the
gradual purchase of thirty-six "rotten boroughs" from their present
proprietors and for the distribution of the seventy-two seats thus

obtained to increase the representation of London, Westminster, the counties, and the new and wholly unrepresented big towns. Wilberforce duly spoke in its support. It was not a great speech: he thought it bad himself: but its main point is interesting in view of the line he was presently to take in politics. The chief merit of the plan, he argued, was the effect it would have on the party system which was largely maintained by the corrupt use of the "rotten boroughs." "By destroying them, the freedom of opinion would be restored, and party connexions in a great measure vanish . . . and for his part, he wished to see the time when he could come into the House and give his vote divested of any sentiments of attachment which should induce him to approve of measures from his connexion with men." But there were too many enemies of Reform in any shape on both sides of the House for even this mild measure to pass. Leave to introduce the Bill was refused by a majority of 74. "Terribly disappointed and beat," comments Wilberforce in his diary; "extremely fatigued—spoke extremely ill, but commended." And next day: "Called at Pitt's—met poor Wyvill."

On the Irish Question the member for Yorkshire was in a far more difficult position. In the West Riding lay the centre of the English woollen industry as well as important ironworks and many allied businesses; and the British manufacturing interest as a whole was up in arms against Pitt's proposal to establish equal trade between Britain and Ireland. But Wilberforce's allegiance to Yorkshire came second to his allegiance to Pitt. He was "extremely anxious" as to the political risk Pitt was running. He suggested to him that the matter might well be postponed. He dreaded, he told him, a conflict between the Irish Parliament and the Irish nation or a conflict between the Irish and British Parliaments, especially in view of the "unprincipled and mischievous" Opposition. "God bless you, my dear Pitt, and carry you thro' all your difficulties!" But, finding Pitt firm, he supported him with a long and closely argued defence of his "propositions." He could not, of course, make light of the manufacturers' apprehensions of Irish competition; he confessed, indeed, in his diary how much it pained him to differ from his constituents; but he suggested that experience would not bear those apprehensions out. The cheapness of Irish labour would be more than compensated by the greater skill, ingenuity, and, above all, the greater capital of British manufacturers. And he warned the Opposition to remember the other side

of the case, the safety of the market for British goods in Ireland.
"For I know," he said, "that, if anything were to interrupt the
harmony between the two nations, this would be the first point at
which Ireland would suffer her jealousy to operate." Protective
duties, he continued, had already been talked of in Ireland; and
perhaps their actual imposition had only been delayed by the introduction of these new proposals. And then he took higher ground.
"I trust," he said, "that these propositions will manifest to Ireland
that we consider her not with the jealousy of a rival but with the
affection of a sister kingdom, and that mutual confidence and goodwill will produce a unity of effort for the promotion of the common
welfare of both countries. And that would infinitely repay us for
any sacrifices we are now asked to make." It was true enough. If
Pitt's scheme had succeeded, something at least would have been
done to appease the tormented spirit of Irish nationalism. But it
was not yet appeased; and Fox could easily evoke its quick instinctive jealousy in order to thwart the Government plan. So on the
Irish Question, as on Reform, the first shoots of Pitt's young
liberalism were promptly nipped and withered. He was compelled
so drastically to amend his proposals at Westminster, that they
were bound to be rejected at Dublin.

When Parliament rose that summer, the first phase of Wilberforce's political career had ended. A new force was beginning to
work on him—a force that was to change his views of politics and
of everything else. But those five years had given to his politics a
colour that they could never lose. They had been years of the closest
intimacy with Pitt. It had been something more than friendship,
it had been a brotherhood-in-arms, especially in those unforgettable
first months of 1784. And inevitably the more adult mind, the mind
that had been trained so long and anxiously for politics and politics
alone, had captured the younger mind, the mind that had so far
never troubled about politics at all. Wilberforce, in fact, had become
the first of the Pittites, and in the root-principles of his politics he
remained a Pittite to the end. But there was an important distinction between Wilberforce and the Pittites of a later generation.
Their hero was the Pitt who fought Napoleon, his the Pitt of 1781
to 1785.

4

Indeed, to fight for Pitt and his new party, with the comfortable assurance that Pitt's supremacy was quite essential to the welfare of the country, was all that politics yet meant to Wilberforce. It was not a highly serious business, not very much more than a fine intellectual game; and as a regular occupation it accorded admirably with the rest of his London life. It was a crowded, varied, exciting, fatiguing life. To be lonely or dull or at a loss for amusement, mental or physical, were impossibilities for a young man in his "twenties" whose means and manners and county standing had won him easy entrance into "Society" in the reign of George III—that brilliant, cultured, extravagant, restless, tireless Society, with its magnificent homes in town and country, its august oligarchic chiefs, its political dames, its *beaux* and reigning beauties; riding, hunting, shooting, dining, dancing, gambling, flirting; out-of-doors all day and up all night, starting with the opera or the play, and on to a midnight masquerade at Ranelagh or Soho Square; modish but quick to change, arrogant but open-minded, many-sided but not unbalanced, not "enthusiastic," not running to extremes; laughing at the new sobriety and thrift at Court, but almost as disdainful of the vulgar excesses of York House; bent on wresting from every hurrying hour all the pleasure it could give to mind and body. Into this aloof, compact little world Wilberforce had plunged with gusto. He had enjoyed his popularity in Yorkshire where, especially after his election for the county, he was a leading social figure, a faithful patron of race meetings and horse shows, a marked man at the county ball. But London left Yorkshire in the shade ; and in London he was scarcely less popular. Society opened its arms to this attractive, responsive little man from the North. If he was shy, he did not show it; and he was never *gauche* or dumb. He was ready, indeed, to talk and laugh with any one in the world. He was a godsend to anxious hostesses. His boyish spirits, his unextinguishable merriment, could melt the iciest company. And he had some valuable drawing-room accomplishments. He was an admirable mimic. His caricature of a speech by Lord North, of its substance as well as its delivery, never failed to bring down the house till his old godfatherly friend, Lord Camden, warned him that mimicry was a dangerous habit for a young politician. And his wonderful voice, untrained though it was, made him a moving singer of parlour-ballads. "We must have you again," they told him at Devonshire House after a *soirée* at which he had first met the Prince of Wales; "the Prince says he will come at any time to hear you sing." He often sang in public in Yorkshire "to please his constituents." So he was very soon right inside the magic circle and very much at home there—equally at ease with statesmen and duchesses and actresses, and they with him. He dined with Fox two or three times and found him "very pleasant and unaffected." Like the other young bloods, he sat at the feet of Mrs. Crewe and burned his incense to Mrs. Siddons. The beautiful Duchess of Gordon, who raised the regiment of Gordon Highlanders, it was said, by giving each recruit a shilling from her mouth, was a frequent guest in his house. He was a member of five fashionable clubs and was very soon an habitual and ardent participator in the gambling which was then the rage in them. "I remember the first day I went to Brooks's," he recalled, many years afterwards, "when I was just twenty, knowing scarcely anybody. Through mere shyness I played a little at the 'faro' table where George Selwyn, of fashionable notoriety, presided, keeping the bank. An acquaintance of mine, who saw me at play and was aware of my inexperience, exclaimed, in a tone akin to pity as though he viewed me as a victim dressed out for sacrifice, 'What, Wilberforce, is that you?' George Selwyn seemed quite disconcerted by this interference, and, patting me on the back, said, 'Don't interrupt him. He couldn't be better employed.'" But the novice was not necessarily a victim. "The first day I went to Boodle's," he used to say, "I won twenty-five guineas from the Duke of Norfolk." He often won larger sums than that ; and, after a time, he was shrewd enough to set a limit of £100 to his losses on a single night. His diary records an occasion when he reached this limit and left the club and then returned and won a guinea, just to keep on the right side of the line. But gambling never gripped him quite as fast as it gripped Fox; and about 1785 he swore off at least the more devastating games like "faro"—for a reason that reveals the gentleness that underlay his gaiety. One night he was challenged by Bankes, who never played himself, to take the bank: he did so, and at the end of the game he had won £600; but among those who had lost most heavily he found young men who had not yet inherited their fortunes and could not easily afford to pay.

Wilberforce had not been long in London before the death of his uncle made him still wealthier and the owner of a spacious house at Wimbledon, with enough bedrooms to entertain eight or nine guests. Always, if he could, he slept there, finding in the quiet and "country air" a much-needed antidote to the racket and fogs and stuffiness of the town; and he would often persuade friends, who came out to dine or sup, to stay the night. Every day while Parliament was sitting, he rode or drove or walked to town. How he spent his time there before a late, sometimes a very late, return to Wimbledon (unless he slept at Bankes's house in town) may best be seen from the brief diary of the period, written up regularly from day to day, with scarcely one omission, in his small, rather illegible, short-sighted handwriting.

Jan. 24, 1783.	At the House—indifferent day—dined Goosetree's. Bankes got drunk and some others—called Eliot's[1]—Home and bed before 12.
Feb. 3.	Very bad morning—feverish—went in carriage to House—obliged to pair off by the heat: dined Pitt's. Home evening.
Feb. 5.	Exceeding rainy bad day. No fever or very little. Missed House. Dined Goosetree's and played billiards afterwards. Home and bed before 12.
Feb. 7 (Sunday).	Morning, Philip Green called at 10 and detained me from church—walked—dined Woodly's . . . afterwards Goosetree's where supped. Bed at 2 o'clock.
Feb. 11.	Morning delightful—carriage to City Custom House. Too late and walked home. House over soon. Dined Advocate's[2] and staid till 11. Goosetree's. At Pharoah, and Pitt—supped late—lost money £100 which had been owed me. Bed about 4.
March 12.	Fine but cold. . . . House. Lord Abingdon's concert. Supped Goosetree's and bed about 2.
March 27.	Walked to House. Dined Lord George's and went with them to Mrs. Siddon's Grecian Daughter.

[1] Afterwards Pitt's brother-in-law.
[2] Dundas, Lord Advocate for Scotland.

March 29.	Morning fine, frosty. . . . Walked for 5 hours —called in Union Club, dined Goosetree's—drank much wine—Pitt, Bankes and Pratt —played Pharoah.
May 20.	Morning, walked — made calls. Dined Woodly's, then Goosetree's and Almack's where danced till 4 o'clock in the morning.
May 26.	Up early. Chaise to East Grinstead where breakfast—then Godstone, 2 old men basking —rode to Croydon and chaise to town— House—spoke—dined Advocate's. Mr. and Mrs. Johnstone, Thurlow, Pepper, Pitt. After the rest went, we sat till 6 in the morning.
Oct. 28.	Morning walked John Villiers—sat at home— then Kemble Hamlet—Goosetree's, no fire there, tried Cocoa Tree, returned Goosetree's. Bed ½ past 1. Began vegetable diet.
Nov. 27.	Great day in the House. Sat till past 4 in morning. Bed without supper at 5.
Nov. 28.	No House. Dined Tom Pitt's.[1] Mrs. Crewe, charming woman.
Nov. 29.	Evening went to Mrs. Siddons—Mrs. Crewe at play.
Nov. 30.	Morning walked. Dined Lord Chatham's. Meeting. Wrote for ladies to get to the Gallery, but disappointed.
Dec. 2.	Up late. Dined Steele, Catch Club. Sandwich. Then opera—Mrs. Crewe there—supped Lord George's—Lord John there, Mrs. Crewe, Duchess of Portland, converts. Mrs. Crewe made the party (promise?) to adjourn to Downing St.[2] next night. Bed 3 o'clock.
Dec. 3.	Dined Goosetree's—played cards and supped Duchess of Portland's, Downing St. Chas. Fox came in—whispering over chair. Heavy evening. Bed about 3.

[1] William Pitt's cousin, afterwards Lord Camelford.

[2] The Duke of Portland was Prime Minister of the Coalition Government (March to December, 1783).

Dec. 6.	Walked. Dined Hamilton's. Opera—supped Burlington House—Mrs. Crewe—Duchess of Portland—Mrs. Sheridan sang old English songs angelically—promised her our votes. Bed about 3.
Jan. 29, 1784.	Windy. House—dined White's by way of forming a Club—then Play and supped Goosetree's.
Feb. 21.	Continued thaw—dined Lord Camden's—Prince of Wales' Levée—opera—supped Goosetree's—took off [1] people—Bed 3.
Feb. 22 (Sunday),	Very much fatigued—church—dined G. Hardinge's. Mrs. Siddons sang charmingly.
Feb. 24.	Very tired—walked—dined Mr. Smith's—then Lady Howe's Ball, danced till $\frac{1}{2}$ past 4.
March 7 (Sunday).	Morning, church—dined Lord Salisbury's. Then with Dundas to Mr. Seaton's to sup with Mrs. Siddons—Sir C. and Lady Dorothy. Bed $\frac{1}{2}$ past 2.
June 21.	Rode in goggles 6 miles, then to town—House—dined Pitt.
August 5.	Dined Pitt's—jolly large party—at night returned to Wimbledon. Bed $\frac{1}{2}$ past 4.

An exacting life. One wonders, indeed, how a man of Wilberforce's poor physique could live it. As it was, the body rebelled. It was not only his eyes, which were frequently indifferent and sometimes "very bad" in cold or dusty weather or after playing cards, so bad now and then that the lines of the diary run into one another. He suffered also from occasional fever and sickness and the *mal du pays*. One suspects that he enjoyed those two meals every night too much, and that the "vegetable diet" was a reluctant and not very long sustained experiment. Brief as it is, there is room in the diary for a mention of duck and asparagus and turtle and venison: and once, it confesses—"ate enormously." He slept badly too. One night, indeed, at Hampstead, there was some excuse; he was "kept awake by fleas": but often at clean, comfortable Wimbledon, when he came home late from the House, he would lie tossing and dreaming about the debate. No doubt it was only his love of out-

[1] i.e., mimicked.

of-door exercise, his walks and rides, that kept him fit at all for this London life; and happily those late sittings and those "heavy evenings" did not run on all through the year. When Parliament rose, Wilberforce was off into the country—preferably to the Lakes, where he had taken a house at Rayrigg on the edge of Windermere—with a great box of books to read, "classics, statutes at large, and history," and, better still, congenial folk to talk to. St. John, who often supped and gamed with him in London, spent several months at Rayrigg in the summer of 1782: other friends, Cambridge contemporaries some of them, came to stay from time to time; and his mother and sister paid visits from Hull. So the books, it seemed, often remained in their box. "Boating, riding, and continual parties at my own house and Sir Michael le Fleming's fully occupied my time," says Wilberforce in one of the many stray notes he kept of his doings. Another year he tried the West Country and found Teignmouth greatly to his liking—"a delightful place in delightful country, mild air, good and cheap provisions, many things in the neighbourhood to see, but lodgings very indifferent and a smell arising from the stagnant sea-water in some of them." One June he drove to Southampton to meet Pitt, visiting Salisbury and Stonehenge on the way and returning by Romsey and Winchester. And sometimes he went to Brighton to take the warm sea-water baths, now coming into vogue, or to Cambridge where he dined in hall at St. John's and drank with his old admirers in the Combination Room, and played cards with them once more. There was plenty of change, therefore, and plenty of fresh air and exercise—enough, apparently, to keep that slight, delicate frame going, and that lively brain working, at full speed through all the noise and dazzle, the drinking and gambling and singing, the debates and *levées*, the balls and routs of those hectic London nights.

5

In all this social side of Wilberforce's early life, just as in his politics, Pitt is the dominant, ever-present figure. There are not many pages of the diary without a mention of his name. They had the same tastes, followed the same pursuits, haunted the same places. Wilberforce was always calling at Goosetree's, and Goosetree's at this time was almost Pitt's home: he dined there every night one winter. They became addicted to gambling about the same time and with the same fervour. "I well remember," said Wilberforce once, "the intense earnestness he displayed." And they gave it up about the same time, though Pitt's reason was characteristically different from Wilberforce's. Cooler headed than Fox, Pitt realised that it was getting so strong a hold on him, taking so much of his time, as to endanger his political career. And there were plenty of other amusements. Wilberforce, for his part, was never happier than when they sat in a circle of intimates, jesting and "ragging" and exchanging witty repartees—*foyning* or *foining* as they called it. It was Pitt's quick and merry wit that Wilberforce admired perhaps more than anything else in him. "He was the wittiest man I ever knew," he declared, long after Pitt was dead; and he recalled one hilarious evening when they joined a party gathered at the Boar's Head tavern in East Cheap to celebrate the memory of Shakespeare. "Many professed wits were present, but Pitt was the most amusing of the party and the readiest and most apt in the required allusions." If Pitt's youth was very short, at least it was—to those who really knew him—very youthful. "When I left the House," noted the old *roué*, George Selwyn, in his diary one day in 1782, "I left in one room a party of young men, who made me, from their life and spirits, wish for one night to be twenty. There was a tableful of them drinking—young Pitt, Lord Euston, Berkeley, North, &c., singing and laughing *à gorge déployé*: some of them sang very good catches; one Wilberforce, a M. of P., sang the best."

Moreover, unable himself to afford a suburban villa, Pitt often made use of Wilberforce's. He too felt the better for a night in the "country air," and Wilberforce would often get a note like the following, hastily scribbled from Pitt's seat in the House of Commons: "Eliot, Arden and I will be with you before curfew, and expect an early meal of peas and strawberries." "Wimbledon," notes the diary for April 3, 1783, "where Pitt etc. dined and slept—Pratt and Bankes foyned Mrs. Hayes etc. etc. Evening walk. Bed a little past 2." And next day: "Lounged morning at Wimbledon with friends. Night foyned and ran about the garden for an hour or two." Sunday, July 6, "Morning fine. Persuaded Pitt and Pepper to church. . . . Pitt and Pepper and Lawrence and Johnson at night—walked ladies on Common." And the following Friday: "Fine hot day—went on water with Pitt and Eliot fishing—came back, dined, walked evening. Eliot went home, Pitt staid." Wilberforce would often bring Pitt home with him when the House sat late; one spring Pitt lived there for three or four months together; and again continuously from April, 1783, when he left the Chancellor of the Exchequer's official residence, till the following December when he entered the Prime Minister's. With some reason, therefore, Wilberforce could claim in after days to have been "the depositary of his most confidential thoughts." "Hundreds of times," he says, "I have roused him out of bed in the morning and conversed with him while he was dressing." And it was by no means a one-sided friendship. Pitt wanted Wilberforce in those days to talk to, to confide in, just as much as he wanted Dundas later on. "Pray come to Wimbledon as soon as possible," he writes in the early days of his premiership to hasten him back from the Midlands: "I want to talk with you about your navy bills . . . and about ten thousand other things." And he adds in a postscript: "For the sake of this letter I am leaving a thousand others unanswered and a thousand projects unread. You will probably think it was hardly worth while."

Once more, the dominant note of this close personal intercourse is the gaiety, the rollicking spirits, of both young men. The note is worth stressing; for it might well seem incredible that Wilberforce and Pitt as history knows them—the revered humanitarian and saint, and the silent, cold, haughty statesman—could ever have behaved like that. Happily the incredible is true. They did engage in interminable bouts of "foyning": they did run about the garden in the dusk: and Pitt did get up early one morning and carefully sow the flower-beds with fragments of an opera-hat which Ryder had worn down from London the night before. And Pitt's letters to Wilberforce, in those years, exhale the same light-heartedness. "I am as well as it is possible," he writes from London in July, 1782, "in the midst of all this *sin and sea-coal*; and for a Chancellor of the Exchequer who has exchanged his *happier hour*, pass my time very tolerably. Even Goosetree's is not absolutely extinct, but has a chance of living through the dog days. I shall be happy to hear from you, whether in the shape of an official dispatch or a familiar epistle." "*Anderson's Dictionary* I have received," he writes next summer from Brighton, "and am much obliged to you for it. I will return it safe, I hope not dirtied, and possibly not read. I am sorry you give so bad an account of your eyes, especially as this very letter looks as if it would put them to a severe trial. . . . The lounge here is excellent, principally owing to our keeping very much to ourselves—that is Pulchritudo, Steele, Pretyman, and myself. The Woodlys have been here in high foining, and have talked me to death. . . . Mrs. Johnstone and Mrs. Walpole are left to dispute the prize here. The first is clearly the handsomer woman, but the husband of the latter looks the quieter man, and the better part of love as of valour is discretion. I conclude as you did by desiring you to write immediately."

Sometimes they spent their holidays together. One Easter, for instance, they went to Brighton, and then immediately and impulsively, so disgusting was the weather, drove off to Bath. "As Pitt was then upon the western circuit," notes Wilberforce of this holiday, "he entertained the barristers. . . . We had, too, abundance of corporation dinners and jollity." And sometimes they met on visits to the same country-houses and walked and rode together. On one such occasion, which Wilberforce was not easily allowed to forget, his bad sight and clumsy handling of a gun nearly cost Pitt his life—or so at least his friends averred. But the best, the longest remembered, of these joint holidays was the great tour in France in the autumn of 1783, just before the Coalition fell and Pitt came in. It was carefully and keenly planned. "The party to Rheims holds, of course," wrote Pitt some weeks beforehand, "at least as far as depends on me. . . . We ought to start within the three or four first days of September. I hope you will recollect that you have to do with punctual men who could not risk their character by being late for any appointment." "Do not verify my prophecy of detaining us a fortnight," he writes on the 22nd, "and jilting us at the end of it": and on the 30th, "Your letter has relieved me from two fears I have for some time entertained; the one of losing the pleasure of your company, the other of being made to wait for it. I am very sorry for the state of your eyes, but I am quite of opinion that the air of Rheims is exactly the thing for you. I hope to find it equally sovereign for toothaches and swollen faces which have persecuted me ever since I have been here [at Burton Pynsent] as if it was the middle of a session. We shall agree excellently as invalids, and particularly in making the robust Eliot fag for us, and ride bodkin, and letting him enjoy all the other privileges of health." But it was not, after all, till September 11 that the three of them met at Canterbury and set out for France via Dover and Calais. The stay at Rheims was a great success, largely owing to the benevolence of the Abbé de Lageard, a high official of the town. The good Abbé was told by the superintendent of police that three strange Englishmen had arrived. They had no servants, he said, and had taken wretched lodgings: and yet they pretended to be *grands seigneurs* and one of them, forsooth, "a son of the great Chatham." "It is impossible," declared the agitated policeman; "they must be *des intrigants*." "Let us be in no hurry," replied the Abbé: "I will inquire about them myself." So he visited the travellers, and was "at once satisfied by their appearance"—so much so that he invited them forthwith to dinner, gave them "the best vintage of the country" (since Pitt had complained that even in the middle of Champagne they could get no "tolerable wine"), and kept them talking for several hours. Nor was this all. "The Abbé," wrote Wilberforce, "was a fellow of such extraordinary humanity that to prevent our time hanging heavy on our hands he would sometimes make us visits of five or six hours at a stretch." Similarly overwhelming was the compliment paid to the Englishmen by a rich wine-merchant of the town at whose house, after supper had been started with a series of light dishes in the French mode, "a vast joint of ill-roasted beef . . . was placed upon the table amongst the winks and smiles of the company." "A sad party," records Wilberforce, "a drunken prior—sang—[*aet.*] seventy-three." And Paris was no less diverting. A week of social activities in the city itself—dinners, receptions, cards, the opera, hunting—and then four days with the Court at Fontainebleau, Marie Antoinette bewitching Wilberforce with her "engaging manner and appearance," Louis, on the other hand, striking him as "a clumsy, strange figure in immense boots . . . worth going a hundred miles for a sight of him, a-boar-hunting." As for Pitt, the men and women crowded round him "in shoals." "He behaved with great spirit, though he was sometimes a little bored when they talked to him about the parliamentary reform." But their stay in Paris was cut short. A special messenger arrived summoning Pitt to London; and before the end of October they were back in town.

They found London agog with "secret plottings—the King groaning under the Ministry which had been imposed upon him"; and in two months the Coalition had fallen and Pitt was in power. Never again could he and Wilberforce have quite so gay and care-free a holiday. "The *foinsters*," as Eliot called their little group, were now on the Government bench; and a short letter from Pitt

to Wilberforce in the next year, discussing co-operation with Wyvill
for Reform, significantly ends, "Adieu: I must conclude, having
no time for *foining*." The same serious note is sounded in a letter
from Wilberforce to Pitt in 1785. "You may reckon yourself most
fortunate in that cheerfulness of mind which enables you every now
and then to throw off your load for a few hours and rest yourself.
I fancy it must have been this which, when I am with you, prevents
my considering you as an object of compassion, tho' Prime Minister
of England; for now, when I am at a distance, out of hearing of
your *foyning* . . . I cannot help representing you to myself as
oppressed with cares and troubles; and what I feel for you is more,
I believe, than even Pepper feels in the moments of his greatest
anxiety; and what can I say more? . . ." For both of them, indeed,
young as they still were, their youth was nearly over. It had been
all too short, but it was very glorious while it lasted.

II

The Call

MIDDLE-AGE came quickly to Pitt. A Prime Minister of twenty-four must needs soon double his years: and beneath the cares of office, and presently of war, his short youth was smothered. But the change was not sudden, nor complete. The method and purpose of his life were unaltered. He still enjoyed such social relaxations as his duties permitted. He could still be merry, now and then, with children and his intimates. And, if, as the strain increased and the weak body, which was to fail him altogether before those twenty-four years had become forty-eight, began to revolt against its exacting master, if his stern self-sufficiency became more marked, if there was a touch of hauteur in his aloofness, if his cold, stiff bearing in the House seemed at times a little stilted, these were but the old manners growing on the man: it was the same Pitt to the end. With Wilberforce it was otherwise. In 1785 he underwent an abrupt and profound psychological change. It was not merely the passing of his youth. He would himself have been the first to admit that he became a different man.

The Evangelical movement was perhaps the most striking event in the domestic life of England in the second half of the eighteenth century: but it was mainly among the poorer classes that Whitefield and Wesley made their conquests; and to the average, comfortable, well-to-do Englishman this new conception of religion, so revolutionary in its simplicity, so extortionate in its demands on a man's whole manner of life, seemed not merely inconvenient but dangerous. No wonder, therefore, that Wilberforce's mother should have promptly summoned her ten-year-old son home to Hull from his school at Putney, when she heard that his aunt, with whom he lodged at Wimbledon, was trying to "convert" him. After anxious consideration the boy was entrusted to the charge of the correct clerical headmaster of Pocklington Grammar School. There he would assuredly be safe: for it was a more expensive and exclusive institution than its name suggests. There, at the cost of some £300 or £400 a year, he would be certain to learn nothing dangerous. And in the holidays he should be left no time for mischief. "Hull," said the victim to himself in after days, "was then one of the gayest places out of London. The theatre, balls, large supper and card parties were the delight of the principal merchants and their families." As the son of a principal merchant, young Wilberforce was deluged with invitations, and his mother saw to it that none of them was needlessly declined. "No pious parent ever laboured more to impress a beloved child with sentiments of religion than my friends did to give me a taste for the world and its diversions." Their labours were not in vain. In the seductive gaieties of Hull, as in the costly seclusion of Pocklington, the temptations of Wimbledon, his aunt's insidious discourses, the hearty chapel services, the long sermons—it was soon all forgotten: and Mrs. Wilberforce could rest content in the belief that she had plucked her brand from the burning.

Yet, had she known it, the train of circumstance which was to lead to her son's conversion—"perversion," she would have called it—had already been laid. Before he went to Putney the boy had attended the Grammar School at Hull, and shortly before he left it, a certain Isaac Milner had become an usher there. Left in poverty on his father's death, this able young man had found in this ushership the first rung of the ladder which was to lead him far from the weaver's loom where he had begun to earn his living. A sizarship at Cambridge presently gave him the requisite scope for his genius in mathematics. In the tripos of 1774 so brilliant were his papers that the examiners placed him first and "wrote the word *incomparabilis* after his name." Two years later he was elected a Fellow of Queens' College and the Royal Society as well. At one time he held the chair of Natural Philosophy and later that of Mathematics; in 1788 he became President of Queens', and in 1792 Vice-Chancellor of the University. In 1778 he was appointed rector of St. Botolph's, Cambridge; in 1791 Dean of Carlisle; and till his death in 1820 he was better known as a preacher and religious writer than as a scientist. Rarely then, since the days when Andrew Marvell's father was its headmaster, can the Grammar School at Hull have possessed so remarkable an usher: and if the youthful "shrimp" was naturally attracted by Milner's energetic personality, by his great size and strength, and by the jovial and sometimes uproarious humour in which, despite the seriousness of his religious views, he indulged

to the end of his life, the remarkable usher was as quick to recognise
the gifts of his remarkable pupil. He noted especially the wonderful
voice: and he used to set the lad on a table and make him read
aloud to the assembled school as a model of elocution. The friendship thus struck up between the two outlasted Wilberforce's excur-
sion to Putney, and his subsequent removal to Pocklington and
later to Cambridge; and it was not forgotten when he found
himself a favourite among people so different from his Yorkshire
schoolmaster as the Duchess of Portland or George Selwyn or Mrs.
Siddons. So it happened that when in the summer of 1784, a year
after his trip to Paris, having celebrated his twenty-fifth birthday
in style at the York races, he met Milner, now a Cambridge don, at
Scarborough, he told him he was contemplating a second visit to
the Continent and asked him to join the party.

The invitation was accepted; and in the autumn they set out
for the Riviera by way of Lyons and Avignon, Wilberforce with
Milner in one carriage, his mother and sister and two female cousins
in the other. Talking is easier in a carriage than in a railway train
and there is more time for it, but it was not during this journey,
nor at Nice, where the ladies of the family settled down in a villa
for the winter, but on the return journey to London, whither Pitt
had summoned Wilberforce to support his Reform scheme, that the
subject of religion was first seriously discussed. Wilberforce had
casually picked up a copy of Doddridge's *Rise and Progress of Religion*;
and since Milner thought it "one of the best books ever written,"
they read it together as they drove slowly along those snow-clogged
roads. When they reached Dartford late on a February night, they
heard that a critical division in the House of Commons on the
unfortunate business of the Westminster Election was expected in
the early hours of the morning; but though Pitt's position might
have been, and indeed was, in danger, Wilberforce did not push on
to London. Was it fatigue? Or had politics and Pitt begun already
to lose something of their hold? At any rate the first symptoms of
a change are soon discernible in the pages of Wilberforce's diary.
The life recorded is outwardly the same—constant social engagements, dinners with Pitt twice or thrice a week: "Sitting up all
night," "Shirked Duchess of Gordon at Almack's," "Danced till
five in the morning." . . . But a new note has begun to sound. Of
a christening ceremony, for instance, he writes, "Very indecent—
all laughing round"; and of the opera, "Shocking dance of Festin

de Pierre, and unmoved audience." Still more significant is this
comment: "Strange that the most generous men and religious do
not see that their duties increase with their fortune, and that they
will be punished for spending it in eating, etc." With such new
thoughts in his mind—disquieting thoughts for a man of his
wealth and his tastes—Wilberforce set out, when the session was
over, to rejoin his family. And Milner was again his companion.
They met the ladies in July at Genoa and travelled thence to Geneva
and the Bernese Oberland. This time, on Milner's suggestion, they
read the New Testament in the Greek; and on the way home by
the Rhine and Spa their discussions became so absorbing that
Wilberforce was taken to task for the infrequency of his visits to
the other carriage. "By degrees," he wrote long afterwards, "I
imbibed his (Milner's) sentiments, though I must confess with
shame that they long remained merely as opinions assented to by
my understanding but not influencing my heart." And now the
change could be detected by his fashionable friends, some of whom
he encountered among the "curious assemblage from all parts of
Europe" at Spa. "Mrs. Crewe," he notes, "cannot believe that I
can think it wrong to go to the play. . . . Surprised at hearing that
halting on the Sunday was my wish and not my mother's." Clearly
the days of Sunday suppers with Mrs. Siddons are now over.
Wilberforce's leisure, indeed, is now more and more occupied with
introspection and reflection. "Began three or four days ago to get
up very early," says the diary for October 25. "In the solitude and
self-conversation of the morning had thoughts which I trust will
come to something." In the following month, besides the diary, he
began to keep a private journal of his inner life. It might help
him, he thought, to be "humble and watchful." And certainly some
outlet was needed for the emotionalism of a nature now wrung
to its depths by a bitter spiritual conflict. "Often while in the full
enjoyment of all that this world could bestow, my conscience told
me that, in the true sense of the word, I was not a Christian. I
laughed, I sang, I was apparently gay and happy, but the thought
would steal across me, ' What madness is all this; to continue easy
in a state in which a sudden call out of the world would consign
me to everlasting misery, and that when eternal happiness is within
my grasp! '" The process of conversion soon reached its climax.
"For months I was in the deepest depression from strong conviction
of my guilt." The London life became wellnigh unbearable; and

the diary at this period is a tragically different document from that of 1783-4. "I feel quite giddy and distracted by the tumult, except when in situations of which I am rather ashamed, as in the stage-coach: the shame, pride: but a useful lesson." "All religious thoughts go off in London." "I must awake to my dangerous state, and never be at rest till I have made my peace with God." "My heart is so hard, my blindness so great, that I cannot get a due hatred of sin." "True, Lord, I am wretched, and miserable, and blind, and naked." "At the levée, and then dined at Pitt's—sort of cabinet dinner—was often thinking that pompous Thurlow and elegant Carmarthen would soon appear in the same row with the poor fellow who waited behind their chairs." "In vain endeavoured in the evening to rouse myself. God grant it may not all prove vain. Oh, if it does, how will my punishment be deservedly increased!" "As I promised, I went to Pitt's—sad work—I went there in fear, and for some time kept an awe on my mind." "I am too intent on shining in company, and must curb myself here." "Sunday . . . I felt sometimes moved in church, but am still callous."

This new seriousness, this constant watching for little faults and stern self-condemnation when he marks them, were to grow into a permanent habit of Wilberforce's life: but happily he was soon rescued from the initial phase of excessive self-distrust and misery. After "a good deal of debate" with himself he decided, early in December, to ask for spiritual advice from the Rev. John Newton, the rector of St. Mary Woolnoth in Lombard Street and one of Whitefield's most celebrated successors in the Evangelical line. Whitefield spent his youth as a tapster at the Bell Inn, Gloucester; but the contrast between the young Newton and the old was even more remarkable. Son of a master-mariner, he had gone to sea at the age of twelve; and after some years of service, partly on his father's ship, partly as a "pressed man" on a man-of-war, he had drifted into the position of an overseer at one of the depots on the Gold Coast where slaves were collected for shipment to America. Himself a slave to dissolute habits and to the brutal caprices of his master and his master's negro concubine, he was fast sinking into that irrecoverable degradation which has often been the doom of an outcast white man among black men, when he was rescued, more or less against his will, by a friend of his father's, brought back to England, and finally given the command of a slave-ship. It was during his career as a "slaver" that "conversion" came upon him; and, oddly enough, the transformation of his beliefs and his morals brought with them no sense of repugnance to his occupation. On one side of a partition in his ship the slaves lay packed in chains, many of them dying, all of them in appalling filth and discomfort, while, on the other side, from time to time, the lord and master of the infernal vessel conducted the prayers of his European crew. He desired, however, to bear witness to a wider circle; and presently he was admitted to deacon's orders and obtained a curacy at Olney in Buckinghamshire where he became an intimate friend of the poet, Cowper. Thence, after sixteen years, he was transferred to London, and, till his death in 1807 at the age of 83, "the old African blasphemer," as he called himself, continued to depict with ruthless candour and in lurid hues the foulness of the pit from which he had been so miraculously lifted. Such was the scarred and seasoned warrior to whom the young novice turned for aid, and not in vain. Doubtless the mere outpouring of his trouble to another was itself a great relief: doubtless, too, the old pastor, though he would rack and harrow his penitents, knew also how to console them. At any rate, now that he is definitely within the Evangelical fold, Wilberforce's spirits begin to mend. The accusations continue: "I go off sadly" . . . "I tremble" . . . "I am in a most doubtful state" . . . "Very wretched—all sense gone." But the sufferer is no longer alone: "Very unhappy—called at Newton's, and bitterly moved: comforted me." And presently, through Newton, he finds other sympathisers in that dangerous aunt of bygone days and in her brother, John Thornton. So gradually the pages of the diary are less profusely strewn with "coldness," "darkness," "weakness," and in place of them there is more of "peace" and "hope"; till, as time goes on, Wilberforce renews his old cheerfulness, almost his old gaiety. If "gravity" indeed, he tells his sister, should be the business of life, "gaiety" should be its relaxation; but, he adds, "I will give it a more worthy epithet than gay. Let me call it serenity, tranquillity, composure which is not to be destroyed."

2

To all his friends the passing of Wilberforce's soul-sickness was a great relief, and to no one greater, we may be sure, than to Mrs. Wilberforce. The rumour had run through Yorkshire that the

young member for the county had "gone mad," and it was with
anxious feelings that the mother awaited her son's first visit after
this strange new fanaticism, which she had tried to fence off years
before, had come upon him. Was it melancholy that possessed him,
or, in the language of the day, "enthusiasm"? Was it some silent,
dreamy anchorite that she would have to welcome home, or, more
likely, some wild hot-gospeller, ranting of hell-fire and Eternity ?
Happily it was neither. It was just her son—older, certainly, and
quieter, but as alert and affectionate and companionable as ever, and
more constantly considerate now than he had once been and less
quick-tempered. "If this is madness," said a friend to whom Mrs.
Wilberforce had opened her heart, "I hope that he will bite us all."

In the judgment of serious-minded people, indeed, the charm of
his personality had been deepened by the change, and the new
Wilberforce made many new friends. It was about this time that
at Bath, whither he was frequently driven by ill health, he made
the acquaintance of Hannah More, whose experience of life had
been so like his own. Born fourteen years before him, she too had
been a delicate and precocious child. During her girlhood at Bristol
she mastered French, Italian, Spanish and Latin. At the age of
seventeen she published an "edifying" drama called *The Search for
Happiness*. When she came to London she soon found herself a
favourite in the world of art and letters. Burke, Reynolds, Garrick
were her constant friends: and Dr. Johnson, who treated her with
playful affection, declared her to be "the most powerful versificatrix
in the English language." Others, it seems, were of a like opinion:
for no less than four thousand copies of her tragedy, *Percy*, were
sold in a fortnight. And then suddenly, in the midst of these social
and literary triumphs, under the influence (it is said) of Garrick's
death in 1779, she began to break away from her London circle and
its manner of life. The theatre, above all, seemed now so evil that
she even refused to be present when her own *Percy* was revived with
Mrs. Siddons as the heroine. And it was divines like Dr. Kennicott
and Bishop Porteus she now made her friends. Finally, withdrawing
from London to live with her sisters at Bath or at a cottage she had
built at Cowslip Green in Somerset, she began with *Thoughts on the
Importance of the Manners of the Great to General Society* that series of
moral writings which were so widely, and so appropriately, read
by her contemporaries. It was a little before the publication of the
Thoughts that she first became fully acquainted with Wilberforce at

Bath: and, soon afterwards, he paid a visit to her and her sisters at Cowslip Green. It was the beginning of a close and lifelong friendship. Like two exiles drawn together by a common patriotism, their spirits had recognised and acclaimed their kinship. "That young gentleman's character," said Hannah More at the outset of the acquaintanceship, "is one of the most extraordinary I ever knew for talents, virtue and piety." "This is truly magnificent," wrote Wilberforce of her devotion to the ignorant rustics of Somerset instead of to London rank and fashion, "the really sublime in character."

What was attractive in the new Wilberforce to Hannah More may well have been repugnant to some of his earlier friends. Writing to one of them many years later—he was then over sixty —he recalls the circumstances with characteristic, if somewhat laborious, sincerity. "I grant," he says, "that, though the interest I took in the well being of my old friends was even greater than it had been before the change I have been speaking of, yet, from natural and obvious causes, we were not likely to be such agreeable intimates to each other as heretofore. There was no longer the 'eadem velle' and 'eadem nolle' in the same degree; and therefore we were likely to retain full as strong a desire to SERVE such friends as formerly, but not to have the same pleasure in each other's society." It was probably true. While Wilberforce, as will presently be seen, never lost contact with the closest and greatest of his old intimates, he could never again be quite at ease in his earlier circle. His tastes, his manner of life, were too completely changed for that. He no longer sat up into the small hours if he could help it. He took his name off all his five clubs. Gossip and aimless wit no longer amused him. *Foyning* and dancing and singing over the wine had gone the way of cards and mimicry. And the play, whether *Hamlet* or *The Grecian Daughter*, had gone too. "I think the tendency of the theatre most pernicious," he writes to his sister in 1787, begging her to set a good example to the people of Hull by abstaining from it. He did not, however, after those first weeks of misery, seclude himself from the world: he was careful, indeed, to keep in touch with it: and if he resolved to devote his mornings to study and reflection, the evenings were to go to society. But society was now a duty rather than a pleasure. Though he was no longer haunted by morbid visions of his fellow guests standing stripped beside the waiters before the Judgment Seat, he was worried by the apparent lack in others of the high seriousness he felt in himself. The diary of the period is all too full of this impatience. "How vain and foolish all the conversation of great dinners: nothing worth remembering." . . . "Dined Lord Chatham's—Duchess of Gordon, Lady Charlotte, Duke of Rutland, Graham, Pitt, Dundas, etc. How ill-suited is all this to me ! How unnatural for one who professes himself a stranger and a pilgrim!" . . . "Obliged to dine at the Speaker's." . . . "Forced out to breakfast at the Bishop of London's." Sociability, it is clear, is no longer the easy virtue it once was; and he is happier when he writes: "Dined at home—Milner and I had some serious talk." His continued interest in society is mainly due, in fact, to the hope that a surreptitious opportunity may be given him at those gay gatherings for a little "serious talk" with others than Milner. Some quiet words of his, in the corner of the drawing-room, may carry through the music and the laughter to a friend's heart, and—who knows—may set the inner forces moving that may lead him, from just such an accidental start as in his own case, to share in the end his own felicity. When, moreover, the Abolition of the Slave Trade became the main purpose of his life, social inter-course provided another field of good work. He could use it to propagate the cause. There is a quaint item in the diary in 1793 which reveals both these motives in combination: "Doubtful whether or not I ought to go to Windsor to-morrow to take the chance of getting into conversation [on the Slave Trade] with some of the royal family. Lady E. may afford me the opportunity. Also I may do good to N. and H."

Yet, at times, the old Wilberforce breaks through. "Dined at E.'s—rout afterwards—what extreme folly is all this! Yet much entertained." And again, after a luxurious country-house party, he writes to Hannah More: "How difficult it is to be merry and wise." Yes; with all his seriousness he can still be merry. And therein lies the clue to what would otherwise be a puzzling mystery. How was it that Wilberforce was still so popular with so many diverse types of men and women? How was it that hostesses still invited him to entertainments which he thought so vain and foolish? Nay, indeed, why was he not regarded as an insufferable prig? Because always, whatever the company, however frivolous to his inner mind its chatter, he was still the same kindly, courteous, engaging little man; not, perhaps, as of old, the source and centre of all the fun, but ready to be "merry"—within the limits of decorum—with the rest. It is only in the diary that he seems a kill-joy at the feast; and many men might be misjudged by later generations if they ventured to keep and to leave unburnt behind them so candid a record of their innermost thoughts. Thus, if cynics smiled at the "convert," if friends "take him to task" over some of his "peculiarities," such as always saying "grace" at meals, or dislike some of his habits, such as that which grew on him in later life, of humming hymn-tunes about the house, nobody seems ever to have spoken of him, or thought of him, as a prig.

It was impossible, too, no doubt, to regard as a prig one whose virtues were so genuine and yet so unostentatious. Those, for instance, who knew of Wilberforce's wealth and how he spent it must perforce have respected him. He soon abandoned his pleasant house at Wimbledon because it entailed unnecessary expense as well as being inconvenient for his servants; and thenceforward his purse was always open to private and public charity—to Hannah More's schools, to which for a time he subscribed £400 a year; to a Yorkshire society "for catching the colts running wild on Halifax Moor . . . and sending them to college"; to the unemployed and destitute at Pudsey; to some hundreds of Lascars stranded in the East End; to sufferers in Germany from the devastations of the Napoleonic War; and so forth without stint. One year he finds that on such objects and in helping friends he has spent nearly £3000 of his capital. So he takes stock of his finances and plans domestic economies which will enable him in future "by management to give away at least one fourth" of his income to the poor. Was this a prig? It was certainly a saint.

3

And what of politics and of Pitt ?

In the first days of his spiritual conflict, as soon as Wilberforce began to realise what was happening to him, he must at once have wondered what effect it would have on his relations with his most intimate friend. Pitt had never, he knew, given much thought to religion; and to his quieter, cooler temperament anything so precipitate, so tumultuous, as an evangelical conversion might well seem strange, if not positively distasteful. Might he not find it hard to understand and to sympathise? Only a few months back Wilberforce had entered in his diary: "Sat up late chatting with

Pitt—his good hopes of the country, and noble patriotic heart."
Could he realise that even patriotism might seem a secondary thing?
Would he see that one who had felt a higher call must needs give
less of time and mind to politics, and in so far as he remained a
politician could no longer render strict allegiance to a person or a
party, but, whatever might be at stake, must speak and vote only
as conscience should prescribe? And must not such independence
mean, if not indeed a "loss of friends," at least a loss of intimacy?
Deeply anxious as to the answer to these questions, Wilberforce
hesitated for several weeks to grasp the nettle. It was not till the
beginning of December, 1785, when his inner struggle had reached
its final stage, that he wrote to Pitt, telling him what had happened
and of his intention to withdraw for a time from public life and
declaring that, though he would "ever feel a strong affection for
him" and though he saw no likelihood of their differing in politics,
he could no longer be "so much of a party man" as he had been
before. But even now, and even with one who had hitherto shared
so freely in his thoughts, he dreaded argument over matters which
he felt could not be argued; he shrank from discussing face to face
the cause and meaning of his transformation. He suggested that,
when next they met, it would be better not to talk about the subject
of his letter.

Pitt's prompt reply, disclosing as it does not only the strength
of his feeling for Wilberforce but, better perhaps than any other
published document, what manner of man Pitt was, must be quoted
in full:

Downing St.
December 2, 1785.

My dear Wilberforce, Bob Smith mentioned to me on
Wednesday the letters he had received from you, which prepared
me for that I received from you yesterday. I am indeed too
deeply interested in whatever concerns you not to be very sensibly
affected by what has the appearance of a new æra in your life,
and so important in its consequences for yourself and your
friends. As to any public conduct which your opinions may ever
lead you to, I will not disguise to you that few things could go
nearer my heart than to find myself differing from you essentially on any great principle.

I trust and believe that it is a circumstance which can hardly occur. But if it ever should, and even if I should experience as much pain in such an event, as I have found hitherto encouragement and pleasure in the reverse, believe me it is impossible that it should shake the sentiments of affection and friendship which I bear towards you, and which I must be forgetful and insensible indeed if I ever could part with. They are sentiments engraved in my heart, and will never be effaced or weakened. If I knew how to state all I feel, and could hope that you are open to consider it, I should say a great deal more on the subject of the resolution you seem to have formed. You will not suspect me of thinking lightly of any moral or religious motives which guide you. As little will you believe that I think your understanding or judgment easily misled. But forgive me if I cannot help expressing my fear that you are nevertheless deluding yourself into principles which have but too much tendency to counteract your own object, and to render your virtues and your talents useless both to yourself and mankind. I am not, however, without hopes that my anxiety paints this too strongly. For you confess that the character of religion is not a gloomy one, and that it is not that of an enthusiast. But why then this preparation of solitude, which can hardly avoid tincturing the mind either with melancholy or superstition? If a Christian may act in the several relations of life, must he seclude himself from them all to become so? Surely the principles as well as the practice of Christianity are simple, and lead not to meditation only but to action.

I will not, however, enlarge upon these subjects now. What I would ask of you, as a mark both of your friendship and of the candour which belongs to your mind, is to open yourself fully and without reserve to one, who, believe me, does not know how to separate your happiness from his own. You do not explain either the degree or the duration of the retirement which you have prescribed to yourself: you do not tell me how the future course of your life is to be directed, when you think the same privacy no longer necessary: nor, in short, what idea you have formed of the duties which you are from this time to practise. I am sure you will not wonder if I am inquisitive on such a subject. The only way in which you can satisfy me is by conversation. There ought to be no awkwardness or embarrassment to either of us, tho' there may be some anxiety: and if you will open to me fairly the whole state of your mind on these subjects, tho' I shall venture to state to you fairly the points where I fear we may differ, and to desire you to re-examine your own ideas where I think you are mistaken, I will not importune you with fruitless discussion on any opinion which you have deliberately formed.

You will, I am sure, do justice to the motives and feelings which induce me to urge this so strongly to you. I think you will not refuse it: if you do not, name any hour at which I can call upon you to-morrow. I am going into Kent, and can take Wimbledon in my way. Reflect, I beg of you, that no principles are the worse for being discussed, and believe me that at all events the full knowledge of the nature and extent of your opinions and intentions will be to me a lasting satisfaction.

Believe me, affectionately and unalterably yours,

W. PITT.

With such an appeal in his hands Wilberforce could not evade discussion: and next morning "the young saint and the young minister" were closeted at Wimbledon for nearly two hours. It was a conversation which neither of them was likely to forget. "He tried to reason me out of my convictions," recalled Wilberforce long afterwards, "but soon found himself unable to combat their correctness if Christianity were true. The fact is, he was so absorbed in politics that he had never given himself time for due reflection on religion. But amongst other things he declared to me that Bishop Butler's work raised in his mind more doubts than it had answered." Clearly Pitt discussed their differences with all the candour he had promised: clearly, too, those differences could not be compounded. So the two parted, one fearing that his country had lost a statesman, the other knowing that he had not lost a friend. And as soon as events put it to the test, Wilberforce discovered that, for the time at any rate, his anxiety lest politics should create a breach was quite unfounded. Whole-hearted converts to any doctrine are apt to expect—almost, sometimes, to welcome—disagreement with the unconverted on other issues: and when a few months later Wilberforce resumed his duties in the House of Commons—his emergence from seclusion hastened, maybe, by Pitt's arguments—he expressed a naïve surprise at finding how generally he agreed with Pitt. Something like the old intimacy could, therefore, be recaptured. Once more the diary records their constant intercourse. "Pitt's before House—dined." "After House to Pitt's—supped." "Dined Pitt's and sat with him." "Went to Holwood with Pitt." "Hurried to House, no business, Pitt having got the gout—saw him." To all appearance the relationship was all it had ever been. "They were exactly like brothers," said one who often saw them together at this time. And yet there was, inevitably, a change. Not only the increasing pressure of business on the Prime Minister's time but Wilberforce's new dread of spending leisure in mere talk or of keeping late hours (and those were Pitt's freest hours) so as to impair his strength for good next day reduced the opportunities of meeting. Again the diary tells its tale: "Called in at Pitt's . . . and stayed supper—Apsley, Pitt and I. Too late, particularly for Saturday—will not again." "Called on Pitt and lounged too long." "A note from Pitt, desiring me to dine and go to Holwood with him, and stay two or three days. Would not do the latter that I might get out of town, and while in it might be quiet and reform." There must have been occasions, moreover, when Pitt could no longer give all his confidence to Wilberforce. Not that Pitt's politics were dirty. He was above a fraud and far above a bribe. The notorious example of his personal incorruptibility in that cynical age was one of his greatest services to England. But the maintenance of a majority, if not so directly mercenary an affair in Pitt's time as in Walpole's, was still an unsuitable subject of discussion with Wilberforce's conscience. On a point of party tactics, too, or in the heat of party combat, Pitt could no longer turn first to Wilberforce for counsel and aid. Would there not be something incongruous now in bidding him "tear the enemy to pieces"? So, in the daily round of party duties, it was the man of the world, not the saint, that Pitt naturally chose for his comrade —Dundas, not Wilberforce. And Wilberforce on his side was, for a time at least, content. He saw all he wanted of Pitt; and the more he saw, just as in the old days, the greater his affection and respect. "In the midst of all these disquieting circumstances," he wrote during the Regency crisis of 1788 (a crisis, by the way, in which party fortunes were deeply involved), "my friend is every day matter of fresh and growing admiration. I wish you were, as constantly as I am, witness to that simple and earnest regard for the public welfare . . . you would love him more and more."

III

Novitiate

I

IN the course of that interesting interlude between the Wars of the American and the French Revolutions it was not so very difficult for a politician with a conscience to support the Government. Only the crudest partisans can withhold their tribute of admiration for the manner in which the "schoolboy," as the Whigs dubbed the young Prime Minister, nursed his country back to health and strength in that critical decade. When the Treaty of Versailles was signed in 1783, British fortunes were at a lower ebb than they had been for centuries. A wretchedly conducted war had ended in a decisive defeat and a humiliating peace. Our kinsmen beyond the Atlantic, weak and divided at the moment, despite their triumph, but bearing in their young untainted vigour and in the unfathomed wealth of their vast country the seeds of a splendid future, had determined not to share that future, for good or ill, with the mother-country. The English-speaking commonwealth, in fact, had split asunder; and to the rival states of Europe it seemed that the blow they had helped to deal had struck Britain down for ever to the second rank. And if they were soon proved wrong, if with the advent of the next war only ten years later—a stubborn long-protracted war, enmeshing, bleeding, exhausting all the Powers —Britain proved herself inferior to none in strength and endurance, it was principally Pitt she had to thank for it. By a steady pursuit of peace abroad he secured just that little breathing-space which his countrymen needed to throw off the despondent mood engendered by defeat and to recover all their old resilient self-confidence. By resolute financial retrenchment and reorganisation at home, he enabled them to lift themselves swiftly and surely from the economic morass in which the American war had left them sunk to the neck. More than that, it was a decade in which, in politics as in religion, a new spirit was abroad; and if Pitt was never a disciple of Wesley or Whitefield, he was an early and zealous disciple of Adam Smith.

He failed, as has been seen, in 1785, to establish commercial equality between Britain and Ireland; but in 1787 he secured a measure of free trade in the famous commercial treaty with France. He never renewed, it is true, his attempt to introduce the new spirit into the heart of the whole political system, but it must not be forgotten that Reform was stubbornly opposed by a majority of his colleagues in the Cabinet and a majority, in which there were Whigs as well as Tories, of the House. It must be remembered, too, that Pitt's insistence on the sovereignty of Parliament and the authority of the First Minister of the Crown did as much as the fiasco of George III's American policy to defeat the last attempt of a king of England to turn back the tide of English liberty.

In all this Wilberforce could support his friend with a single mind. Peace, public frugality, freer trade—it was an honest and not un-Christian programme. And the resolve to live up to his faith in politics as in everything else had not carried Wilberforce quite into the clouds. He was no fanatic, and the fanatic's inclination to embrace the rigours of the logical extreme made no appeal to him. He remained a good man of the world, seeking peace but not a quietist, a champion of the weak but not an enemy of all government, considerate to the poor but dreaming no dreams of primitive Christian communism. Save only in the matter of Slavery and the Slave Trade he had no radical propensities. But on Reform, with Yorkshire behind him, he could venture a little farther than Pitt, or, rather, he could do what Pitt would have done in his place. Thus his first achievement on his return to politics in 1786 was the successful conduct through the Commons of a Bill which "aimed directly at purifying county elections by providing a general registration of the freeholders and holding the poll in various places at the same time." It was not Wilberforce's fault that this useful little measure never became law: the country magnates in the Lords, Tory and Whig, combined to kill it. In 1793, again, more free as a private member than Pitt to prove himself unshaken in his principles by the tremors of the cataclysm across the Channel, he kept in close touch with his fellow Yorkshireman, Wyvill, and declared his sympathy with "all moderate Reformers." It was right, he said, "to pay great regard to them and to the object of bringing them to act cordially for the constitution and against the republicans." He intended to express these sentiments openly during the Reform debate of that year, but he failed repeatedly to catch the Speaker's eye. Some notes have been preserved, however, which may have been jotted down in preparation for the speech he meant to make. They reveal, at any rate, the trend of his thought and especially the dominance of moral ideas. To argue from the actual results of the existing machinery of election, he notes, and not to consider how corruptly it works is "the expediency gentleman's system" and it "has this grand vice inherent in it—that national morals [are] of no account whatever in it." Again, "many boroughs now, where interest (often family interest) must either be at once abandoned or maintained by the most unjustifiable means. How wrong to reverse the Divine procedure and make duty and interest incompatible."

High notions, likewise, inspired Wilberforce's support of the Commercial Treaty with France. He did not neglect the material arguments—that the British business world was in favour of it, that the free exchange of British manufactured goods for French raw materials would tend to prevent France from setting herself to develop new industries in competition with Britain, and so forth. But "the most pleasing view he had of the Treaty," he told the Commons, "was in the tendency which he hoped it would have to check destructive contentions between the two countries by making the preservation of a harmonious intercourse the mutual interest of both." And in the course of this speech, not for the first time, he crossed swords, on Pitt's behalf, with Fox. It was a curious encounter; for by opposing a measure which, except for the fact that the government of France was still the most famous embodiment in Europe of the principle of absolutism, was in accordance with all his liberal sympathies, the great Whig had enabled his opponent to use language which might more naturally have fallen from his own lips. Is it necessary, asked Wilberforce, to remain perpetually at feud with France, simply in order to maintain the tradition of the Balance of Power and the policy of allying ourselves always with the weaker states against the stronger in order to maintain the liberty of Europe? "This principle," he said, "has made us splendid in the page of history; but I wish the country could at length learn that important lesson—that the greatness and happiness of a people are not the same. . . . If the right honourable gentleman's system has made us often reap the laurels of victory, yet has it not loaded us with 250 millions of debt? Has it not laid us under the necessity of abridging every cottager in the kingdom of his comforts? And what are the feelings of the poor creature who, with his windows stopped up, with scarce food to eat or a house to live in, by the miserable light of a candle he can scarce afford to burn, is to be compensated for all his distress by reading over a speech of the right honourable gentleman in which he is dignified by the honourable appellation of the Adjuster of the Balance of Power and Guardian of the Liberties of Europe!" Yes! Fox was forced to answer, such *is* the poor cottager's compensation. "That it is that enables him to bear his poverty with cheerfulness, and to feel the satisfaction, amidst all his distress, of reflecting on the thought of his being one of the subjects of a free country, whose characteristic it is to balance the power of Europe." And he belaboured Wilberforce for belittling the power and prestige of England. "Is not his country, then, in a situation to take a part in preserving the liberties of Europe? Does the honourable gentleman mean to hold that language to the world?" Effective debating stuff, no doubt, but it sounds more like Pitt's voice than Fox's. And indeed from time to time hereafter Pitt, as well as Fox, was to find himself somewhat embarrassed by the conscientious Wilberforce's habit of transcending the authoritative party arguments. It can never be very comfortable for Ministers to have their policy earnestly vindicated in the language of the Opposition.

Two other causes taken up by Wilberforce in this first phase of his new political life were not so much exposed to party contention. He had made friends with Samuel Romilly and had been much impressed by the pamphlet which heralded his great crusade against the barbarities of the English penal law. In 1786, therefore, he himself introduced an amending Bill, and carried it through the Commons. It was a mild measure, considering how wide was the scope for humane improvement. Its most striking provision was the substitution of hanging for burning as the capital punishment for women convicted of murdering their husbands. But Lord Loughborough denounced it on points of law, although, or rather because, it had been drafted by Pitt's Law Officers; and on Lord Loughborough's high authority his fellow peers rejected it. The subject, however, had set Wilberforce thinking along another line. He had been brought up against the old problem of the effectiveness of punishment as a preventive. "The barbarous custom of hanging," he wrote to Wyvill in the following year, "has been tried too long, and with the success which might have been expected of it. The most effectual way of preventing the greater crimes is by punishing

the smaller and by endeavouring to suppress that general spirit of
licentiousness which is the parent of every species of vice." But by
what special means, beyond the customary agencies of school and
church and penal code, was this end to be sought? A perusal of
Dr. Woodward's *History of the Society for the Reformation of Manners
in the year 1692* gave Wilberforce his cue. He proposed to found a
similar society. It was to assume the rôle of "the ancient censorship,"
to be "the guardian of the religion and morals of the people." The
project was well received in high quarters. The Archbishop of
Canterbury blessed it. The Duke of Montagu undertook to be the
society's first president. And we are informed by his filial biographers that Wilberforce "spared no labour to attain his object,
visiting in succession the episcopal residences of the prelates of
Worcester, Hereford, Norwich, Lincoln, York, and Lichfield, and
gaining many of the bishops as the first promoters of his scheme."
Influential lay support was also forthcoming on both sides of politics. Pitt was ready to help. Fox, seemingly, was not approached;
but Lord North gave his name. Finally the royal sympathies were
engaged. The conduct of the Prince of Wales had been more than
usually embarrassing of late; rumours of his secret marriage with
Mrs. Fitzherbert were abroad; and it was only when the Prince had
authorised Fox to give the House a direct, quite untrue, but convincing denial of the marriage—"that miserable calumny, that low
malicious falsehood . . . which had not the smallest degree of
foundation"—that the Commons had consented to pay his debts
from the nation's purse to the tune of £161,000. The King, however,
was still sane; it was a year later that his mind gave way; and
since Wilberforce's plan appealed strongly to his genuine domestic
piety, a Royal Proclamation against Vice and Immorality was
issued on June 1, 1787, to provide the new society, which was consequently known as the Proclamation Society, with a pretext and a
programme. Its activities, in which Wilberforce took a vigorous
part for many years, were mostly directed against blasphemous and
indecent publications, but it busied itself also with attempts to
enforce a stricter observance of Sunday among the poor, to suppress
such indecorous rustic festivities as "wakes," and so forth. In 1802
its place was taken by the better-known Society for the Suppression
of Vice—better known if only as the butt of Sydney Smith's mor-
dant humour. "A corporation of informers," he called it, "supported
by large contributions" and bent on suppressing not the vices of the

rich but the pleasures of the poor, on reducing their life "to its regular standard of decorous gloom," while "the gambling houses of St. James's remain untouched." These were well-aimed shafts; and they hit the Proclamation Society as truly as its successor. It was fortunate, surely, that Wilberforce's fine enthusiasm was soon to find a wider and worthier field.

2

There was one vastly wider field of human relations in which any one who believed, like Wilberforce, in the application of Christian principles to politics was bound sooner or later to find himself profoundly interested. From the Age of Discovery onwards the peoples of Europe had been brought into contact with the peoples of Asia and Africa—a multitude of races, infinitely dissimilar in their capacities and in their standards of civilisation, but all alike in this: they were the weaker and the white men the stronger. To any candid Christian mind there could be no clearer case of the eternal issue between might and right. Asia and Africa lay at Europe's mercy—ever more helplessly as her material power grew. Her treatment of them was a palpable test of the validity of her moral and religious professions. And of all the European peoples the test was especially applicable to the British. Masters of the sea-ways of the world, they had already assumed in Wilberforce's day the leading rôle in the relations between Europe and Asia and, in one respect at least, the leading rôle also in the relations between Europe and Africa.

It so happened that, when Wilberforce first entered Parliament, the British connexion with Asia had reached a critical stage. Since the middle of the eighteenth century the East India Company had slipped with rapid and dangerous momentum into a new phase of its career. It had started, at the beginning of the seventeenth century, as a purely commercial concern. For more than a hundred years it had confined itself, almost without a break, to the peaceful routine of trade. Its foothold on Indian soil had been limited to the two or three settlements it had established, with the permission of Indian rulers, for the purpose of carrying on its business. But all this had suddenly been changed. The Mogul Empire, by which the unity and peace of India had been more or less effectively maintained, had collapsed. Released from its binding rim, the kaleidoscopic pattern of Indian races, dynasties and creeds had broken into a tangle of discordant fragments. That huge country, those millions of men and women, had drifted helplessly towards anarchy and chronic warfare. And to make confusion worse confounded, the French Company had sought to make use of the general disorder for an attack on its British rival. The subsequent struggle, with Clive as its protagonist, is a familiar chapter of British history. At its close the members of the East India Company had found themselves no longer merchants merely but the virtual rulers of Bengal and possessors of a great—it might soon be the greatest—political power throughout India. It was a drastic transformation, and it had come about much too swiftly. The Company was unable to face its new obligations. Political power, in Bengal at any rate, it could not now evade, but it would have nothing to do with political responsibility. Its sole object in India was still to be the Indian trade; the maintenance of law and order, the welfare of the Indian people, these were not its affair, these were to remain the business of Indian princes and officials. True, the Bengal Government was entirely the Company's creature. The Company controlled the revenue; paid its puppet rulers; called their tune. Yet, all the time, the Company declined to hold itself responsible for the manner in which they ruled. The results were inevitable. Power divorced from responsibility offers a temptation which human nature cannot easily resist. There were men of honour and humanity in the Company's service in India—and there were others. The opportunities not only for legitimate or illegitimate private trading but for corruption and extortion were almost infinite ; and presently a stream of men, with the bronzed faces and luxurious habits of the East, began to trickle back to England, still in the prime of life but already owners of enormous fortunes. They were not altogether welcome. The old landed families looked askance at the invasion of Mayfair and the countryside by these *nouveaux riches*. The man in the street shook his head at their extravagance and ostentation. And politicians, observing how keenly and with what inexhaustible purses the "nabobs" pushed into the borough market, recalled the precedent of the Proconsuls and the fate of the Roman Republic.

The British Commonwealth, in fact, was standing at the crossways. If the true principles that should control British relations with India had not now been quickly recognised and applied, imper-

fectly and haltingly at first, but with increasing conviction and
consistency as time went on, to the concrete problems of Indian
government, the consequences would have been disastrous both for
India and for Great Britain and in the long run for all the world.
That the worst did not happen, that Britain presently took the right
path, gave the right lead, was mainly due to one Irishman. Burke's
vivid pictures (not always accurately drawn) of the sufferings of the
Indian people and his flaming denunciations (not always scrupu-
lously just) of British misrule in India awakened the public conscience and created the atmosphere of reform. More than that, he
was the first to state in unequivocal terms the new doctrine on
which the reconstruction of British rule in India was to rest. In
his great speech on Fox's India Bill he declared that "all political
power which is set over men . . . ought to be some way or other
exercised ultimately for their benefit," and that the rights and
privileges derived therefrom "are all in the strictest sense a trust."
Truisms, no doubt, of political thought in England, but startlingly
novel in their application to India. In fact, it is not too much to
say that Burke's publication of that idea marks a decisive moment
in history. The principle of trusteeship as the governing rule in
the relations between strong and weak, advanced and backward,
peoples had been set before the world.

Even in his unregenerate days, Wilberforce must have been
shocked, like most Englishmen, at the revelation of the Indian
scandal. He had been in the House when the famous Reports of
the two Committees of 1781, on one of which Burke had been the
outstanding figure, were laid on the table, with their overwhelming
mass of black and authoritative evidence. He had probably voted
for the damnatory resolutions, moved by Dundas in 1782, one of
which had demanded the recall of Warren Hastings, whom Burke
was not alone in regarding as the villain of the piece. And he had
probably supported Dundas's challenge to the Coalition in its early
days of office, when he introduced a Bill to transfer the power of
recall from the Company to the Crown and urged that Hastings
should be the first to suffer under it. And yet he had joined quite
happily in the denunciation of Fox's India Bill by Pitt and his party.
It was only natural. The Bill might be, as impartial critics have long
recognised, a not unworthy embodiment of Burke's ideals. It might
at least attempt to do the essential thing—to force responsibility
for British rule in India on the British Parliament and people by

entrusting the supreme authority over the personnel and conduct
of the Company to a Commission appointed in the first instance
by Parliament and after four years by the Crown. It might be
supported by Fox at his best and by Burke in a speech which ranks
among his masterpieces. But quite naturally—for those were his
unregenerate days—Wilberforce would have none of it. It was the
product of the Coalition, a child of that unseemly marriage. It
was Fox's Bill, not Pitt's. So, as we have seen, he was content to
match his cheap witticisms and his party clap-trap against Burke's
burning sincerity and the purple and the thunder of his eloquence
—content, too, to go all lengths with Pitt in exaggerating the weak
point of the Bill, the appointment of the first Commissioners by
Parliament, into an incredible intrigue to give to Fox and his
friends a really effective and lasting stranglehold on the whole of
British public life. As every one knows, these tactics were gloriously
successful. No need to tell the King that to let the Bill go through
was to surrender his crown to Fox. He jumped at his chance, secured
the Bill's defeat in the Lords, and promptly dismissed the Coalition.
And so, when, next summer, another India Bill was introduced,
which was grounded on the same cardinal principle as Fox's Bill
and which, if it was on the whole a better Bill, differed from it in
form rather than in substance, Wilberforce was free to support it.
It was Pitt's Bill, not Fox's.

But the Act of 1785 had by no means shelved the Indian Question.
It had initiated a new era. It had placed the exercise of the British
"trust" in India under the supervision and control of British
Ministers and the British Parliament. With modifications in detail,
it was to remain the governing Act till the great re-settlement of
1858. But Burke and those who felt as he did were not satisfied. The
future of India might be brighter now, but what of the black past?
Could a new era be built up on unredressed injustice? It was impossible, doubtless, to mark what had been done amiss by every
Englishman in India—impossible to wrest from every guilty
"nabob" his ill-gotten gains. But there was one of them whose
punishment could atone for the immunity of the rest—the man
who had been primarily responsible for British policy in India
since 1772, the man whose recall Parliament had demanded in 1782
and who, a year after the passing of Pitt's Act, was still Governor-
General of Bengal. In 1785-6, therefore, the Indian Question was
right to the front again in the guise of the Hastings Question; and

the Wilberforce of 1786 was not the Wilberforce of 1784. What was the man who had severed all party ties going to think and say about it?

Few *causes célèbres* have occasioned such cross-swearing as the Hastings case. And the reason is not far to seek. In the first place the case became, all too quickly, a party question; and, secondly, the presentation of it was lamentably one-sided. For years past, Francis had been pouring his stream of jealousy and spite into the ears of the Whigs till they had come to conceive Hastings as a monster of iniquity; and, while his enemies were ransacking the archives for evidence that could be twisted into proof of his guilt, Hastings was too much occupied with his overwhelming task in India, and perhaps too proud, to busy himself with propaganda in his own defence. There is something ironical, indeed, in the alliance of Burke's untainted moral passion with so much that was mean and malignant. For in two main respects Hastings had been trying to do in India what Burke wanted done. He had striven from the beginning to awaken and enforce a sense of responsibility among the Company's officials. He could not abolish the bad custom of private trading; but he had cleansed it of its worst impurities. He had reorganised the collection of the revenue under the more direct supervision of his Council. He had established law-courts in Calcutta and in the outlying districts of Bengal to make justice more easily accessible to the Indian population. Hastings, in fact, more than any other man, was the initiator of the tradition of efficient and just administration for the common people of India which was one day to become the unquestionable hall-mark of the British Raj. Moreover, it was due to Hastings that the British Raj continued to exist, and whatever Burke might think of the Company's government, he never desired that Britain should abandon altogether the trust with which Providence, so he held, had charged her. In the dark days of the American War, when France was once more striving for mastery in the East and Britain was no longer in undisputed command of the sea, that far-off British outpost in India would have been overwhelmed but for Hastings's vigour and tenacity. But if Burke could scarcely disapprove the end, the means appalled him. Hastings could not fight without money for his troops. When his official treasury was exhausted, he could get none from England, where, indeed, his own Directors were clamouring for dividends. Yet he had to find it, not for himself, as so many lesser men had

done in India, but for his country. And he found it, in one case at
least, by methods which, like the power behind them, were those of
an Oriental despot, except that the rich man, not the poor, the
prince, not the peasant, was the victim of his extortion. When Raja
Cheyt Singh, the wealthy *zemindar* of Benares, refused the payment
of £50,000 which, in addition to his regular annual tribute, Hastings
had demanded of him in accordance with the Indian custom that
vassals might be called on to assist their paramount chief in time
of emergency, Hastings treated the refusal as proof of disaffection
and determined (as he said himself) "to exact a severe vengeance for
his delinquency and to draw from his guilt the means of relief to
the Company's distress." So, after giving him more than one
warning, he fined him £500,000. On his continued recalcitrance,
Hastings ordered his arrest, and when this was met by rebellion, he
deposed Cheyt Singh and installed a new *zemindar*. Equally notorious was Hastings's treatment of the Begums of Oudh. Those
exalted ladies were unfortunate in being nearly related—one of
them as grandmother, the other as mother—to the Nawab of Oudh
whose tribute to the Company had fallen heavily in arrears. To
enable him to pay this debt the Nawab demanded that the Begums
should surrender to him a share of the family treasure which they
had unjustly been allowed to appropriate; and at the instigation of
the British Resident the sum of £300,000 was grudgingly paid out,
a pledge being given by the Governor-General-in-Council, that no
further claim should be made. Six years later, the Nawab was again
in arrears; and Hastings, in serious financial straits, acceded to his
request that the family wealth should be tapped once more. Since
the Begums had undoubtedly favoured Cheyt Singh's rebellion,
Hastings was able to maintain that the pledge had been invalidated;
and when they resisted, British troops were dispatched to assist the
Nawab's forces, and the treasure was seized. These things happened
in 1780 and 1781, but another of the leading charges against Hastings
belongs to an earlier date. In 1774 he had allowed the Nawab of
Oudh the use of British troops wherewith to conduct an attack on
a border hill-tribe, the Rohillas. They had been sternly suppressed
and the survivors driven from the country.

The assault came to a head in 1786. From the moment when
Hastings landed in England in the previous summer the great body
of public opinion had ranged itself in opposing camps. The Court
at once took Hastings's part, so did influential peers like Lord

Mansfield and Lord Thurlow. Burke and Fox and the Whig party as a whole stood already committed on the other side. Every one was wondering what Pitt would do, for on Pitt's attitude, every one knew, the fate of Hastings depended. But never was Pitt's reserve more baffling. It was thought that the influence of Dundas, his intimate adviser, who, man of the world as he was, could scarcely change the colours he had worn so openly four years before, must go far with Pitt; but, if this were so, he gave no sign of it. And when Burke presently forced the question on the House of Commons, his official declaration was studiously impartial. "I am neither a determined friend nor foe of Mr. Hastings," he said, "but I will support the principles of justice and equity. I recommend a calm dispassionate investigation, leaving every man to follow the impulse of his own mind."

The curtain was now rung up and the drama rapidly developed. In the early months of 1786 Burke brought forward a series of motions for papers. To all of them, save two which involved the publication of confidential matter, Pitt promptly assented, and the motions were carried without a division. The prosecution then demanded that certain witnesses should be called before the House. To this Pitt demurred on the ground that the accused should in justice be heard before his accusers. At this point Wilberforce first intervened. He applauded Pitt's steady course and he begged him not to be driven from it by intemperate attacks. Then came Hastings's appearance at the Bar of the House. It would have been a notable opportunity for an orator. But Hastings was a man of action, and all he could do was to try to set the facts, as he saw them, before his judges. So throughout, not one sitting only, but two, he prosed away from a long written narrative of his thirteen-years' administration. But the House could not be bothered with all those details. It yawned and emptied. Then, after a month's respite, during which both sides were busy with the papers, the climax came. On June 2 Burke propounded the first of his definite charges against Hastings—his conduct with regard to the Rohilla War. Whatever its merits, the charge was weakened by its staleness, and to those members of the House who had not resolved *a priori* to vote for Hastings or against him on every point it seemed unreasonable to press it. Wilberforce spoke before the Government had given a lead. He agreed with the censure passed on the Rohilla War, but he was not prepared to make it the ground of an impeachment. It was Lord North's duty, he argued, to have recalled Hastings at the time. Twelve years had since gone by, and during those years Hastings had spent his life and health in the public service, and had left our affairs in India in a more prosperous state than they had been for long before. To punish him now for his earlier mistakes was "like eating the mutton of a sheep which we had previously shorn of its fleece." The argument was obviously equitable, and Dundas, seizing the chance of a little trimming, strengthened it by pointing out that Hastings had received in the interval "what might be considered as a parliamentary pardon"; he had been reappointed Governor-General of Bengal by statute. Pitt spoke only on a technical point arising from the wording of the motion, and the House, assuming from his silence that the Government was on the whole opposed to the charge, rejected it by 119 votes to 67.

So far Hastings was safe, and his friends were hopeful. If Pitt holds to this moderate line, they thought, there can be no impeachment. And Pitt, for his part, was well aware of his peculiar responsibility. Only eleven days supervened before the second charge—as to Hastings's treatment of Cheyt Singh—was raised, and every moment of those days which he could spare from other pressing business at Downing Street he gave to the study of the case. "I have had hardly hours enough," he wrote to a friend, "to read all the papers on that voluminous article." And when, all too soon, the day arrived, he was still not perfectly certain of his judgment. On this charge he knew he must break silence, and if the Prime Minister spoke, it would be proper that he should not wait till the end of the debate. It opened with a long and vehement speech by Fox, followed by a shorter and more bitter one from Francis. Pitt sat stiffly in his seat, attentive to every word, and, as he winnowed the justice from the rhetoric, the wavering balance of his mind began to settle. But before he spoke the irrevocable words, on which, more than on any others uttered in the House, the fate of a great public servant must depend, he determined to take one man's advice—the only man, perhaps, in that assembly whose conscience he could absolutely trust. Catching Wilberforce's eye, he beckoned him to his place, and they retired together behind the Speaker's chair. "Does not this look very ill to you?" asked Pitt. "Very ill indeed," said Wilberforce. It was enough. The scales had settled. And when Francis had been followed by an unflinching advocate of Hastings who declared downright that he had acted very properly, Pitt rose

to deliver one of the most candid and unequivocal speeches ever
made by a front-bench politician on a burning issue. He frankly
told the House that, if he had followed his inclinations rather than
his duty, he would not have been there, such was the difficulty and
uneasiness he felt at having to form a judgment on the question.
But by a most laborious investigation he had satisfied himself as
to the vote which in his conscience he was bound to give. . . . At
last, then, the decisive word, for which both sides had so long been
waiting, was to be spoken. And soon the friends of Hastings were
rubbing their hands. For Pitt, with the quiet logic of which he was
a master, was busy tearing up Fox's plea that in all his transactions
with Cheyt Singh, from first to last, Hastings had been wrong. He
had been right, he declared, to demand the *zemindar's* feudal aid,
over and above the tribute, in an emergency. Such was the old-
established custom. And the sum required had not been too high.
Cheyt Singh was admittedly capable of paying it. Hastings had
been right, too, in inflicting punishment when the payment was
contumaciously refused. . . . But presently it was the turn of
Hastings's enemies to rejoice. For Pitt went on to say that the
actions of Englishmen in India must conform to other standards
besides those of Oriental custom. "Though the constitution of our
Eastern possessions is arbitrary and despotic, still it is the duty of
every administration in that country to conduct itself by the rules
of justice and of liberty as far as it is possible to reconcile them to
the established government." And in fixing the fine which he had
levied on Cheyt Singh Hastings had not been "guided by any
principle of reason or justice." It was "beyond all proportion
exorbitant, unjust, and tyrannical." Since, then, in this respect he
had committed "a high crime and misdemeanour," if an impeachment should be preferred against him upon the whole of the charges
—and as to that he did not now commit himself—this must be one
of its articles. A few words more—on the subsequent deposition of
the *zemindar*, which was, he held, the inevitable result of his rebellion—and, without any peroration to break the cool judicial tenor
of the speech, Pitt resumed his seat.

From that moment the impeachment of Hastings was a certainty. A few Tories spoke, several voted, against their chief; but
there could be no question of a general revolt, and the motion was
carried by 119 votes to 79. The raising of the charge relating to the
Begums of Oudh a few weeks later was scarcely necessary, for after

what had happened Pitt's vote and the consequent result were a foregone conclusion. The decisive moment had come and gone on June 13 behind the Speaker's chair.

There was uproar, of course, among the Hastings faction, and bitter recriminations were heaped on the young Prime Minister's head. Never, it was said, had a British statesman committed so gross, so coldly calculated, an act of treachery. He had waited to see which way the current of opinion was going to flow, and at the chosen moment he had sacrificed a far greater man than himself to his petty love of popularity and power. Nay, it was worse than that. He had thrown Hastings to the wolves merely to appease a mean Scot's jealousy. Had he not been closeted with Dundas for hours on the morning of the debate? And was it not a well-known fact that Dundas regarded Hastings as a dangerous rival; that Lord Chancellor Thurlow had a "scheme for making him a peer, perhaps a minister"; that the King was bent on obtaining his admission to the Cabinet? . . . What matter that the evidence for these calumnies was of the slightest? It was enough for the passions of the time; it was enough for the magisterial eloquence of Macaulay; it has even been enough for partisans of our own day. But Wilberforce knew better. One evening, many years afterwards, the old man was recalling, as he loved to do, the memories of his long, eventful life. "Oh, how little justice," he exclaimed, "was done to Pitt on Warren Hastings's business! People were asking what could make Pitt support him on this point and that, as if he was acting from political motives, whereas he was always weighing in every particular whether Hastings had exceeded the discretionary powers lodged in him. . . . He paid as much impartial attention to it as if he were a juryman."

3

If the European record in Asia in Wilberforce's day had its dark spots, in Africa it was wellnigh wholly black. It might almost seem as if Nature had decreed that the destiny of Africa should be sacrificed to that of other continents. Cut off from Europe by the vast Sahara, the great mass of it lay for centuries outside the stream of history. Its unindented, harbourless, inhospitable coast, the bars and rapids of its few great rivers, the deadly climate of its tropical belt made exploration difficult and unattractive. And if, as old rumour ran, somewhere in its dark interior immeasurable wealth was to be found, the difficulty of finding it, of getting it away, of developing any systematic commerce in such an impenetrable country and with so primitive a population, repelled the pioneers of European trade. Africa was little more to them than a gigantic obstacle to a straight sea-voyage to Asia. Diaz and da Gama attempted and achieved its circumnavigation merely as a means of reaching India. The Dutch settlement at its southern extremity was only established, and for some centuries of its existence was only valued, as a strategic outpost on the sea-road to the East and a port-of-call for Indian merchantmen. Only in one part of Africa (save where it fronted Europe across the Mediterranean) had Europeans begun to settle and trade in those early days. In the fifteenth century the Portuguese crossed from Madeira to the West coast, planted trading stations along it towards the Equator, and trafficked with the natives for gold and ivory and pepper. But the African trade would never have been very lucrative, it would never have been worth a fraction of the Indian trade, if other products than those had not been found there—products for which there presently developed an almost inexhaustible demand among the leading European nations, and the exploitation of which brought Africa at last into the main current of the world's business.

While Africa was yet barely known, Europe, still groping for the East, had found America: and soon from Carolina through the West Indies to Brazil a chain of European colonies had been created which promised their creators an infinite supply of sugar and tobacco and other desirable commodities, provided only they could find the labour wherewith to till the soil. Unhappily it could not be found in America. The redskins of the North were not of the type to be persuaded or compelled to give up hunting buffalo and take to digging on the pale-faces' plantations. The feebler Indians of the South had been decimated or driven deep into the forests by their Spanish conquerors, and in any case they were not physically fit for the work. Yet somehow or other civilised Europe must have its sweets and solaces: if Nature had imposed obstacles thereto, civilised Europe must use its strength and ingenuity to break them down. And not much ingenuity or strength was needed. The idea came straight from those Portuguese traders who had found something else in Africa than gold. The first cargo brought to Lisbon by the first European company for the exploitation of West Africa had consisted of two hundred negro slaves: and if negroes could work in Portugal, they could work in Brazil. Simple, childlike folk, hot-blooded but docile under the whip, inured to tropical heat, very strong and tough, they might almost seem to have been created for the special needs of colonial planters. Nor was it difficult or dangerous to get them. They could be got, in fact, more easily and in more paying quantity than gold or ivory. So the dilemma was quickly overcome; and in due course the men, women, and children of West Africa were being bundled across the ocean, not in hundreds merely, but in thousands and tens of thousands. The life of America had been saved, so to speak, by a transfusion of blood from Africa.

The merchants of other countries were soon sharing the trade with Portugal and Spain: but it was not till the middle of the sixteenth century that an Englishman first took a hand in it. In 1562 that notable buccaneer, Sir John Hawkins, shipped 300 negroes from Sierra Leone and sold them to Spanish planters in St. Domingo; but for many years after that the English took little, if any, part in the Slave Trade. The agent of the African Chartered Company, established in 1618, told a dealer who offered him slaves that Englishmen did not buy or sell "any that had our own shapes." But when the demand occasioned by the establishment and growth of English colonies in North America and the West Indies increased, these high sentiments were soon forgotten. The main object, it is true, of the first African Company to obtain a charter (1660) was to discover the "golden mines"; nothing was said about slaves; but the new charter granted to the Company in 1663 gave it a monopoly of the trade in West African negroes—the first official recognition of the Slave Trade as a branch of English commerce—while the Company undertook to supply 3000 slaves a year to the West Indian colonies. From that time onwards the expansion of the Slave Trade was steadily encouraged by English statesmen as an integral factor in the commercial and naval strength of England. Forts were built on the Gold Coast, and in 1713 a treaty was concluded with Spain, which transferred from French to English merchants the notorious *Asiento*, the monopoly of the supply of slaves to the Spanish colonies. By the beginning of the eighteenth century the rivalry of the Dutch and the French was overcome, the largest share of the Trade was in English hands, and English traders were dumping about 25,000 negroes on the other side of the Atlantic every year. About 1770,

out of a rough total of 100,000 slaves exported annually from West
Africa by traders of all nations, British ships were carrying from
40,000 to 60,000: and though the British figure dropped as the
result of the American War, it was still the highest on the list in
1787, standing at 38,000, with France a good second at 31,000. Of
the English ports engaged in the Trade Liverpool easily held the
lead. In 1771, for example, 107 ships cleared from Liverpool to
carry 29,250 slaves, 58 from London to carry 8136, 23 from Bristol
to carry 8810, 4 from Lancaster to carry 950. At the beginning of
the nineteenth century, Liverpool had captured six-sevenths of the
whole English trade with West Africa.

The slaves were obtained in three ways—by direct seizure, by
purchase from professional traders, or by barter from a chief. If
it was an unfrequented part of the coast, or if the inhabitants could
be taken by surprise, a sudden armed landing might be made and
the natives kidnapped by force or guile. The grossest treachery was
regarded by some slave-captains as legitimate. On one occasion the
British military Governor of Goree was entertaining a merry party
of over a hundred natives—men, women, and children—when three
slave-captains, who chanced to be present, suggested to him that
the whole party should be seized and carried off to their ships,
alleging that a former Governor, on a similar occasion, had consented. The professional traders, mostly Arabs of old-established
"firms," which had carried on the traffic in the heart of Africa for
ages past, obtained their slaves in the interior and brought them
down to the coast for sale. But a deal with a native chief was the
easiest and most productive method of getting the goods. British
agents would be sent up-country with orders "to encourage the
chieftains by brandy and gunpowder to go to war and make slaves,"
and a chief was rarely to be found who could long hold out against
such encouragement, particularly against the lure of the raw, fiery
spirit. The usual result was an order to his soldiers to round up a
neighbouring village in the night and bring back all the captives
they could make; but sometimes, if his greed were desperate, a
chief might sell his own subjects into slavery. And there was yet
another way of doing business. Enslavement, it was observed,
became an increasingly favourite penalty for crime—not only for
witchcraft and adultery, but for petty offences. Or again, a fine
would be levied in slaves, and if the offender had none to pay it
with, he would be himself enslaved. Even *agents provocateurs* of a

sort were not unknown: if an unwary fellow tribesman could be
tempted astray, there would be brandy and gunpowder for somebody. Inevitably, therefore, the season of the coming of the slave-
ships was a season of terror and violence all along the coast. When
a slaver was seen in the offing, the inhabitants left their work in the
fields and gathered together for safety in armed groups. Raids
meant reprisals. Chief went to war with chief and tribe with tribe
—each victory rewarded by a sale of slaves—until at last, their holds
filled by one means or another with living cargo, the ships set sail
for the West and peace, for a season, settled down again on Africa—
on villages lying wrecked and empty among the neglected corn, on
childless parents and orphaned children, on a people decimated as
by some demoniac visitation.

Meantime the sufferings of the slaves themselves had only
begun. The direct voyage to the West Indies might take three or
four weeks or more in unfavourable weather, and if the complement
was not yet complete the ships might hang about along the coast.
The "hunting-ground" from Cape Verde to the Gulf of Guinea lay
close to the Equator and the route thence to the West Indies was
entirely within the tropical belt. On a luxurious modern steamship
it would be a trying voyage. For the slaves in their small sailing-
ships this "Middle Passage" was an inferno. The bigger the cargo,
the bigger the profit—it averaged between £2 and £3 per slave in
the eighteenth century—and a boat of 100 to 150 tons was made to
carry from 300 to 600 slaves. The space between decks was usually
about five feet, and this was divided into two by a broad shelf on
each side with a passage-way in the middle. On the floor and on
the shelves the male slaves were laid, manacled together in pairs
and so closely packed that often they had not room to lie flat on
their backs. Suddenly torn from their homes, wholly unused to the
sea, terrified by their present fate and the prospect of unknown
sufferings to come, squeezed together, like sardines, in sultry heat
and rank air, fed on the coarsest food—it is not surprising that
numbers of them fell ill. Dysentery of a kind was always rife among
them; and there was no sanitary equipment. In fine weather they
would be taken on deck for a time, and forced to dance in their
chains for exercise, while their quarters below were being cleaned.
In rough weather they had to stay where they were. What the
conditions must have been like in a severe Atlantic gale of some
days' duration it is impossible to imagine. No wonder that some-

times as many as a quarter of the slaves died on the voyage. No wonder that sometimes a slave took advantage of a chance release from his fetters and his captors' surveillance to leap into the sea. The women and children were not chained together or so closely imprisoned, but the women were habitually exposed to the lust, and the children to the cruelty—sometimes the fatal cruelty—of the captain and crew. John Newton used to tell the story of a mate "who threw a child overboard because it moaned at night in its mother's arms and kept him awake." Nor were the slaves the only sufferers. The captains of the slave-ships were a peculiar class: and their crews suffered in a special degree from the hardships and the brutal treatment which in those days were more or less a regular part of the sailor's life at sea. And the contagion of disease was unescapable. The death-rate among the white men engaged in the Slave Trade was far higher than in any other field of the merchant service.

As the end of the voyage approached, the slaves were examined and prepared for sale. Wounds, caused by storm or ill usage, were doctored up and, as far as possible, concealed. But all traces of the Middle Passage could not always be removed; and the reports of the agents at the ports in the early records are full of complaints: "The parcel of negroes were very mean." "Very bad, being much abused." "These . . . included some little boys and dying negroes." Strong men were singly and quickly disposed of at good prices—as much as £40 apiece—but the sick and injured would be lumped with women and children in a batch and sold off cheap. "Refuse" such were called. And so, at last, those wretched Africans found in far-away plantations oversea their second "homes," where some of them might in time be happy—happier, perhaps, than they had ever been in Africa, if the master were kind-hearted and the meaning of freedom forgotten—and some of them might not. . . .

4

How was it—we may well ask—that eighteenth-century Englishmen, who, whatever their faults, were not devilishly cruel, could tolerate the continuance of this hideous scandal? Doubtless the facts were not very widely known. Doubtless the public as a whole knew as little and cared as little about Africans as Indians. And it

required, no doubt, an unusual effort of imagination to realise the
sufferings of those remote black men. But why was there no
organised attempt to enlighten the public, to awaken its imagination and its conscience? Why did the leaders of State and Church
do nothing? Partly, no doubt, for economic reasons—because the
Slave Trade was a profitable element in British business (the Liverpool slavers, for instance, between 1783 and 1793, carried over
300,000 slaves to the West Indies, sold them for over £15,000,000,
and made a net profit of 30 per cent.) and because the productivity
of the West Indies and hence of the West Indian trade seemed indis-
solubly linked up with it. "The impossibility of doing without
slaves in the West Indies," wrote a London publicist in 1764, "will
always prevent this traffic being dropped. The necessity, the absolute
necessity, then, of carrying it on, must, since there is no other, be
its excuse." Partly, again, for political reasons—because the withdrawal of Britain alone from so large a field of the carrying-trade
might greatly injure her maritime strength in comparison with
that of less scrupulous European rivals; partly because any interference with the Trade by the mother-country would arouse the
bitterest resentment in the colonies; even because—so it was
actually argued—the filling-up of the islands with a slave population
would tend to keep them more loyal to the imperial connexion than
if, like those tiresome New England colonies, they developed into
little democracies of white men with English notions of political
freedom. Doubtless all these reasons helped in different degrees to
keep the humaner feelings in their proper place. But there was one
other check, and that not the least effective. The agents and connexions of the Slave Trade on the one hand and the colonial planters
on the other constituted in course of time a powerful vested interest
in England. The "West Indians" became as well known and almost
as formidable a body in politics and in society as the "nabobs"; and
it must be a bold man who would face their anger and their
influence.

This was a powerful array of arguments and interests, powerful
enough to keep the leaders of English opinion and the makers of
English policy from interfering with the Slave Trade for a very long
time. But the silence of consent was not unbroken. No sooner had
the Trade firmly established itself than individual protests began to
make themselves heard. The first of them, it is safe to assume, were
made not in England itself but in the American colonies. In

America imagination was not needed. The thing was there. It was to maintain Slavery in the southern continental colonies as well as the West Indies that the Trade existed; and if the plantations which required slave-labour lay only in the South, they were very close to the Puritan consciences of the middle and northern colonies. In 1688 both the two allied questions—the Slave Trade and Slavery itself—were raised at a meeting of German Quakers in Germantown, Pennsylvania. "Tho' they are black," it was said, "we cannot conceive there is more liberty to have them slaves as it is to have other white ones. . . . Those who steal or robb men and those who buy or purchase them, are they not all alike?" In 1696 the Yearly Meeting of the Quakers of Pennsylvania advised "that Friends be careful not to encourage the bringing in of any more Negroes." This warning was constantly repeated, but without complete effect, until in 1774 a decree of expulsion from the Society was passed on any Friend who should persist in concerning himself with the Trade. At the same time, manumission of existing slaves was recommended to all Friends and in 1776 it was made compulsory. But in America as in England the claims of justice and humanity were no match for economic interests. To the planters of the South and the merchants of the North the Trade was a "necessity"; and such restrictions on it as were imposed by the colonial legislatures, usually in the form of import duties, were mainly inspired by fear, by the alarming results of the great influx of black men into their small white communities, by occasional negro risings in Carolina and even by a "negro plot" in New York. And those restrictions were mostly disallowed by the British Government in the interests of the British element in the Trade.

Meantime Englishmen at home had not been silent. As early as 1680 an Anglican clergyman, named Godwyn, who had been a student of Christ Church, Oxford, and had gone out to Barbados, published a tract entitled *The Negro's and Indian's Advocate, suing for their admission into the Church*, in which he asserted that the planters excused their brutal treatment of their slaves by the plea that they were brutes, proved by sundry arguments that as a matter of fact they were not apes or drills but men, and incidentally described the traffic in them as "a Cruelty capable of no Palliation, and for which *Vengeance* cannot be long expected ere it fall upon the *inhuman Authors*." About the same time, Richard Baxter, the great Nonconformist, roundly declared in his *Christian Directory* that slave-pirates ought to be regarded as the common enemies of mankind. Similar protests were made at intervals by individual preachers and publicists of lesser note; and in 1766 Bishop Warburton, an outstanding figure in more than one crucial question of his time, proclaimed from the pulpit that "the infamous traffic for slaves directly infringes both divine and human law." But there was no organised movement, religious or secular, against the Trade till in 1727 the Quakers, the first Christian community in England as in America to make a stand collectively and consistently against this negation of Christianity, passed a resolution condemning Slave Trade and Slavery together. In 1758, in step with their brothers in Pennsylvania, they proceeded to warn, and in 1761 to disown, all Friends who continued to participate in the Trade. The Wesleyans, meantime, had followed the Quakers' lead. In 1774 John Wesley himself entered the lists with his widely read *Thoughts upon Slavery*. In the secular world, too, voices, somewhat lonely voices, were raised from time to time against the whole slave-system. Locke, for instance, opened his first *Treatise on Civil Government* (1689) with a denunciation of Slavery, and Adam Smith cut at the root of its economic defence by arguing in the *Wealth of Nations* (1775) that slave labour was dearer than free.

Nor was it only in religious or academic circles that attention was being drawn to the African scandal. Already before the end of the seventeenth century the tragedy of enslavement had begun to figure in fashionable literature. *Oroonoko*, by Mrs. Aphra Behn, the first novel with a negro for its hero, was posthumously published in 1696 and afterwards dramatised by Southerne. Early in the eighteenth century Defoe took up the cudgels. He condemned the Slave Trade in his poem on *The Reformation of Manners*; he pleaded for kindlier treatment of the negroes in his *Life of Colonel Jacque*; and in *Robinson Crusoe* (1719) he drew a picture, to be adored by every English child for centuries to come, of a coloured man who could prove himself a shrewd, devoted, lovable comrade to a white man. Pope's *Essay on Man*, published in 1733, contained the famous lines on the "poor Indian," dreaming of

> Some happier island in the watery waste,
> Where slaves once more their native land behold,
> No fiends torment, no Christians thirst for gold.

And Thomson broke the homely quietude of the *Seasons* (1726-30) with a grim picture of a shark as it follows a slave-ship,

> And from the partners of that cruel trade,
> Which spoils unhappy Guinea of her sons,
> Demands his share of prey.

"Why must I Afric's sable children see, Vended for slaves?" wrote Richard Savage a few years later; and "See the poor native quit the Libyan shores, Ah! not in love's delightful fetters bound," sang Shenstone, not without bathos.

Meantime something more practical than the poets could do was being done for the slaves by the cold machinery of English law. It may seem strange to the present generation of Englishmen that less than two hundred years ago a negro slave was a commonplace sight in England. Till past the middle of the eighteenth century, planters and merchants resident in the colonies were accustomed to bring some of their domestic slaves with them in their visits to the home-country. It was more comfortable, no doubt, and cheaper than hiring English servants; but it had its drawbacks. Many masters were kind to their slaves; many slaves were devoted to their masters: but slaves in less happy households, observing the freedom of white servants, and the opportunities of escape afforded by a crowded town, frequently absconded; and their masters were put to the trouble of hunting after them and bringing them back, if necessary by force. And this, though they can never have suspected it, did more than anything else to set in motion a train of events that was ultimately to bring not only the Slave Trade but Slavery itself to an end. For it thrust realities, hitherto far off, under the very eyes of the English people. In the streets of London now, just as if it was in Georgia or Jamaica, Englishmen and Englishwomen could see miserable negroes dragged along to captivity and punishment. For the most part they did not like the spectacle. It startled their imagination. It stirred their sympathies. It was unseemly, un-English. It hurt their pride in the tradition of personal liberty which was rooted so deep in English soil. It was repugnant to their general notions of English law. Surely, they muttered behind their windows, every one in England was free, provided, of course, he had been baptised.

Whether this was indeed the law or not, it was an idea that

intelligent slaves were quick to appreciate and to act upon. And
they had no difficulty, if once they could slip away, in finding
Christian ministers to baptise them and warm-hearted citizens to
be their godfathers. By this means they obtained at least some
measure of protection, ineffective as it often might be, against the
arbitrary power of their masters. Godfathers could not always
prevent the recapture of fugitive slaves; but, if they were stout,
contentious Englishmen, they could, and often did, threaten their
masters with a suit at law if they attempted to remove the slaves
from England. Interference of this kind became in fact so frequent,
so tiresome, and, in the uncertainty of the law, so menacing that
in 1729 the West Indian community appealed for an opinion to the
Law Officers of the Crown. It got all it could want. Attorney-
General Yorke and Solicitor-General Talbot pronounced that
neither residence in England nor baptism affected the master's
"right and property" in the slave and that "the master may legally
compel him to return again to the plantations." Naturally the
masters gave all the publicity they could to this reassuring doctrine;
and now that the law was unequivocally behind them, they abandoned such reticence and discretion as they had hitherto observed
out of deference to English taste. They saw no reason now why the
whole slave-business should not be treated with the same frankness
in England as in the colonies. They advertised the sale of slaves by
auction in the newspapers. They advertised, too, for runaways, and
offered rewards for their apprehension. To capture slaves and put
them safe on board ship at a price became almost a regular trade in
the East End of London. But again the West Indians had not
reckoned with the instincts of stay-at-home Englishmen. Slave-
hunts, slave-auctions! Such things might happen every day in
Africa or America; but they could not go on in England. Before
very long, they had jolted the nascent movement against Slavery
and all its concomitants one stage farther: they had created the
first of the Abolitionists.

  Granville Sharp was born in 1735 of an eminent ecclesiastical
family. Though his grandfather was Archbishop of York and his
father Archdeacon of Northumberland, he started life himself in
the humble station of apprentice to a linen merchant. In 1758,
however, he obtained a clerkship in the Ordnance Department,
where he employed his leisure in writing treatises on the text of
the Old Testament and the use of the English tongue. It happened

one day in 1765 that he was in the house of his brother, William Sharp, a surgeon, noted for his readiness to help the London poor, when a slave, called Jonathan Strong, appealed for medical aid. He belonged, he told them, to a certain David Lisle who had brought him from Barbados and had so maltreated him in his lodgings at Wapping, especially by beating him over the head with a pistol, that his eyesight had become affected; then he had been attacked by an ague which had left him lame in both legs; and finally, being useless for work, he had been deserted by his master. William Sharp soon cured him; and Granville, whose sympathies had been keenly excited, provided him temporarily with money and presently found him a situation with an apothecary. Unfortunately, some two years later, Jonathan was observed by his old master, while he was taking medicine to a customer's house. Too obviously, he was quite fit again for work or for sale. So David Lisle procured two men to kidnap him and promptly sold him to John Kerr, a Jamaican, for £30. Jonathan Strong at once appealed to his godfathers, and they to Granville Sharp, who hastened to the Lord Mayor, Sir Robert Kite, and persuaded him to intervene. Kite sent for Strong, and, after some legal debate, discharged him on the ground that he had been deprived of his liberty without a warrant. As the parties were leaving the court, the captain of the ship that was to carry Strong to Jamaica attempted to drag him away, but on being charged by Sharp in formal terms with an assault, he released his hold. So Strong went off in safety with his protector, and apparently Kerr made no further effort to recover his property.

This case, though it had ended happily, had made a deep and permanent impression on Sharp's mind. The wretched Jonathan, despite the desertion and the two years' interval, had still been legally Lisle's to sell and Kerr's to buy—and this in England! The ruling of the Crown lawyers had been quoted in the court and the Lord Mayor had not ventured to contest it. But was that ruling inexpugnable? Sharp applied to no less an authority than Blackstone and was told it was. Still he would not accept it. He would study the law himself. And after two or three years of hard work he produced a book on *The Injustice and dangerous Tendency of tolerating Slavery in England* in which he resuscitated the earlier opinion of Chief Justice Holt that every slave entering England became free and supported it with a learned exposition of the principles of villeinage and of the Common Law. Soon after the publication of this book, he rescued another slave from a ship on the point of sailing for the West Indies by means of a writ of *Habeas Corpus*. Neither in this case nor in Strong's had the broader legal issue been faced; and the continual evasion of it—for there were other cases besides those in which Sharp was concerned—began seriously to disquiet the legal authorities, until, in 1772, Sharp brought up the case of James Somerset, a captured runaway, as a test case for definitely resolving the conflict between Holt's ruling and that of Yorke and Talbot. Naturally the West Indian community was alarmed. Planters and merchants rallied to the side of Somerset's owner, Stewart, and put up the money for engaging the professional services, if not the personal sympathies, of the brilliant Whig barrister, Dunning. The case was heard at three sittings, and at each the court was crowded. For it was far more than a West Indian concern. The general interest of the public had been roused. English history, it was felt, was in the making; and certainly when Chief-Justice Mansfield, the greatest lawyer of his day, delivered judgment on June 22, a conspicuous piece of English history was made. "Tracing the subject to natural principles," he said, "the claim of slavery never can be supported. The power claimed never was in use here or acknowledged by the law." Slavery was still to exist, for more than sixty years, on English soil overseas; but from that moment it ceased to exist on the soil of England.

Religion, literature, individual philanthropy, and finally the law had thus played their part in the gradual awakening of English opinion to the anachronism of Slavery and the Slave Trade. But the only positive result of it all was the Somerset judgment; and that in itself had done no more than prevent slaves being brought to England. The whole inhuman business on the Guinea Coast, on the Middle Passage, in the island slave-markets, could go on exactly as before. Neither churchmen nor professors nor poets nor lawyers could stop it for an hour. Only Parliament could do that. No one questioned its legality outside England: it could only be stopped by an Act of Abolition. And Parliament, through all those years, had done virtually nothing. It had, indeed, in 1750, passed an Act to regulate the Trade, which, after reciting its advantages to Britain and its necessity to the colonies in the preamble, had solemnly pronounced any deed of "fraud, force, or violence" committed against a native in the process of carrying him off from Africa to be an offence punishable by a fine of £100. Palpably the preamble was more important than the clause. Parliament continued to regard the advantages and necessity of the Trade as unquestionable; but Parliament did nothing to enforce the punishment of a single trader for any of the countless acts of fraud and violence without which the Trade—as everybody knew—could not be carried on. It was not that the sympathies of the average Englishman, in Parliament or out of it, had been quite untouched. When he read about the wrongs of Slavery or the Trade or saw some faint reflection of them on the stage, he was moved to pity and sometimes perhaps to indignation. And at close quarters, of course, he could not endure them. But as long as they were out of sight, he could. He came, in fact, to regard them as part of the inevitable evil in the order of creation. Men were but men; everybody was involved in it; every other maritime nation was as eager as England to profit by the Trade and envied her the lion's share of it. The American colonists, it was true, protested at having it forced on them by the disallowance of their restrictions; but there was more politics than morals in their indignation. When Congress banned the Trade in 1774, it was mainly as a part of the general policy of severing all commercial connexion with the mother-country, a move in the preliminaries to rebellion. And when the war itself had come, when the Declaration of Independence was being framed, it was not only morals that inspired the charge levied against the King in the first draft of the document, of waging " cruel war against human nature itself, violating its most sacred rights of life and liberty in the persons of a distant people who never offended him, captivating and carrying them into slavery in another hemisphere or to incur miserable death in their transportation thither." Jefferson, the draughtsman, himself confessed later on that this clause " was struck out in complaisance to South Carolina and Georgia who had never attempted to restrain the importation of slaves and who, on the contrary, still wished to continue it. Our northern brethren also, I believe, felt a little tender under those censures; for though their people had very few slaves themselves, yet they had been pretty considerable carriers of them to others." In any case, as soon as the war was over, the Trade was complacently and profitably resumed in Georgia and the Carolinas and New England, just as it was resumed in England as soon as the seas and the markets were reopened. It made no difference that some of the most notable men of the day had joined,

during the war period, in the attack upon the Trade—that Adam
Smith, as has been seen, had demonstrated that slave-labour was
uneconomic; that Robertson's widely read *History of America* had
denounced the Trade as equally repugnant to humanity and religion;
that Paley in his *Moral Philosophy* had expressed the fond hope that
"the great revolution which had taken place in the western world
may conduce (and who knows but that it was designed?) to accelerate
the fall of this abominable tyranny"; that Bishop Porteus had
preached a sermon on the wrongs of the negroes before the Society
for the Propagation of the Gospel. Nor did it matter much that
the thorny question had been revived in Parliament. It had been
quickly shelved again by the appointment of a Commission in 1775
to take evidence on the conditions of the Trade. And in 1776 the
House of Commons had promptly rejected the first of the long
series of ineffective resolutions against the Trade moved by Hartley,
a predecessor of Wilberforce's in the seat for Hull, and seconded by
that generous Yorkshireman, Sir George Savile. All this was of
small account. The sacrifice of Africa was still a "necessity" for
Europeans across the Atlantic. The Trade, indeed, could never
satisfy the planters' needs. Conditions of slave-life on the plantations were not conducive to any large natural increase in the stock.
Always more imported slaves were wanted, and some day more
islands might be British, more land available for cultivation. There
seemed no reason why the Trade should ever come to an end.

5

   Thus resigned, thus fatalistic was the attitude of the House of
Commons when Wilberforce became a member of it. And he was
soon enabled to judge its temper for himself. The Quakers were not
minded to let the matter drop; and, when in 1783 a Bill was introduced to prevent servants of the Crown from engaging in the
business of the African Company, they took advantage of this
incidental reference to the Slave Trade to present a petition against
it. The Coalition had just come into office, and Lord North responded with urbanity. "The object and tendency of the petition,"
he said, "ought to recommend it to every humane breast; and it
did credit to the feelings of the most mild and humane set of
Christians in the world. But still he was afraid that it would be

found impossible to abolish the Slave Trade . . . for it was a trade which had, in some measure, become necessary to almost every nation in Europe; and as it would be next to an impossibility to induce them all to give it up and renounce it for ever, so he was apprehensive that the wishes of the humane petitioners could not be accomplished." Two years later, another appeal was made to Parliament. The inhabitants of Bridgwater petitioned for "the extinction of that sanguinary traffic." The petition was presented by Poulet and Hood, the members for the borough; and in due course they reported to their constituents that it had been ordered to "lie on the table." "There did not appear," they said, "the least disposition to pay any further attention to it." What Wilberforce thought is not recorded.

The Quakers, meantime, had not by any means resigned themselves to Parliament's cool *non possumus*. In 1784 the Meeting for Sufferings, a sort of standing committee to which the matter was entrusted, prepared a written statement entitled *The Case of our Fellow-creatures, the oppressed Africans, respectfully recommended to the serious Consideration of the Legislature of Great Britain, by the people called Quakers*. Copies were sent to the King and Queen and the Prince of Wales, to Pitt, who was now Prime Minister, to Lord Chancellor Thurlow and Chief Justice Mansfield, to Lord Howe, First Lord of the Admiralty, to the Speaker, and to the members of both Houses of Parliament. Twelve thousand copies in all were printed and circulated. In 1785 they likewise promoted the circulation of a book by Anthony Bezenet, an American Quaker, on "the calamitous state of the enslaved negroes in the British Dominions," and deputations waited on the head masters of Winchester, Eton, Harrow, Westminster, Charterhouse, and other schools to ask them to allow their scholars to be given copies of it. Since 1783, moreover, a small committee of six—William Dillwyn, George Harrison, Samuel Hoare, Thomas Knowles, John Lloyd and Joseph Woods— had been acting as a sort of permanent executive "for the relief and liberation of the negro slaves in the West Indies and for the discouragement of the Slave Trade on the coast of Africa" by means of personal influence, publication of books, and propaganda in the newspapers. This little body soon found itself drawn into collaboration with other pioneers outside the circle of Friends—chief among them Granville Sharp, who had continued ever since the Somerset case to work for the cause on his own account, corresponding with

Bezenet and other Abolitionists in the United States and with the leaders of the established Church in England. Another useful ally was the Rev. James Ramsay, who had spent nineteen years in St. Christopher and had returned to take up a living at Teston in Kent burning to redress the negroes' wrongs. His *Essay on the Treatment and Conversion of the African Slaves in the Sugar Colonies*, published in 1784, was the first of a series of outspoken pamphlets from his pen. And presently a recruit was found who was ready to devote the whole of his life to the cause. Thomas Clarkson, son of the headmaster of Wisbeach Grammar School, had come into residence at St. John's College, Cambridge, about the time that Wilberforce went down. He was evidently a "sap"; he had come up with an exhibition from St. Paul's; he worked hard for his degree; and in 1784 he won the first prize for the Latin Essay for B.A.s of "middle" standing. It so happened that in 1785 the Vice-Chancellor, whose duty it was to choose the subjects for the Latin Essays, was Dr. Peckard, Master of Magdalene College and a determined foe of the Slave Trade; and the subject he set for "senior" B.A.s was *Anne liceat invitos in servitutem dare?* or *Is it right to make men slaves against their will?* Clarkson again competed. "In studying the thesis," he afterwards said, "I conceived it to point directly to the African Slave Trade, and more particularly as I knew that Dr. Peckard (in a sermon in the previous year) had pronounced so warmly against it." It was a safe assumption; and Clarkson, having devoured all the books about West Africa he could find and discussed the question with military friends who had served in the West Indies, won the first prize. In due course he read his essay in the Senate-house; and as he rode back to London he found himself unable to think of anything but the Slave Trade. "I became at times very seriously affected," he records, with the zest for personal detail which protracts but enlivens his *History of the Abolition of the Slave Trade*. "I stopped my horse occasionally, and dismounted and walked. I frequently tried to persuade myself in these intervals that the contents of my essay could not be true. . . . Coming in sight of Wades Mill in Hertfordshire, I sat down disconsolate on the turf by the roadside and held my horse. Here a thought came into my mind—that, if the contents of the essay were true, it was time some person should see these calamities to their end. Agitated in this manner, I reached home." The agitation continued. When he set himself to translate his essay into English for publication, the truth of the evils it described once more stared him in the face, stared him out of countenance. Presently he made Dillwyn's acquaintance and learned from him—what he had not hitherto suspected—that other Englishmen were troubled by those facts and had banded together to deal with them. Then he met Granville Sharp and Ramsay. Finally, in 1787, he came to his decision. He would abandon the clerical career he had begun—he was already in deacon's orders—and devote the whole of his life to the destruction of the Slave Trade.

In the summer of 1787 this band of fellow workers formally consolidated itself, with the original group of Quakers for its kernel, into a Committee for the Abolition of the Slave Trade, with Granville Sharp as its first chairman. It was well manned for its initial task—to elicit, to master, and to spread broadcast the widest possible amount of evidence as to the realities of the Trade. But that was not enough. If the country must first be schooled and roused, the second step must be to break through the apathy of Parliament, to defy such fatalistic doctrine as Lord North's, to introduce and— tremendous task!—to carry a Bill for the abolition of the Trade. And for this a politician was needed, and a politician endowed with very rare gifts indeed. He must possess, in the first place, the virtues of a fanatic without his vices. He must be palpably single-minded and unselfseeking. He must be strong enough to face opposition and ridicule, staunch enough to endure obstruction and delay. In season and out of season, he must thrust his cause on Parliament's attention. Yet, somehow or other, Parliament must not be bored. He must not be regarded—and the planters, no doubt, would do their best to cultivate this idea—as the tiresome victim of an *idée fixe*, well-meaning possibly, but an intolerable nuisance. Somehow or other he must be persistent, yet not unpopular. Secondly, he must possess the intellectual power to grasp an intricate subject, the clarity of mind to deal with a great mass of detailed evidence, the eloquence to expound it lucidly and effectively. He must be able to speak from the same brief a score of times without surfeiting his audience with a hash of stale meat. And, since the Slave Trade is his theme, he must have a certain natural delicacy of feeling. He will have terrible things to say; they will form an essential part of his case; but in the choice of them and in the manner in which he says them he must avoid the besetting sin of the professional humanitarian. He must never be morbid. He must not seem to take a pleasure in dwelling on the unsavoury vices of his fellow men. He must not pile up the horrors and revel in atrocious details. He must shock, but not nauseate, the imagination of his hearers. Finally, he must be a man of recognised position in society and politics. It must be impossible for wealthy West Indians to deride him in London drawing-rooms as an obscure crank, a wild man from beyond the pale. And he must have, or by some means must obtain, a footing in Downing Street. For without at least some shadow of support from Government his task might well prove desperate.

Such were the requisite qualifications for the politician needed to lead the movement for the abolition of the Slave Trade in Parliament; and, as we know, a politician so qualified was available. Like many other Englishmen of good feeling, Wilberforce had early been impressed with the abuses, actual and potential, of Slavery and the Trade. Indeed the precocious boy had written, at the age of fourteen, a letter to a York newspaper "in condemnation of the odious traffic in human flesh." But the subject had not haunted or depressed him, and it was not till he was twenty-one that his active interest was reawakened. A friend of his chanced to be going to Antigua, and Wilberforce wrote to ask him to collect some first-hand information as to the treatment of slaves in the West Indies. "I expressed," he said afterwards, "my determination, or at least my hope, that some time or other I should redress the wrongs of those wretched and degraded beings." Three years later, in 1783, he first met Ramsay, but it was not till 1786 that the acquaintance bore fruit. In the interval Ramsay had published his first pamphlet, and among its many readers were his old friend and patron, Sir Charles Middleton, afterwards Lord Barham, First Lord of the Admiralty in the days of Trafalgar, and his public-spirited wife. So shocked was the latter at Ramsay's revelations that she entreated her husband to take the matter up in Parliament and cast about in her mind as to which of the front-rank politicians might be prevailed upon to undertake the championship of the cause. Her choice fell on the young member for Yorkshire whose ability and eloquence were already well known and who was, moreover, so usefully intimate with Pitt. So Wilberforce was invited to Teston; Ramsay was reintroduced to him; and to the rector's torrent of appalling facts Lady Middleton added her own earnest prayers.

It has sometimes been asserted that Lady Middleton's initiative decided the issue. "The abolition of the Slave Trade," wrote the venerable Ignatius Latrobe in 1815, "was, under God and when the time was come, the work of a *woman*." But Wilberforce himself put the case in truer perspective when he said in after life that "it was just one of those many impulses which were all giving to my mind the same direction." One such impulse was certainly the intercourse he had with Clarkson in 1787.

> On my first interview with him [the latter's faithful prose records] he stated frankly that the subject had often employed his thoughts and that it was near his heart. He seemed earnest about it and also very desirous of taking the trouble of enquiring further into it. Having read my book, which I had delivered to him in person, he sent for me. He expressed a wish that I would make him acquainted with some of my authorities for the assertions in it, which I did afterwards to his satisfaction. He asked me if I could support it by any other evidence. I told him I could. I mentioned Mr. Newton, Mr. Nisbet, and several others to him. He took the trouble of sending for all these. He made memorandums of their conversation, and, sending for me afterwards, showed them to me. On learning my intention to devote myself to the cause, he paid me many handsome compliments. He then desired me to call upon him often and to acquaint him with my progress from time to time. He expressed also his willingness to afford me any assistance in his power in the prosecution of my pursuits.

John Newton's name suggests another "impulse." No one at this period was more intimate with Wilberforce; none had greater influence over him; none knew better what torments the young penitent had lately passed through, what vows he had made to prove himself worthier of grace. Is it not likely that the old pastor seized the opportunity and spoke long and earnestly to Wilberforce of the field in which, as he knew too well, a great redeeming work was crying to be done? At any rate it was Wilberforce's "conversion," whatever the personal suggestions which followed it, that primarily accounts for his fateful decision. He returned to his place in the House of Commons, as has been seen, with quite a new conception of his political career. He felt that in previous sessions he had been merely wasting his time. "The first years that I was in Parliament," he once said, "I did nothing. . . . My own

distinction was my darling object." Now he was determined—
partly, maybe, owing to Pitt's kindly and practical sympathy—at
any rate to do *something*. But what was it to be? What cause could
pass the test of his new conscience? It must be something outside
or above the party programmes, untainted and unwarped by the
pretences and compromises of party strife. It must be something
big; for otherwise the talents which he knew had been given him
to use had better be used elsewhere than in politics. Up to a point
the notion of a great campaign against vice might seem to satisfy
these conditions. But was this enough? It did not readily lend itself
to parliamentary treatment; and surely some more tangible, more
exacting, more drastic task was needed than the constricted and
rather humdrum activities of the Proclamation Society. To Wilberforce, in some such questioning mood, the thought of taking up
the cause of the slaves must at once have made a strong appeal.
Here was a cause which no party had cared or dared to touch. Here,
if you like, was a big cause—a cause on which depended the moral
and physical welfare of hundreds of thousands of human beings.
Here, above all, was a challenge which no Christian could evade.
Coming when it did, in fact, the idea seemed to Wilberforce to be
charged with higher than human inspiration; and his mind was
soon made up. "God Almighty," he wrote in his journal, "has set
before me two great objects, the suppression of the Slave Trade and
the reformation of manners." The order is significant. The Proclamation Society may still claim part of his thoughts and his
time, but most of them will henceforward be occupied elsewhere.

Wilberforce promptly set himself to master the facts. He sought
out and closely questioned the London merchants in the African
and West Indian trade. "I found them," he says, "at this time ready
to give me information freely, the Trade not having yet become
the subject of alarming discussion." Any one, indeed, who knew or
cared anything about the matter became the prey of his tact and
charm and curiosity. There were constant interviews at the house
he had now taken in town in Palace Yard. Clarkson called to report
progress at least once a week. And there were breakfast-parties at
Sir Charles Middleton's and long talks over the fire, and finally
regular meetings at Palace Yard between Granville Sharp, Ramsay
and Clarkson on the one side and one or two friendly members of
Parliament on the other. Thus, in the course of 1787, Wilberforce
began to feel that, though he had a great deal more to learn, he

was sufficiently equipped to open the case in the House of Commons. But one thing remained to be done before he finally committed himself to political action. Just as Pitt had consulted him before making his decisive speech on the Hastings case, so now he consulted Pitt. The opportunity came when he was staying at Pitt's country-house at Holwood; but he hesitated, it seems, from modesty or shyness, to raise the question himself. And Pitt, who was doubtless aware of what had been occupying so much of Wilberforce's mind for many months past, may well have hesitated too. The political championship of Abolition was not a task to be lightly urged upon a friend, especially upon one so sensitive and seemingly so fragile. It might leave him broken in health, and isolated and crippled in politics. Had not Burke himself, before he became engrossed in India, contemplated the task, but refrained from undertaking it for fear of rousing a storm that might rend and shatter the Whig party? And was not Pitt himself, *mutatis mutandis*, in the same position as Burke? But he knew that the plea of party loyalty and unity did not apply to Wilberforce. He knew, too, how closely the cause must harmonise with his new religious zeal; and to his practical mind this was probably the determining argument. The task might be painful and exhausting; but, once absorbed in it, Wilberforce would be safe at least from the temptation, which not so long ago he had confessed to him, of secluding himself altogether from the world of affairs; safe from drifting into extravagant or ineffective pietism; safe from spending all his days on nothing more fruitful than the Proclamation Society. In a sense, indeed, the idea must have seemed as providential to Pitt as it had to Wilberforce. And so, as they sat one day, with Grenville for a third, "at the root of an old tree just above the steep descent into the vale of Keston," Pitt asked the question which his friend wanted most to hear. "Why don't you, Wilberforce," he said, "give notice of a motion on the subject of the Slave Trade?" Had he not "taken great pains to collect evidence?" Was not the credit therefore his due? And was not the subject admirably "suited to his character and talents?" "Do not lose time," he added, with a touch of worldly wisdom, "or the ground may be occupied by another."

There was now no reason why Wilberforce's decision should not be made known to the world of politics and business; and Clarkson, so he tells us, was conspiring to bring this very thing about, anxious doubtless to get the brilliant young politician committed beyond

W.   F recall. Accordingly he arranged with his old friend, Langton, a well-known London host whose table had been honoured by Johnson and Burke and most of the great men of the day, that Wilberforce should be invited to a dinner-party and tactfully drawn into a positive declaration. The party duly assembled. Joshua Reynolds, Boswell, Windham and Middleton were among the seven guests. And the subject of the Slave Trade was duly broached. It was a rich subject for the dinner-table; and Boswell expatiated on the planters' plea that the negroes were happier on their plantations than they had ever been in Africa. "Be it so," he sagely remarked, "but we have no right to make people happy against their will." "But what about the welfare of the West Indies and the prosperity of Liverpool?" suggested someone. That fired Windham. "Rather let Liverpool and the Islands be swallowed up in the sea," he said, "than this monstrous system of iniquity be carried on." And then Langton delivered his attack on Wilberforce "in the shape of a delicate compliment." There had been, of course, no need whatever for all this finesse. Wilberforce had committed himself at Holwood; and he at once replied to Langton's question that he was quite prepared to take up the cause in Parliament "provided no more proper person could be found." Nor, of course, had he any objection to Clarkson's mentioning this avowal to his "friends in the City." So the news was quickly spread. With very different feelings Abolitionists and West Indians heard that the Prime Minister's intimate friend had taken the field against the Slave Trade.

IV

Crusade

I

WHEN Pitt recommended Wilberforce to take up the Slave Trade question, he had not washed his hands of it himself. He must already have felt that the Trade was an outrage on Africa and a disgrace to Europe and that it ought to be, and could be, stopped: for he would scarcely have encouraged Wilberforce to divert his talents and enthusiasm into a blind alley. At the same time, with his cooler judgment and his closer knowledge of the political world, he probably realised better than his sanguine friend what a long and laborious task it well might be. If he did not know already, he very soon discovered that his own colleagues and followers were by no means prepared to risk the fortunes of the Government and the party on such an idealistic and controversial issue: that Sydney, his Secretary of State who dealt with colonial questions, was stubbornly opposed to it: that Thurlow, his cynical and disloyal Chancellor, whose influence with the King was almost as strong as his own, was dead against it: that the King himself would do all he could to prevent his admirable young Minister from disturbing the present comfortable adjustment of political forces. And Dundas, who had now become Pitt's most intimate and influential political adviser, though, like most people, he had a warm liking for Wilberforce, was the last person to encourage Pitt to go crusading with him. One thing, therefore, was very soon plain. Pitt could not commit his Government to an official assault on the Trade for the simple reason that his Government was not agreed on it. Presently, perhaps he might prove himself so indispensable to the King and to the country as to be able to do as he chose. Some day, perhaps, he might contemplate resignation in the Cabinet with indifference: he might break outright with Thurlow: he might impose Abolition on the King. But not yet. To force the issue now would probably mean his own dismissal or, at the best, another General Election; and with his party divided, with Thurlow and his pack and possibly the King against him, with the currents of corruption working quite incalculably, an Election might mean downfall and the breaking-off of his patient, systematic work for the restoration of his country. Those critics who maintain that Pitt betrayed his littleness by refusing in so great a cause to stake all and face the consequences, should reflect that Wilberforce, to whom also, as it happens, the cause seemed a great one, had no suspicions of Pitt's littleness. Whatever he may have thought later on, he never supposed at the outset that Pitt should have done anything more than he did. He quite understood, he fully concurred, he had never expected anything else, when Pitt told him that the opening move of his campaign—a motion in the House of Commons calling for consideration of the Trade—must be a non-party move; that Ministers and their following must be left free to speak and vote on the motion as they pleased.

Of course this did not mean that Pitt himself was going to be neutral. He would be as free as anybody else; and he can have had no doubt from the first which way he would speak and vote. Having settled that the motion should come on early in the following year, he gave a good deal of his time during the autumn and winter of 1787 to studying and discussing the case. He saw almost as much of Wilberforce as in the Wimbledon days; witness the diary. "Called at Pitt's and staid supper—Apsley, Pitt and I." "Pitt, Bearcroft, Graham, &c. dined with me." "Pitt's before House—dined." "After House to Pitt's—supped." And one entry shows that Pitt was going to first-hand sources for his information: "Unwell and so did not dine at Pitt's, but met Ramsay there in the evening and discussed." "It would delight you to hear Pitt talk on this question," Wilberforce told Wyvill in January; and in the same month Pitt wrote from Holwood begging Wilberforce to give him yet more talk. "If you could contrive to come here to-night or to-morrow, I would stay another day quietly in the country, and should like extremely to have a full prose on all this business. Remember you owe me at least a week." And there was more than talk. Pitt's political insight had instantly seized on the argument which the defenders of the Trade would make the most of—the economic folly and the national danger of giving up the Trade as long as other countries continued to pursue it: and in the course of the autumn he began, in concert with Wilberforce, to make soundings abroad. Obviously, it would cut a big slice of ground from under the West

Indians' feet if some sort of provisional agreement could be made
with foreign Governments; and in this hope, this rather desperate
hope, Pitt was ready to thrust the thorny question into the delicate
field of international diplomacy. "You have had a letter from my
friend Wilberforce," he wrote to Sir William Eden, British Ambassador at Paris, on November 2, "on a scheme which may appear to
some people chimerical, but which I really believe may, with proper
management, be made practicable. If it can, I am sure it is an
object well worth attending to, and perhaps you may be able to
learn the private sentiments of the French Government upon it, in
a general way; so as to enable us to judge whether it can be carried
further. I mean the idea of the two nations agreeing to discontinue
the villainous traffic now carried on in Africa." A few days later
Pitt wrote again: "The more I reflect upon it, the more anxious
and impatient I am that the business should be brought as speedily
as possible to a point"; and since Eden was shortly to be transferred
to Madrid, he added: "If you see any chance of success in France,
I hope you will lay your ground as soon as possible with a view to
Spain also. I am considering what to do in Holland." Eden cannot
have relished the task. His relations with the French Government
were not of the smoothest. M. de Montmorin, indeed, had just
been telling him that France had recently been "much nearer going
to war than from a view of the circumstances I might suppose"
and was now complaining bitterly of the effect on French industries
of the new Commercial Treaty which, it had been hoped, would
initiate a real *entente*. "He says," Eden informed Pitt, "that the
representations from the different parts of Normandy, and even
from Bordeaux also, against our pottery and against the cottons
are again urgent to a degree of clamour and violence. . . . In
Normandy above 4000 manufacturers are begging in the streets."
Eden cannot, therefore, have welcomed his rather imperious Prime
Minister's move; and he would have been still more uneasy if he
had known that Wilberforce was impulsively bent on a visit to
Paris, and was only dissuaded by Grenville's tactful suggestion that
"the appearance of our being over-solicitous upon the subject would
not forward the attainment of our point." But Eden's diplomacy,
however free from amateur intrusion, however correct and cautious,
could get little out of Montmorin. "It is in a more hopeful way
than I expected," he reported to Wilberforce on December 19; "but
I am not sanguine as to the success of any proposition, however just

and right, which must militate against a large host of private
interests." And he went on to suggest half-measures—an agreement
with France and Spain to denounce the Trade and to prepare
measures for its abolition or to suspend it temporarily with a
view to its final cessation later on. But these half-measures were
firmly combated by Wilberforce in his reply, and he was as firmly
backed by Pitt. "On the subject of the Slave Trade," the latter
wrote to Eden on January 7, "you will hear from Wilberforce more
at large than I have time to write, and it is the less necessary for
me to do it as I concur entirely in his ideas. I am persuaded a temporary interruption of the Trade would be as full of difficulty and
inconvenience as to abandon it entirely. . . . Besides this, if the
principle of humanity and justice, on which the whole rests, is in
any degree compromised, the cause is in a manner given up. I
therefore trust you will find the French Government in a disposition to concur with the measure in its full extent." But Eden's
further efforts were quite unavailing. M. de Montmorin was vague.
"It is one of those subjects," he said, "upon which the interests of
men and their sentiments are so much at variance that it is difficult
to learn what is practicable." And he repeated grave opinions he
had heard as to the ruinous effect of Abolition on the French West
Indies. He said in fact precisely what Sydney would have said,
mutatis mutandis, to the French Ambassador if he had raised the
question in London. And, apart from other arguments, the French
Government was naturally unwilling to commit France to Abolition
until it was quite certain that England was committed. That was
in fact, the cardinal crux in all these negotiations, not to be overcome by the most confident assertions on Wilberforce's part. He
told Eden about the activity of the Quakers, about the Abolition
Committee and its increasing influence, about the enthusiasm for
the cause at Manchester, about the foundation of an Abolitionist
Society at Birmingham with "a liberal subscription." He even
declared that, so far as he could judge during the recess, "there
appears an universal disposition in our favour in the House of
Commons." "On the whole, therefore," he concludes, "*assure
yourself that there is no doubt of the success.*" It may be questioned if
even those italics convinced Eden; and certainly in the light of
after events, M. de Montmorin cannot be blamed for requiring
some rather more positive proof of the British Government's and
Parliament's intentions. So Pitt's assault on France proved ineffec-

tive; and, if France held out, it was useless to press the matter on Spain or Holland.

Meantime Wilberforce was better engaged in London than he would have been in Paris. Since the impending motion was to be "unofficial," it was decided that he should move it rather than Pitt: and throughout those winter months he was busy arming himself with more facts. The diary is full of it. "Mr. Hartley, African, &c. breakfasted with me." "Dined Sir C. Middleton's—Ramsay and Collins." "Collins, Ramsay, Edwards, Gordons supped—Slave Trade discussed." And he was corresponding with friends of the cause in the provinces. "At this place," writes one from Manchester, "large subscriptions have been raised for the slave business, and *te duce Teucro* we are warm and strenuous." But it was from the Abolition Committee, which Wilberforce was not yet invited to join on the ground that his influence would be greater if he acted independently, that he obtained the best and fullest information, and particularly from Clarkson. That autumn Clarkson set out on the first of those laborious missions of inquiry which were to do so much—more, indeed, than anything else—to give the Abolition movement its essential basis of hard fact. Bristol, Liverpool, and Lancaster, the three ports outside London concerned in the Trade, were naturally his first quarry. At Bristol he found the subject "in everybody's mouth." "Everybody seemed to execrate it, though no one thought of its abolition." Of the evidence he was hunting there was enough and to spare. He discovered, by checking the muster-rolls, that the proportion of deaths among British seamen on slave-ships was exceptionally high. He was told some gruesome stories, one at least at first hand, of the cruelty of captains to their crew. He took the measurements of the slaves' quarters in two small ships then in port and worked out the allowance of space for each slave as two square feet in one and four in the other. At Liverpool, and at Lancaster too, the muster-rolls told him the same tale of high mortality. He saw in the window of a Liverpool shop the leg-shackles, handcuffs, thumbscrews and mouth-openers used on slave-ships, and wisely purchased a specimen of each. And everywhere and all the time he was asking questions, disagreeable questions, questions that presently gave rise to the idea that this mad busybody was actually proposing to destroy the traffic which had made Liverpool the great and wealthy place it was! The atmosphere grew warm. Traders and captains and their friends began to frequent the "King's Arms," where Clarkson habitually dined; they talked loudly at him; they drank provocative toasts to the Trade; they tried to engage him in argument. Fortunately Clarkson had always with him a companion of the martial name of Falconbridge, who could explain, if counter-attack were needed, his own experience of the Trade on the African coast. Better still, he was, says Clarkson, "an athletic and resolute-looking man." And he had a pistol in his pocket. But before he left Liverpool Clarkson had a narrow escape. He had got on the track of the murder of a seaman by his captain; and one day a gang of eight or nine men, the suspected murderer among them, tried to hustle Clarkson into the sea as he was watching a big gale from the pier-head. "I escaped, not without blows." And so back to London by way of Manchester, where he preached one of his few sermons, and Birmingham, where he stimulated the local zeal of which Eden had been told. A letter from George Rose to Wilberforce reveals him still at work on his return. "It is quite unprecedented," he writes, "to allow any one to rummage the Custom House papers for information, who has no employment in the revenue. I will, however, without delay obtain for Mr. Clarkson all the information which he wants—though I am a West Indian planter, would I were not!" It was at this time, too, that Wilberforce arranged for Clarkson to lay his evidence before Pitt. He went twice to Downing Street and his minute account of the interviews shows that Pitt was well acquainted with the statesman's art of eliciting information. He was rather cold, thought Clarkson, and uncertain in his sympathies. He confessed to doubts about the validity of the case for Abolition and was not easily to be satisfied. It was not till Clarkson had fetched his copies of the muster-rolls and Pitt had himself, "looked over about a hundred pages accurately," that he admitted conviction. Not unnaturally, perhaps, Clarkson was deceived by these tactics. He knew nothing of Pitt's earlier talk with Ramsay, nothing of the negotiations with France; and he came away with the conviction that the interviews "had given birth to an interest in favour of our cause." He found Grenville better informed and troubled by fewer doubts: so it is probable that Grenville got much less out of him than Pitt.

But the activity that winter was not all on one side. The representatives of the Trade had awakened to the gravity of the danger implied in Wilberforce taking the field as a champion of Abolition

—Wilberforce the popular, the eloquent, the unimpeachable, the member for Yorkshire, the friend of Pitt. Anxiously they began to set the machinery of the African and West Indian vested interest in motion. Wherever they had influence, they tested and strengthened it—in Society, in Parliament, at the Court. In all quarters conversation began to turn upon the Trade. Its value to England, it seemed, had never been adequately estimated. Did critics realise, it was asked, what the cessation of the Trade would mean to the West Indies? Nay, were they aware of the unsuspected blessings it bestowed on the people of Africa? As the case for the defence took shape, it became clear to Pitt, clear to Wilberforce too, that the obstacles to Abolition were greater than they had at first foreseen. "Called at Pitt's at night," says the diary early in 1788; "he firm about African trade, though we begin to perceive more difficulties in the way than we had hoped there would be." It was soon obvious that the attack could not be opened as early as February 2, the date originally fixed for the motion. More time was needed, and, despite Clarkson's energy, more information. Nothing could so damage the cause at the beginning as unsubstantiated accusations: and Wilberforce agreed with Pitt that, in face of the concerted opposition of the Trade, some more authoritative evidence was required, whatever delay it might entail, than could be obtained by the private efforts of Clarkson or himself or anybody else. And here the Prime Minister could help officially without violating his Government's neutrality. Pitt directed the Trade Committee of the Privy Council to make an inquiry into the conditions of British commercial intercourse with Africa. It was a straight challenge to the Trade, and the Trade met it squarely. They could prove, said the African merchants, that the traffic in slaves was at once necessary and humane. On the other side the Abolition Committee, with which Wilberforce kept in constant touch, prepared its evidence and marshalled its witnesses.

2

At this exciting moment, when the opposing forces were already lining up for the first battle, the Abolitionists were suddenly deprived of their parliamentary leader. Wilberforce's frail physique had mutinied. In the course of February and March his recurrent indigestion developed into serious intestinal trouble. He could eat little and assimilate nothing. Intermittent fever and tormenting thirst robbed him of sleep. He rapidly lost weight. "There's Wilberforce," said one Cambridge acquaintance to another, pointing out the enfeebled invalid: "he can't last three weeks." And when his friends compelled him to summon the fashionable Dr. Warren to consult with Dr. Pitcairne, the great man came to much the same conclusion. Whether or not they diagnosed the case in the drastic language of Wilberforce's biographers as "an entire decay of all the vital functions," the doctors shook their heads and gave it up. "He has no stamina to last a fortnight," they told the family, and advised the prompt removal of the dying man to Bath on a desperate chance that its mysterious waters might work a miracle beyond the reach of human skill. It was practically a death-sentence, and Wilberforce was not deceived. He was ready to go and die at Bath if such was God's will. But there was one thing he must do before he went. He sent for Pitt and, fighting down the physical languor and mental exhaustion which had begun to assail him, he entreated him to undertake, if he should die, the cause to which he had meant to give his life. Would he, in any case, he asked him, move the resolution in Parliament which, whatever happened, he would not now be able to move himself? Pitt's answer came straight from his heart. His innate political caution, his party difficulties, the problems of his own career were forgotten. "With a warmth of principle and friendship," as Wilberforce said afterwards, "that has made me love him better than I ever did before," he promised not only to introduce the motion but to do anything, if his friend so wished, which it "would be proper for him to do himself." The sick man was deeply moved. This was more than he had dared to hope. If the greatest statesman of the day should succeed him in the conduct of it, the cause would lose nothing—might it not even gain? —by his own dismissal. And so, the one thing done and so well done, Wilberforce prepared for his journey with a quiet and thankful mind.

He reached Bath on April 5 in a state of collapse; and a week later, since he was now unable to attend to business, a letter was written on his behalf to Pitt, saying the time had come for the formal commitment of the Abolition cause into his hands. And then the miracle began to happen. Not indeed by drinking the Bath waters but by taking minute doses of opium—a drug which Dr.

Pitcairne had had the greatest difficulty in forcing on his scrupulous patient—Wilberforce began to mend. And his progress, once the corner had been turned, was astonishingly rapid. On May 5, exactly a month after his arrival *in extremis*, he was strong enough to leave Bath for a visit to Cambridge, travelling mostly in a carriage, but at times—a miracle indeed!—on horseback. There followed a peaceful month in comfortable quarters in the Master's Lodge at St. John's. "Lived more regularly and quietly," he wrote in the Journal, "than I had done for a long time. Chiefly with Milner [1] in the evenings. Dined commonly in Hall. . . . In health mended." But he was not yet fit for London and politics, and in June he left Cambridge for the Lakes, where he settled down for the summer in his house at Rayrigg. He was able now to continue his correspondence with the Abolition Committee in London, and he had hoped to find in his retirement an opportunity for unbroken study and contemplation; but his days were soon encroached on by a stream of visitors. "The tour to the Lakes has become so fashionable," he wrote to John Newton, "that the banks of the Thames are scarcely more public than those of Windermere. . . . At this moment my cottage overflows with guests." And there was one day in the week on which this constant irruption was especially irksome. "Sadly taken up on Sundays," he complains, "with company in the house." But there were precious hours he could still make his own. Early in the morning, before any of his guests were stirring, he would take a boat and row out by himself and "find an oratory under one of the woody islands in the middle of the lake."

3

While Wilberforce was thus gathering strength to return to the stage he had nearly left for ever, Pitt was faithfully playing his part as understudy. From the moment of Wilberforce's departure from London he began to devote yet more time and thought to the question than he had hitherto assigned to it. He at once arranged to superintend the Privy Council inquiry henceforth in person; and on receiving the letter from Bath, he promptly invited Granville

[1] Now Fellow of Queens'.

Sharp to come to Downing Street and discuss with him the policy
of the Abolition Committee. The invitation was eagerly accepted,
and the conference was held on April 21. Sharp had decided to
state the Committee's case without reserve, and he told Pitt that
its object was nothing less than the complete abolition of the Trade.
Pitt replied "that his heart was with them and that he considered
himself pledged to Mr. Wilberforce that the cause should not sustain any injury from his indisposition." But he pointed out that
success could not be won in an instant. No Bill could be introduced
before the Privy Council inquiry was completed; in other words,
till next session. To Sharp this delay was doubtless irksome; for
already the Committee's propaganda in the country was bearing
fruit and impatient supporters were demanding that, since Wilberforce was out of action, another parliamentary leader should at
once be chosen to press the business on. Pitt's attitude, on the other
hand, was manifestly as sincere as it was practical; and Sharp could
use the knowledge of his pledge to Wilberforce to propitiate the
hotheads.

A few days later, on May 9, Pitt fulfilled the first and smallest
of the promises he had made. In a short speech he moved a resolution binding the House to consider the circumstances of the Slave
Trade early in the next session. It was a short speech because Pitt
"studiously avoided," as he frankly told the House, giving his own
opinions on the Trade at this stage. A full discussion of the question,
he declared, was now neither useful nor desirable. Some held that
the Trade should be abolished outright; others that it only needed
regulation. The matter must be considered deliberately and in
detail, and this was impossible until the result of the inquiry instituted by his Majesty's Ministers elsewhere was known. He alluded
to Wilberforce's illness, and expressed the hope that his honourable
friend would be able to "resume his charge" and introduce the
question himself next session: for in no one's hands could "any
measure of humanity and national interest" be better placed. But
if he were still too unwell, he (Pitt) would undertake the task again
himself. In this tribute to Wilberforce Fox promptly concurred.
He had meant himself, he said, to raise the question of the Slave
Trade, but "when he heard that the member for Yorkshire had
resolved to take it up, he was unaffectedly rejoiced, not only knowing
that gentleman's purity of principles and sincere love for the rights
of humanity, but because, from a variety of considerations as to the

characters and situations in which different men stood in that House, there was something that made him honestly think that it was better that the business should be in the hands of the honourable gentleman than in his, and that it would come from him with more weight, more authority, and more probability of success than from himself." But his faith in the cause was as strong as Wilberforce's own; and in contrast to Pitt's official caution—a contrast he was careful to bring out—he openly asserted it. "I have no scruple to declare, at the onset," he said, "that my opinion of this momentous business is that the Slave Trade ought not to be regulated but destroyed." Burke also spoke. He, too, had previously thought of taking up the question of the Slave Trade, and he, too, at once committed himself to the full, clean course of Abolition. Of the other speeches Sir James Johnstone's was the most interesting. He was the first to raise the question of the effect of these discussions at Westminster on the minds of the slaves themselves. Others were presently to point to restlessness among the negroes on the plantations as a reason for doing nothing and even saying nothing; but to Johnstone, who declared himself an Abolitionist, it was a reason for doing something and doing it without delay, lest "the poor creatures' hopes might be raised too high and bad consequences follow." The slaves, he told the House, were already aware of the Abolitionist movement in England. He had recently heard from Grenada that they were going about invoking the champions of their cause in a crescendo of excited hope and faith—"Mr. Wilberforce for negro. Mr. Fox for negro. The Parliament for negro. God Almighty for negro." The rest of the debate was only remarkable for the silence of the West Indian group. They had decided, it appeared, to reserve their defence. Only one member had the impatience to assert that Abolition was "unnecessary, visionary, and impracticable"; and not one voted against the resolution. It was carried *nem. con.*

The general question of Abolition was thus temporarily shelved; but the session was not to close without one at least of the particular scandals of the Trade being forced on Parliament's attention. Old Sir William Dolben, member for Oxford University, had been moved to go on board a slave-ship that was lying in the Thames and had been so horrified at the arrangements for packing the slaves between decks—"like books on shelves," as Lord Stanhope put it—that he had promptly given notice of a Bill for limiting the number of slaves in proportion to the tonnage which a ship should be allowed to carry. The Bill was read a first time on May 26, and in the debate on the second reading, since the House was not now discussing the theoretical rights and wrongs of slave-trading but a single, definite abuse connected with it, the champions of the Trade were forced into the open. Lord Penrhyn flatly denied the cruelty and unhealthiness alleged. "It was absurd to suppose," he said, "that men, whose profit depended on the health and vigour of the African natives, would purposely torment and distress them during their passage so as to endanger their lives." But when, in support of the petition Lord Penrhyn presented the Liverpool merchants were heard by counsel at the bar, their representatives were compelled to admit that the average death-rate on the Middle Passage was at least 10 or 5 per cent. according to its length and that in one case no less than a third of the slaves had died. It was useless, after that, to plead that "the voyage from Africa is the happiest period of the slave's life." These disclosures made a marked impression on the House; and Pitt showed that he had made up his mind on this particular aspect of the Trade at any rate by moving and carrying the unusual proposal that the Bill, if passed, should operate retrospectively from June 10. The partisans of the Trade would have been wise if they had taken the hint, made as graceful a retreat as possible, and dug their trenches farther back against the next attack. But they were not wise. They declared that they would have none of these regulations. To regulate the Trade would ruin it. Every negro lost by regulation to a British ship would be a negro won by a French ship. To argue thus, at this stage, was a tactical mistake. It raised the general question and raised it in a provocative manner. It amounted to a claim that, so far from contemplating the abolition of the Trade, Parliament must put no limits on it at all. And this was more than Pitt could stomach. At the outset of the debate he had asked the House to judge the particular regulations proposed in the Bill on their own merits, and not to go back on its previous decision to reserve the broader discussion on the fate of the Trade as a whole till next session. But now he himself was provoked into taking the wider ground. "I have no hesitation to declare," he said in the closing speech of the debate, "that, if the Trade cannot be carried on in a manner different to that stated by the honourable members opposite me, I will retract what I said on a former day against going into the general question, and, waiving every other discussion than what has this day taken place, I will give my vote for the utter abolition of a trade which is shocking to humanity, is abominable to be carried on by any country, and reflects the greatest dishonour on the British senate and the British nation. The Trade, as the petitioners propose to carry it on, without any regulation, is contrary to every humane, to every Christian principle, to every sentiment that ought to inspire the breast of man."

This discharge of high explosive seems to have blown the opponents of the Bill right out of Westminster Hall. Only five members in a thin House voted against the third reading, while fifty-six voted for it. But the Trade had still a chance, and a good chance, in the House of Lords. It mattered not at all to Lord Chancellor Thurlow that the Prime Minister had given the Bill such wholehearted support in the Commons as almost to make it his own measure. He derided it as the product of a "five days' fit of philanthropy." It might well teach the slaves "to proceed of their own accord to an abolition of this Trade." Unhappy merchants who had embarked their all in ships already sailed would be ruined by it. The Duke of Richmond and Lords Carlisle, Stanhope, Hopetown and Townshend supported the Bill: but the rest followed Thurlow's lead. Lord Heathfield had ascertained by careful calculations that a negro in a slave-ship had nearly twice as many cubic feet of air to breathe as a British soldier in a tent. The Duke of Chandos was convinced by a letter he had just received from Jamaica that the passage of the Bill might very well lead to a negro rising in the West Indies and a universal massacre of the whites. More reasonable and more respectable was Lord Rodney's blunt anxiety at the prospect of losing commerce to the French. Obsessed by the idea that to tamper with the Slave Trade might somehow mean a weakening of our strategic hold on the West Indies, the great sailor not only minimised the hardships of the Middle Passage, but went beyond his brief to repudiate current notions of the sufferings of the slaves on the plantations. He had never heard of a negro being cruelly treated, he avowed, in all the time he had been at the West Indies; and he had often expressed the wish that the English labourer might be but half as happy. Finally, Lord Sydney, the Secretary of State primarily concerned, declared his preference for leaving the matter over for the general discussion in the next session. It seemed, indeed, as if the Bill was lost; and it would have been lost if the Lords had been left to themselves. But

Pitt's back was up. When he heard how the debate was going, he told Grenville that, if the Bill were defeated, he would not remain in the same Cabinet with its opposers; and he used all his personal influence with individual peers to save it. By a narrow margin he won and Thurlow lost. On June 30 the Bill was carried, with certain useful amendments of its hasty drafting, by 14 votes to 12. It was said that Pitt did not "allow" the King to prorogue Parliament till he had given his assent.

4

Events at Westminster during the summer of 1788 were thus calculated to hasten Wilberforce's convalescence, and in October he returned to town and dined with Pitt. But he was soon off again to Yorkshire and to Bath; and it was not till the beginning of December that he finally settled down again in London and resumed his parliamentary duties. It was a critical moment in politics. The King had gone out of his mind. The Whigs were demanding the automatic assumption of the Regency by the Prince of Wales, whose first act, they assumed, would be to dismiss Pitt and send for Fox. And Thurlow, scurrying betimes from the ship, all gratitude for his sick master's past favours forgotten, had sold his support to the Prince, and continued to sell him the secrets of the Cabinet to which he still belonged, at the price of retaining the woolsack in the new Ministry. But Pitt had still to be reckoned with. He was determined that if and when the medical evidence should leave no doubt as to the need for the appointment of a Regent, it should be made by the will of Parliament and under such conditions as Parliament might desire. And Wilberforce, now quite himself again, joined eagerly in the struggle on Pitt's side, admiringly convinced that his friend was standing, not only for constitutional right, but for plain honesty and patriotism in a world of selfish intrigue. Before Christmas the crisis was practically over. The Prince had acknowledged the sovereignty of Parliament—"the sacred principles which seated the House of Brunswick on the throne"—and Thurlow in the House of Lords had prayed God to forget him if ever he should forget the loyalty he owed the King. In the following February Pitt introduced a Bill to confer the powers of Regent with certain restrictions on the Prince, but it never became law. Before the end of the month George III recovered his reason as quickly as he had lost it.

The Regency crisis over, Wilberforce could concentrate once more upon the Slave Trade; and from the beginning of the new year he was occupied all day and every day in preparation for the imminent parliamentary struggle. Somehow or other his health, though he refused to play the invalid and spare it, kept up to the old indifferent level of the days before his breakdown. "House till near six," says the diary for January 26: "slave business all the evening, with only biscuit and wine and water—nervous at night, and dreamed about slavery." Again, a month later: "Slave business till near bed, and slept ill, as I commonly do when my mind is occupied before bedtime—nervous and tossing, haunted by thoughts about trifles." But there was one thing he could do, and do willingly enough, to ease the pressure. After dining one night in February at Lord Salisbury's he sets down this characteristic resolution: "On full conviction from experience that it is impossible for me to make myself master of the slave subject and to go through my various occupations except I live more undistractedly, I determine scarce ever to dine out in parties, and in all respects to live with a view to those great matters till the slave business is brought to some conclusion. May God bless the work and my endeavour."

But abstention from parties meant no rest. The insatiable "slave business" streamed into the vacuum. Almost every day the diary bears witness to it. "Evening. Eliot staid and we looked at slave business." "Very unwell—kept the house all day—slave business, Eliot." "Frewen and Clarkson at dinner—Jonas Brown, Muncaster, and Eliot at night—slave business, but interrupted often and much by people on other matters which sadly obstruct my progress." "Morning to Pitt's on business. Then Slave Trade. Dined Bay-ham's. Slave business evening." "Obliged to dine at Speaker's. Found Ramsay and Clarkson at home, so kept up." And all the time those "other matters" were pressing and obstructing. There were the various duties he had to perform as member for Yorkshire and the calls on his time of his numerous private charities. Not many public men can have spent busier days. Already while he sat at breakfast—to which some Abolitionist colleague was often invited to discuss the latest evidence—his ante-room began to fill with callers, the earliest of whom was generally summoned to the breakfast-room before the meal was ended. It was a queerly mixed

W.   G

company that gathered in that ante-room. "On one chair sat a
Yorkshire constituent, manufacturing or agricultural; on another
a petitioner for charity or a House of Commons client; on another
a Wesleyan preacher; while side by side with an African, a foreign
missionary, or a Haytian professor, sat perhaps some man of rank
who sought a private interview and whose name had accidentally
escaped announcement." That is the description of Wilberforce's
biographer-sons—a little pompous, a little early-Victorian. Hannah
More's was more succinct: "Noah's Ark, full of beasts, clean and
unclean." And certainly not all the callers were immaculate; for
it appears the small books which had originally been kept in the
room had to be exchanged for heavy folios "which could not be
carried off by accident in the pocket of a coat." The morning calls
disposed of, Wilberforce was off to a meeting of the Abolition
Committee or to the House of Commons; or if nothing took him
from home, he was closeted with his collaborators in his library,
examining, winnowing, tabulating the gigantic mass of detailed
evidence that was to smash the Trade. It was at this period that he
first became acquainted with James Stephen, who had lived for the
past eleven years as a barrister at St. Kitts, and had been so deeply
stirred by the evils of slavery as he saw it at close quarters that he
had refused, in the teeth of universal custom, to own a single slave
himself. Such experience, such burning convictions were the best
credentials; and Wilberforce promptly took Stephen to his heart—
and to his library. As likely as not, he would find Clarkson there,
or Ramsay who was often up from Teston, staying in the house.
As the date of the debate drew near, this little band of zealots were
labouring at their papers for eight or nine hours every day. "Wilberforce's white negroes," Pitt once dubbed them; but, if Wilberforce
was in a sense their master, he toiled no less than they. Their
presence and their example, indeed, made it almost impossible for
him, even if he had wished it, to slacken the strain. To return home
from some tiring business was not to find an easy-chair and restful
solitude. Once, towards the end of March, he thoroughly exhausted
himself travelling to Cambridgeshire and back between nine at
night and noon next day. "Reached London about twelve very
faint," he says. The rest of the day's record in the diary is brief
but significant. "Ramsay and Clarkson"—that is all, and quite
enough.

Meantime the other side was also hard at work. The debates on

Dolben's Bill, and especially Pitt's uncompromising attitude, had convinced the Trade of the reality of the danger threatening it. At public meetings all over the country, in the newspapers, in a host of pamphlets, the British people were assured that their interests were inextricably interwoven with the interests of the Trade. Abolition meant the end of our colonial empire—more, it meant the commercial downfall of the mother-country. Not only from Liverpool, but from Bristol and from London also, though neither of these latter ports enjoyed a quarter of Liverpool's share in the Trade, came the same lurid warnings. Even Alderman Sawbridge, that old, robust exponent of the City's traditional devotion to liberal causes, was induced to confess his belief that any further tampering with the Trade would spell ruin for his constituents. And while Abolition would cripple England, it would do no good to the negroes. Those morbid tales of cruelty and suffering, those fantastic statistics of mortality were only the hysterical inventions of pietistic old women who knew nothing about the West Indies and less than nothing about Africa.

It is well known [wrote the author of a pamphlet entitled *Slavery no Oppression*] that the eastern and western coasts of Africa are inhabited by stupid and unenlightened hordes; immersed in the most gross and impenetrable gloom of barbarism, dark in mind as in body, prodigiously populous, impatient of all control, unteachably lazy, ferocious as their own congenial tigers, nor in any respect superior to these rapacious beasts in intellectual advancement but distinguished only by a rude and imperfect organ of speech, which is abusively employed in the utterance of dissonant and inarticulate jargon. Such a people must be often involved in predatory battles, to obtain a cruel and precarious subsistence by the robbery and destruction of one another. The traffic has proved a fortunate event for their miserable captives.

Not all the apologists of the Trade were quite so dishonest or so imbecile as that. There were candid merchants who did not deny the hardships of the negroes, but held that business is business and that the weak must suffer for their weakness in this hard world. Some, indeed, were willing, if not anxious, that everything should be done to improve the conditions under which the Trade was carried on—anything, that is, which would not diminish its profits. Others, like Rodney, thought first and foremost of British sea-power and set their faces stubbornly against endangering it for a sentiment. Others, again, like Admiral Barrington, had seen only the happier side of the slave's life in the West Indies and were as unconvinced of its evils as were many of the better slave-holders in the Southern States of America in the nineteenth century. And behind all these was the English legal mind. When negroes were suffering in London, the legal mind had concentrated—after some hesitation —on the slave's right to freedom; but when negroes were suffering on the Guinea Coast or in mid-Atlantic, the legal mind was more concerned with the owner's right of property. Were numbers of Englishmen to be suddenly deprived of what the law allowed them to possess, of a livelihood, which, unpleasant though it might be, they had so long been permitted to pursue by public opinion and with at least the tacit authority of Parliament?

Amid all this discussion, public and private, passionate and sober, the Privy Council Committee was quickly finishing its inquiry. Before the end of April its Report was presented to Parliament in a stout sub-folio volume. It did not state any conclusions on the Committee's part for or against the Trade; it was simply a collection of the evidence given before it and of information otherwise obtained —declarations submitted to it, tables of statistics, and so forth. These materials were marshalled in five sections: (1) on the civilisation of West Africa and the manner in which slaves are made; (2) on "the manner of carrying slaves to the West Indies"; (3) on the treatment of slaves on the plantations; (4) on the extent of the trade and population, slave and free, of the West Indies; (5) on the Slave Trade and Slavery as practised by other nations. Of these sections the first three, and of their contents the statements of the witnesses, were the most interesting and important. A variety of persons gave evidence—ex-governors, naval officers, captains of slave-ships, surgeons, traders, travellers. One of these last, Dr. Andrew Spaarman, Professor of Physics at Stockholm, the record of whose travels in South Africa has long been known and valued by geographers and historians, is worth quoting because of his palpable disinterestedness. On the question as to how slaves were obtained, he gave evidence as follows:

When the kings of the country want slaves for the purchase

of goods they send their horsemen in the night to the villages
to make as many slaves as they can. In the neighbourhood of
Goree he saw one of these expeditions. The King of Barbessia
came to him in the night to tell him that he was going to send
out a party to make slaves as he wanted brandy to encourage
his officers. In the course of the conversation, the King became
so intoxicated with madeira by Dr. Spaarman's bedside that he
was carried away speechless. Dr. Spaarman saw the party set
out and saw them return with some slaves they had made. They
conceal part of those they make on these occasions in order to
enhance their price.

A good deal of evidence was given on both sides, but rather more
against the Trade than for it. Clarkson's first journey had not been
taken in vain. He gave evidence himself on what he had discovered
at Liverpool and Bristol, and he is named as presenting several of
the other witnesses. The most whole-hearted defender of the Trade
was Robert Norris, a slave-captain, whose rose-coloured caricature
of the Middle Passage was to be dealt with presently by Wilberforce
in Parliament. Its most outspoken assailant was James Arnold, one
of Clarkson's witnesses, a Bristol surgeon who had served on slave-
ships and told a ghastly story of a captain's fiendish cruelty not
only towards the slaves, male and female, in his power, but towards
his white crew too. But, apart from the more extreme statements,
if half what the moderate men said was true—as they took oath it
was—it was more than enough. On the issue of bare humanity,
uncrossed by political or material considerations, any ordinary
kindly human being who read the Report must instantly, by simple,
instinctive standards, have condemned the Trade.

The Report presented, there was no reason for further delay;
and already on April 10 Pitt had written to Wilberforce to fix the
day for the debate. "Grenville and I," he said, "have formed a
project of reducing the case, as it appears from the Report, into a
string of resolutions, which we will send you as soon as they are
complete. . . . The more we consider the case, the more irresistible
it is in all its parts." Wilberforce was now at Teston, making his
final preparations away from the interruptions of town; but he
went to Holwood twice in the next few weeks to discuss the campaign with his chief. "Pitt very earnest about the Slave Trade," he
notes. And now at last the day came—May 12. Its events are thus

typically recorded in the diary. "Tuesday very indifferent. Came
to town sadly unfit for work, but by Divine grace was enabled to
make my motion so as to give satisfaction—three hours and a half
—I had not prepared my language, or even gone over all my matter,
but being well acquainted with the whole subject I got on. My
breast sore, but *de ceteris* pretty well. How ought I to labour, if it
pleases God to make me able to impress people with a persuasion
that I am serious, and to incline them to agree with me!"

Who would suppose from this entry that its author had made
that day one of the finest speeches in all that golden age of Parliamentary oratory? The greatest of the orators had been quick to
acclaim it. "The House, the nation, and Europe," said Burke, "are
under great and serious obligations to the hon. gentleman for
having brought forward the subject in a manner the most masterly
impressive, and eloquent. The principles were so well laid down,
and supported with so much force and order, that it equalled anything I have ever heard in modern times, and is not perhaps to be
surpassed in the remains of Grecian eloquence."

5

Considering the nature of the subject, the most remarkable
quality of the speech was its studied moderation. "It is not your
passions I shall appeal to," said Wilberforce at the outset: "I ask
only for your cool and impartial reason." And he deprecated any
special condemnation of the people directly concerned with the
Trade. "We are all guilty: we ought all to plead guilty and not
to exculpate ourselves by throwing the blame on others." After
this preface came a full and lucid account, with well-chosen illustrations from the evidence submitted to the Privy Council Committee, of the manner in which the slaves were obtained. The most
striking case cited was that of certain traders who, finding that two
African townships had abandoned their traditional feud and initiated
a new era of peace with intermarriages between the chiefs' families,
set themselves to undermine a compact which so clearly tended to
reduce the supply of slaves. Next came a harrowing but by no means
an overstrained description of the Middle Passage, in the course of
which Norris's evidence was dealt with as it deserved. He had drawn
a romantic picture of the comfort enjoyed by the slaves on ship-

board, of the profusion and variety of their food seasoned "with the best sauces of African cookery," of their happy life, the men singing and dancing, the women and girls making ornaments with beads "with which they are plentifully supplied." Wilberforce tore this nauseating fantasy to shreds. The dancing, for instance, he explained, was compulsory dancing to improve the slaves' health. "I was employed," said one witness, "to dance the men, while another person danced the women." But there was no need, said Wilberforce, to dwell on the details of what happens on those dreadful voyages. "Death is a sure ground of proof," and "exclusive of those who perish before they sail, not less than 12½ per cent. perish on the Passage, and not less than 4½ per cent. die on shore before the day of sale."

Wilberforce then told the House how the discovery of these ghastly facts had affected his own mind. He had at once decided that the Trade must be abolished whatever the consequences might be; and, when he was told that it meant the ruin of the West Indies, he had refused to believe it. "It naturally suggested itself to me how strange it was that Providence, however mysterious in its ways, should so have constituted the world as to make one part of it depend for its existence on the depopulation and devastation of another. I could not help, therefore, distrusting the arguments of those who insisted that the plundering of Africa was necessary for the cultivation of the West Indies." And he went on to argue that "in truth the West Indies have nothing to fear from the total and immediate abolition of the Slave Trade." On the contrary, the bad economy of the slave-system—the unhealthy conditions, the over-work, the low fertility—was mainly due to the fact that the planters could always obtain fresh slaves to replace their losses. Abolish the Trade, and they would be compelled to raise the standard of living among the existing slaves, to guard their health, to promote the requisite conditions for natural increase, till in the end they found themselves with a larger and more efficient labour force than they had ever got from the Trade.

The three other objections to Abolition were similarly assailed. It was absurd to say that Liverpool and other British cities would be paralysed: only a small group of Liverpool merchants had made fortunes out of it; only one-fifteenth of outward-bound shipping from the Mersey was employed in it. And it was no less absurd to suppose that Abolition would injure the merchant-marine, since "more sailors die in one year in the Slave Trade than die in two years in all our other trades put together." Lastly, France. Was not France "too enlightened a nation to begin pushing a scandalous as well as a ruinous traffic at the very time when England sees her folly and resolves to give it up?" In any case the iniquity of the Trade was unaffected by what France might do, and it was England's duty to give a lead. For England, as chief participant in the Trade, had done most thereby not merely to prevent the emergence of Africa from barbarism but to make it still more barbarous. "Let us make such amends as we can for the mischiefs we have done to that unhappy continent."

After arguing that no regulations or palliatives could meet the case, Wilberforce concluded with a direct appeal for total abolition on the twofold ground of policy and religion. The economic advantages would be felt not only in the West Indies but also in the growth of a new African trade conducted on the orthodox lines of honest commerce.

> Policy, however, Sir, is not my principle, and I am not ashamed to say it. There is a principle above everything that is politic; and, when I reflect on the command which says "Thou shalt do no murder," believing its authority to be divine, how can I dare set up any reasonings of my own against it? And, Sir, when we think of Eternity and of the future consequences of all human conduct, what is there in this life that should make any man contradict the dictates of his conscience, the principles of justice, and the laws of God?

Wilberforce then moved twelve resolutions, recapitulating the main facts as to the operation of the Slave Trade on the African coast and the effects of its methods on the civilisation of the natives, as to the hardships of the Middle Passage and the loss of life entailed among both slaves and seamen, and as to the lack of natural increase among the slaves in the West Indies and the causes of it; and declaring that the interests of the planters would suffer no considerable or permanent damage from the discontinuance of the Trade and that for the merchants engaged in it a substitute might be found in the export of those special products of the African soil which were required for the manufactures of this country.

6

So forcible, yet so moderate, an appeal, the fruit of so many months' unresting labour, deserved a better fate. But almost from the moment of its delivery the long, intolerable sequence of Wilberforce's disappointments began. It made no difference that the few great men in the House of Commons of that day were on his side. Burke devoted not only his incomparable eloquence but all his powers of lucid reasoning to show that the threatened loss of commerce would not be great enough to justify, on the plea of necessity, the terrible inhumanity of the Trade: and if some loss there must be, "were they not prepared," he asked, "to pay the price of virtue?" Pitt followed Burke with the frank avowal which everybody had expected since his outburst on Dolben's Bill. Though he was willing, he said, to listen to arguments for the continuance of the Trade, he did not believe that any of them could be reconciled with the principles of justice and humanity. One particular plea—that Abolition would simply lead to the smuggling of slaves into the British West Indies by traders of other nations—he dealt with in advance. "Should that be the case," he said, and it was the Prime Minister speaking, "our language must be that Great Britain has resources to enable her to protect her islands and to prevent others carrying on a traffic which she has thought it for her own honour and character to abandon." And Fox followed Pitt, applauding Wilberforce's clear demand for Abolition, applauding, too, Pitt's firm attitude on the question of smuggling by foreign slavers, but avowing the hope that other countries would follow our example and the belief that France, at any rate, might be expected "to catch a spark from the light of our fire and to run a race with us in promoting the ends of humanity." But it made no difference that Fox and Pitt and Burke were all with Wilberforce, nor that the case against him was feebly put by lesser men—by Alderman Newnham, who predicted in all seriousness that Abolition "would render the City of London one scene of bankruptcy and ruin"—by Mr. Dempster, who asked whether Wilberforce or Pitt or Fox possessed plantations of their own, and declared that, though sugar could indeed be grown more profitably by free labour than by slaves, Parliament had no pretence of right "to prescribe to the gentlemen of the West Indies by what hands their plantations should be cultivated"—by Mr. Drake, who insisted that Abolition would be in the highest degree unjust unless everybody who might lose by it were fully compensated from the public purse—by Mr. Henniker, who read a very long letter, which purported to have been sent by the King of Dahomey to George I, in order to prove that the cruelties practised in Africa could not be ascribed to the operation of the Slave Trade—by Mr. Molyneux, who asked whether they meant "to swallow all the property of the planters in order to gratify a humane disposition towards the Africans" and produced what he described as a proof that slaves were not cruelly treated, to wit, a letter from his agent in the West Indies, complaining that a certain Rev. Mr. Frazer, who was paid £50 a year by Mr. Molyneux for looking after his slaves, had neglected to give proper attention to "a negro that was ill in the hot-house with a sore throat"—by Viscount Maitland who, cleverer than the rest, appealed to the jealousy of the Commons on a point of privilege and urged that they would be surrendering their historic rights if they accepted the evidence submitted to the Privy Council and did not insist on its being given all over again at their own bar.

None of these arguments, except the last, had much effect. What mattered was the disinclination of the average silent member of the House to screw himself up to a definite decision on such a controversial subject. The brief report in Hansard of one speech from a back bench may be taken to illustrate the mood of the great majority.

> Sir Guy Cooper confessed himself a friend to the inquiry. He thought, however, that the representatives of a generous and brave people might be carried by too rapid steps to the adoption of a measure which introduced such novelty in the commercial concerns of the West Indies. Men distinguished for philanthropy might be hurried to the adoption of a measure which tended to the injury of our West India islands. He confessed he entertained much doubt and perplexity on the subject.

A jejune, perfunctory report of what was probably a poor enough speech: but it may serve as a not unfair reflection of the frame of mind that defeated Wilberforce. They were not insensible, nor inhumane, these country gentlemen. They were not unmoved by Wilberforce's unimpeachable sincerity. Indeed, he had sharply pricked their consciences. But between conscience and the interests of the State and of the planters and of the innumerable individuals whose livelihood, one way or another, depended on the Trade, they were most uncomfortably perplexed. And, for once, the traditional way of escape from such a dilemma was barred. Compromise, for once, was impossible: for had not the Trade declared that further regulation would be as fatal as Abolition itself? Puzzled and uneasy, therefore, they leaped at the chance, obligingly suggested by Lord Maitland, of at least postponing a decision. Yet; let the evidence be recited all over again. Then, surely, they would be able to make up their minds.

It was useless for Pitt and Fox to expose the flimsy pretext of privilege. The great majority on both sides, if they could decide nothing else, had decided to procrastinate. So it was agreed, without a division, to go into committee on nine specified days. And when those days had passed with the long task of hearing evidence still far from finished, the end of the session was close at hand, and further discussion of the subject was squeezed out by other business. This did not mean, of course, that the twice-told evidence had convinced the House that the Trade was right and Wilberforce wrong. It meant nothing so definite as that. And indeed, when Wilberforce displayed anxiety at the possibility of the whole question being shelved, a motion was promptly brought forward "that this House will, early in the next session of Parliament, proceed to consider further the circumstances of the Slave Trade." Alderman Newnham himself proposed it, and the House carried it *nem. con.* And there was time for one more good deed. A Bill for amending and continuing Sir William Dolben's temporary Act of the previous year was quickly and smoothly passed before the session closed. Then members, their duty done, carried off their consciences for a holiday.

Time was to prove abundantly that Wilberforce possessed a wonderful patience. Throughout these disappointing debates he maintained the same temperate, conciliatory attitude he had shown in his opening speech. Bitter things were said by some. One champion of the Trade, in particular, was so violent in his personal abuse of Wilberforce that the Prime Minister himself rebuked him. But however violent the invective, its object remained unruffled. And when the session from which he had hoped so much ended with so little done, Wilberforce quietly resumed his labours. At any

rate he had learned something from those otherwise futile debates.
The opposition had declared its hand. There were new arguments
to be met, new evidence to be sought for, weak points in the
Abolitionist case to be strengthened. Above all, some further
attempt might be made to win the co-operation of France, and thus
to nullify the most weighty, genuine and respectable argument
against Abolition. To its weight even young Charles Grey, the
most promising of the Whig cadets and more liberal-minded than
most of the older members of the party, had yielded. "If France
alone," he had written in answer to a letter from Wilberforce
appealing for his support, "would consent to abolish this detestable
and inhuman traffic, the proposed plan would not have a more
zealous supporter than myself." But, without that condition, he
confessed that he would probably cast a silent vote against his
feelings and for the Trade. Wilberforce, accordingly, again proposed that he should go himself to Paris, and this time no official
objection was raised. For the moment relations with France were
friendlier; and M. Necker, who was now Chief Minister, was
known to favour Abolition. Unofficial conversations might, therefore, be more effective than formal diplomacy. But before Wilberforce was ready to start there was a sudden change in the whole
political situation. The first rumbles of the great earthquake
became audible across the Channel. "The news came of Necker's
being out," he records in his diary for July 14, "and of insurrections,
firing, &c." For one so eminent in British political circles as himself to visit Paris just at this crisis seemed obviously unwise: and
it was decided that Clarkson should go in his place. So, on August 7,
Clarkson set out, accompanied by a French secretary and interpreter,
and furnished by Wilberforce with written instructions and a
considerable sum of money from his private purse. Of the results
of this mission, more anon.

Meanwhile there had occurred in England an event which must
have strained even Wilberforce's patience. The vicar of Teston,
whose knowledge and zeal had been such important factors in
determining Wilberforce to take up the cause, and who had worked
so unsparingly and in such close intimacy with him ever since, had
been singled out by the more violent of the West Indian planters as
the special victim of the bitter and revengeful feelings which the
attack on them and on their fortunes had excited. Hard things had
been said about their indifference to the horrors of the Trade and

their treatment of the slaves on their plantations—not without occasional distortion and exaggeration of the facts. And they meant to repay the debt with interest. If Wilberforce himself was beyond their reach, too popular and influential, too famous, and too notoriously good, at any rate the obscure Kentish clergyman could be assailed with impunity. So the sewers were opened, and a stream of calumny poured out on Ramsay. His life in the West Indies, it would seem, had been one black story of depravity. By such a merciless assault the sturdiest spirit might well have been shaken, and Ramsay, a sensitive man, never robust, and now suffering from his excessive labours, bent to the storm. His character, indeed, could easily be cleared. James Stephen, on his return to the West Indies, carefully inquired into the accusations and reported the results to Wilberforce. "I have not heard," he wrote, "a crime or a blemish imputed to Mr. Ramsay which has not been refuted afterwards in my presence by some of his most inveterate enemies, better acquainted with the facts." But the damage could not be undone. Ramsay's health was completely broken, and Wilberforce's diary for July 21 thus records the end: "Heard that poor Ramsay died yesterday at ten o'clock. A smile on his face now." Not such the victor's comment. "Mr. Molyneux," wrote Stephen, "announced the decease of the public enemy to his natural son in this island in these terms ' Ramsay is dead—I have killed him.'"

7

When Parliament reassembled in the New Year, Wilberforce made an attempt to speed up the procedure of taking evidence. On January 27 he proposed that the witnesses should henceforth be heard before a Select Committee instead of before a Committee of the whole House as in the preceding session. The spokesmen of the Trade opposed it, for the wiser heads in their party had realised that the case against them was too strong to be met by simple contradiction and that their best policy at the moment was delay— delay on the plea of fair-play, delay in the interests of national security, delay on any grounds and at any price. And delay, as has been seen, was by no means unpalatable to the average member of Parliament. But to insist on devoting the meagre space of time of the whole House to witnesses whose statements would have just as much or as little weight in committee "above stairs" was palpably to shelve the business almost indefinitely and was dangerously suggestive of a definite decision in favour of the Trade. So on this occasion, at any rate, Wilberforce and Pitt and Fox and Burke had their way. A Select Committee was appointed, and during the next three months steady progress was made.

The evidence in defence of the Trade was taken first: it was completed during April; and then came an unexpected interruption. The Trade party had decided on a daring change of tactics. Having only heard one side of the case, the Committee was presumably at that moment in a more favourable mood towards the Trade than it was ever likely to be again. Might it not be worth while, then, to drop the policy of procrastination and press for an immediate decision? A vote snatched now for the maintenance of the Trade as it stood might smash the Abolitionist movement for years to come! The news of this audacious plan took the Abolitionists by surprise and filled them with alarm. As soon as it reached Wilberforce's ears he hastened straightway to Downing Street. "Saw Pitt in bed," he notes on April 20, "and talked with him on the enemy's impudent attempt to resist our calling evidence." Pitt suggested that he should go at once to Fox, since the proposal for the vote was to come from Lord Penrhyn and his friends on the Whig side of the House. So Wilberforce hurried off to the Leader of the Opposition, who, no less determined than the Prime Minister to keep the Slave Trade question above the party conflict, undertook to make inquiries and to do what he could to prevent the threatened move. He was apparently successful; for he told Pitt, two days later, that the forthcoming motion—so he was informed—was not intended to force a decision at once but merely to fix a day, in about three weeks' time, for closing the evidence, on the supposition that by then all the witnesses against the Trade would have been heard.

But Fox had been deceived. When the House got to business next day, Alderman Newnham at once rose to protest against the calling of any further evidence. The House, he argued, must already be convinced that Abolition was quite impracticable. Further evidence, therefore, was unnecessary and would merely cause delay from which—he coolly confessed—the question had already suffered too much. Let the House give forthwith a manly and decisive vote and so put an end to these protracted and dangerous discussions. This plea was underlined by Lord Penrhyn with a frank appeal to fear; he begged for an immediate decision on the ground that the vast negro majority in the West Indies might be so excited by the continuance of these debates as to rise and massacre the whites. This was not the first time that this argument had been used: nor was it by any means the last. At every stage of its slow progress the cause of the negroes was to be damaged and obstructed by the cry that Englishmen and Englishwomen were in danger. And at times, as will be seen, they were in danger.

With the whitewashing evidence fresh in their minds, members were doubtless more susceptible to such arguments than they had been in the previous year. But, their ingrained sense of fair play combining with their inveterate irresolution, they declined to be hustled into conceding to Lord Penrhyn the swift decision they had refused to Wilberforce. So the indecent manœuvre failed. The House decided, without a division, that the evidence should be continued. "Our opponents, blessed be God, fairly beat," says the diary.

All through May and on into June the Committee was meeting almost daily, and Wilberforce was invariably present, watching and assisting his witnesses. "I am almost worn out," he writes, "and I pant for a little country air and quiet." But even the close of the session on June 10 did not bring him rest. A General Election was imminent, and the member for Yorkshire hurried off on the 9th to conduct a three-weeks' canvass. In the last few years he had become almost a stranger to his constituents. He had no country house on his scattered Yorkshire property and he rarely visited the county. In the biographical notes he left behind him, he confesses and excuses his neglect. "I must mention," he says, "the uncommon kindness and liberality which I experienced from my constituents. In former times the county members displayed their equipages annually at the races and constituted a part of the grand jury at the summer assizes; the latter, indeed, I should have been glad to attend but for the unseemly festivities which annually take place at that period. I was not, however, wanted; the number of gentlemen of larger fortune in the county were far more than sufficient to constitute a most respectable grand jury, both at the spring and summer assizes. I could not consistently with my principles frequent the theatre and the ball-room, and I knew I should give offence by staying away, were I actually at York; but no discontent was ever expressed at my not presenting myself to the county on those occa-

sions. My friends appeared tacitly to admit my claim to the command of my own time during the recess." And Wilberforce was no
more subservient to his constituents' political opinions than to their
social conventions; more than once, he was to set himself against
the popular tide. It is to the credit of the Yorkshire electors that,
under these circumstances, his seat was always safe.

The election over—a dull election, increasing, as every one
expected, Pitt's hold on the House of Commons—Wilberforce was
able to spend the rest of the summer in the country, taking the
waters at Buxton and touring in Wales with Mr. Babington, a
zealous Abolitionist, and now one of his closest friends. In October
they both settled down at Yoxall in Staffordshire, where, on the
fringe of Needwood Forest, the Rev. Thomas Gisborne had his
home—Gisborne the "mere sap," the receptacle of Wilberforce's
midnight loquacity at Cambridge, but now and for the rest of his
life a far more intimate friend of his than he ever could have been
in those old gay days at St. John's. For a whole month the two
labourers stayed at Gisborne's, wrestling with the Privy Council
Report and with the evidence—nearly 1400 folio pages of it—given
before the House of Commons. "Mr. Wilberforce and Mr. Babington," writes a visitor in the house, "have never appeared downstairs
since we came, except to take a hasty dinner and for half an hour
after we have supped; the Slave Trade now occupies them nine
hours daily. . . . They talk of sitting up one night in each week.
. . . The two friends begin to look very ill, but they are in excellent
spirits, and at this moment I hear them laughing at some absurd
questions in the examination." That one of them, at any rate, was
once more taxing his strength to the limit is clear enough from the
diary; Oct. 8: "Unwell. Hard work—slave evidence." Oct. 9:
"Eyes bad. Hard at work." Oct. 11: "Slave evidence, and very
hard at it with Babington all this week: wherein by God's blessing
enabled to preserve a better sense of heavenly things than for some
time before." Nov. 1: "Continued to work very hard at the evidence
all this week. Slept ill, not being well, partly through working
too much."

On November 19 he is back in London, "plunging at once into
a dinner-circle of Cabinet Ministers"; and the diary resumes its old
complaint of wasted hours. Many men might have envied Wilberforce an evening spent with Pitt, Chatham, Grenville, Dundas, and
Ryder, discussing Burke's newly published onslaught on the French

Revolution—Pitt, Chatham, and himself on one side, Grenville and
Ryder on the other, Dundas apparently on neither—but his characteristic comment is merely, "kept up late, and unfit for prayer."
"Oh! how I regret Yoxall Lodge," he cries a little later. And, when
the new session began and the hearing of evidence in committee
was resumed, not without renewed opposition, the hours available
for work were still further curtailed. Yet work was more imperative
than ever; for the evidence was drawing to an end, and then, surely,
Parliament must give its verdict. At last, in the early spring of
1791, Wilberforce was forced to retreat from Palace Yard to Clapham
where he prepared, as at Teston two years before, for the imminent
debate. The prospects of success were certainly no more favourable
than in 1789. Abolitionist enthusiasm in the country had begun to
lose its edge as the novelty of the crusade wore off. Pitt was still
warm in its support, like Fox and Burke, and his dominion over
the House of Commons was now stronger than it had ever been; but
he was still unable to commit the Government to Abolition, still
unable, therefore, to compel his followers to vote with him. In the
House of Lords there was one change for the better. Sydney had
resigned because he felt that, differing, as he did, from the Prime
Minister on the Slave Trade, he could not remain in charge of the
department in which colonial matters were then dealt with. And
Pitt had made the most of this opportunity. He had appointed
Grenville, a staunch Abolitionist, Home Secretary in Sydney's place
and had raised him moreover to the peerage in order that he might
act, on the Slave Trade question amongst others, as a check to
Thurlow in the Upper House. But what was one friend among so
many enemies? And if Wilberforce was hopeful, it was not to
human allies that he looked. He had received, late in February, a
letter from the aged Wesley—written a week before his death,
perhaps the last he every wrote—which echoed his own inmost
convictions. "Unless the Divine power has raised you up," it ran,
"to be as *Athansius contra mundum,* I see not how you can go through
your glorious enterprise. . . . Unless God has raised you up for
this very thing, you will be worn out by the opposition of men
and devils; but if God be for you, who can be against you? . . .
Go on, in the name of God and in the power of His might, till even
American slavery, the vilest that ever saw the sun, shall vanish
away before it." In the same spirit in which the old crusader put
off his armour, the young crusader girded his on. "May I look to

w   H

Him," he writes in his spiritual journal a few days before the debate, "for wisdom and strength and the power of persuasion . . . and ascribe to Him all the praise if I succeed, and if I fail, say from the heart ' Thy will be done.'"

He had need to pray for resignation; for the debate of 1791 followed much the same course as the debate of 1789 to a worse end. Wilberforce opened it—moving for "leave to bring in a Bill to prevent the further importation of slaves into the British islands in the West Indies." His speech was as eloquent as its predecessor, as moderate in tone, as careful not to underestimate the strength of the opposition's case, but now more closely packed with detailed evidence. The fruit of those long laborious hours with Babington, it stands as the clearest, most circumstantial, and yet most succinct account, given then or since, of the case against the Slave Trade. And again the great trio supported Wilberforce. Burke's speech was short and sharp, but both Pitt and Fox made longer and bigger efforts than in 1789. Others might be squeamish but certainly not Fox; and whether he won votes by it or lost them, he forced the House to listen to the grim realities which Wilberforce had mostly left to the imagination. He told them of the planter who had ordered his surgeon to cut off a fugitive negro's leg, and, on his humane refusal, had broken the leg himself; and of the young female slave, tied naked to a beam by the wrists and burnt about the body as she writhed and swung. Was there not, he asked, in the cruelty of the little despots of the slave-ship and the plantation a streak of insanity as in the cruelty of the great Roman despots, of Caligula and his like? And he bade each doubtful member of the House to "make the case his own." "What would any of us say, and how would we feel, if conquered and carried away by a tribe so savage as our countrymen on the coast of Africa show themselves to be? How would we bear the same treatment ourselves which we do not scruple to inflict on the Africans?" Pitt's speech, as usual, was the antithesis of Fox's. It was not primarily a question of humane feeling, he insisted at the outset, but a question of moral justice. "It is impossible," he said, "for me to support the Slave Trade unless gentlemen will, in the first place, prove to me that there are no laws of morality binding upon nations and that it is not the duty of a country's legislature to restrain its subjects from invading the happiness of other countries and from violating the fundamental principles of justice." Intent on gaining votes, he devoted most of his speech to removing the objections of those members who desired the Trade to cease but feared that the labour supply in the West Indies could not be maintained without it. Coolly setting forth the facts and figures and reviewing separately the different circumstances in each of the islands, he repeated Wilberforce's argument that, if the Trade were abolished, better conditions in the life of the plantations would nullify the need of further importation. And in this connexion he touched on what he called "a rather delicate point," the possibility of emancipating the slaves— not rashly, not at once—it was madness to talk like that—but when they had been raised from their present degradation and made capable of freedom. But perhaps the most important feature of the speech was the unequivocal lead it gave. He said nothing now of his willingness to listen to the arguments on the other side. He had listened to them—to all the elaborate defences the West Indian party had put up in the committee—and they had not shaken his previous opinions in the least. At the beginning of his speech, he declared that never, since he entered the House, had there been a question in which his heart was so deeply interested. "How can we hesitate a moment," he asked at the end of it, "to abolish this commerce in human flesh which has too long disgraced our country and which our example will contribute to abolish in every corner of the globe?"

But, as in 1789, the great men pleaded in vain. This time the opposition was better managed. The Trade had realised that something more was needed than bluster and *gaucherie* from the back benches. Quiet, not unreasonable, effective speeches were made by Sir William Yonge, Colonel Jackson, and Lord John Russell. Mr. Molyneux was wisely silent. One fool, only, was irrepressible—a colonel who had spent ten months in the West Indies and solemnly contended that the slaves must be happy because they were fond of ornaments. But folly, no more than wisdom, could now affect the issue. At last the country gentlemen had made up their minds. There were some on both sides of the House who were ready to take the leap of Abolition—all honour to them. But there were more, on both sides, who had come to the conclusion that the Trade must go on. Property, precedent, prescription—these were stronger forces than Pitt's justice or Fox's humanity; and the strongest of them was property. A little speech towards the close of the debate put the whole case with admirable brevity and candour. "The leaders, it is true," said Mr. Drake, "are for Abolition. But the minor orators, the dwarfs, the pygmies, will, I trust, this day carry the question against them. The property of the West Indians is at stake; and though men may be generous with their own property, they should not be so with the property of others." Mr. Drake's trust was justified. After two days' debate, prolonged till half-past three in the morning of April 20, the House of Commons rejected Wilberforce's motion by 163 votes to 88.

V

Check

I

WITH his defeat in the session of 1791 Wilberforce had lost his last chance of carrying Abolition for a long time to come. Why this was so will be clear if we return to Clarkson and follow him on his visit to Paris in 1789. For it so happened that this zealous Abolitionist was present in person at the beginning of two interlinked series of events, which in their consummation were to have the effect of stopping dead the progress of his cause for fifteen years.

Clarkson, of course, was unaware of this. The fact that the Bastille had fallen only a few weeks before his arrival in Paris was for him the best of good omens, signifying the advent of a new era in which Slavery and the Trade could have no place. While the foundations of the society in which he moved began to quiver and crack around him, he devoted himself to his mission with single-minded and confident industry. He was greatly encouraged at the start by the sympathetic reception accorded him. In France as in England, it need scarcely be said, there were sensitive philanthropists as well as cynical business-men and timid politicians. "Men are born free and with equal rights," proclaimed the first article of the Declaration of the Rights of Man in 1789: "free and equal they remain." And there were Frenchmen prepared to apply the doctrines of Rousseau beyond France, to black men no less than white. The Abbé Raynal had denounced Slavery at the same time as Dr. Paley was denouncing the Slave Trade. Within a decade of the *Wealth of Nations* had appeared Necker's *De l'Administration des Finances de la France* in which he suggested the possibility of abolishing the Trade within a generation by a general European compact. And the foundation of the Abolition Committee in 1787 had at once attracted attention in Paris. Brissot, whom the new dispensation was bringing to the forefront of French politics, had written to congratulate the Committee and to ask that he and his friend Clavière might be regarded as associates in its work; and, when passing through England on his way to visit the United States, he had attended a meeting of the Committee in London. Lafayette had also communicated with the Committee and announced that he proposed to found a similar society in France. Accordingly, in 1788, *Les Amis des Noirs* had come into being. It was a more distinguished body than its prototype of quiet Quakers and the like. Condorcet was its president, and Rochefoucauld and Lafayette were enrolled as its first members.

Clarkson, therefore, was not coming to preach in a wholly heathen land; and he was promptly and warmly welcomed by the *Amis des Noirs* as the representative of the sister society in England and as a useful ally in France. A joint deputation was arranged to lay the case for Abolition before Necker; and Clarkson, at any rate, was pleased with the result. The Minister was kindness itself. He flattered Clarkson with the suggestion that better progress would be made if they discussed the matter privately, without the distinguished Frenchmen of the deputation, and he begged him to dine with him from time to time for the purpose. If it should happen by ill luck that he were called away on business of state, Madame Necker—she promised it herself—would take her husband's place and would receive and converse with Clarkson "on all occasions in which this great cause of humanity and religion might be concerned." And Madame Necker, if not so useful, was at least as ardent as the Minister; like the Marquise de Lafayette, she was one of the *Amis des Noirs*. The Archbishop of Aix, the Bishop of Chartres, the Abbé Grégoire were as keenly interested as the churchmen of England. The Abbé Sieyès presented Clarkson with a set of his works and expressed his pleasure at making the acquaintance of "the friend of man." Rochefoucauld, "the most virtuous man in France," held a meeting of sympathisers at his house. Mirabeau welcomed Clarkson with open arms. He had just drafted the outlines of a speech on the Slave Trade for the Assembly; the only think lacking to complete it was the "circumstantial knowledge" which Clarkson was just the man to supply. Clarkson supplied it. Every other day for a month he wrote him a letter of sixteen to twenty pages; and Mirabeau, he tells us, "usually acknowledged the receipt of each." But there was one piece of information available in more graphic and compendious form; for Clarkson had with him some copies of a plan printed for distribution in England, showing a section of a slave-ship's interior with its shelves of human cargo. Mirabeau was delighted. He summoned a carpenter, gave him the plan, and told him to make forthwith a wooden model of a slave-ship as an ornament for his dining-room. It was about a yard long, we are told, and it contained the authoritative number of little men and women, painted black, and stowed tightly in their proper places. . . . Mirabeau, Rochefoucauld, Lafayette, Condorcet, Brissot, Sieyès, Necker, Madame Necker—these were great French names, and Clarkson proudly capped the list with Louis XVI himself. His Majesty, Necker informed him, was desirous of making himself master of the question and had expressed a wish for two copies of his *Essay on the Impolicy of the Slave Trade* (published in 1788), one in French and the other in English. The volumes were duly presented together with specimens of native African handicrafts. The plan of the slave-ship was not submitted, since Necker "thought it would affect His Majesty too much, as he was then indisposed." The outcome was highly gratifying. Louis admired the specimens, "particularly those in gold," and he devoted himself, it was said, to an "unwearied" perusal of the book.

Clarkson's temperament was at least as sanguine as Wilberforce's; and perhaps it is not to be wondered at that so kindly an interest, in quarters so varied and so high, should have excited fond delusions in his mind. Quite early in his mission he wrote that the question of Abolition would be raised in the National Assembly in eight or ten days' time. And once they were at it, these quick Frenchmen would put slow, deliberate England to shame. "Evidence will not be necessary," he declared, "and I should not be surprised if the French were to do themselves the honour of voting away the diabolical traffic in a single night." Some weeks later he is less confident as to speed but not as to the ultimate result. "I am convinced in my own mind," he writes, "that the Slave Trade will, in a couple of months, fall in France." When, in the autumn, after nearly six months' stay, he at last left Paris, the sympathy of his French allies had been as cordial as when he came; Lafayette had condoled with him in his disappointment; Mirabeau had told him that he had won over at least a quarter of the members of the Assembly and had given him a letter for Pitt; Brissot had accompanied him to his carriage—but the Slave Trade had not fallen. In France, as in England, though supported by some of the best and ablest men of the day, the cause had failed, and largely for the same reasons. Bordeaux and Havre had defended the Trade as stoutly as Liverpool and Bristol. The planters had fought as hard in Paris as in London, and their weapons were as sharp. The press had been virulent. Clavière had been anonymously threatened with assassination. Clarkson himself had been personally denounced as, among other things, an English spy. And the average Frenchman had been confronted with the converse of the argument which had weighed so much with the average Englishman. If France relinquished the Trade before England, would not England sit still and reap the profit? Nay, how was it that England, peaceful and prosperous, unshaken by the throes of Revolution, having considered the question coolly and at length, had not given the lead herself?

Revolution! There, though nobody, perhaps, and certainly not the busy English visitor could then have guessed it, lay the insuperable obstacle to the success of Clarkson's cause, not only for the moment in France but for years ahead in England. It was actually while he was in Paris that Versailles was invaded by the starving mob and the King and Queen escorted, prisoners of the people, to the Tuileries. And from that instant the tragedy proceeded to its climax with the seeming certainty of Fate—first, a year of illusory calm; then the flight to Varennes and the conference of the despots of Central Europe at Pilnitz; next, the gathering of the *émigrés* and their allies on the frontier; and then, in quick succession, the outbreak of war, the September Massacres, and the execution of the King.

Already in 1791, still more darkly in 1792, the shadow of this tragedy was falling over England, dimming the light and distorting the perspective along the whole range of British politics. No great stir had been created at the first appearance of Revolutionary France on the European stage. Observers on this side of the Channel had looked the new actor up and down and concluded that he was not unlike themselves—almost an Englishman, a very old-fashioned Englishman, about a century behind the times. It was Burke's shrill cry of "wolf" that first roused alarm, not very deep or widespread to begin with, till presently those seemly garments of the orthodox cut fell off and a new and utterly un-English figure was disclosed, gaunt, ferocious, in rags and a red cap, with bared teeth and dripping knife. And then, indeed, throughout the political classes of England, excepting only a tiny minority of unrepentant Whigs and a negligible handful of Republicans, alarm stiffened into a complex of anger, fear and hate. Thenceforward it was impossible for the

British people to determine British questions on their merits. Cases were still elaborately argued at Westminster. Fox answered Pitt. Whig voted against Tory. But appeals to logic, to justice, to humanity, even to party principles were now of secondary importance. The grim figure of the Jacobin brooded over every debate. It was he, not really Pitt or Fox, that dominated the discussion; inspired, chiefly by reaction, the arguments; decided, mostly by repulsion, the votes. Inevitably, under these conditions, that little burst of liberalism, which had broken out so hopefully since 1783 and might, if peace had lasted, have gained strength to do the work of the Reform Act forty years before its time, was promptly and utterly suppressed.

The cause of Abolition was among the first of good causes to suffer from this process of reaction. It was not only affected, in general, like all other questions, by the results of the Revolution in France; it was affected, also, in particular, by the results of the Revolution in the West Indies. And in the approaches to this second tragedy we meet again the busy, rather self-important, very English Clarkson, not this time merely a silent spectator as when the doomed King and Queen drove by, but in close and constant intercourse with one of the principal actors. Dining one day with Lafayette, he met the six representatives of the mulatto or "coloured" population of the French half of St. Domingue, who had been sent to Paris with a gift of six million *livres* to the National Assembly, a request to Lafayette to accept the post of Commander-in-Chief of the people of Colour in the island, and a mission to obtain from the Assembly a pledge that, when, as was shortly expected, it framed a new constitution for the colony in accordance with the new ideas, the mulatto population should be put on the same political footing as the Europeans. Clarkson was naturally interested in these indirect products of the Slave Trade. As he sat among them at the dinner-table, he noted that their behaviour was "modest" and their appearance "genteel"—they had donned the uniform of the French National Guards, and one of them wore the Cross of St. Louis—and that their complexion, though "sallow and swarthy," was "not darker than that of some of the natives of the south of France." On several subsequent occasions Clarkson met and talked with these "Deputies of Colour"; and their mutual acquaintanceship ripened into something like a transient friendship. When Clarkson left Paris one of them, he says, "gave me a trinket, by which I might remember

him." And indeed there was much common ground between them.
The six men were ardent Abolitionists and Clarkson was in genuine
sympathy with their claim to political equality. But he was somewhat disturbed at the growing impatience they displayed as week
after week went by and their mission remained unfulfilled. Soon
after their arrival, they had been called before the National Assembly,
in which the European delegates from St. Domingue had already
taken their seats, and the President had bidden them take courage
since the Assembly "knew no distinction between Blacks and Whites,
but considered all men as having equal rights." But when they had
pressed for admission as regular members, they had met with
nothing but evasion and delay. The whole colonial interest in Paris
was up in arms against them; and even in that new sanguine atmosphere interest was still a match for principle. Six times a day was
fixed for the discussion of their claim; six times it was postponed;
and the disappointed deputies grew more and more restive. At last
their leader, Ogé, confided to Clarkson that he no longer cared what
the Assembly did. "But let it beware of the consequences," he added.
"Dispatches shall go directly to St. Domingue and we will soon
follow them. We can produce as good soldiers on our estates as
those in France. Our own arms shall make us independent and
respectable." Clarkson—so he tells us in his book—begged them to
be patient, to make allowance for the domestic difficulties of France,
to reflect on the miseries which hasty action might bring to their
own island. "At my last conference with them I recommended
moderation and forbearance as the best gifts I could leave them."

But before Clarkson's departure Ogé, heedless of this pacific
counsel, had angrily shaken off the dust of Paris and returned to
St. Domingue. Some months later, he put his threat into execution; he armed his slaves and called on his fellow mulattoes to rise
and fight for their rights. The rebellion was quickly suppressed.
Ogé himself escaped to a Spanish port, but was surrendered to the
French authorities and broken on the wheel.

The second act of the tragedy was a conflict among the Europeans themselves. Since the first days of the Revolution in the
mother-country the partisans of the Assembly and of the King in
the island had been on the brink of civil war; and early in 1791,
encouraged by some mutinous French regulars, recently sent from
France, the soldiers of the garrison of Port au Prince tore off their
white cockades, murdered their Royalist colonel, and set the

Government at defiance. The situation was clearly very delicate and very dangerous. At the back of the 40,000 divided whites were 40,000 embittered and revengeful mulattoes; and at the back of the mulattoes were 450,000 negro slaves. And this complex of inflammable human nature was perilously isolated from the civilised world, shut in upon itself by the encircling sea. Yet the left wing of the National Assembly took a recklessly precipitate course. It began at precisely the wrong end. It made no attempt to restore order in the island or to establish a single effective government. Brushing aside the opposition of the colonial party, it straightway applied the principle of equality for which Ogé had pleaded in vain, and applied it in a manner which was bound to be regarded as invidious and provocative. On May 15, on the motion of the Abbé Grégoire, a decree was carried bestowing on mulattoes born of free parents an equal political status with the whites. At once the great majority of the mulattoes, whose mothers had been slaves, were up in arms. Treated like slaves themselves, they summoned the slaves to make common cause with them against the whites. And this time the revolt was far more formidable. The call was answered by 100,000 slaves; within two months, in the early autumn of 1791, 2000 whites, of both sexes and all ages, had been massacred, more than 1000 plantations destroyed, and 1200 planters' families reduced to beggary. Bestial cruelties were perpetrated by the blacks; and the whites, sinking to their level, gave like for like. The beautiful, fertile colony had become—and was long to remain—a little hell on earth.

Thus a second and more direct argument was established against the cause of Abolition. To the Red Terror in Paris was added the Black Terror in St. Domingue; the one an awful warning of the perils of idealism in general, the other of its perils as applied particularly to the negroes. And when the contagion of rebellion spread to Martinique and the smaller French islands, and finally to the British island of Dominica—where a small and soon-suppressed slave-rising occurred in 1791—the case, to the cautious conservative temper of the British Parliament at any rate, seemed proved. The reasoning might be weak. It might, indeed, have been argued that, if the slaves in the West Indies were in a rebellious mood, it was better not to let the Trade bring more of them from Africa. But into the minds of British legislators, stiffened and hardened by the impact of horrible events, logic could now scarcely penetrate.

2

The petrifying effects of the French Revolution were slower to reach the rank and file of the British people than their so-called representatives at Westminster; and it is a significant commentary on the character of the unreformed Parliament that, at the very time when its attitude to Abolition was at freezing-point, the country at large had never been so hot for it. This recovery of all and more than all the initial enthusiasm for the cause was mainly due to the indefatigable propaganda of Wilberforce and Clarkson and the Committee. The torments of the slave-ships were not only popularised by the Committee's literature and by the publication of the debates in Parliament; other means of the most diverse kind were employed. The poet Cowper, who had already attacked the Slave Trade, somewhat heavy-handedly, in *The Task*, was inspired to write three shorter pieces on the theme. Of these *The Negro's Complaint* was perhaps the best calculated to appeal to the popular taste. The following are three of its seven stanzas:

> Still in thought as free as ever
>   What are England's rights, I ask,
> Me from my delights to sever,
>   Me to torture, me to task?
> Fleecy locks and black complexion
>   Cannot forfeit Nature's claim;
> Skins may differ, but affection
>   Dwells in black and white the same.

> Why did all-creating Nature
>   Make the plant, for which we toil?
> Sighs must fan it, tears must water,
>   Sweat of ours must dress the soil.
> Think, ye masters, iron-hearted,
>   Lolling at your jovial boards,
> Think how many backs have smarted
>   For the sweets your cane affords.

> Is there, as you sometimes tell us,
>   Is there one, who rules on high;

> Has he bid you buy and sell us,
>   Speaking from his throne, the sky?
> Ask him if your knotted scourges,
>   Fetters, blood-extorting screws,
> Are the means which duty urges
>   Agents of his will to use?

The Abolitionists made prompt use of a poem which, as Clarkson puts it, "gave a plain account of the subject with an appropriate feeling." It was printed on the finest paper, and thousands of copies, neatly folded and aptly superscribed *A Subject for Conversation at the Tea-table*, were circulated throughout the country. It was also set to music, and presently the unhappy negro could be heard complaining in the streets of London and many provincial towns. Another propagandist device was due to the ingenious generosity of Wedgwood, the famous master-potter and an ardent Abolitionist. He had a cameo made depicting a negro in a posture of piteous entreaty on a white ground and distributed hundreds of them among the supporters of the cause. The cameo soon became as popular as the poem. It was to be seen everywhere—inlaid in gold on the lids of gentlemen's snuff-boxes, inserted in ladies' bracelets or worked up into heads of ornamental hair-pins. The wearing of it, it is said—and it is not incredible—became quite the fashion. Even more significant was the success of a campaign against the use of West Indian sugar. All the more zealous Abolitionists had resolved to abstain from it on the morrow of the parliamentary failure of 1791. "We use East Indian sugar entirely," wrote Babington to Wilberforce, "and so do full two-thirds of the friends of Abolition in Leicester." The venerable John Newton, on the other hand, regarded this move as premature and likely to alienate moderate men; and Wilberforce decided not to make it an essential part of the official programme. But when Clarkson travelled through the country in 1792 he found that numbers of individual Abolitionists in all parts had adopted the ban. He estimated—probably somewhat over-estimated in his sanguine way—an average of 200 to 500 abstainers in the larger towns "who had made this sacrifice to virtue." He came upon grocers who had ceased to sell West Indian sugar, and children old enough to be persuaded to abstain, on principle, from sweets.

These symptoms of popular zeal were not to be disregarded;

and after the signal defeat in the House of Commons in 1791 and
when in the subsequent months the damaging effects of the French
Revolution and the St. Domingue affair became increasingly manifest in political circles, Wilberforce and his colleagues decided that
the time had come to appeal from Parliament directly to the people
on a comprehensive scale. Then, with an emphatic popular mandate
behind him, Wilberforce was to return to the charge in the Commons. "The best course will be," he wrote at the beginning of
1792, "to endeavour to excite the flame as much as possible in a
secret way, but not to allow it more than to smoulder until after
I have given notice of my intention of bringing the subject forward.
This must be the signal for the fire's bursting forth." So a new
abstract of the evidence against the Trade was prepared by Clarkson
and this, together with the report of the last debate, was circulated
broadcast. On its heels Clarkson set out on another of his exhaus-
tive and exhausting tours through England, while Dr. Dickson was
dispatched to Scotland. The results of this mission were immediate.
Corresponding Committees, linked to the parent body in London,
sprang up at Newcastle, Nottingham, Glasgow, and then all over
Britain. The second step was the organisation of public meetings;
the third and last the presentation of petitions to Parliament. For
three months the flame was thus kindled according to plan. And
there was no doubt whatever as to its heat. Throughout the Midlands and the North enthusiasm for Abolition ran riot. It was
reported from Scotland that "the clergy to a man were favourable
to the cause," and in Scotland the opinions of the clergy were the
opinions of the people. Even the City of London returned at last
to its old liberal traditions. The proposal of a petition in the
Common Council was stifled by the Lord Mayor and a majority of
the Aldermen, but they could not override a meeting of the Livery.
The Liverymen attended in full strength, drowned their protests in
groans and hisses, and triumphantly carried the motion.

The campaign was controlled by the London Committee, with
which Wilberforce was closely associated, though not actually a
member till 1794. His own duties were heavy, for his lieutenants
in the country were always asking how they should proceed even
in details. Should they raise the question of the sugar ban? What
were they to say about St. Domingue? When was the precise
moment for launching a petition? How was a public meeting to
be organised? "Give us precise instructions," wrote one agent on

this last point: and precise instructions were forthcoming day after day. Never was Wilberforce's intimate knowledge of society more useful. He could warn one man of Lord Harrowby's dislike of public meetings, advise another how best to approach Lord Fitz-william, suggest to a third that the father of a Staffordshire M.P. might persuade his son to propose the motion for a petition if he were informed that by so doing his son would secure the votes of the Wedgwood interest at the next election. And, in the intervals, there was his own speech to be prepared—the culminating effort of the whole campaign. Once more the physical strain was severe. "I thank God I keep well," he wrote.

Meantime the enemy were not idle. Paris and St. Domingue had given them two new cards to play, and they played them for all they were worth. And there was a weakness in their opponents' hand of which they were quick to take advantage. It may be a salutary dispensation that human progress is always retarded not only by the people who want to go too slow, but also by the people who want to go too fast. The history of all great causes is full of set-backs from the "Left"; and the cause of Abolition was no exception to the rule. The Abolitionists in the mass were not fanatics, but every fanatic was an Abolitionist and a great deal more. It was an easy game, then, for the Trade to spy out the Jacobins among the British *Amis des Noirs*; to suggest that the good, simple-minded Wilberforce was unaware of the sinister forces that had enlisted under his banner; to give out that, however moderate and respectable their leaders might be, the mob behind them was bent on securing Abolition only as a lever wherewith to thrust the British Empire down the primrose path of Equality into the flames of St. Domingue. The danger of these insinuations was clear to Wilberforce; and when, in this year, the Convention made him and Clarkson—together with George Washington, Joseph Priestley, Jeremy Bentham and Tom Paine—citizens of France, he quickly parried the unwelcome compliment by joining, on Burke's sugges-tion, a committee in aid of the French emigrant clergy. But Clarkson was not so wise. He failed to realise that a public expres-sion of his eager sympathy with the Revolution might damage the cause of Abolition, the triumph of which was, after all, the supreme, the single motive of his life. His friends realised it well enough. After a long talk with him Milner wrote to Wilberforce, "I wish him better health, and better notions in politics." "You will see

Clarkson," wrote Wilberforce to Lord Muncaster: "caution him against talking of the French Revolution; it will be the ruin of our cause." Clarkson, wrote Samuel Hoare, is making inquiries as to whether there are "many friends to the French Revolution" in various places. "I hope thou wilt lose no time in giving him a hint upon this subject, or our cause will be essentially injured." But hints were thrown away on so sanguine an apostle, and there was rejoicing in the enemies' camp when it was known that he had ventilated Jacobinical opinions at a meeting at a pothouse in the Strand. And it was not only the Trade that marked his indiscretion. Government circles, already sniffing the scent of a Republican bogey in England, were annoyed; and Dundas wrote a sharp note to Wilberforce. "What business had your friend, Clarkson, to attend the ' Crown and Anchor ' last Thursday? He could not have done a more mischievous thing to the cause you have taken in hand." And if Dundas was angry, Pitt must have been more so, and for a better reason. He was a confessed Abolitionist—and Prime Minister; and since, at this time, he was maintaining the strictest official neutrality towards the French Revolution, it was not pleasant for him to find a cause, which he had so notoriously supported, tainted ever so little with Jacobinism.

The incident, indeed, may well have been one reason for Pitt's betraying, at this time, the first faint touch of embarrassment at the conflict between his personal sentiments and his official position. St. Domingue had made it difficult enough, without any gossip about Jacobins, for the Prime Minister to reassert, just at this moment, his uncompromising condemnation of the Trade. "People here are all panic-struck with the transactions in St. Domingue," wrote Wilberforce: "I am pressed on all hands . . . to defer my motion till next year." And, to his dismay, one of those who pressed for delay was Pitt. There is a painful note in the diary of a committee-meeting on the question. "Pitt threw out against Slave motion on St. Domingue account. . . . I could hardly bring myself to resolve to do my duty and please God, at the expense (as I suspect it will turn out) of my cordiality with Pitt, or rather his with me." The little storm was over in a moment: Pitt was willing still to yield to Wilberforce and his own instincts: but the entry was sadly prophetic. If Pitt should retire from the conflict, the friends would part; for Wilberforce assuredly would stay behind. "Do not be afraid," he said to Babington at this time, "lest I should give ground. . . . This is a matter wherein all personal, much more all ministerial, attachments must be as dust in the balance."

And now the campaign had reached its climax. Wilberforce had given notice of his motion, and on this, the appointed signal, the well-prepared machinery for the launching of petitions for Abolition all over the country was instantly set in motion. It went like clock-work. Petitions poured into Westminster—312 from England and Wales, 187 from Scotland. On the other side only five petitions were presented—two of them from individuals and a third in favour at least of regulation. "You will perhaps be surprised," wrote one of Wilberforce's correspondents, "that Liverpool does not petition for the Trade. Liverpool will never again, I think, petition on this subject; conviction of the truth has spread amongst us widely." And he hinted that the vehement support of the Trade by Tarleton, the local member, might cost him his seat at the next election—as indeed it did. Never before had the politically passive, quiescent, oligarchic Britain of the eighteenth century witnessed such a lively and widespread movement. It had shown how much could be done to mobilise public opinion outside the walls of Parliament, yet strictly within the liberties of the constitution. It was a new and a great fact in British politics. "Its methods," says G. M. Trevelyan, "became the model for the conduct of hundreds and even thousands of other movements—political, humanitarian, social, educational —which have been and still are the chief arteries of the life-blood of modern Britain." And not the least effective part of its organisation was the admirable timing, so as to bring the maximum of pressure on the House of Commons at the latest possible moment. The last of the petitions, that from the Livery of the City, was presented on April 2 at the very hour at which Wilberforce rose to make his motion.

Meantime, only a fortnight earlier, something had happened outside England that was bound to affect the question. On March 16, Christian VII of Denmark had signed an edict declaring that "with the beginning of the year 1803, all traffic in the Slave Trade by our subjects shall cease." The Danish possessions in the West Indies were few and small. On a yearly average, only some fifty or sixty ships of from 80 to 120 tons were engaged in trading with them. Denmark's share in the Slave Trade was thus incomparably less than Britain's. But, none the less, that enlightened country had achieved the honour of giving the lead to Europe. And from the point of view of British Abolitionists the edict might at first sight have seemed peculiarly timely. The preamble to it bristled with their arguments—the conditions of the Trade were undesirable: the plantations could be cultivated by labourers born and trained in the islands instead of by imported slaves, and this would eventually prove a benefit to the masters themselves. But there was a dangerous flaw in the plan—the date. Wilberforce and Sharp and Clarkson, Pitt and Fox and Grenville, the Abolition Committee and all that host of petitioners desired immediate Abolition. Not so the King of Denmark. He had indeed condemned the Trade: but he had postponed the execution of the sentence ten whole years.

3

The invasion of the eighteenth-century House of Commons by such an undesirable stranger as Public Opinion was somewhat disconcerting to the representatives of the people. In the last session they had achieved, not without throes and twinges, a decision; and now it appeared that this decision was repudiated by a very large number of their countrymen, less properly impressed than themselves by those plain warnings from oversea. For those members, at any rate, whose seats were not positively secured by influence or bribery, it meant at least a reconsideration of the thorny question. And another full-dress debate meant for all, or most of them, a reopening of their minds to the Abolitionist logic and a re-exposure of their consciences, still a little raw, to the painful facts of the Trade case. To the spokesmen of the Trade the spectacle of the heaped petitions on the table might have been even more unpleasant if they had not known what was coming. But they had known, and they were ready. The possibility that this volume of public protest might just succeed in turning the scale against them had compelled them to reconsider their strategy. Their old policy of direct and complete opposition to Abolition had been discarded and a new and skilful plan concocted. And, to make victory certain, they could count for the chief part in its execution on the services of a very big man indeed. A few weeks earlier Wilberforce had jotted down this characteristic note in his diary, quite unsuspicious of its irony: "January 21. Went with Pitt to Wimbledon. . . . A long discussion with Dundas after dinner *tête-à-tête*—most excellent man of business.

Oh, what a pity he is not alive to what is best!" It was indeed a pity. This excellent man of business, the most indispensable of Pitt's colleagues, the most powerful and *rusé* of his party managers, the master-broker of Scottish seats, was to be the mainspring of the Trade's device. It was not true, though it was often to be said, that Dundas was the West Indians' tool. He was nobody's tool. He had his own reasons for opposing immediate Abolition. Above all he dreaded its effects on the solidarity of the Government and the party. But, if the Trade did not actually choose its champion, no better choice could have been made. Not only was the House of Commons bound to be impressed by this professional exponent of plain horse-sense, this personified antithesis and antidote to Wilberforce's sensibility and Fox's passion; but his performance would also rub in the important point that, if Pitt still spoke for Abolition, he would not be speaking for his Government. So the enemies of Abolition could face the debate, despite those piled petitions, with a fairly easy mind. Let Wilberforce make the most of Pitt: they had a Roland for his Oliver.

Wilberforce's opening speech was a masterly example of the art of variation on a familiar theme. He was bound, as in his previous speeches, to make the same two cardinal points—that the Slave Trade was an abomination and that its continuance was not essential to the welfare of the planters. But there was no hackneyed clap-trap in his arguing of them, no sentimental *clichés*, no stale illustrations. It was to the first of the two points that he paid most attention, bent on convincing the House that the inevitable concomitants of the Trade were so hideous that no civilised community could know of them and let it be; and for this, of course, the evidence was so voluminous that there was never need for him to tell the same story twice. One striking phrase deserves quotation. "Europeans," he said, "are hovering round the coast like vultures: and like vultures they feed on blood." And of the two or three telling incidents he chose to recount, one made a peculiarly sharp impression. Six British slave-ships, he told the House, had anchored off the little African coast-town of Calabar: and their captain, on learning that the native traders were obstinately demanding more than the usual payment for those of their countrymen whom they were willing to sell as slaves, took counsel together and decided to open fire on the town in order to compel a lowering of the price. Some time was wasted in discussion with a French slave-captain who happened to be present and who, being ready to pay the higher price, declined to take part in the operation; but in the course of the morning fire was opened with sixty-six guns. Not a shot was fired in reply, but the inhabitants could be seen running in all directions like ants in a broken nest. The bombardment was continued for three hours and resumed again in the evening, until at last, some twenty people having been killed and many injured, the natives consented to sell their slaves at any price the captains fixed. . . . The Abolition debates had accustomed the House to horrors; but this particular story created a sensation. There was—says sober Hansard in one of his rare interpolations—"a sudden burst of indignation." The House rang with cries of "Name! Name!" "Mr. Wilberforce," the chronicler continues, "resisted for a long time; at last the cry overpowered him and we heard the names." Those of the captains may well be left in obscurity. The ships were *Thomas*, *Recovery*, *Amacree* of Bristol, *Betsy* and *Thomas* of Liverpool, and, more appropriate than these humanities, *Wasp*, her port not stated.

Wilberforce was followed by orthodox champions of the Trade —Baillie, agent for Grenada, and Tarleton, member for Liverpool. Their part was to state the case against Abolition as clearly as before and to make all possible capital out of St. Domingue. Baillie indeed, detecting in the irresponsible propaganda of Wilberforce and his friends a more sovereign source of evil for the world than the French Revolution itself, declared that "the causes of all these calamities have originated in Great Britain." But it was not according to plan that the opposition should be quite inexorable. These first speakers were to show themselves not impervious to reason, not altogether unmoved by the weight of evidence against them, not quite irresponsive to the popular clamour. Accordingly they were readier to make admissions than in earlier debates. Baillie was "far from denying that many acts of inhumanity have been committed." Tarleton even confessed that, if the Trade were not an old-established interest but about to start *de novo*, he would himself be its most strenuous opponent. And then, when one or two minor Abolitionists had had their say, Dundas got up. Those of his honourable friends, he said, with whom he was most closely associated, knew very well that he had long shared their opinion as to the desirability of abolishing the Slave Trade. In fact, he fully agreed with all the material parts of the honourable mover's argument. But he differed as to method. His friends' plan was precipitate abolition, a plan which showed their zeal for a great object. But was it prudent? Was it practical? Might it not run counter to an equally great object, "the sacred attention which Parliament had ever shown to the interests of individuals?" And the speakers on the other side had been no less rigorous, no less unequivocal: they had asserted that the Slave Trade must continue for ever or the West Indies be ruined. Let no one suppose that he admitted that. He was for abolition, total abolition, but by a method no less speedy, nay, even speedier, than that of his friends. The most direct method. Indeed, the only method. He would proceed by regulations. "What regulations?" interjected Fox. Regulations, replied Dundas, to promote the breeding of negroes in the West Indies; to put an end by a gradual process to hereditary slavery; to improve the conditions of the existing slaves; and to provide for the education of their children. Two results would accrue: not only would the practicability of abolishing the Trade without injury to the planters' interests be proved by experience, but in course of time a transition would be effected from slave labour to free. Having thus outbidden the Abolitionists both in immediate respect for the rights of property and in prospective philanthropy, Dundas turned to the defenders of the Trade and begged them in their own interest to accept his proposal. Let them only try his regulations, and in a few years' time they would be of one mind with him. The speech concluded with a plain appeal to all "gentlemen of the moderate or middle way of thinking" to form a coherent group in favour of this policy and so "reduce the question to its proper bounds."

Two gentlemen of the moderate or middle way of thinking, both destined, possibly on that account, to become Prime Ministers, responded to this shrewd proposal. Addington at once left the Speaker's chair to thank Dundas for relieving him from "the utmost anxiety," torn as he had been between his hatred of the Trade and his respect for individual rights. The new method, he declared, could hardly be improved on. Certainly the Trade "ought to exist a few years longer, perhaps for a period of eight . . . or ten . . . or twelve years," but under regulations. And he suggested a few more of these—a heavier duty on male slaves than on female, to increase the importation of the latter; a bonus to slaves for large families; a premium on the introduction of agricultural machines. The second "moderate," Jenkinson, who was one day to bear a title taken from the greatest Slave Trade port, showed himself decidedly more averse to Abolition that Addington; but he, too, welcomed Dundas's method and added his quota to the stock of regulations—premiums to such planters and overseers as promoted an increased birth-rate among the slaves; liberty for every female slave who reared five children to the age of seven; a bounty of £5 a head to every slaver whose cargo contained more young females than males.

It may be that these moderate men—Addington, at any rate, if not Jenkinson—really believed that regulation was a "method" of abolition. But they were not to be allowed to salve their consciences without hearing some sharp home-truths. Fox was too old a parliamentary hand to let Dundas's specious promises go by unquestioned; and when Addington returned to his chair, he let fly at the policy of "moderation" with all his incomparable debating skill. Moderation in the slave trade, he said, reminded him of a passage in Middleton's *Life of Cicero*—"To break open a man's house and kill him, his wife, and his family in the night is certainly a most heinous crime and deserving of death; but even this may be done with moderation." Moderation in atrocity, in robbery and murder, in the pillage and destruction of a country! The real question was not whether that execrable Trade required regulation, but whether it was fit to be continued at all. And it seemed to him that in the scheme proposed something like a foundation had been laid for preserving it not only for years to come but for ever. "I note the terms in which the Trade has been reprehended by the two last speakers, but where is the proof that they will ever vote for the abolition of it?" And meantime, year after year, the Africans were being plundered and murdered and sold into slavery. The rest of the speech was occupied with a further exposition of the horrors of the Trade, with a rebuttal of the suggestion that immediate Abolition would involve the British West Indies in the fate of St. Domingue, and with a reminder of the constitutional importance of the petitions, which Dundas had carefully disparaged. "I am certain of this," he said. "The table is never loaded with petitions but when the people of England feel an actual grievance and when the House ought to feel itself bound to give a remedy." And for peroration he summed up his opinion of the Trade in terms that were certainly not "moderate." "I believe it to be impolitic. I know it to be inhuman. I am certain it is unjust. I find it so inhuman and unjust that, if the colonies cannot be cultivated without it, they ought not to be cultivated at all. . . . As long as I have a voice to speak, this question shall never be at rest . . . and if I and my friends should die before they have attained their glorious object, I hope there will never be wanting men alive to do their duty, who will continue to labour till the evil shall be wholly done away."

Dundas was used to Fox's eloquence and knew how to deal with it. When Fox sat down, he rose again, made a few dry, simple remarks in defence of his own position, and, to carry the question to an issue, coolly moved an amendment to insert the word *gradually* in Wilberforce's motion in favour of Abolition. Then came Jenkinson's speech; and when he had done, the night was already over and dawn near breaking. But the debate could not conclude without a speech from the Prime Minister; and, exhausted as he confessed himself to be after listening for so many hours to such a host of words, Pitt spurred himself to an effort which even his critics admitted to be the finest he had ever made. His continued devotion to the cause of Abolition, unlike Fox's, had been widely doubted. "From London to Inverness," Dickson had written to Wilberforce from Scotland, "Mr. Pitt's sincerity is questioned; and unless he can convince the nation of his cordiality in our cause, his popularity must suffer greatly." And Wilberforce himself had not forgotten that little disquieting outburst of impatience about St. Domingue. But when, after speaking for over an hour, Pitt sat down, all doubt had been dispelled.

The first part of his speech was typically logical. He went straight to the main contention of the "moderates" that "a gradual and in some degree a distant Abolition" would better serve the interest of the West Indies than the more "immediate and direct" course. Immediate Abolition, he argued, would compel the planters to improve the conditions of their existing slaves and so increase their numbers and their labour. It would improve their finances by reducing their debts which—it was admitted—were due to speculation in slaves. And it would minimise the danger of insurrection which—again it was admitted—arose from the contact of newly imported negroes with the older and more resigned slaves. "Surely, Sir, when gentlemen talk so vehemently of the safety of the islands and charge us with being so indifferent to it, when they speak of the calamities of St. Domingue and of similar dangers impending on their own heads, it ill becomes them to cry out for further importation. . . . Let us vote that the Abolition of the Slave Trade shall be immediate. Will my right honourable friends answer for the safety of the islands during any imaginable intervening period?"

From the argument from expediency Pitt then passed to the argument from legal prescription—an argument which, he pointed out, applied as much to gradual as to immediate Abolition and was in any case unfounded. Was it suggested that "the Slave Trade had received any such parliamentary sanction as must place it more out of the jurisdiction of the legislature for ever after than the other branches of our national commerce?" Every new commercial regulation, every new tax, every prohibitory duty affected some man's property or some man's expectations. "If for the sake of moral duty, of national honour, or even of great political advantage, it is thought right by authority of Parliament to alter any long-established system, Parliament is competent to do it." And it would be particularly offensive to suppose that Parliament had ever bound itself to maintain such a scandal as the Slave Trade. "As well might an individual think himself bound by a promise to commit an assassination!"

"And now, Sir," said Pitt, "I come to Africa"; and in the second half of his speech he cut, as a statesman should, to the very root of the question—the relations between the two continents, one civilised and strong, the other weak and savage. Why, first and last, he asked, ought the Slave Trade to be abolished? Because of its incurable injustice to the Africans. So much the "moderates" admitted and, so doing, give away their case for delay. "If on the ground of injustice it ought to be abolished at last, why ought it not now? Why is injustice suffered to remain for a single hour?" What have we done for Africa—save robbing her of fifty thousand people every year?

Long as that continent has been known to navigators, the extreme line of its coasts is all with which Europe is yet become acquainted, while other countries in the same parallel of latitude, through a happier system of intercourse, have reaped the blessings of a mutually beneficial commerce. . . . But Africa is known to you only in its skirts; yet even there you are able to inject a poison which penetrates to its very centre, corrupting every part to which it reaches. . . . What astonishing, I had

almost said, what irreparable, mischief have we brought upon
that continent! . . . How shall we hope to obtain, if it be
possible, forgiveness from Heaven for the enormous evils we
have committed, if we refuse to make use of those means which
the mercy of Providence has still reserved for us for wiping
away the shame and guilt with which we are now covered?
. . . Shall we not count the days and hours that are suffered to
intervene and to delay the accomplishment of such a work?
. . . If you go into the street, it is a chance but the first person
who crosses you is one, *vivendi recte qui prorogat horam*. We may
wait: we may delay to cross the stream before us till it has run
down; but we shall wait for ever, for the river will still flow on
unexhausted.

Pitt then briefly combated the argument that the Trade relinquished by Britain would be at once absorbed by other countries.
Would France take it, he asked, in the light of events in St. Domingue?
Would Spain, Portugal, Holland? He doubted if they would have
the will to go against our lead; he was certain they would not have
the money to purchase the 30,000 or 40,000 slaves bought annually
by us at £40 or £50 a head. "From what branch of their commerce
will they draw together a fund to feed this monster?"

And so he returned to Africa and to his final plea. It was for
Britain, he declared, to make amends for the past by doing what
she could to promote the civilisation of Africa. Let no one say that
she "labours under a natural incapacity for civilisation," that such
practices as human sacrifice prove that "Providence has irrevocably
doomed her to be only a nursery of slaves for us free and civilised
Europeans." Human sacrifice had once been practised in these
islands, and Britons had been sold for slaves in Rome. With equal
justice some Roman senator might have pointed to "British barbarians" and said, "*There* is a people that will never rise to civilisation—*there* is a people never destined to be free."

We were once as obscure among the nations of the earth, as
savage in our manners, as debased in our morals, as degraded in
our understandings, as these unhappy Africans are at present.
But in the lapse of a long series of years, by a progression slow
and for a time almost imperceptible, we have become rich in a
variety of acquirements and favoured above measure in the gifts

of Providence. . . . From all these blessings we must for ever
have been shut out, had other nations adopted in their conduct
towards us the principles laid down as applicable to Africa.
. . . Ages might have passed without our emergence from
barbarism: and we, who are now enjoying the blessings of
British civilisation, British laws, and British liberty, might, at
this hour, have been little superior in morals, in knowledge, or
in refinement to the rude inhabitants of the coast of Guinea.
. . . If we shudder to think of the misery which would still
have overwhelmed us, had Great Britain continued to the
present times to be the mart for slaves for the more civilised
nations of the world, through some cruel policy of theirs, God
forbid that we should any longer subject Africa to the same
dreadful scourge.

It was now nearly seven o'clock in the morning; and while Pitt
had been speaking, the climbing sun had begun to throw its rays
through the windows of the House. It must have made singularly
impressive, it may even have suddenly suggested, the prophecy of
dawn in Africa with which Pitt closed his speech.

If we listen to the voice of reason and duty, and pursue this day
the line of conduct which they prescribe, some of us may live
to see the reverse of that picture from which we now turn our
eyes with shame and regret. We may live to behold the natives
of Africa engaged in the calm occupations of industry, in the
pursuit of a just and legitimate commerce. We may behold the
beams of science and philosophy breaking in upon their land,
which, at some happy period, in still later times, may blaze with
full lustre, and, joining their influence with that of pure religion,
may illuminate and invigorate the most distant extremities of
that immense continent. Then may we hope that even Africa,
though last of all the quarters of the globe, shall enjoy at
length, in the evening of her days, those blessings which have
descended so plentifully upon us—

>   Nosque ubi primus equis Oriens adflabit anhelis
>   Illic sera rubens accendit lumina Vesper . . .

It is in this view, Sir; it is as an atonement for our long and
cruel injustice towards Africa, that the measure proposed by

my honourable friend most forcibly recommends itself to my mind. . . . I shall vote, Sir, against the amendment; and I shall also oppose to the utmost every proposition which in any way may tend either to prevent or even to postpone for an hour the total abolition of the Slave Trade.

"For the last twenty minutes," said Wilberforce, who had himself suggested the theme of the civilisation of Africa to Pitt the day before, "he really seemed to be inspired." And as Fox walked away from the debate with Grey and Windham, the three Whigs, none of them lovers of Pitt, agreed that the speech was "one of the most extraordinary displays of eloquence they had ever heard." And indeed throughout its closing passages the whole House had sat spellbound. Never had Pitt so nearly reached the level of his father's magic art. But when it was over, when the young orator had at last sunk back into his seat, the spell was broken. Back into members' minds thronged the memories of Paris and St. Domingue, not easily effaceable by any eloquence or logic; back, too, came their old love of compromise and the deep impression made by Dundas's exhibition of blunt common sense. And so, hurriedly dividing, they carried his amendment by 193 to 125; then the motion as amended —"That the Slave Trade ought to be *gradually* abolished"—by 230 to 85; and then trooped out into the April sunshine in search of breakfast.

4

The great debate of 1792 was the last of a series which formed the crowning experiences of this period of Wilberforce's life. They were to him like the battles at which the whole of the strategist's career is brought to an issue. Most of the steady, uneventful labour of the intervening days had been spent in preparing for them. On their result the success or failure of his lifework mainly turned. What, then, were his feelings at the close of this particular debate? Sanguine as ever and little knowing what lay ahead, he was not greatly disappointed. Something after all had been gained. A motion for Abolition, gradual alas! but still Abolition, had been carried for the first time and by a great majority. He was not alone in his opinion. Many of his friends regarded the vote as a signal triumph, and letters of congratulation poured in on him. But one

old friend saw farther ahead. "I thought of you most unremit-
tingly," wrote Milner from his deanery at Carlisle, "the whole day
of April 2 and a good deal of the night which to me was a very
restless one. . . . I think there can be no doubt that you have
gained some ground . . . as far as respects public opinion; the
opposers are plainly overawed and ashamed. The worst circumstance is this Dundas—nobody thinks well of him—duplicity and
artifice are esteemed parts of his character—he is judged to do what
he does unwillingly and with design, in the worst sense."

The Dean was soon proved right in his belief that the direct
opposition to Abolition had been weakened and in his recognition
of the strength of the indirect opposition headed by Dundas. On
April 23 and 27 the House discussed the resolutions proposed by
Dundas in execution of his policy. The interval had enabled him
to expand and polish up the "method of regulation"; and the
resolutions prohibited the carrying on of the Trade with foreign
countries or in ships not hitherto employed in it, forbade the
exportation of males over twenty years old and females over sixteen,
and laid a lower customs-duty on females than on males. But the
most vital resolution was that which, outbidding Denmark, fixed
the date for Abolition at January 1, 1800. Wilberforce, Fox, and
Pitt stood manfully by their guns; and the House was told by its
Leader that it need not feel itself prevented by its previous decision
from changing its mind and voting now for an immediate Abolition. But their highest efforts had been made on April 2-3, and the
most notable speech of this debate came from another of the great
young men of those days, as great in his way as Pitt and Wilberforce
in theirs and a year younger than they. An amendment was moved
by Lord Mornington, to be better known in time as Marquess
Wellesley, substituting 1793 for 1800. "We cannot modify injustice," he declared; "the question is to what period we shall prolong
it. . . . Some think we should be unjust for ten years: others think
it is enough to be unjust for five years; others . . . that the present
century should continue in disgrace and that justice should com-
mence its operation with the opening of another." These sarcasms
went home. The House was undoubtedly uncomfortable; and it
was soon evident that many of those who voted in the majority on
the morning of April 3 really meant Abolition by gradual Abolition.
Dundas's seven-year period was thrown out; and after some hag-
gling over the exact date, it was fixed at 1796 by 151 votes to 132.

"On the whole," wrote Wilberforce, "this is more than I expected two months ago, and I have much cause for thankfulness. We are to contend for the number of slaves to be imported; and then *for the House of Lords*." He might well italicise the words. The obstructionists had still a trump-card in their hand. The King had still his "friends" in the Upper House; and the King, who used once to chaff Wilberforce about his "black clients," had become with the progress of the French Revolution an obstinate defender of the Trade. And Dundas, too, had his friends among the Lords—on both sides of the House. "Dropped in one day at Dundas's," runs a naïve entry in the diary about this time, "and much surprised to find Lord Loughborough there"—Loughborough, *alias* Wedderburn, one of Dundas's Tory colleagues not so long ago, but now among the Whigs in the hope of finding there a less encumbered access to the Woolsack, a cynical careerist not likely to be moved by arguments of justice or humanity. And in the Lords, presiding over them, though near the end of his tether now, was the perfidious Thurlow, bitter enemy of Pitt and of every liberal idea. On this "unofficial" subject of Abolition, moreover, the attitude of the rank and file of the parties was not the same in the Upper House as in the Lower. Tory peers could vote more freely against Pitt than Tory Commoners, who, however un-Governmental the matter might be, could not but be influenced by the lead, the logic, the mere Olympic presence of the saviour of their party and the mainstay of the Crown. And of the Whig peers very few were "Foxites"; for the most part they were landed magnates of the Portland faction and dead against Abolition. Only one circumstance could conceivably have undermined these bulwarks of vested interest. If Dundas's "method" had never been suggested, if the full weight of the popular campaign—with electors' votes behind those petitions—and the full force of the Abolitionist speeches, especially Pitt's, had not been broken by that one conscience-saving word, *gradually*, it is conceivable that immediate Abolition might have been carried on April 3. And if this clean, uncompromising decision had come up from the Commons, it is just imaginable, though not at all likely, that the Lords would have accepted it. As it was, the result, despite Wilberforce's spirited battle-cry, was a foregone conclusion.

The debate of May 3 was distinguished by the maiden speech of William, Duke of Clarence, an honest young Tory, who, like Rodney, had formed his own opinions of the slave business during naval service in the West Indies. So far from accepting gradual Abolition, he was against Abolition altogether. "He had been an attentive observer of the state of the negroes, and had no doubt but that he could bring forward proofs to convince their Lordships that their state was far from being miserable: on the contrary, that, when the various ranks of society were considered, they were comparatively in a state of humble happiness." And he ventured on another argument, little dreaming of the far-off day when he would give his royal promise to create, if need be, sufficient Peers to carry the Reform Bill. "An implicit obedience to the House of Commons," he said, "much as I respect that House, would make the House of Peers useless, and thus the natural and constituent balance in the constitution would be endangered." But the Peers did not require this princely lead. With a great parade of undertaking a burdensome duty, they repeated the solemn farce which had been played with such effect a few years earlier in "another place." Just as the Commons had repudiated the evidence given before the Privy Council Committee and insisted on hearing it anew for themselves, so now the Lords repudiated the evidence given before the Commons. Grenville vigorously protested, declaring that the removal of a national disgrace brooked no delay, and pleaded that, if evidence must be taken afresh, it at least should be heard by a Select Committee, as in the Commons, to save time. But in the Lords the tactics of obstruction were pressed to their limit. Lord Chancellor Thurlow had the face to assure his fellow Peers that a Committee of the whole House would not involve delay; and, amongst others, the Archbishop of Canterbury had the folly to believe him and to vote accordingly—on which account (for he was a sincere Abolitionist) he had presently to write a remorseful letter to Wilberforce. So the comedy proceeded without a hitch. Seven witnesses were heard at such intervals as the whole House could spare; and then, on June 5, ten days before the session closed, it was resolved to continue the hearing of evidence in the following year.

Sentence had been pronounced. A hundred thousand natives of West Africa had been condemned to death or penal servitude. Before another witness could attest their sufferings in the House of Lords, war had broken out between Great Britain and France. Year after year now, it was less and less possible for English ears to hear the far, faint cry of Africa beyond the guns in Europe.

VI

Interruption

I

"HEARD of the militia being called out and Parliament summoned," notes Wilberforce on December 3, 1792. "Talked politics, and of the state of the country which seems very critical." Modern opinion, wiser after the event, is sometimes tempted to make light of the anxieties of our forefathers in that troubled period. There was no cause for panic, it is true; but, none the less, strange things were happening. Working men were betraying an interest in politics which, save locally and transiently, they had never shown before. Radical clubs were springing up like mushrooms, proclaiming allegiance to Tom Paine, spreading cheap copies of his subversive pamphlets, and even demanding the suppression of a Parliament that had refused Reform by a National Convention on the French model. "After the example given by France," wrote the London Corresponding Society to the French Convention, "Revolutions will become easy." As the rupture with France approached, the symptoms became slightly more feverish. French emissaries conducted a little futile propaganda among British artisans. "No war with France" was chalked up here and there on the walls. Attempts were made to tamper with the army. At Sheffield a crowd, ten thousand strong, marched in procession with the tricolour at its head. In one or two towns there were riots. Even more disquieting was the emergence of the Scottish people from half a century of political apathy. All the chief towns followed the English lead. A Convention, representing forty-five societies, met at Edinburgh. A *liaison* was established with Wolfe Tone's United Irishmen. In Dundee, the hottest point, an effigy of Dundas, garbed with singular prodigality in satin waistcoat and breeches, was burnt by a cheering mob. And in both countries, while nothing very terrible was done, very terrible things were said. Hot-headed orators revelled in the sanguinary language of the Terror.

Now in all this there was little, if any, positive danger. There was no comparison between the social evils of France and Britain. There was no real question of a British Revolution, no more likelihood of the mass of Englishmen becoming Jacobins in 1793 than of their becoming Bolsheviks in 1919; and Burke's theatrical "dagger-scene" in the House of Commons was as much out of tune with the realities of the situation as with the British temperament or his own earlier sanity. The Radical agitation of the war-period was due to temporary and remediable causes—dear corn, enclosures, low wages, unemployment, and the new recognition of the impurities and inequalities of the existing system of representative government. It was relatively mild in operation; not a life was taken by the British Jacobins; and it was confined to a very small circle. Nevertheless the anxiety of Wilberforce and his contemporaries is not unintelligible. Never before had they seen anything like this turbulence, heard anything like these threats against English society, these greetings to England's enemies. And, as they watched with horror the holocaust in Paris, they remembered how quietly the fire had started and how swiftly it had spread.

Wilberforce's attitude at the outset was a typical blend of practical insight and a kind of spiritual fatalism. "I will frankly own," he wrote at the end of 1792, "that I entertain rather gloomy apprehensions concerning the state of the country. Not that I fear any speedy commotion—of this I own I see no danger. Almost every man of property in the kingdom is of course the friend of civil order, and if a few mad-headed professors of liberty and equality were to attempt to bring their theories into practice, they would be crushed in an instant. But yet I do foresee a gathering storm, and I cannot help fearing that a country which, like this, has so long been blessed beyond all example with every spiritual and temporal good, will incur those judgments of an incensed God which in the prophets are often denounced against those who forget the Author of all their mercies." "I think," he writes again, "of proposing to the Archbishop of Canterbury to suggest the appointment of a day of fasting and humiliation." On its secular side, at any rate, it was a pity that this attitude was not shared by Pitt. It would have been well for his country and for his reputation if he could have regarded those "mad-headed professors" with Wilberforce's calm indifference instead of letting loose on them the ferocity of a Judge Braxfield and his kind. It would have been well, too, if,

following the same guide, he had not left his old Reform plans on
the shelf to await more tranquil times, but at least had tried—
though the prospects of support in Parliament were far worse now
than in 1785—to counter anticonstitutional agitation with constitutional reform. "Unless some reforms be made," said Wilberforce,
"though we should get well through our present difficulties, they
will recur hereafter with aggravated force"; and for a man of
his day and of his conservative proclivities it was a singularly wise
saying. Who could have guessed in 1793 that the British people
would be nearer Revolution in 1832 than they were then?

On the second great question of the moment Wilberforce's
standpoint was nearer Fox's than Pitt's. To most historians, the
outbreak of war between Britain and Revolutionary France has
seemed almost as inevitable under the circumstances as it seemed
to the great majority of Englishmen at the time. It is not to the
point to argue that the terrible change which came over the methods
and objects of the French Revolution in the autumn and winter of
1792 was largely due to the menacing attitude of unregenerate
absolutism in Central Europe. The change was no less a fact. It
is not to the point to argue, either, that Pitt ought to have shown
something warmer than his strict neutrality to the Revolution at
its onset, that he ought to have won over Parliament to a policy
of holding the ring and forbidding Austria and Prussia to cross
the French frontier, and that then the change might never have
occurred. For, Pitt and Parliament—and, let it be added, the British
people—being what they were, to argue so is to argue *per impossibile*.
Nor is it to be wondered at that the beginnings of the Terror should
have seemed to throw Europe back into the atmosphere of St.
Bartholomew's Eve and to have reproduced in English minds the
passionate antipathy of the Elizabethans to an alien Antichrist. It
was hatred of the Jacobins, not panic, that made Englishmen all
too ready to fight them. And when the easy triumph of Jemappes
made Frenchmen all too ready to fight England, when a war for
saving the Revolution from extinction in France became a war for
imposing it on all the rest of Europe, something like a miracle was
needed to prevent the open breach.

To Wilberforce, with his one supreme test for every thought and
deed, the weeks before the rupture were weeks of ferment. He hated
the excesses of the Revolution, hated especially its anti-religious bias;
but he also hated war. One reassuring fact he clung to through

the autumn—Pitt's genuine desire for peace. He repeatedly assures his correspondents of "the error of imputing to Mr. Pitt a war-system, as if it were his plan, his wish, his predilection to engage in war, and that he had set himself to consider how he could effect his purpose." And, many years later, he reasserted his conviction and cited what was and is the best proof of its truth—Pitt's famous budget-speech of February 17, 1792, prophesying the continuance of peace for fifteen years. It was this trust in Pitt's pacifism that enabled him, after many searchings of his conscience, to support the Government in the debate on the Address when Parliament met in the middle of December. He spoke last and briefly.

> He frankly declared that, as at all times war ought to be depre-cated as the greatest of human evils, so there never was a period when it appeared more likely to be injurious to this country than the present. . . . If we should find ourselves compelled by the obligations of solemn treaties to engage in war, as men of conscience and integrity we must submit to the necessity; but nothing less than this necessity would justify the measure.

A few days later the French Government disclosed its intention of violating the neutrality of Holland, Britain's ally, and French ships sailed up the Scheldt in defiance of the treaty, signed by Britain, which reserved its navigation to the Dutch. The necessity, it would seem, had arisen; yet Wilberforce still shrank from war. He clung desperately to the policy of holding the ring; but, if that was impossible at an earlier stage, it was still more impossible now. The French were in Flanders. Mere neutrality, mere diplomacy, on Pitt's part could not turn them out; and, if they stayed, Pitt could not long be neutral. Yet Wilberforce believed that a public declara-tion of the fact that Britain was negotiating a pact of neutrality would have checked the intoxicated victors of Jemappes on the road to the Dutch frontier. "I never was so earnest with Mr. Pitt on any other occasion," he afterwards declared. And since Pitt could not be persuaded, he determined to urge his policy on the House of Commons. But he had not realised how strong the ties of friend-ship were; he had not yet steeled himself to reject a personal appeal from Pitt, to face an open breach with him. "I was actually upon my legs to open my mind fully on the subject," he writes of the debate of February 1, on the need for military preparations, "when

Pitt sent Bankes to me, earnestly desiring me not to do so on that day, assuring me that my speaking then might do irreparable mischief, and pledging himself that I should have another opportunity before war should be declared." "Sat very late," the diary adds, "and much disturbed afterwards." It was not Pitt's fault that he never had his opportunity. For the next few days no business could be transacted for lack of sufficient members in the House; and then the news came that on February 1, the very day on which Wilberforce had wanted to "open his mind," France had declared war on Great Britain and Holland.

Wilberforce was not one of those who interpret Christianity as vetoing the use of force in any circumstances. He believed that the war might have been prevented; but now it had come, he had no doubts as to his duty. "I deemed it," he says, "the part of a good subject not to use language which might tend to prevent the unanimity which was so desirable at the outset of such a war." And he sat silent when the House discussed the French declaration and Fox argued that the conduct of the British Government had done much to provoke it—silent, but uneasy. He did not love the Revolution, but neither did he love the *ancien régime* or its champions in Vienna and Berlin. He realised the dilemma we were in. It was one thing to stand by our treaty and our ally against the Jacobins' assault on the public law of Europe. It was another thing to set Englishmen shoulder to shoulder with Austrians and Prussians, champions of the old absolutist order, and as greedy on their part as the Jacobins for territorial aggrandizement. If Wilberforce could have seen the long years of war ahead, the rise of Napoleon, and Britain forced to pay those continental legions to wage a war on land which she could not wage successfully alone, he might not have been so anxious to escape from the dilemma. As it was, he hoped to wriggle out of it, to have Britain's cause somehow or other dissociated at the outset from the cause of Austria and Prussia. "Vexed at Pitt and Dundas," the diary says of the debate, "for not being explicit enough."

2

It was, of course, impossible for Britain to act quite independently of her associates on the Continent, and Wilberforce's distrust of them was quickly justified. The First Coalition was a sorry failure. The chance of stamping out the Revolution by a swift combined move on Paris was missed; and while the lives of British troops were muddled away in Flanders and eaten up in the poisonous swamps of the French West Indies, Prussia was mainly preoccupied, and Austria not much less, in butchering and dismembering Poland. And when, in 1795, Prussia drew off to masticate her share and so brought the First Coalition to an end, the only satisfactory event for Britain had been the demonstration on the Glorious First of June that, whatever might happen on land, she was again supreme at sea.

War is a stern ordeal for any statesman. For Pitt, it was a tragedy. It had cut right across his career, shattering his dream of peace, bringing to a sudden end the steady work of reconstruction for which he was so admirably fitted and which, as he knew, he had so far done so well, and thrusting on him a new and tremendous task—a task he faced with all his father's patriotism and fortitude, but with none of his father's genius for war, and with a growing consciousness, as the years went by and peace still eluded him, that his proper life-work would never be accomplished. Hitherto so self-sufficient, so easily successful, he needed his friends now as he had never needed them; and at the outset of his war-government his association with Wilberforce was almost as close and intimate as it had been at the outset of his peace-government nine years before. Nor was it only Wilberforce's earnest disinterested sympathy he valued, or his practical aid in counsel, though this he rated high. He recognised that Wilberforce was now a power in the country, that his opinion would have weight with all impartial Englishmen, and particularly with those religious-minded people who had been his most devoted followers in the Abolitionist crusade and amongst whom might be found the most dangerous, because the most impeccable, opponents of the war. Pitt strove, therefore, to win his old friend's mind as well as his heart. And since at first there was nothing in his conscience to forbid it, Wilberforce eagerly responded. A few months before the outbreak of war he had disclosed his golden opinion of Pitt to a friend who had sharply criticised his policy. "Faults he has," he had written, "as who is free from them? But I most solemnly assure you that I am convinced, if the flame of pure disinterested patriotism burns in any human bosom, it does in his. I am convinced, and that on long experience and close observation, that in order to benefit his country he would give up not situation merely and emolument, but what in his case is much more, personal credit and reputation, though he knew that no human being would ever become acquainted with the sacrifice he should have made. . . . Believe me, who am pretty well acquainted with our public men, that he has not his equal for integrity as well as ability in the *primores* of either House of Parliament." "I am almost ashamed," he had added, "of being drawn into this long panegyric, but I will not burn it; it is the language of the heart." It is easy to imagine, then, with what keen, serious pleasure he resumed, at such a crisis in the country's history, his old constant intercourse with its patriot leader, stood at his side through the early disappointments of the war, shared in his thoughts and discussed his plans—or those of them, at least, which were not kept for Dundas's less sensitive ears. The diary is full of it. "To Holwood with Pitt in his phaeton—early dinner and back to town." "Pitt's birthday, 34 (May 28). . . . Dined Dundas' (with Pitt and friends) and up too late." "To town to see Pitt—a great map spread out before him." "Dined *tête-à-tête* with Pitt—he disengaging himself to do so." "Slept at Pitt's—he very kind." "Off to Holwood. Pitt and I *tête-à-tête*—he very open and we discussed much." "Long political discussion with Pitt on the King's speech."

The last-quoted entry is for January 18, 1794, and so far their minds had moved as one. The Saint had become as militant as the Statesman. "House—Pitt uncommonly fine on armed nation, etc.," says the diary for February 3. But, as the year drew on, the harmony, daily scrutinised and tested in the sanctuary of Wilberforce's conscience, began sensibly to weaken. The cause of the Allies in Europe went steadily from bad to worse. By the end of the year they had evacuated Belgium; and the French, having occupied the whole of the left bank of the Rhine, were overrunning Holland and forcing the States-General to sue for peace. This unbroken record of failure made a deep impression on Wilberforce. Clearly the war had brought, seemed likely to bring, no tangible results. Was it wise, then, for statesmen, was it right for Christians, to persist in it? For a time, however, the intimacy with Pitt continued. In July Wilberforce is at Holwood and makes the usual entry in the diary —"Dined *tête-à-tête* with Pitt, and political discussion"; but in a letter to his old confidant, Lord Muncaster, written before he left Pitt's house, he strikes a new note. "Pitt's speech," he confesses, "both from the Treasury Bench and the Throne, was too pugnacious for me. It required our friend Hawkins Brown's nerves and warlike propensities to stand it. May God protect us!" By the autumn Wilberforce's peaceful propensities have hardened. Writing again to Lord Muncaster in November, "Little as one could hope," he says, "for a secure peace with such a set of fellows as the French Conventionalists . . . I begin to think we can look for no good from the prosecution of the war; and if so, it is time to stop for a while the ravages of that scourge of the human species." Wilberforce was now well on to the diverging path; and he was pushed a little farther down it, as it happened, by a Frenchman. Fugitives from France had been steadily trickling into England since the war began, and among them there arrived, that autumn, the Abbé de Lageard, who had shown such "extraordinary humanity" to the three young Englishmen in those far-off light-hearted days at Rheims. Hunted for a year and a half through thirty Departments of France, he had slipped away at last from the guarded coast and, a pauper now and a pessimist, had found a refuge in London. His old acquaintances seized the opportunity of repaying his hospitality; they feasted him as he had feasted them; they discussed the war with him and enlarged on the sea-power of Britain, on her reserves of strength, on the tenacity of her people. But the weary exile shook his head. "Only the French," he said, "can conquer the French. *Dieu vous garde, messieurs, d'une revolution.*"

There was another aspect of the war which confirmed the drift of Wilberforce's mind away from Pitt's. It was questioned at the time and it has been questioned ever since whether Pitt was right to lay so much stress on the acquisition of the French West Indies and to squander in those malarious islands British troops which might have been put to better use in Europe. And, considering how many thousands of British lives were sacrificed and how little the loss of the islands affected the war-strength of France, the verdict has usually gone against him. But it is only fair to Pitt, and to Dundas, who was Pitt's chief prompter in the matter, to recognise how tempting the adventure must have seemed. Tropical "sugar-islands" were regarded in those days as the richest plums of empire; and if the French West Indies could be won and retained at the peace, it would deprive France of a great branch of her old commerce and reimburse Britain for the cost of the war. But Wilberforce did not want his country to acquire more sugar-islands,

however valuable, for the simple reason that their acquisition and
increased development by British settlers would create a new demand
for slave-labour and heavily reinforce the case for an indefinite
postponement of Abolition. It was a question, therefore, which
touched the nerve-centres of his life. As time went on, it deflected
him from concentrating on the main issues of the war as much as,
for opposite reasons, it deflected Pitt.

Once Wilberforce had come to a decision he felt bound to declare
it publicly, though from the consequences of openly demanding
peace from a Government still bent on war a smaller man might
well have shrunk. War makes no allowances. "He who is not
with us is against us" is its watchword. And the war-mind moves
easily along the sequence of ideas from "pacifist" to "coward,"
"defeatist," "traitor." It needed no little moral courage to pass
from the warm friendship of 10 Downing Street out into the bleak
frost of popular suspicion and abuse. "Perhaps my differing from
Pitt," is Wilberforce's comment, "by lessening my popularity and
showing me my comparative insignificance, may not be bad for
me in spiritual things." But it was the personal breach that mattered
most. To change from Pitt's intimate to something like his enemy!
To work for his downfall? Even that might be his bitter duty.
"I would gladly get an end put to this war," he writes, "without
Pitt's being turned out of office, which will hardly be possible I
fear, if it continue much longer."

In the last six weeks of the year the decision was reached,
"cautiously and maturely." "Off at ten to Pitt's," records the diary
for November 19. "Heard that Parliament would be prorogued
until December 30, giving me time to make up my mind—strongly
at present disposed to peace. . . . Threw out some hints of my state
of mind, and accepted Pitt's invitation to dine." On the 21st he
met Pitt at dinner again, and on the 27th breakfasted with him to
"discuss politics." That Pitt was clearly using all his powers of
argument to win Wilberforce back is evident from an entry a few
days later: "At nine, Pitt's for political discussion till near one,
and not bed till near two. Head and mind full, and could sleep but
very distractedly." But other influences were also brought to bear.
Christmas came with its special message; and then, on the two
following days, "much political talk with Grant and Henry Thornton [two of his closest Evangelical allies], making up my mind."
On the 29th, at a dinner-party of friends—Duncombe, Muncaster,

Henry Thornton, Bankes and Montague—his course of action was agreed on. On the 30th, after "a disturbed night," in what he calls "a very incoherent speech" he moved an amendment to the Address, declaring that it is "advisable and expedient to endeavour to restore the blessings of peace upon just and reasonable terms," but that, if such efforts should be "rendered ineffectual by the violence and ambition of the enemy . . . the burdens and evils of a just and necessary war will be borne with cheerfulness by a loyal, affectionate and united people."

The language of the Address, he argued, by its reference to "that violent and unnatural system which is equally ruinous to France and incompatible with the tranquillity of other nations," had suggested that we intended to prosecute the war until a counter-revolution had been effected. But was it feasible to impose a change of government by force on a high-spirited people? A republic had now existed for some years in France; it had acquired a sort of stability; there were no signs of disaffection to it in the army; the royalist insurrections had been easily put down; and now that "the furious and bloody tyranny of Robespierre" was over, a "somewhat milder" system had been introduced. If anything could bring about a counter-revolution, it was peace more likely than war. Moreover, it was not so much to crush the Revolution that we had begun the war as to defend Britain from invasion by its evil principles; and with the easy suppression of Jacobin agitation this danger had passed away. The other object of the war had been the defence of our ally, Holland; but the Dutch were now on the point of making a separate peace. As to our other allies, "it would be the extreme of dishonour to steal alone out of the general confederacy," but Prussia, who was already giving us little active aid, and Austria, who could not go on fighting without our financial backing, were readier for peace than we were; and if the war continued, we should find ourselves alone. It was true, perhaps, that no secure or lasting peace could be attained. No trust could be put in the good faith of France. It would be necessary to maintain our forces in being on a costly scale. But war would be costlier still; and cost was not war's only evil. Finally, it might be hoped that the French would also "be glad of a little quiet," and, however bitter their antagonism, would not be so hasty a second time to force a quarrel on their powerful neighbour.

It was harder for Pitt to answer Wilberforce's speech than to

answer one of Fox's. It came from his own side of the House; it
was moderate in tone; it was untainted by any suspicion of sympathy with the principles of the Revolution. But it had one weak
point—its admission of the insecurity of any peace with the existing
French Government. And on this Pitt fixed. He denied that the
Address implied that we would never make peace with a French
Republic; it simply meant that, till our resources were exhausted
and all hope dead, we would never make peace without security.
"It had pleased inscrutable Providence that this power of France
should triumph over everything that has been opposed to it. But
let us not therefore fall without making any efforts to resist it;
let us not sink without measuring its strength." What is to be
gained by a temporary peace? It would enable the Revolutionaries
to strengthen a system of government, which, though Robespierre
were dead, had not changed its principles nor abandoned its ambition of dominating Europe. It would give them a free hand to
work their will on Holland. It would leave them in the possession
of the Austrian Netherlands;[1] and "will my honourable friend say
we ought to consent to that? He will not say so." Finally, it would
dissolve for ever the Alliance of Europe. How could we hope to
bring it back at our summons, when we had proclaimed our own
weakness to the world? When the war was resumed, we should be
exposed alone to the fury of France. The Alliance may have
weakened, but what then? If Holland falls, if Prussia withdraws,
we must throw more British troops on to the Continent to fill the
gap and hope for a diversion on the part of Italy and Spain. We
can maintain, if not increase, our present efforts, but—and this is
the main argument for fighting on—France cannot. Her incredible
efforts have been financed by the confiscation of property and the
issue of paper money. This system in turn has rested, could only
rest, on fear. Now that the Terror is over, it must collapse. Let us
carry on the war, then, "if not with the certainty of faith, yet at
least with the confidence of expectation."

A resolute, but scarcely a cheering speech. The majority voted
down the amendment, as a matter of course, by 246 to 73, but they
had received cold comfort; and Wilberforce, voting uneasily with
the Opposition, was unshaken. A month later, he repeated his case
in the debate on Grey's motion in favour of opening peace-negotiations, and voted accordingly once more—in a minority of 86 to 269.

[1] Roughly equivalent to the modern Belgium, created in 1830.

3

It is said that only two public events in Pitt's life were so disturbing as to rob him of his sleep—the mutiny at the Nore in 1797 and Wilberforce's first open opposition. Strictly accurate or not, there is truth in the tradition. Pitt's administration might be secure enough; but the defection of Wilberforce, notoriously disinterested and conscientious and in no man's eyes a fool, was a more serious blow to it than that of any other man in politics could have been. No one else could have given such a handle to his critics, so enhanced the daily strain of meeting the watchful, expert opposition of Fox and his Whig "die-hards" and the growing discontent in the country at a war which brought nothing but bad trade and unemployment and defeat. And the breach was more than political: it was personal. Only a Gallio, at such a moment, could have remained in intimate fellowship with the defaulter. So the lonely bachelor, who had found in Wilberforce some touch of spiritual kinship which he could rarely find in the obedient throng of hard-headed or second-rate men about him, became lonelier still. And Wilberforce, on his part, was hit more hardly than by anything in his life before except the first pangs of his "conversion" or by anything after except family bereavement. He had foreseen that he would suffer, and suffer he did. Twenty-five years later the memory could still sting him. "No one," he told a friend in 1820, "who has not seen a good deal of public life and felt how painful and difficult it is to differ widely from those with whom you wish to agree, can judge at what an expense of feeling such duties are performed." "I felt queer, and all day out of spirits," confesses the diary for February 4: "wrong, but hurt by the idea of Pitt's alienation." A week later comes this poignant little entry: "Party of *the old firm* at the Speaker's: I not there."

He minded less the misconceptions and hostilities which the very moderation of his policy aroused. Everybody must be black or white in war-time, and he was grey. On the main question of peace-negotiations he would vote against the Government, but not on anything else if he could help it. As long as the war continued, he would support its measures for maintaining the British forces abroad and keeping order at home. To most men such a logical compromise seemed impracticable; and at first the Whigs were openly triumphant at the accession to their resolute but small minority of so considerable a turncoat. Fox was prompt to pay a friendly call. "You will soon see," he told Wilberforce, "that you must join us altogether." But Fox was quite mistaken. Seven years later, in the breathing-space of the Peace of Amiens, Wilberforce committed to paper, but not for publication, his opinions on the "hard and difficult case of a private member of Parliament in time of war and violent opposition" with particular reference to the circumstances "in which our country was placed during the last war."

There was an Opposition, able, vigilant, active, inveterate, powerful from their talents, formidable from their principles, not very scrupulous in their means, and bitter and uniform in their hostility, between whom and myself there existed a differ-ence not merely as to the mode of prosecuting the war of which we all recognised the necessity, but a fundamental difference as to the main principles not only of political conduct but even of moral practice—in whom I thought I saw (though neither in private nor in public did I ever impute to them that they were not really intending the good of the country, etc.), that pre-judice and passion had so blinded them that they could see nothing to be apprehended in those principles and proceedings which appeared to me likely to sap the vitals of our country and to produce an explosion in which the whole fabric of our political and social edifice was likely to be buried in one common ruin. If by stating my doubts as to the wisdom of our counsels and the prudence of our measures, I should strengthen the cause of a party like that, how could I have made amends for the mischief I might have done, while, as before alleged, I could not have effected the purpose I had myself in view?

A few years later Wilberforce would have spoken in somewhat less alarmist terms of the radical proclivities of Fox and Sheridan and Grey; but that was what he was thinking while he talked to Fox—very courteously and pleasantly, no doubt—on the occasion of that friendly call. And Fox soon had reason to abate his confi-dence. On January 5, 1795, less than a week after his "pacifist" amendment, at the end of the long and bitter debate on Sheridan's motion for the repeal of the recent Act suspending the right of

Habeas Corpus, Wilberforce briefly stated his opinion that "the hands of Government ought to be strengthened at such a time for the repression and punishment of faction," his belief that "Government had not abused the power committed to them," and his intention to vote against the motion. The significance of this little speech could not be missed. Independent, Pittite-pacifist—whatever Wilberforce was—he was evidently not a Foxite.

It seems curious, at first sight, that Wilberforce should have accepted so calmly the initial severities of Pitt's *régime* of repression. Few gentlemen were democrats in those days, and he was assuredly not one of them. But the French Revolution had inspired no class-antagonism in him. He had none of Society's uneasy distaste for the "lower orders." He was constantly giving time and money privately to help the poor. There was no hidden streak of hardness in his nature. He was keenly sensitive to injustice. He could not be cruel. It has been seen, moreover, that though he hated Jacobinical doctrine and dreaded its influence on English morals and religion —"God defend us from such poison," he exclaimed after reading Paine's *Age of Reason*—yet, until the black October of 1795, at any rate, he had no panic fears that the "professors of liberty and equality" could sweep the country headlong into Revolution. Why then did he not protest against, why did he positively or tacitly accept the Government's harsh measures in 1793 and 1794? Did he approve the prosecution of the English Radicals? Did he tolerate Braxfield's grim mockery of justice in Scotland? From his public record, from what he said and left unsaid in Parliament, it would seem so. As to his private opinions, he speaks in the diary for December 19, 1794, of a "conversation on the pending trials for high treason" at Pitt's and makes no comment—and that is all.

But the puzzle has its key. Something must be allowed for his confidence in Pitt, which, though the coming years were now and again to strain it, had by no means been destroyed by the difference of opinion on the war. Any action on his part, again, which might be publicly construed as sympathy with Jacobinism, could only be undertaken at the risk of far more serious damage to the cause he had most at heart than that already done by Clarkson's impulsive tongue. But probably the strongest motive for his acquiescence in Pitt's "terrorism" lay in his understanding of the special responsibilities of public criticism under war-conditions. "In war-time," he says in that private memorandum already quoted, "often an honest man cannot [speak out], because he knows he will or may thereby do much public injury. Suppose him to see abuses. If by pointing them out he should, without procuring a reform of them, lessen, as far as his influence may extend, the estimation, attachment, and confidence which difficult times and times of war . . . render necessary to be had in Government, will he not be injuring the public interests?" And he enumerates particular abuses that might call for remedy—mismanagement and misconduct in the military and naval establishments, the need of parliamentary and municipal reform, "corruption in our judicial system," and so forth. He is jotting down his thoughts on paper in this memorandum—stating the difficulties, not solving them—laying down no hard and fast rule; but it is clear that he feels the difficulty of opposition to be greater than the difficulty of acquiescence. Thus, on the simpler problem of criticising the actual conduct of the war he has no hesitations at all. The honest man may differ from Government as to the best measures and, if so, he should state his alternative; but, that done, it only remains for him, "if he cannot procure the adoption of the plan he would wish to see pursued, to endeavour to give effect to that which is preferred to it—not to thwart, not to impede, not to cripple."

This line of conduct, while it made him useless to the Opposition, did not palliate Wilberforce's defection on the peace issue in the eyes of the war-party. It was, after all, the supreme issue; and the one lapse was enough to make him abominably grey. The King gave the lead which Tory society expected of him. He studiously cut Wilberforce at the first *levée* he attended after moving his pacifist amendment. Acid references to "Citizen Wilberforce" began to appear in the political correspondence of the day. Windham, as befitted a convert, let loose his bitter tongue. "Your friend, Mr. Wilberforce," he remarked to Lady Spencer, "will be very happy any morning to hand your ladyship to the guillotine." Even Burke, so close a brother-in-arms to Wilberforce in the cause of humanity anywhere outside Europe but only living now on the desperate longing to see the *ancien régime* triumphant over a punished and humbled France, could not resist a sarcasm. "Mr. Wilberforce is a very respectable gentleman," he said to Pitt, "but he is not the people of England." Naturally the country at large was no more tolerant than Burke, and faithful Yorkshire was dismayed and angry. In the summer of 1795, when the worst of the storm was over and

Wilberforce toured the county in order to explain his conduct and re-establish his popularity, he found the fires of resentment still smouldering. Women in politics are apt to be more outspoken or less easygoing than men; and there were women in Yorkshire who were determined that the refractory county-member should know what they thought of him. "In one family of my most zealous partisans," he records, "the ladies would scarcely speak to me." At another house, while "the coldness of the others seemed to give way by my being quite unaffected and undiscerning," the hostess refused to come downstairs.

And if acquaintances were cold, friends were puzzled and disquieted. One of his most constant correspondents, Mr. Hey, wrote vigorous expostulations. Dr. Burgh, an old and tried adviser, told him frankly that "above all evils he most deprecated a peace, in whatever form the present moment could obtain it." "Faction begins to claim you," he wrote; "you are quoted and are growing into the subject of a panegyric. It is of infinite importance that you should not appear to the country as a leader of opposition. . . . Strange as it may sound, it is not so much the war that is in the mind of many of its supporters as the individual person of Mr. Pitt. Though they like not his new connexions, yet still they attach themselves to him and do not love to see him opposed." And no one was more anxious than Dean Milner. As soon as he heard at Carlisle the news of Wilberforce's forthcoming amendment he wrote an appealing letter, and another was soon posting at its heels. "I do not perceive," he says in the first, "the nature of the opposition to Pitt which you are likely to make. Weigh it well, my dear friend. I hope you will not prove a dupe to the dishonest Opposition who will be glad to make use of you in hunting down Pitt and for no other purpose." The second letter is written when the report of the debate has told him all. "I can truly say," he groans, "I never was so much concerned about politics in my life; I was quite low, and so I continue. . . . I never conceived that you had intended to take so decided a part in this business as to lead the opposition against Pitt." A few days later the loyal friend is at Cambridge, putting up an eloquent defence of Wilberforce in hostile combination-rooms.

It was a black, lonely time for Wilberforce. Solace indeed he could find and comradeship, in privacy, on his knees. But, little as he loved promiscuous society, he had none of the anchorite's self-sufficiency. The daily sitting in the House of Commons had lost half its fascination with Pitt there, so cold now and far away. And, however congenial the company of his less political associates, the thought would come and come again that, in Downing Street or at Holwood, the "old firm" were gathered and he was not there.

4

Wilberforce's ordeal of isolation was happily short. In fact, the breach with Pitt had hardly opened before it began to close, for the simple reason that Pitt became gradually converted, as the year 1795 drew on, to the desirability of negotiating for peace. Presently, therefore, the broken threads could be tied up again, rather clumsily and comically, as befitted Englishmen. Pitt was shy and stiff, Wilberforce self-conscious and diffident. The diary for May 21 records their first meeting at a dinner-party—"I think both meaning to be kind to each other—both a little embarrassed." Then, on April 15: "Called at Pitt's the first time since the beginning of the session—he having the gout." And on April 25 this quaintly typical entry: "Called Eliot's, knowing that Pitt was there, and that Pitt knew I knew it, and thinking, therefore, that it would seem unkind not to do it." But there was soon no need for these awkwardnesses and hesitations. Their relations responded like a barometer to the steady rise of Pitt's pacifism. "All Pitt's supporters," says the diary for May 2, "believe him disposed to make peace." A few days later the mischievous Thurlow—still snarling at his expulsion three years earlier from the Woolsack and seeking to damage Pitt in the eyes of his more warlike followers by hinting that he has been in secret agreement with Wilberforce all along—lays a bet for five guineas with the Dukes of Leeds and Bedford that Pitt will vote with Wilberforce when the latter moves the next peace-resolution. And certainly the Dukes might well have hesitated to take the bet if they could have overlooked the garden of Eliot's house at Battersea on the afternoon of May 12, and seen the two men, whose sharp estrangement was so recent and so notorious, with Eliot and Ryder, "walking, foining, laughing, and reading verses, as before."

There was indeed some substance in Thurlow's jibes. If Pitt was not prepared for some months yet to move publicly for peace him-

self, he was no longer unwilling, much less aggrieved, that Wilberforce should do so. Events seemed steadily to be proving him the
better prophet of the two. Prussia made her selfish peace. Holland,
under her new masters, declared war on her old ally. The British
troops evacuated Flanders. The French consolidated their hold on
Belgium, and in the autumn annexed it finally to France. The
"First of June" and the capture of Corsica, Martinique, St. Lucia,
Ceylon and the Cape of Good Hope were inadequate off-sets to the
enemy's triumph on land. And Pitt's chief hope—the collapse of the
French finances—seemed as far from fulfilment as ever. Moreover,
the reaction of the Moderates against the Terror was proving lasting
and substantial. The Convention recovered its old authority. The
leading Terrorists were executed or exiled. And, in the autumn,
when young Bonaparte had whiffed away the feeble royalist rising
in Paris with his grape-shot, the new constitution of the *Directoire*,
with its bicameral legislature, was successfully established. It
looked, indeed, as if Revolutionary France had at last put her house
in order; and it became increasingly more difficult to plead that
peace with security was unattainable. Finally, the serious dearth of
corn and the growing destitution and discontent on this side of
the Channel became daily stronger arguments for peace than they
had been at the beginning of the year. But these developments were
gradual, and Pitt was no hastier than Wilberforce in making up
his mind. Its doors, however, were open to the idea of peace from
the spring of 1795 onwards; and it seemed not only harmless now,
but positively advantageous, that Wilberforce should fly his kite.
So, although Pitt declared in the House on May 27 that we must
fight on a little longer and "lamented and deplored" Wilberforce's
motion in favour of an honourable peace, he had actually discussed
it with its author a day or two before the debate. "I had shown my
motion to Pitt on Saturday—he very kind now and good-natured;
he wrung from me to show it to others; so I showed it to Grey
and Fox"—a backstairs proceeding which Thurlow would doubtless have given his ears to ferret out. Pitt's colleagues, however,
were not quite so ready as Pitt himself to make it up with the
defaulter; and when he called at Downing Street to settle the time
for his motion and found Grenville and Dundas there, he noted that
while Pitt again was "very kind," Grenville was "shy" and Dundas
"sour." And Windham was too passionately imbued with the anti-
Jacobinism of his master, Burke, to follow Pitt's lead as to peace

or the men who preached it. In his reply to Wilberforce's motion he derided his illusions and mocked bitterly at the "Christian conscience" of one who lauds his friend's ability to the skies and, in the same breath, is not too humble to oppose that friend's policy and to suggest that he could govern the country better himself. "Too much hurt by Windham's personalities," the diary confesses, not unnaturally perhaps. But there is balm now in Gilead. Once more, like a refrain, came the salving words—"Pitt kind."

The summer passed, and nothing happened to check the reviving harmony. In the autumn Pitt showed how nearly he had reached a decision to try for peace by making advances to Wilberforce for the renewal of their interrupted habit of constant political discussion. On October 24, twenty days after the monarchist fiasco of *Vendémiaire*, he wrote to urge him to come to London a few days before the opening of the session.

I cannot help being more anxious for this, as I think our talking over the present state of things may do a great deal of good, and I am sure at all events it can do no harm. It is hardly possible to form any precise opinion as to what is to be done, till we see the immediate issue of the crisis just now depending, but I cannot help thinking that it will shortly lead to a state of things in which I hope our opinions cannot materially differ. I need not say how much personal comfort it will give me if my expectation in this respect is realised. Yours sincerely and affectionately, W. Pitt.

Between the lines of this guarded letter Wilberforce read all he longed for. He hurried to town, breakfasted with Pitt, and "had a most satisfactory conversation with him." Two days later he repeats "another confidential and satisfactory conversation." The fruits of this cabal were visible to all the world when Parliament met on October 29. The King's Speech declared that, if the termination of the constitutional crisis in France should be such as to afford "a reasonable expectation of security and permanence in any treaty which might be concluded," Britain would be prepared to reciprocate a disposition on the part of France towards a just peace. On December 8, the Directory being now firmly in the saddle, these overtures were renewed, and next day Pitt reaffirmed his willingness to treat with the Republican Government.

W.

L

Meantime the renewed *entente* had been cemented by Wilberforce's stalwart support of Government at one of the two moments during the war when the tide of internal discontent rose nearest to actual danger-point. The crowds that clamoured for peace in the autumn of 1795 were no more Jacobin in spirit and motive than those that cheered the Radical demagogues in 1793. They wanted a more immediate necessity than Revolution; they wanted bread. The bad harvest of the previous year had been followed by a peculiarly cold summer which blighted the corn and killed the shorn sheep; and heavy storms of rain in August increased the loss. So, while unemployment was as rife as ever, the food-shortage became more serious. In the middle of the summer a mob of hungry men at Birmingham was dispersed by the military, not without bloodshed. "Are we to be starved to death?" they had shouted. "War and Want or Peace and Plenty" were the catchwords of a crowd in St. George's Fields in July. And all over the country the suffering poor grew more and more resentful at a war which brought such hardships and which, till Napoleon roused the instinct of self-defence, they never understood or cared about, and more and more exasperated with Government which gave them neither victory nor peace. In July the windows of Pitt's house in Downing Street were broken by an angry mob. But it was not till the autumn that the unrest became seriously alarming. On October 27 a vast meeting was held at Islington under the auspices of the London Corresponding Society. Nearly 150,000 people, it was said, attended it; and those of them at least who were within earshot of the platform accepted a resolution declaring that they were ready to take up arms, if need be, for peace and constitutional reform. The circulation in London of a leaflet on "King-killing" was less positively dangerous; but it gave a sinister colour to the unprecedented scene on October 29 when George III drove to Westminster to open Parliament through the hoots and hisses of the great crowd that packed the Mall. "Peace," "Bread," "No Pitt," "No Famine," they yelled. The state coach was struck by a stone, and a pebble or some other small missile pierced the window. On the way back to St. James's the curses and threats were redoubled. The Guards could scarcely hold the people back; and when the King had entered the palace, they wreaked their fury on his empty coach. It was as well that the mob, in this mood, saw nothing of Pitt. Certainly it was an ugly affair. The King had been shouted at before, notably by a "No Popery" crowd on the occasion of the passing of the famous Quebec Act in 1774; but never had such bitter and violent animosity been displayed. And coming in such close conjunction with the Islington meeting, if it gave no solid reason for panic, it at least gave some excuse. George III himself behaved throughout with admirable *sang-froid*; but Parliament and Society were shocked and frightened, and two severe measures of repression, the Treasonable Practices Bill and the Seditious Meetings Bill, were hurriedly framed and passed.

These Acts were unquestionably effective. There were no more monster meetings, no more riots—a fact which class-warriors like Lord Malmesbury regretted, now that Government was so well armed for their repression. Reformers could only meet now in numbers that would fill a small room. One or two leading spirits were arrested. The Corresponding Society wilted away. Indeed the Acts were too effective, since, continuing in force when any real danger had passed over, they could be used, and were used, to keep the poor in sullen silence, to prevent the escape of much honest Reform steam, and to suppress the legitimate efforts of the workers to combine not against their country but against the taskmasters of the new and primitive industrial system. None the less, Pitt's violation of the British heritage of personal freedom may well have been justified at the time the Acts were passed. It is for the hardened controversialist to say for certain they were not.

Wilberforce, at any rate, had no doubt whatever about the Acts. It was not now merely his enthusiasm for Pitt nor his shrinking from opposition in war-time that led him to support the Government. He had forgotten his cool reckoning of the invincible sobriety of "every man of property in the kingdom." He was alarmed—as much alarmed as any member of the Government. There is an anxious note in the diary on "papers dispersed against property" and "prints of guillotining the King and others." And when Pitt introduced the Bills in the House on November 10, Wilberforce showed once more the gulf that lay between his political temperament and Fox's. Amid Tory cheers he declared that Parliament, not those newfangled clubs and assemblies, was the custodian of British freedom; that in the right of petition—which, not forgetting the Abolitionist crusade of 1792, he insisted must be left inviolate—lay the only legitimate and effective safety-valve for popular grievances; and that the Bills should, therefore, be regarded "as a temporary sacrifice by which the blessings of liberty may be transmitted to our children unimpaired." Next day he was closeted with Pitt at No. 10 over the draft of the Seditious Meetings Bill— "altered it much for the better by enlarging." And the day after, he attended a further meeting "at Pitt's about the Sedition Bill— after which supped with him and Mornington." "Never was a time," he comments, "when so loudly called on to prepare for the worst." And, a little later, comes a note of personal anxiety—a note which, be it remarked, would never have been sounded elsewhere than in the privacy of a deliberately introspective and candid diary: "The people, I hear, are much exasperated against me. . . . I greatly fear some civil war or embroilment; and with my weak health and bodily infirmities, my heart shrinks from its difficulties and dangers." Strange as it seems to us who know the quiet sequel, Pitt shared in these alarms. "My head would be off in six weeks," he said to Wilberforce at this time, "were I to resign."

It was in this almost Parisian atmosphere that a summons came to Wilberforce to face what seemed—groundlessly, perhaps, but none the less substantially at the time—a personal danger. Yorkshire, it was reported, was up in arms against coercion. "The Bills," wrote Dr. Burgh, "are obnoxious in this part of the world to an extreme degree." The opposition party, determined to make its protest heard before the Bills became law, requested the High Sheriff, Mr. Mark Sykes, to call a county-meeting, and, on his refusing for fear that it would cause a riot, it hurriedly organised a private meeting of its own. "Come forth in the spirit of your ancestors," ran Wyvill's stirring appeal, "and show you deserve to be free!" Wilberforce had already written to his friend, Hey, deploring the High Sheriff's timidity and asking for prompt news of further developments. "I shall ride at single anchor," he said, "ready to sail at a moment's warning." The warning came as he was setting out to church one Sunday morning. It gave him little time, for it told him that the opposition meeting had been fixed for Tuesday. Sending his carriage to be prepared for the journey, he attended the service—he noticed that Sir George Shuckburgh "talked," and thought it a "sad sermon"—then hurried off to Pitt, whom he found "much disquieted," and since Pitt's carriage was ready for instant use, he accepted his offer of it and, by half-past two, was off on the Great North Road, behind four horses, his secretary beside him. "Almost the whole of Monday," says the latter, "was spent in dictating; and between his own manuscripts and the pamphlets which had followed him, we were almost up to our knees in papers." If Wilberforce had not been so busy with his speech, his reflections might have been disquieting. "If he ventured down," he had been told by Yorkshire friends, "it would be at the hazard of his life." And one of the party at No. 10 had cheered him on his way by suggesting he would certainly be murdered "if they find out whose carriage you have got." Meantime the milestones were passing. He reached Doncaster on Monday night and early next morning set out for York.

A multitude of Yorkshiremen were converging on the same point. All Monday the roads to York were thronged. Over 3000 horsemen were counted passing through Halton turnpike alone. Many spent the night by the roadside, and next day they still came trooping in. The whole county, it seemed, was going to be there; and the High Sheriff and all those responsible for the maintenance of order grew hourly more anxious as the crowd within the city gates increased and no one knew to which faction the great mass belonged. But the friends of the Government had not been idle; and when, on the Tuesday morning, the two forces drew apart into separate camps, it was clear that the "Loyalists" were more numerous than the "Reformers." Some of the former gathered in the Castle Yard, the usual place for a large-scale public meeting. Others forced their way into the Guildhall where the meeting of protest was to be held; and a somewhat disorderly discussion was in progress there, when suddenly, above the general tumult, a great roar of cheering was heard outside the building. A chariot and four was slowly making its way along the street. The crowd was yelling itself hoarse. The air was thick with hats. Wilberforce, whom almost every one believed to be in London, had arrived. "What a row I made," he said to his son as they entered York by the same road thirty-two years later, "when I turned this corner in 1795. It seemed as if the whole place must come down together."

Making his way through the throng in the Guildhall and mounting the platform. Wilberforce entreated his old ally, Wyvill, to bring his minority to the Castle Yard for a joint discussion. "He hoped," he said, "to have met his opponents that day face to face and convinced them of the feebleness of their prejudices." But Wyvill and his followers refused to move; and Wilberforce withdrew without them to the Castle Yard. The crowd that packed itself round him as he stood on the old stone steps was over 4000 strong, "perhaps the largest assemblage," said the local newspaper, "of gentlemen and freeholders which ever met in Yorkshire." His speech was brief. "I should have said much more," he told Hey, "if we had got into debate." But it was enough to win once again the popular triumph which the "shrimp" had won on the same spot ten years before. "A most incomparable speech indeed," said one of his listeners. "I never saw you but once," wrote another, fifteen years afterwards, "and that day you won my heart and every honest heart in the country. . . . You made my blood tingle with delight." To the malcontents who had stayed in the Guildhall the speaker might not have seemed so eloquent; but there were still many doubters in his audience who doubted no more when he had done. There was only one discordant incident and that in the vein of burlesque rather than of serious politics. An officer stood up in full uniform—"that mad fellow, Colonel Thornton,"[1] said the chairman—informed the crowd that "many of the soldiers were ready to join them whenever they should rise," and then, "after throwing off his regimentals to the rabble," was borne away in a chair to the Guildhall. The supporters of the Government were thus left in possession of the field even more completely than before, and an address and a petition against seditious meetings and in favour of the King and Constitution were carried with scarcely a dissentient voice.

The lead thus given at York was promptly followed by the West Riding as a whole. Bells were set ringing, exuberant meetings held, petitions signed in all the big towns. And, according to Wyvill, it was Wilberforce's personal intervention which had turned the current of opinion. "Many who, to my personal knowledge, came decidedly hostile to the Bills," wrote Dr. Coulthurst, "were induced, on hearing your speech, to sign the address and petition. You have gained over almost every man in the five great commercial towns of the West Riding." And one of the leading merchants in Leeds bore witness to the same effect. Yorkshire's lead, moreover, was followed in turn by other counties, "proving," said Wilberforce, "the justice of what Fox would often say—' Yorkshire and Middlesex between them make all England.'"

There is, no doubt, a note of exaggeration in the mutual congratulations of the "loyalists"; but there was enough at least in

---

[1] Thomas Thornton, colonel of the West Riding Militia : see his life in *D. N. B.*

what happened to dissipate Pitt's worst anxieties. Clearly the electorate had not been irrevocably estranged by his measures of repression. Clearly the country had not reached the brink of Revolution. November had been darkened by the shadow of the guillotine; in December it was gone. It was with real gratitude, therefore, that he welcomed the traveller back to London. That their fears had proved groundless detracted nothing from the instant courage with which Wilberforce had set out to face the unknown in the North. And whether or not its actual effects were as decisive as they seemed to some, he had dealt a great stroke for the Government. The personal reunion had been sealed and crowned.

5

The effort and excitement of the Yorkshire adventure had proved somewhat exhausting. "The last fortnight or three weeks," writes Wilberforce on December 19, "have been severe trials to a man weakly like me, and I have lost ground in health which I must recover." But this Christmas was far more cheerful than the last. The clouds of popular disfavour had blown away. Society smiled once more on the intrepid champion of law and order. Majesty no longer turned its back. The King, indeed, so far unbent at the *levée* as to discuss with Wilberforce a current theological disputation between Gisborne and Paley. But the renewed note of happiness in the daily record of his life has little to do with Society or the Court. The vital entries are those which tell of Pitt—how "very friendly" he is now; how "very affectionately" he accosts him when he calls; how they dine alone together and have "long discussions about politics and people"; how he stays at Holwood and goes for country walks with his host; above all, how "very kind, open and fair" he is "about peace, and I think wise too."

On this cardinal issue, indeed, they could not quarrel now. During the next two years, while the course of the war abroad and the distress and discontent at home went steadily from bad to worse, Pitt was anything but bellicose; and in the spring of 1796 he made the first of a series of overtures for peace. Informal negotiations were set on foot at Basle; but they soon broke down because the Directory demanded that France should retain all she had won in Europe while Britain surrendered all she had won elsewhere. By the autumn the situation was still less promising. Bonaparte's astonishing career of victory had begun and the Austrians were fast being driven out of Italy. In October Spain, with her considerable fleet, entered the war on the side of France. So far from contemplating peace, the Directory were now proclaiming their intention of invading England. To many of Pitt's supporters, to Windham and the "Portland Whigs" who had joined forces with him in 1794, and of course to all the stubborn Royalists like Burke, this new provocation was a summons to fight on. But there was no such militant ardour among the people at large. Wilberforce's correspondents in the country all told the same tale. "My good Wilberforce," wrote Henry Duncombe, "pray make Pitt conclude a peace; the country is quite tired of fine speeches." Moved by these appeals and by his own convictions, Wilberforce, who was spending August and September in industrious retirement at Buxton, determined to see Pitt; and, cutting short his "holiday," he drove up to town and on to Holwood. "Full talk of all politics," he records: "pleased with my interview on the whole."

Pitt, indeed, needed no pressing towards peace. He had decided to make another effort, though the terms must now be hard for Britain if France were to be persuaded to accept them. In October Lord Malmesbury made his slow journey over the neglected roads to Paris—"No wonder it was slow," sneered Burke, "for he went all the way on his knees"—with authority to offer the return of most of Britain's acquisitions overseas if France would only restore the conquests she had made from Austria in Europe. But he was soon back without a treaty in his pocket. The Directory had utterly refused to consider the severance of Belgium from France which Pitt, like every British statesman before him, regarded as essential to the balance and stability of the European system. There was nothing for it, therefore, but to carry on the measures already begun for strengthening the forces in England for defence against invasion. And Wilberforce was fully as convinced as Pitt that, for the moment at any rate, peace was unattainable. In the debates on the Militia and Cavalry Bills and on the subsidy to Austria he vigorously supported the Government, and on one occasion, exasperated by what seemed to him the almost criminal factiousness of the Opposition, he let himself go. "I will not charge them," he said, "with desiring an invasion, but I cannot help thinking that they would rejoice to see just as much mischief befall their country

as would bring themselves into office." Sheridan at once replied
with a bitter protest against Wilberforce's "malice" and "insults"
and "cant," and with a violent counter-attack on ministers "be-
grimed and black with infamy." But the chief object of Wilberforce's insults was a bigger man than Sheridan. Next day the diary
admits a fear lest the speech "had gone too far. . . . But Fox very
good-natured."

With the New Year the gloom thickened. Britain could hold
her own at sea against the four next strongest naval powers in
Europe. St. Lucia (for the second time) and Demerara had been
captured in 1796, and now in February, 1797, came Jervis's defeat of
the Spanish fleet off Cape St. Vincent with its first great example of
the "Nelson touch." But, though the mistress of the seas might
still defy invasion, it was clear that she would soon be left without
a friend or foothold on the Continent; for Austria was evidently
weakening under Bonaparte's continued blows in Italy. Meantime
a far graver domestic crisis than that of November, 1795 was
gathering to a head. Its prelude was a sudden and startling shock
to the old prim self-confidence of the British business-world. "This
morning," writes Wilberforce on February 26, "Eliot came in and
told me of the Bank going to stop payment to-morrow." "It disturbed my sleep at night," he adds—and no wonder, for the suspension of cash-payments at the Bank of England by order of the
Government seemed to herald a general financial crash. "Anxious
about great event," notes Wilberforce next day. "Went to General
[Pitt's *soubriquet* among his closer followers]. . . . Letter from Lord
Carrington stating that all going on well and stocks rising. They
seemed cheerful and gay." Ten days later Wilberforce was appointed
on the Parliamentary Committee which took possession of the Bank
and inquired into its solvency.

The financial danger soon passed off, but there was worse to
come. On the morning of April 17 Wilberforce, who had gone
down to Bath, was visited by Hannah More's sister, Patty, who
brought with her a letter she had just received from Captain Bedford
of the *Royal Sovereign* at Portsmouth. It contained the news of the
mutiny in the fleet at Spithead. Since Burke was also at Bath,
Wilberforce hurried off to his lodgings. It was, as it happened,
their last meeting; for Burke's fatal illness was now within a few
weeks of its end. "The whole scene is now before me," wrote
Wilberforce some time after. "Burke was lying on a sofa, much

emaciated; and Windham, Lawrence, and some other friends were round him. The attention shown to Burke by all that party was just like the treatment of Ahitophel of old. It was as if one went to inquire of the oracle of the Lord. I repeated to them the account I had received, and, Burke being satisfied of its authority, we held a consultation on the proper course for Government to follow. Windham set off to London the same night with the result of our deliberations." Burke's advice, continues Wilberforce, was much the same as Sir Charles Middleton's when he was told on a previous occasion that a ship had mutinied. "You know how ill I think these poor fellows have been used," he had said, "but . . . you must order a 90-gun ship on each side of her and sink her on the spot if she does not at once submit." In this case no such measures were practicable, for the whole fleet was soon flying the red flag. By reasonable concessions, however, to the sailors' reasonable grievances and by the personal intervention of the popular old admiral, Lord Howe, discipline was ultimately restored without bloodshed. But, meanwhile, a more dangerous mutiny—more dangerous because more seditious in its origin and better led—broke out in the fleet at the Nore. And that was not all. At the moment when England's "wooden walls" had ceased to protect the country from invasion, there was trouble among the troops quartered in London. On May 13 Wilberforce received an urgent message from Pitt and a personal call from Windham, Secretary at War. One of the fomenters of disorder, it appeared, was a certain Williams, an Anglican parson who, having drunk himself into destitution, had become one of the many recipients of Wilberforce's private charity. But "wicked Williams," as he was popularly called, had proved irreclaimable; and Wilberforce at last had written to tell him to expect no further aid. Whether from sheer malice or from incipient insanity he had taken this letter to various barracks, read out from it a warm expression of sympathy with the soldiers' discontents and a promise to bring their case before the House of Commons, and then showed Wilberforce's signature to confirm what he had read. On hearing this queer story, Wilberforce wrote to Pitt, recommending that Williams should be closely watched and that, since, it seemed, he had already confessed contrition to Windham, he might perhaps prove useful in Government service. "I dare say he is hungry," wrote the Saint. The absurd incident was soon closed, but not before the gossips had buzzed it about London that the Abolitionist fanatic had been trying to excite a mutiny. A day or two later the diary records yet another alarm: "Pitt awaked by Woolwich artillery riot, and went out to Cabinet." There were rumours abroad, too, that even the Guards were planning a revolt. But by midsummer this perilous fit of distemper in army and navy alike had run its course and Pitt was relieved of the worst strain he ever had to face.

To Pitt and Wilberforce, though not to Windham and the war-party, these grave internal troubles seemed to strengthen the case for peace. At the time of the Bank crisis Wilberforce had pressed for the reopening of negotiations. "Called at Pitt's," says the diary for March 31; "a most earnest conversation about peace, and degree in which I may fairly differ from Ministry about it. Pitt exceedingly moved." But after the mutinies Pitt needed no pressing. It was not indeed to be expected that the French Government would prove more accommodating than in the previous autumn. Camperdown had followed St. Vincent. Trinidad had been added to Britain's island captures. But there was heavier weight in the other scale. Bonaparte's magic soldiership in Italy had achieved its certain goal. Already in April peace-preliminaries between France and Austria had been discussed at Leoben; and the cynical bargain of Campo Formio was about to be concluded, leaving Belgium firmly in the grip of France, and Britain alone without an ally. Nevertheless, since the French, it was rumoured, were growing tired of the war despite its triumphs, it was worth while to make one more attempt at peace. But the terms Malmesbury offered, when he crossed to France for the second time in July, were bound to be humiliating terms for Britain. If Austria were willing to leave her Netherlands in the grip of France, Britain would no longer insist on their release: and while France might retain her new frontiers, Britain would give up all her acquisitions except the Cape and Trinidad—Ceylon being set aside for exchange. And even as to this residue of British conquests Pitt was prepared in the last extremity to yield. It was a fine offer for France. Pitt had only wrung it from his Cabinet after two stormy meetings, with Grenville, Windham, Portland, and Spencer against him and the King behind them in the back-ground. And yet it was rejected—though not by France. The majority of Frenchmen, both in the legislature and in the country, belonged to the moderate or "constitutional" party; and their representatives were on the point of coming to terms with Malmes-

bury when the minority or Jacobin party, inspired and directed by
Bonaparte, "purged" the Directorate by the *coup d'état* of *Fructidor*
and plunged France into a new phase of terrorism at home and a
new period of aggressive and unceasing war abroad. Before long
the whole situation had been changed: the French Revolution had
reached its transforming climax in the virtual absolutism of
Napoleon; and Britain was fighting not only for the general
liberties of Europe, but for her own existence as an independent
state.

6

Meantime the question of the Slave Trade had inevitably fallen
far into the background. From the moment war broke out,
Englishmen had interests and troubles to think about nearer home
than the Guinea Coast and Mid-Atlantic. Moreover, the actual
rupture with Jacobin France at once sharpened and concentrated
the vague suspicions and antagonisms that had begun to cloud the
field of liberal and humane ideals. Already, therefore, in 1793 public
opinion in the country as a whole had become as cool towards the
Abolitionist cause as Parliament had been in 1792. From the reports
that reached Wilberforce it might well have been difficult to believe
that the great petition movement of the previous year had ever
taken place. "I do not imagine," wrote a Yorkshire correspondent,
"that we could meet with twenty persons in Hull at present who
would sign a petition, that are not Republicans. People connect
democratical principles with the Abolition of the Slave Trade, and
will not hear it mentioned." It was the same story in Norfolk. In
Suffolk it was said that "a damp and odium" had fallen on the idea
of "collective applications." So Parliament was no longer out of
harmony with popular opinion when it continued the solemn
business of killing Abolition by delay.

On February 26, 1793, Wilberforce proposed that the House
should go into Committee on the Slave Trade in a few days' time.
The attendance was thin; and though a similar resolution had been
carried in the previous year and though Fox and Pitt both warmly
supported Wilberforce as before, the motion was lost by 61 to 53,
and an amendment, postponing the question for six months, was
carried. Undaunted by this rebuff, Wilberforce determined that, if

no progress could be effected with wholesale Abolition, at least some effort should be made to destroy that part of the Trade which had nothing to do with the British colonies. On May 14, accordingly, he moved, and carried by seven votes, a motion for leave to introduce a Bill to suppress the British trade in slaves with foreign territories; and the Bill actually passed its first and second readings. But it got no farther. The debate on the third reading was only attended by the few who, for different reasons, retained a lively interest in the question. Hansard dismisses it in a sentence. Pitt and Fox, it is elsewhere reported, were eloquent once more, and Warren Hastings's old enemy, Francis, made one of his able speeches. Sixty members sat out the debate, and rejected the Bill by 31 to 29.

The House of Lord, it will be remembered, was supposed in the meantime to be examining witnesses with a view to considering the resolution passed by the House of Commons in 1792—that the Slave Trade should be abolished in 1796. They had made no further progress with this task in the session of 1793, when, on April 11, the anti-Abolitionists made a vigorous effort to strangle the question for good and all. The Earl of Abingdon led off with a remarkable speech. He began with a fierce attack on the people of France, "monsters in human shape," "wolves and monkeys," as Voltaire had rightly called them, from whom proceeded, as from Pandora's box, "all the evils and vices that human nature or the world can be inflicted with." "Better were it for us that we were created toads to live on the fumes of a dunghill" rather than endure the fruits of their philosophy. "And what does the Abolition of the Slave Trade mean more or less in effect than Liberty and Equality? What more or less than the Rights of Man? And what is Liberty and Equality and what the Rights of Man but the foolish fundamental principles of this new philosophy?" The Abolitionist agitation proves in fact, that "we too have in this country our Condorcets, our Brissots, our Abbé Grégoires, and our Robespierres." And then, with a fierce jibe at Dr. Priestley's levelling (and Unitarian) teaching to his levelling (and dissenting) flock, the noble naturalist adds one more specimen to his Zoo. It means, he says, that "all being equal, blacks and whites, French and English, wolves and lambs, shall, 'merry companions every one,' promiscuously pig together, engendering a new species of man as the product of this new philosophy, a nondescript in the order of human beings." Finally, he swept aside the noxious bundle of petitions. What was the ground of them?

Humanity! "But humanity is no ground for petitioning. Humanity is a private feeling and not a public principle to act upon. It is a case of conscience, not of constitutional right. And if petitions are to be admitted for conscience' sake, why not petition to alter the liturgy of the Church of England and to change the established religion of the country?" These petitions "are consequently illegal, and being illegal, ought not to have been received, but, being received, ought wholly to be disregarded." With this strenuous logic his lordship moved the postponement of the question for five months. He was seconded by the Duke of Clarence who breezily abused the Abolitionists, dead or alive. Mr. Ramsay, he declared, was "one of the most tyrannical men who ever governed a plantation," and as to the present promoters of Abolition, "they are either fanatics or hypocrites, and in one of those classes I rank Mr. Wilberforce." The Duke, and the Earl before him, had gone a little too far. It was more than the House could stomach. When Grenville, very grave in word and manner, protested against the attack on Wilberforce, there was general applause; and the Duke at once responded with a frank apology. "He respected that gentleman's very high character and certainly meant no personal or political insult." And Lord Abingdon, aware that the feeling was against him, accepted Lord Mansfield's suggestion that he should withdraw his motion. This did not mean, of course, that the peers had changed their views on Abolition. It was not till May 6 that they found time to continue the evidence; and then only seven witnesses were examined before the session closed.

To these repeated blows even the stalwarts of the Abolition Committee began at last to yield. In the winter of 1793 they sent Clarkson on yet another journey through the country in order to bring their body of evidence against the Trade up to date. But they held few meetings in 1794 and only two in each of the next three years. After 1797 they did not meet at all till the spring of 1804. Meantime they had temporarily lost the services of their almost indispensable agent. Clarkson's busy, impulsive, high-strung spirit was harnessed to an inelastic constitution. In the last few years he had done far more than any other man in the collection of evidence and the informing of public opinion. His book is full of calculations as to the thousands of miles he traversed, the thousands of people he conversed with, the hundreds of his correspondents. To search out and to register minutely the sordid horrors of the Trade had been almost the only, and not a healthy, occupation for his mind. He began to brood about it. And he was specially harassed, too, by a sense of responsibility for the misfortunes of many of the witnesses whom he had personally persuaded to give evidence. Pursued and persecuted by sundry champions of the Trade, deprived sometimes of their livelihood, they appealed for aid to Clarkson as "the author of their miseries and their ruin." And, since Clarkson over and above the funds he drew for expenses from the Committee and from Wilberforce's private purse, had spent money for the cause out of his own very moderate means, he was at his wits' end how to help them, until, to ease his mind, Mr. Whitbread undertook to recompense all the victims of this persecution for the future. The winter journey of 1793-4 proved the last straw. In the spring he broke down completely. "The nervous system," he says in his profuse, punctilious manner, "was almost shattered to pieces. Both my memory and my hearing failed me. Sudden dizziness seized my head. A confused singing in the ears followed me wherever I went. On going to bed the very stairs seemed to dance up and down under me, so that, misplacing my foot, I sometimes fell." A long rest from his obsessing duties was clearly called for, and a subscription of £1500 was quickly raised towards his support in retirement among the friends of the cause. Unfortunately Clarkson's own activity in this matter jarred rather sharply on Wilberforce's delicacy of feeling. Not long before, he had received a petulant letter from his old collaborator complaining that he had not sufficiently used his influence, as requested, with Lord Chatham to procure the promotion of his brother to a captaincy in the navy. "I can have no doubt," Clarkson had said, "but you have frequently written to my Lord Chatham . . . but you have not, I apprehend, waited on him often or insisted on his promise in strong language. . . . I never will believe but that your own want of firmness is the true reason why my brother has not succeeded before." Doubtless Wilberforce had made allowances for Clarkson's strained health; and he had replied, courteously and at length, explaining that he was used to such remonstrances since, though he was ready to help his friends as far as he could with propriety, he had always considered it a matter of principle not "to truck and barter away any personal influence I may possess with some of the members of Administration, which ought to be preserved entire for opportunities of public service." And now Clarkson bombarded him with letters, pressing him to canvass this man or that. "You do not know what ten days may produce, particularly if we act together." Wilberforce did as he was bid. His begging letters were full of Clarkson's praises and of the debt the Abolition party owed him. The money was duly raised. And Clarkson withdrew to ease his shattered nerves and to contemplate the composition of the *History of the Abolition of the Slave Trade*, published in 1808, in which (it is only fair to state) he devoted less than 25 out of 1160 pages to the eleven years of his personal inactivity. But the begging business, coming on the heels of that other matter of promotion, left the relations between Wilberforce and Clarkson a little strained; and the seed was sown from which one day, when the first of them was dead, was to spring an unedifying controversy as to which had done more service to the Abolition cause—a controversy which was only closed in 1844 when Robert and Samuel Wilberforce acknowledged to Clarkson, then in extreme old age, that they had not treated him justly in their biography of their father. It may, perhaps, be added that, while Wilberforce never spoke slightingly of Clarkson, the converse was not the case. Two years after Wilberforce's death, Clarkson remarked to the poet Coleridge that Wilberforce "cared nothing about the slaves, nor if they were all damned, provided he saved his own soul."

Clarkson disabled, the Committee dormant, the generality of his supporters despondent or preoccupied, it would not have been surprising if Wilberforce too had made a truce with the Trade, at least for the duration of the war. If he had done so, he would have been in many ways more comfortable. So long as he persisted in fighting for Abolition, he had to face an increasing measure of resentment or ridicule in political circles; for in war-time the most good-humoured men are apt to be irritated by the persistent agitation of a controversial question not directly concerned with the winning of the war. And such little connexion as there was between the Slave Trade and the war told against Abolition. On the one hand, the war diminished the volume of the Trade; only 7157 slaves were carried from Africa to the West Indies in 1795 as against 26,971 in 1792. On the other hand, the war strengthened the argument for doing nothing to weaken the British mercantile marine. More tiresome, perhaps, for Wilberforce, and at times more alarming than the general atmosphere of opposition, was the hostility of individuals. Early in the campaign his life had been threatened by a Mr. Morris, a witness who had lost his temper under Wilberforce's effective cross-examination. A few months before the war a Captain Rolleston, of the Trade, had challenged him to a duel. He had evaded it on principles of which something will be heard later on; and the incident was closed. About the same time he was assailed by another slave-captain, one Kimber, whom Sir James Stenhouse described as "a very bad man . . . who would swear to any false-hood and who is linked with a set of rascals like himself." He had been charged with barbarous cruelty by Wilberforce in the debate in Parliament in the previous April, and since then he had been tried for the murder of a negro girl and acquitted "through the shameful remissness of the Crown Lawyers," according to Wilber-force's doubtless somewhat partial judgment, "and the indecent behaviour of a high personage who from the bench identified him-self with the prisoner's cause." Thereupon Kimber wrote to Wilberforce demanding a public apology, £5000 in cash, and "such a place under Government as would make me comfortable." Wilberforce consulted Pitt and on his advice dispatched a summary refusal. Kimber then lay in wait for his enemy in the street and accosted him, civilly enough at first, but, finding Wilberforce would give him nothing, he became loudly abusive. "Very savage-looking," reported Wilberforce's servant, Amos, when he came twice in one morning to the house. "He went away muttering and shaking his head." Wilberforce's friends took a serious view of Kimber's threats; and Lord Rokeby insisted on sharing his coach, with a pistol in his pocket, when he made a journey to Yorkshire. "I can't say I appre-hend much," wrote Wilberforce himself to Lord Muncaster; "and I really believe that, if he were to commit any act of violence, it would be beneficial rather than injurious to *the cause*." But the nuisance persisted. In the spring of 1794, the diary refers in what is now a rather anxious tone to "this awkward business of Kimber's . . . in which my life perhaps is at stake." But the desperado was presently placated or intimidated into quiescence by the kindly offices of Lord Sheffield, one of the chief and most uncompromising defenders of the Trade. Less alarming, but somewhat irritating until he got quite used to it, was the ridiculous gossip about Wilber-force's private life inspired by the more unscrupulous members of the West Indian party. Once, when Clarkson was on his travels, and making the most of his opportunities of propaganda in a stage-coach, a fellow-passenger took him up. "Mr. Wilberforce," he said,

"is no doubt a great philanthropist in public; but I happen to know
a little of his private history, and can assure you that he is a cruel
husband and beats his wife." Scandal, indeed, insisted that the
young bachelor was really married. His wife was a negress, said
one report; a lady's maid, said another. And one of his Yorkshire
constituents, who himself had married his cook, wrote to congratulate him on defying "the common prejudices of society" and
following "his own path to happiness."

Threats and libels, however, had no more effect on Wilberforce's
determination than the discouraging indifference of the country
at large. "It is said," his friend, Dr. Currie, had written at the
outset of the war, "that at length you faint in your course; that
tired of the obstacles which present themselves and fearful of
embarrassing the Minister in his present difficulties, you are about
to give up the cause of the poor African until a quieter season."
Wilberforce had at once denounced the "calumny." "When the
actual commission of guilt is in question," he had written, "a man
who fears God is not at liberty." There lay the key to his perseverance and its spring. The pursuit of Abolition might now seem
to others an unprofitable, almost unpatriotic diversion, or, at the
best, a noble waste of energy; but Wilberforce could still hope on,
because, as Currie put it, his trust was not in man.

7

In 1794 the prospects were, if anything, less promising than in
1793. The coalition of the Portland section of the Whigs with Pitt
and the entry of its leaders into the Cabinet weighted the scale still
further against Abolition. Windham was still for it, but the group
as a whole, including Portland himself, were strong supporters of
the Trade. In 1792 Pitt had confessed to Loughborough that, in
order to form a national administration, he would have to make
concessions to the Whig magnates on Abolition; and whether or not
any definite assurances were given at the moment of coalition, it
was now more obvious than ever that no sort or kind of Abolition
could figure as a Government measure.

Wilberforce, however, was soon pressing once more for the
cessation of the foreign Trade. Again he carried the Bill past its
second reading in thin Houses. And there was now a new point in

its favour. It was known that some of the West Indian party, realising that the Bill could not directly injure their interests, were willing to accept it. "It is a compromise," wrote a planter to Wilberforce, "which ought to attach every West Indian to you." But very few of his *confrères* were so clear-headed; and the intransigeant majority had Dundas's heavy weight behind them. In vain Wilberforce privately appealed for his support. The cautious Scot had discovered a reason for opposing even this apparently innocuous instalment of Abolition. "I know with absolute certainty," he replied, "that the Bill will be considered by the colonies as an encroachment on their legislative rights and they will not submit to it unless compelled." Not so many years ago, Dundas had ridiculed the claims of the thirteen American colonies to legislative independence; but apparently he had taken the lesson of the Revolution deeply to heart. And if it was doubtful whether those little groups of planters would ever actually resist the sovereignty of the Imperial Parliament, it was true enough, as the future was to show, that they would bitterly resent its exercise over their domestic concerns. Anyhow Dundas was very much in earnest. He told Wilberforce he had used all the influence he possessed with Pitt personally and his other colleagues, "to prevent any question on the subject being agitated, at least during the war." As it was, he could only make one concession to Wilberforce's plea. He would not publicly oppose the Bill; he would keep "perfectly quiet on the subject"—"and even to that I should feel it very difficult to reconcile myself if I did not believe that your Bill will not pass the House of Lords."

Dundas's conscience was not in serious jeopardy. This time, indeed, the Bill did pass its third reading in the Commons; but it had no chance whatever in the Lords, and on May 2 it was swiftly done to death by 45 votes to 4. Only Lord Stanhope apparently supported it. Lord Abingdon told the bench of bishops that the Bill contained seeds of "other abolitions" which would one day grow up to their own downfall, and sustained his zoological reputation by quoting, *à propos* of those who drew profit from the foreign Slave Trade, the fable of the frogs and the boys who pelted them with stones—"this is sport to you, my boys, but remember it is death to us." The result was a surprise to nobody. But there was one unexpected and very discouraging incident. Grenville, the soul of honour and solidity, who had championed Abolition as earnestly as Pitt since the day of that historic conversation beneath the Holwood oak, declined to press the Bill on the Lords as Pitt had pressed it on the Commons. It ought to wait, he said, till the conclusion of the general inquiry on which the House was then engaged. "I am half vexed at Grenville," wrote Wilberforce to Muncaster. Only half-vexed? The friendly self-restraint sounds a little studied; for did anybody still believe in the inquiry? Two weeks earlier the Lords had rejected a renewed proposal, on Bishop Horsley's motion, that the hearing of evidence should be delegated to a Select Committee, and had done nothing since. But Grenville's argument seems to have reminded them of their neglected duty. Four days later they summoned a witness to their bar. They listened to him and to one more. Then they shelved the tedious business for good and all.

At the beginning of 1795 the outlook was, if possible, still gloomier; for it was the time of Wilberforce's break with the Government. His pacifism, as he knew well, was bound to strengthen the enemies' hands; it was easy to imagine the gusto with which Lord Abingdon would say, "I told you so—all Abolitionists are Jacobins." And what would Pitt do? At Christmas, just when Wilberforce was making up his mind for peace, Pitt had written him an encouraging letter. He was intending, he had told him, to instruct Lord Effingham, who was shortly going to Jamaica, to clear up certain doubtful points in the Slave Trade case. "If any queries occur to you, pray send them to me." But when, a few days later, the gulf had opened, when the friends were no longer on speaking terms, was it to be expected that Pitt would support the cause with the same warmth as before? Might not his personal resentment move him to pay the defaulter back in his own coin? Might he not, at any rate, sit stiff and silent at the next Abolition debate? Such conduct would have been natural enough for the small mean Pitt of partisan lampoons; but for the Pitt of history it was quite impossible. When Wilberforce moved on February 25 that the Slave Trade be considered, and pointed out that the date fixed for Abolition (1796) by resolution of the House was near at hand—and when Dundas, with almost disarming candour, declared himself still wedded to the doctrine of the "middle way," still admitted that Abolition was "absolutely necessary," still insisted that it must be gradual, and then moved an amendment postponing the process till after the war—Pitt supported his recreant friend and combated his loyal colleague as firmly as he had ever done. He was at pains, further, to vindicate Wilberforce and his cause from the current imputation of Jacobinism. "I know not where to find," he said, "a more determined enemy of such delusions than my honourable friend, the proposer of this notion." But Pitt's constancy availed as little as before. "Beat," notes Wilberforce: "78 to 61. Shameful." And he confesses to Wyvill that this "infamous vote" has strengthened his belief in the need for parliamentary Reform.

In the next session it seemed for a few short weeks as if at last the tide was beginning to turn. The successful attempts of French agents to stir up slave rebellions in the British West Indies had stimulated the anti-Jacobin cry; but, on the other hand, Wilberforce had completely dissipated all suspicion as to his own political orthodoxy by his vigorous support of the Government in the November crisis. He was quick to make what capital he could from his renewed popularity. On December 15, fresh from his triumph at York, he gave notice of his intention of renewing his plea for Abolition after the recess. "Now," he declared, "when we are checking the progress of licentiousness, now is the very time to show our true principles by stopping a practice which violates all the real rights of human nature." And when on February 18 he moved for leave to introduce a Bill abolishing the Trade by a fixed date, the House, or at least the Government side of it, was readier to respond than it had ever been since war broke out, and Tarleton's motion for adjournment was negatived by 93 votes to 67. The diary is naturally jubilant. "Surprise and joy in carrying my question. Speaker [Addington] asked me and Pitt to come to sup—thought it would be unkind to Pitt to refuse. He delighted with having carried it—very kind, and seemed vexed when I mentioned our little heat."

It seemed, indeed, as if Wilberforce's perseverance was at last to be rewarded. He quickly drafted the Bill in close consultation with Pitt. On February 22 he heard it read a first time without opposition. On March 3 he thwarted an attempt to snatch a hostile division on the second reading by hurrying from his dinner-table to the House, and speaking against time till his supporters were in a majority of 32. When the Bill emerged from committee, where the date for Abolition was fixed at March 1, 1797, the majority rose to 45; and when it came up for third reading on March 15, its final passage seemed assured. But Fortune had still a trick to play on Wilberforce. Most of his new supporters, though prepared to attend and vote in ordinary circumstances, could scarcely be described as enthusiasts for Abolition; and by a queer chance they were subjected that very night to a more powerful appeal than that of Wilberforce's eloquence or the far-off lamentations of the victims of the Trade. It happened that the evening of March 15 had been fixed for the first performance of a new comic opera, *I dui Gobi* or *The Two Hunchbacks*. Portugallo had composed the music. Vignoni, a favourite of playgoers in pre-war days, was to sing. "There was a large and splendid audience," reported the newspapers next day. And somewhere among that audience, their whole minds happily absorbed in the jests and melodies of the opera, had been sitting some ten or twelve of Wilberforce's allies, while in the dull House of Commons the Bill was being rejected by 74 to 70. It was an infuriating disappointment for Wilberforce. His austere views of the theatre must have made the frivolity of his truant supporters seem positively shocking. "I am personally hurt," he said. And the worst of it was that the loss of the Bill, so far from stinging the backsliders into repentance, confirmed their apathy. A few weeks later an attempt was made to palliate the unabolishable Trade by stiffening the regulations for the transport of slaves. The Abolitionists, Pitt among them, of course supported it, and some of the foremost champions of the Trade, such as Sir William Young and Mr. Barham, were willing to accept it. But it soon perished of neglect. Three times it was brought up; three times the House was "counted out"; and then Parliament was dissolved. It was indeed "enough to try the patience of a saint." "This week," notes Wilberforce on May 15, "I have occasionally felt a sinful anger above the Slave-carrying Bill and the scandalous neglect of its friends."

The following year was even more disheartening. Not only was the public mood more than ever averse in those black days from worrying about the negroes; but it now became apparent that the greatest of the Abolitionists—the one indispensable man without whose support, as time showed, the cause was literally hopeless—was beginning to relax his efforts. From the outset of the crusade, in every important debate, Pitt had been at his post and fought his hardest. Every time he had pleaded unequivocally for immediate Abolition, in the teeth of more than half his Cabinet and in open

conflict with his closest political comrade, Dundas. But early in
1797 a change began to come over him. The worst crisis, so far,
of the war, at home and abroad, was at hand; and the unceasing
burden of work and care, far heavier for him than for any other
man, was beginning to weigh him down. Was it inexcusably faint-
hearted or disloyal, then, was it not natural enough, that he should
want to ease the strain by compromising on the Slave Trade? His
own best efforts for Abolition had proved quite fruitless. Whether
or not he continued them, it was now most improbable that the
Commons would accept it, and it was quite certain, if they did, that
the Lords would reject it. On the other hand, a settlement of the
controversy, if only a temporary makeshift, would remove an
awkward bone of contention between himself and his colleagues
and so far strengthen the Government for the prosecution of the
war.

Such, no doubt, were the reflections which induced Pitt to welcome the new proposal made in the spring of 1797 by Mr. C. R. Ellis,
a member of an old West Indian family. He declared himself a
pupil of Dundas. Like his master, he desired gradual Abolition;
and he was convinced that the West Indian colonists would not
assent to Parliament legislating over their heads in a matter which
so closely affected them. He suggested, therefore, that the Colonial
Governors should be instructed from Whitehall to urge upon their
respective Councils and Assemblies the propriety of laying down
such ameliorative measures for the treatment of the existing slaves
as would promote their natural increase and so in time destroy the
Trade by making it unnecessary. Here was a compromise far more
attractive to the planters and the traders than the Foreign Slave
Trade Bill. It was warmly supported by their representatives. And
no wonder. The West Indian Councils and Assemblies—so at least
it was suspected—were not likely to respond very briskly to recommendations from their Governors as to the treatment of their
slaves; and in any case—it was notorious—they were inexorably
opposed to Abolition. As Fox frankly put it in the ensuing debate,
the plan was just another "indirect attempt to perpetuate the Slave
Trade." "Abominable," Wilberforce called it. And yet Pitt was
anxious that Wilberforce should accept it in some form or other.
"Called at the Speaker's," says the diary for April 1, " . . . Discussed about Ellis's motion till very late—much hurt—Pitt wanted
me to close with it modified, but when I would not, stood stiffly

by me." In the debate on the 6th, Pitt maintained this rigid loyalty. The proposal meant, he declared, that Parliament was formally to sanction the Trade for a quite indefinite period, to go back on its resolve to end the Trade by a fixed date, and to accept an ineffective substitute for that total abolition which the honour of the country and the safety of the islands so badly called for. But he was only wasting argument once more. The motion was carried by 97 votes to 63. Ten days later, Pitt likewise supported Wilberforce's motion for leave to bring in a Bill for Abolition—now a regular annual incident—but he might as well have stayed in Downing Street. The motion, of course, was lost—by 82 to 74.

So Pitt still loyally "stood by" his friend; but, as Wilberforce was well aware, the loyalty was now a little forced. It was against his own inclination. And every month now the strain which had pushed him the first steps along the path to compromise told more heavily. That significant discussion with Wilberforce had taken place in the middle of the financial crisis. It was followed by Leoben, the mutinies, Malmesbury's second mission, *Fructidor*, Campo Formio. Pitt met each blow as it came with unflinching courage; and nobody who marked his cool demeanour could have guessed that those months of anxiety were the beginning of a premature old age. After that turning-point Pitt seems never to have recovered his resilience; henceforward he was a tired man; and when, nine years later, the next crisis came, the patriot's heart-strings were as taut as ever, but this time they were to snap beneath the strain. In that same year, too, he suffered grievous personal blows. At its beginning he felt himself obliged, probably for financial reasons, to put an end to his one brief love-affair—if anything so shy and correct as his approaches to Lord Auckland's daughter can be so described—and in September, at the moment of Malmesbury's disappointing return from France, he lost his brother-in-law, Edward Eliot. "Pitt has been almost overwhelmed with it," wrote Wilberforce of the latter blow to Hannah More; and one element in his own grief was the loss in Eliot, the "robust Eliot" of the Rheims holiday, of "a bond of connexion, which was sure never to fail, between me and Pitt."

Through all these troubles Pitt's fortitude deceived his friends. Eliot's death, indeed, so shook him that he had to postpone his interview with Malmesbury, just returned from France; but next day, to all appearance, he was himself again. And this illusion of unbreakable strength and spirit explains what would otherwise seem to be inconsiderate importunity on Wilberforce's part in pressing the claims of his cause. Thus, when Pitt refused to encumber the negotiations with France by introducing the extraneous question of the Slave Trade, Wilberforce remonstrated with a petulance that now seems oddly out of keeping with his quick, perceptive, affectionate spirit.

> I must honestly say [he wrote], I never was so much hurt since I knew you as at your not receiving and encouraging this proposal. . . . Do, my dear Pitt, I entreat you, reconsider the matter. I am persuaded of your zeal in this cause, when, amidst the multitude of matters which force themselves on you more pressingly, it can obtain a hearing; but I regret that you have been so drawn off from it. Indeed regret is a very poor term to express what I feel on this subject. Excuse this, from the fulness of my heart, which I have often kept down with difficulty and grief.

James Stephen put it more bluntly. "Mr. Pitt," he wrote to Wilberforce, "unhappily for himself, his country, and mankind, is not zealous enough in the cause of the negroes to contend for them as decisively as he ought, in the cabinet any more than in Parliament." But Stephen was not strictly just. It is unnatural to suppose that Pitt no longer desired Abolition; that when he spoke of the need of stamping out the ghastly cruelties of the Trade and ridding British honour of its stain, he no longer meant what he said. But Stephen, and Wilberforce too, had seen half the truth. Pitt could desire Abolition. He could still declare his old convictions to the world. He could, and did, still "stand by" Wilberforce, time after time, in debate. But the spring, the spontaneity, of his earlier efforts were gone. Never again could his speeches be inspired by the passion and the hope with which, five years ago, he had acclaimed the coming dawn in Africa.

VII

The Saint

I

TWELVE YEARS had now passed since the supreme event of
Wilberforce's life: and the capacity it had given him to meet
the "blows of circumstance" not merely with resignation but
—in moments, at any rate, of solitude and contemplation—with
serenity, had lost nothing of its power. We must understand this,
indeed, if we would understand the man at all; and it will help us,
perhaps, though it seems a little intrusive, a little like eavesdropping,
to watch him while the process is at work. Observe him, then, for
example, in the last week of August, 1796. It has been a bad year
alike for his country and his own special cause. The last few months
have brought the news of Bonaparte's first string of victories in
Italy. And the last session of Parliament has been distinguished
above its predecessors by the eleventh-hour betrayal of the Foreign
Slave Trade Bill to *I dui Gobi* and by the repeated, humiliating failure
to obtain a quorum for the Slave-carrying Bill. It is in a despondent
mood, therefore, that Wilberforce writes to his old friend, Hey.
"Public affairs look worse and worse," he says; ". . . our national
sins force themselves into my mind. . . . I scarce dare hope for
better tidings." And then, on the following Sunday, which is set
apart, as usual, for reflection, he shuts himself up and carries his
mind back to the transfiguring ordeal of 1785—to "the singular
accident, as it seems to me, of my asking Milner to go abroad with
me" and all that followed. And as he jots down his thronging
thoughts pell-mell in his spiritual journal, the disappointments and
anxieties of the times fade quickly into nothing. "How much it
depended on contingencies!"—that tour with Milner. "If he had
been ill as he was afterwards or if I had known his character, we
should not have gone together. . . . Doddridge's *Rise and Progress*
having fallen in my way so providentially whilst abroad. . . . My
being raised to my present situation just before I became acquainted
with the truth, and one year and a half before I in any degree

experienced its power. . . . What a mercy to have been born an Englishman, in the eighteenth century, of decently religious parents, with a fortune, talents, etc.! Even Gibbon felt thankful for this; and shalt not thou praise the Lord, O my soul? . . . My being providentially engaged in the slave-business. I remember well how it was. What an honourable service! . . . How often protected from evil and danger ! Kept from Morris' hand and Kimber's. . . . Rolleston—and my coming away from Bath so providentially— the challenge never cleared up. . . . My illness in the spring, which might have been fatal, well recovered from. My going into York- shire in the winter. My election over with little trouble and expense. . . ." And when he turns from these happier events and records the troubles and discouragements and failures of his life, these too seem now no less "providential," no less for his good because they help him to humility. "Do not I owe all to the good- ness of God? It is Thou, O Lord, that has given the very small increase there has been and must give all if there be more." And so he closes his confession and, reassured and reinforced, goes out into the world again to face the fortunes of the coming week.

There lies the secret of Wilberforce's indomitable perseverance. These religious devotions would seem, indeed, to have become an almost indispensable tonic for his mercurial temperament. They steadied, refreshed, inspired him; and he was always trying to secure more leisure for them from the obsessions of his busy life in London. There are innumerable items in the diary like the following: "Alas! what a hurrying life I lead, with little time for serious reflection!" "Some serious thought this morning, and found the benefit of early rising, but it sadly wears my frame." Above all, he depended on his methodical observance of the Sabbath. "Often on my visits to Holwood," he wrote in old age, "when I heard one or another speak of this man's place or that man's peerage, I felt a rising inclination to pursue the same objects, but a Sunday in solitude never failed to restore me to myself." Never, if he could help it, would he let the day be used for work. Once or twice—when, for instance, he was toiling against time in preparation for the Abolition debate of 1791—he was obliged to break his rule. "Gave up Sunday to slave business," he confesses: "I hope it was a grief to me the whole time to turn it from its true purpose." He liked best to spend the day alone and hated going off for the week-end to less sabbatical homes, even to Holwood. "Though I never see *company* (so to be

called) on a Sunday," he prefaces an invitation to a new acquaintance, "yet I sometimes ask a friend or two, who likes our way of
going on, upon that day." The way of going on was regularly prescribed. Family prayers, as usual, before breakfast; and after breakfast, "morning church." Then a stroll and a talk before three
o'clock dinner. After dinner guests were left to themselves while
their host withdrew for an hour and a half. "I almost seem at this
moment," wrote Dr. Harford, many years after Wilberforce's death,
"to behold him on one of these occasions passing through the ante-
room of his library, when about thus to retire, with a folio under
his arm, and stopping me with a smile to tell me that his companion was a volume of Baxter's Works." After this preparation,
"evening church"; then supper and talk or sometimes a reading of
poetry by Wilberforce till bed-time.

Twentieth-century England takes its week-ends differently, and
so did the great majority of Wilberforce's contemporaries. Few
signs of the times, indeed, dismayed or vexed him more; for in
his eyes it was one of the most unmistakable symptoms of a faint
or forgotten faith. "Looked into Swift's *Letters*," he says once;
"what a thoroughly irreligious mind—no trace of Sunday to be
found in his journals or letters to his most intimate friends." Public
duties he regarded as no excuse for the profanation of the Sabbath,
unless they could not conceivably be performed on any other day.
In after days he drew this moral—and physicians might, perhaps,
agree with him—from the suicides, in terrible succession, of Whitbread, Romilly, and Castlereagh. "It is very curious," he writes to
Stephen after the last of the tragedies, "to hear the newspapers
speaking of incessant application to business, forgetting that by the
weekly admission of a day of rest, which our Maker has graciously
enjoined, our faculties would be preserved from the effects of this
constant strain. I am strongly impressed by the recollection of your
endeavour to prevail on the lawyers to give up Sunday consultations
in which poor Romilly would not concur. If he had suffered his
mind to enjoy such occasional remissions, it is highly probable
the strings would never have snapped as they did from over-tension."
It was Wilberforce, again, who persuaded the devout Perceval,
when he was Prime Minister, to abandon the old custom of fixing
a Monday for the reassembling of Parliament on the ground that
it involved members travelling on Sunday. It was he, too, who
persuaded Speaker Addington to hold his *levées* on Saturday instead

of Sunday evenings. When Sunday drilling was made compulsory for the inhabitants of the Channel Islands in 1798 and the Jersey legislature, confronted with the passive resistance of certain Wesleyan Methodists, passed a Bill to banish from the island any one who refused the obligation, Wilberforce promptly responded to the Methodists' appeal and succeeded in persuading Dundas to get the Bill vetoed by the Crown. Even when Napoleon was camped at Boulogne and every one expected a landing on the Kentish coast, Wilberforce was still vehemently opposed to the drilling of volunteers on the only day when men of all occupations were at leisure. "I am worried to pieces," he wrote to Hannah More. It was simply "shameful." The recommendation of it was a stain on the statute-book—for England at any rate: the military men had confessed that "Scotland would not have it." And presently he induced Parliament at least to cancel its positive encouragement of the practice. He was shocked, too, at the popularity of Sunday newspapers; and in 1799, in conjunction with Lord Belgrave, he promoted a Bill for their suppression, but without success. "I got the nineteen Sunday newspapers once for all the other day," the diary records in his later years, "that I might the better judge of their contents; and assuredly such a collection of ribaldry and profaneness never before disgraced my library."

It was largely owing to these personal efforts on Wilberforce's part that a stricter observance of the Sabbath came into general vogue by the end of the eighteenth century. It became more and more the correct, almost the fashionable, thing. And the new custom lasted. Wilberforce's Sunday was the precursor of that orthodox Victorian Sunday which seems nowadays as stiffly decorous as our grandmothers' crinolines—almost an historical curiosity—a day of leaden, listless hours, such as our elders have told us of, with not overmuch regret at their passing—a day when girls might do no needlework and boys read nothing but the Bible. A grey day in truth it was in many a stern household not very long ago. And a grey day it might have been in Wilberforce's home but for Wilberforce, who could be devout and yet no prude, earnest and yet no prig. "There was nothing of affected seriousness in his deportment or manner on this day," writes a solemn admirer: "all was easy, natural and cheerful." Wilberforce would have smiled at this description. It was his smile, indeed, that saved that careful Sabbath routine from pedantry and cant and gloom. On Sunday, at any rate, he was incorrigibly happy. Indeed, whatever else the cynics might say of his religion, they could not accuse it of making him miserable. "You must allow that Mr. Wilberforce is cheerful," a sceptical friend was asked. "Yes," she replied, "and no wonder! I should be always cheerful too if I could make myself as sure as he does that I was going to heaven."

None the less, his was an exacting creed. We have seen him "wearing his frame," like any monk, with religious exercises in the early hours. And just as in the first days of his "conversion," so all through his life, he belabours himself for his failure to live up to his ideal. "What a mystery of iniquity is the human heart!" he cries. And why, particularly? Because "thoughts of worldly pursuits" so often force themselves into his mind during "devotional exercises." And, conversely, at other times (he complains again and again), devotional thoughts are far too rarely present. The "other-worldliness" of the Evangelical revival had given the desperately poor something to hold on to and endure by through the miseries of the Industrial Revolution; but it was not easy for fortunate, vivacious, busy Wilberforce to bring himself to regard all the colour and movement of his happier world as transient shadows against a background of eternity. "How little do we talk," he says, "like passengers who are hastening to a better country and here are in a strange one!" Yet few religious men could carry the logic of this conviction to such rigorous extremes. In 1797 he was once more very ill. "Feared I was about to be as bad as the former time," he notes in the diary; "Suffered much—had death, as probable, in view, and felt, I hope, resigned, but no ardour or warmth." After that, we need not be astonished at the following disclosure of the severity of his spiritual ordeal. "My eyes are very indifferent—tears always make them so, and this obliges me to check myself in my religious offices." Such emotionalism is, perhaps, a little distasteful to our modern temperament. To the masculine-minded it savours of monkish morbidity; and the up-to-date psychologist will promptly diagnose it as a neurotic complex. But let it be remembered that these "religious offices" were not the whole of Wilberforce's life. He was not a saint of the pillar or the gate. His agonies and ecstasies were the secrets of the inner chamber. And they did not enervate, they braced him, for the business of the active world outside. Whatever we may call it, it was not morbidity which enabled this chronic invalid to fight down fatigue, to work as hard, day in, day out, as most stronger men; to brush aside the worry of hostility and insult; to hold up, year after year, often almost single-handed, the drooping banner of his cause; and finally to achieve as great a thing as any of his great contemporaries achieved for the good name of his country and the welfare of mankind.

2

Wilberforce's religion was certainly not self-centred. He had the missionary spirit. He was eager to bring others, through the same experience as his own, to lose and save themselves. And those gentle assaults upon his friends, which had been one of the earliest symptoms of his "conversion," became a regular and methodical business of his life. A curious document, dated January 12, 1794, has been preserved, bearing the title, "Friends' paper," and the instruction, "To be looked at every Sunday." It consists of a list of thirty of Wilberforce's friends with the appropriate notes; for example

S—— and Mrs. What books reading? To give them good ones
   —Walker's Sermons. Call on Mrs. S. and talk a little. Lend
   her Venn's last Sermon. Education of their children, to
   inquire about. Prayer, etc. Their coming some Sunday to
   Battersea Rise to hear Venn. Call often, and be kind.
Lady A—— and Sir R. Has he read Doddridge? Be open to her,
   etc.
Mr. and Mrs. M——. Encourage to family prayers, etc.
Lord and Lady J——. See them. Get at them through G. Dis-
   cover what books reading.
V——. Try what he believes and speak home truths.
The J——s. Call and sound them on religion. Give them
   money to give away, etc. Little presents.
Lady E——. Speak pretty openly, yet tenderly.

Little could these ladies and gentlemen have known what careful preparation their lively friend was making for their good. Little, too, could those who listened with delight to Wilberforce's fluent talk, with its mingled current of merriment and gravity, its unpre-

tentious knowledge of the great world, its shrewd judgment of
men and things, have guessed that he made a habit of keeping
certain topics of conversation at the back of his mind which, if he
could once introduce them, might be insensibly developed into a
discussion of first principles. He would often spend a quiet hour
thinking out these "launchers" as he called them; and he sometimes chastises himself in his diary for having attended some social
party without "fitting himself for company" with a good quiverful
of them. There is an instinct in most civilised human beings which
makes them react to such well-meaning friends like a hedgehog to
a dog. And Wilberforce, of course, had many disappointments,
frankly chronicled in the diary. For example, "Dined at Mrs. N.'s
to try to do her good, but I fear it did not answer." "The ladies all
good-natured," he says, again, of a visit to a country-seat, "but
alas! I make nothing of it. . . . I think Lady Y. has a feeling of
religion. . . . Though with Lord Y. I had some serious conversation, I had no opportunity of any such intercourse with the others,
and I fear I seemed a gay, thoughtless being." And doubtless, then
and often, he *did* seem "gay." How otherwise, indeed, could his
benevolent advances which, however carefully prepared, must often
have been evident enough, have failed to offend the somewhat
cynical taste of eighteenth-century Society? No doubt they smiled
at his pietism. There is a story Wilberforce used to tell against
himself of a visit to his "old friend, Lord N——," when he was ill:
how he had sat some time chatting with him, but without alluding
to religious matters, when another friend came in and asked the
invalid how he was. "As well as I can be," was the answer, "with
Wilberforce sitting here and telling me I am going to hell." But
if they smiled at "the saint" they never derided him, nor ever voted
him a bore. When the little man came in late to a dinner-party,
bristling, maybe, with "launchers," every face, says a contemporary,
"lighted up with pleasure at his entry."

But Wilberforce's sense of mission could not be satisfied with
the spoken word. He could not rest till he had told his secret to a
far wider circle than that of his friends and acquaintances. So in
the summer of 1793, after many months of study and contemplation, he began to write. On August 3, says the diary, "I laid the
first timbers of my tract." It was not an auspicious moment for a
public man to undertake an exacting literary task; and the author
would have been starved into silence by the busy politician, if the

busy politician had not conceived the task as an essential part of his business. The "advancement or decline (of religion) in any country," wrote Wilberforce in the preface, in answer to the possible charge that his work was outside the layman's field, "is so intimately connected with the temporal interests of society as to render it the peculiar concern of a political man." Thus, preoccupied as he was by the war and the Slave Trade, by his conscientious daily attendance at the House of Commons, by the local interests of his county, and by his charities and visitors and friends, he contrived now and again to get an evening undisturbed in his library and write another page or two, and occasionally, when Parliament was not sitting, he would break away into the country and devote a few untrammelled days entirely to the work. And so, in the course of three or four years, the tract grew gradually into a book of nearly 500 pages. By the beginning of 1797 the first draft was finished. Staying at Bath in February, he "manages to be pretty diligent in the mornings" in the work of revision: and when he returns to London, the manuscript is ready for the printers. "April 12. My book out to-day."

The book bears one of those long expository titles which were fashionable in the tractarian literature of the eighteenth century—*A Practical View of the Prevailing Religious System of Professed Christians in the Higher and Middle Classes in this Country contrasted with Real Christianity*. Its main object, says Wilberforce at the outset, is "not to convince the sceptic or to answer the arguments of persons who avowedly oppose the fundamental doctrines of our religion; but to point out the scanty and erroneous system of the bulk of those who belong to the class of orthodox Christians and to contrast their defective scheme with a representation of what the author apprehends to be real Christianity." The purpose, therefore, of the earlier chapters is to show how inadequate is the average Christian's conception of his faith—inadequate, first and foremost, in its failure to realise the supreme, the immeasurable importance of the subject, dwarfing to insignificance everything else in the world; in its strange indifference to the fact that "this present scene, with all its cares and all its gaieties, will soon be rolled away, and 'we must stand before the judgment-seat of Christ '"; in its "utter forgetfulness of its being the great business of life to secure our admission into heaven and to prepare our heart for its service and enjoyments." Inadequate, next, because of its

W.   N too easy confidence in salvation; in its notion that a man can be a true Christian without taking pains; in its refusal to face the reality and the awful consequences of "original sin"; in its abuse of the idea of divine mercy to cover even unrepentant sinners, despite the "clear and decisive" warning of the Scriptures that "the wicked shall be turned into hell." Inadequate, too, because of its readiness to accept works without faith, because it regards "amiable tempers and useful lives" as if they constituted practical religion by themselves. All this, says Wilberforce, is "only nominal Christianity." The true Christian recognises that the doctrine of grace is "the cardinal point on which the whole of Christianity turns"; that only by "an absolute surrender of soul and body to the will and service of God" can he hope for salvation; that every purpose he has in his life must be tested by the pattern of the life of Christ.

And so he comes to what he himself regarded as one of the most "practical" parts of the book, to the chapter headed "A brief inquiry into the present state of Christianity in this country . . . and its importance to us as a political community." True religion, he maintains, has been steadily declining in England. The growth of prosperity, the multiplication of great cities, the splendour and luxury of London, the prevalence, "much as we are indebted to it," of the commercial spirit—all this has led to "the discontinuance of the religious habits of a purer age." Christianity now "seldom occupies the attention of the bulk of nominal Christians"; it is "scarcely at all the object of their study." And to be lukewarm is a stage towards unbelief. The tone of current literature is already sceptical. "The time is fast approaching when Christianity will be almost as openly disavowed in the language, as in fact it is already supposed to have disappeared from the conduct of men; when infidelity will be held to be the necessary appendage of a man of fashion, and to believe will be deemed the indication of a feeble mind." If any one doubts this, let him look at France, where the same causes have produced their inevitable result—"manners corrupted, morals depraved, dissipation predominant, above all, religion discredited and infidelity, grown into repute and fashion, terminating in the public disavowal of every religious principle which has been used to attract the veneration of mankind." Against that picture set the ideal of a community whose members all lead Christian lives.

If any country were indeed filled with men, each thus diligently discharging the duties of his own station without breaking in upon the rights of others, but on the contrary endeavouring, so far as he might be able, to forward their views and promote their happiness—all would be active and harmonious in the goodly frame of human society. There would be no jarrings, no discord. The whole machine of civil life would work without obstruction or disorder and the course of its movements would be like the harmony of the spheres.

For the supreme political value of Christianity is its direct hostility to selfishness, "the moral distemper of political communities," the cause wherever it appears—among governors or governed, rich or poor—of political disorder and decay.

In whatever class or order of society Christianity prevails, she sets herself to counteract the particular mode of selfishness to which that class is liable. Affluence she teaches to be liberal and beneficent; authority to bear its faculties with meekness and to consider the various cares and obligations belonging to its elevated station as being conditions on which that station is conferred. Thus, softening the glare of wealth and moderating the insolence of power, she renders the inequalities of the social state less galling to the lower orders, whom also she instructs in their turn, to be diligent, humble, patient: reminding them that their more lowly path has been allotted to them by the hand of God; that it is their part faithfully to discharge its duties and contentedly to bear its inconveniences; that the present state of things is very short . . . that the peace of mind which religion offers indiscriminately to all ranks affords more true satisfaction than all the expensive pleasures which are beyond the poor man's reach . . . and finally that all human distinctions will soon be done away, and the true followers of Christ will all, as children of the same Father, be alike admitted to the possession of the same heavenly inheritance.

It is on the thought of England as she thus might be and England as she is that the seventh and final chapter closes. It appeals to all "true Christians," laymen and clerics alike, to devote the whole of themselves to stemming the tide of unbelief by precept and example.

Let them consider as devolved on them the important duty of serving, it may be of saving their country, not by busy interference in politics (in which it cannot but be confessed there is much uncertainty), but rather by that sure and radical benefit of restoring the influence of religion. . . . Let them be active, useful, generous towards others; manifestly moderate and self-denying in themselves. Let them be ashamed of idleness as they would be of the most acknowledged sin. . . . Let them cultivate a catholic spirit of universal goodwill and of amicable fellowship towards all those, of whatever sect or denomination, who, differing from them in non-essentials, agree with them in the grand fundamentals of religion. . . . Let them pray continually for their country in this season of national difficulty. We bear upon us but too plainly the marks of a declining empire. . . . It would be an instance in myself of that very false shame which I have condemned in others, if I were not boldly to avow my firm persuasion that *to the decline of Religion and Morality our national difficulties must, both directly and indirectly, be chiefly ascribed; and that my only solid hopes for the well-being of my country depend, not so much on her fleets and armies, not so much on the wisdom of her rulers or the spirit of her people, as on the persuasion that she still contains many who love and obey the gospel of Christ; that their intercessions may yet prevail; that, for the sake of these, Heaven may still look upon us with an eye of favour.*[1]

When Wilberforce submitted this book to Mr. Cadell the publisher, it was not very warmly received. Mr. Cadell was aware that the current demand for religious literature was meagre; and though he accepted the book, he shook his head over its commercial prospects. "He evidently regarded me," reports the author, "as an amiable enthusiast." "You mean to put your name to the work?" he asked, "Ah! . . . Then I *think* we may venture on 500 copies." His daring was rewarded. The 500 were sold out in a few days. By midsummer the book had become almost a "best-seller." In August the fifth edition appeared, making a total of 7500 copies. And year after year the demand continued. By 1837 only one more edition had been produced; but fifteen impressions, some of them running into thousands, had been struck off in England, and in America no less than twenty-five. It had been translated, moreover, into French, German, Italian, Spanish, and Dutch.

[1] Italics in the original text.

The book's success surprised others besides Mr. Cadell. Many of Wilberforce's friends had feared that it would add nothing, or less than nothing, to his reputation. Dean Milner had earnestly tried to dissuade him from undertaking the "tract" at all. "A person who stands so high for talent," another friend had written, "must risk much, in point of fame at least, by publishing upon a subject on which there had been the greatest exertions of the greatest genius." But all such doubts had been instantly dispersed. Such criticism as there was did but stimulate discussion and increase the sale. A Socinian attack in the *Monthly Review* made admirers of the book identify it with the very cause of Christianity. Nonconformist dissatisfaction with its Anglicanism endeared it all the more to the Church of England. "The bishops in general," wrote Henry Thornton to Zachary Macaulay, to whom he was sending a copy, "much approve of it, though some more warmly, some more coldly." And first among the warm ones was Bishop Porteous, Wilberforce's Abolitionist ally. "I am truly thankful to Providence," he told him, "that a work of this nature has made its appearance at this tremendous moment." And, of course, it was particularly welcome to divines of his own Evangelical persuasion. "I deem it," wrote the venerable Newton, "the most valuable and important publication of the present age, especially as it is yours"; and the old pastor adds a touching compliment to his disciple of twelve years ago. He had continued to write him letters of spiritual advice from time to time; "but now," he says, "I shall be glad to look to you (at least to your book) . . . to strengthen my motives for running the uncertain remainder of my race with alacrity."

And what of the folk to whom the book had more directly been addressed? What did Society, what did his own circle, think of it? At any rate they did not ignore it. In Bath, to quote a friend who was staying there with Wilberforce, it produced quite a "sensation" and "drew upon him much observation." "Many of his gay and political friends admire and approve of it," wrote another, "though some do but dip in it." A dip, we may suppose, was enough for the Lord Chancellor. "I sincerely hope," wrote Loughborough, *alias* Wedderburn, "that your book will be read by many, with that just and proper temper which the awful circumstances in which we stand ought to produce." Some of the author's acquaintance found an intriguing personal interest in the book: several, it is said, recognised in its pages the likeness of themselves. But for many of its thousands of readers the book satisfied a real spiritual need. Arthur Young was helped by it to something akin to the "experience" which Wilberforce himself had undergone and which he had hoped through the book to impart to others. "I read it coldly at first," he says in his autobiography, "but advanced with more attention. It brought me to a better sense of my dangerous state; but I was very much involved in hesitation and doubt, and was very far from understanding the doctrinal part of the book. This was well, for it induced me to read it again and again, and it made so much impression upon me that I scarcely knew how to lay it aside." An anonymous reader told Wilberforce that he "had purchased a small freehold in Yorkshire that by his vote he might offer him a slight tribute of respect." Unhappily the opinion of the man, whom, above all others, Wilberforce would have liked to influence, is not on record. Of course he had sent a copy at once to Pitt, recommending him "to open on the last section of the fourth chapter" (entitled *Mistaken conceptions entertained by nominal Christians of the terms of acceptance with God*). "You will see wherein the religion which I espouse differs practically from the common system. Also the sixth chapter has almost a right to a perusal, being the basis of all politics, and particularly addressed to such as you." It was the eve of the mutinies in the fleet: and whether the busy Minister did as he was told must remain a matter of surmise. At any rate his letter of acknowledgment—if there was one—was not warm enough to be quoted by Wilberforce's loyal biographers. There was another great man, however, of whose opinion there can be no doubt. Windham once told the House of Commons that Burke was comforted in his dying hours by reading Addison; but we are also told by Mrs. Crewe, who was with him, that he spent a great part of the last two days of his life on the *Practical View*. "If I live," he said, "I shall thank Wilberforce for having sent such a book into the world." And one of the last messages he gave to Dr. Laurence was a word of gratitude for it to Wilberforce.

The publication of this book, then, must be reckoned as one of the outstanding achievements of Wilberforce's life. He could not himself be blind to its immediate and great success: but—it goes without saying—the buzz of interest, the chorus of congratulation, the admiring throng at Bath made no shade of difference to his demeanour. His chief satisfaction was to have declared his own opinions so frankly that in nobody's eyes in future need he fear to seem other than he was. "I cannot help saying," he confessed to Newton, "it is a great relief to my mind to have published what I may call my manifesto—to have plainly told my worldly acquaintance what I think of their system and conduct and where it must end."

3

The most malicious cynic could not accuse the author of the *Practical View* of failing to practise what he preached. We have seen something of his unsparing devotions, his untiring benevolence, his strict observance of the Sabbath; and he applied the same stern standards to all the details of daily life. Wilberforce at thirty-eight had left very far behind the care-free young man of the world who idled at Cambridge and sported in London in the "eighties." Once upon a time he had noted in his diary, "My horse won at the Harrowgate races." "Oh, what folly!" is his comment now on the Newmarket meeting: "What forgetfulness of God!" So strongly had he come to feel on the point that he refused the formal office of steward at the York races which custom had always bestowed on a member for the county, and even diverted the member's usual subscription to the funds of the county hospital. He was distrustful, too, of less extravagant amusements. He shunned the theatre. He shied at cards. Quite late in his life, he can still comment, of a dinner-party at the Duke of Gloucester's, "I felt awkward about cards, though I declared I did not make a point of conscience of not playing." He was uneasy, too, about dancing. At a big party at Bath, for instance, he was once painfully surprised by a gentleman who had been discussing with him the discipline of the Calvanist church breaking off to join in a *cotillon*. And, indeed, to have told his easygoing world in his book what he thought of it may have soothed his conscience, but it had not made him any more at home in it. Time and again he complains of his discomfort. "Taken in to dine at W. Smith's, with a vast company. . . . I was not sufficiently guarded in talking about religion after dinner. . . . Came home, as if hunted, to Thornton's quiet family party, and much struck with the difference." "Dined at Dundas's: Lady —— and great party. The conversation on natives of New South Wales, duels, etc. I felt strongly how little I was fit for these people or they for me. ('What does thou here, Elijah?')" Again, of that brilliant annual festival, the Royal Academy dinner, he notes: "Sat near Lord Spencer, Windham, etc.—too worldly minded—catches and glees, they importunate for *Rule Britannia*—I doubt if I had much business at such a place. . . . Yet what a gay dream!" Of course, too, on more ordinary occasions the broad conversational taste of our forefathers must often have jarred on those Puritan ears; and the diary bears frequent witness to the "improprieties" and "profanities" of the fashionable company he moved in.

When one is confronted with such comments as some of the above—quoted as they are so profusely by the filial biographers and clearly without the faintest qualms as to the effect on their readers —the old suspicion forces itself back on one's mind. This calm, superior aloofness! This self-conscious Elijah among the idolaters! Surely the man was brimful of spiritual pride? Surely he was a prig? Well, the answer is the old answer—his contemporaries did not think so. There were others than the slave-traders—and there will be occasion presently to speak of them—who disliked Wilberforce, hated his politics, railed at his religion; but none of them seems to have regarded him as arrogant or insincere. That confident, full-blooded, supercilious *fin-de-siècle* Society, moreover, would have given short shrift to a prig: no prig could conceivably have won from it the genuine and kindly respect it showed to Wilberforce. It is, indeed, remarkable that these fashionable folk, who regarded the enthusiasms and inhibitions of the new and very *bourgeois* Puritanism with mild amusement or positive distaste, should have treated Wilberforce's notorious fads with such singular deference. "Dined at the Duke of M.'s," records the diary one day. "Many improper things said, which G. told me afterwards *they were themselves regretting on my account*." One other instance out of many is yet more striking. In the year of Waterloo it chanced that Wilberforce was at Brighton during one of the Prince Regent's frequent visits to his favourite watering-place. He was invited to dine at the Pavilion; and on his refusing on the ground of ill health, the Prince was told by one of his companions that the Saint would never dine with him. But the Prince persisted. When Wilberforce came to pay his respects a few days later, he treated him with marked urbanity and reminded him of their first meeting at the Duchess of Devonshire's ball in 1782, and of the particular song that Wilberforce had sung on that occasion. It was a rash opening. All unawares the Prince had provided Wilberforce with a "launcher," and the result was delightful. "We are both, I trust, much altered since, Sir"—was the startling reply. The Prince took a strong hold on himself. "Yes," he responded with somewhat laboured gravity: "the time which has gone by must have made a great alteration in us." "Something better than that, too, I trust, Sir." Even now the Prince was not deterred. He repeated his invitation to dinner and assured Wilberforce, with an engaging candour, that "he should hear nothing in his house to give him pain." And so it was, both on that occasion and at another dinner-party later on. There were times when "the first gentleman in Europe" could live up to his title.

A sincere and unpretentious virtue commonly commands respect, but not so commonly affection. Those qualities in Wilberforce, however, which had kept the young "convert" still lovable at the outset, persisted throughout his life. The confessions in the diary do not mean that he felt himself personally, innately superior to his fellows. His moral standards were not, so to speak, of his own prescription. A revelation had come to him, without any conscious volition on his part, and in the light of it he was bound to try to live as he did. To any of those others, any day, he believed, the same call might come and with the same results. And his piety was no more tinged with the sourness of conventional Puritanism than with its arrogance. It would seem—there has been more than a hint of it in these pages—that he had little real sense of humour: but he had something almost as good—a lightness and sweetness and simplicity of manner which enabled him to obey his conscience in any society without offence. Fashionable hostesses were never afraid of his creating "awkward moments." He could refuse to conform without seeming to condemn—a rare gift.

Meantime, in the world outside the society in which he moved, Wilberforce's reputation for saintliness grew and grew. Englishmen in those days had good reason to doubt the disinterestedness of their politicians, but they never doubted Wilberforce's. His association with any enterprise was accepted by the public as a proof, not always of its wisdom, but always of its honesty. And when the world gave him and his little group of friends in Parliament the nickname of "the Saints," it was a genuine tribute: there may have been a touch of mockery in it, but none of sarcasm. Wilberforce's name, in fact, became a by-word for scrupulous virtue —as witness Byron's famous anecdote. Sheridan, so he writes to

Moore, was found by a watchman in the street one dark night, "fuddled and bewildered and almost insensible. 'Who are *you*, sir?'—no answer. 'What's your name?'—a hiccup. 'What's your name?'—answer, in a slow, deliberate and impassive tone . . . 'Wilberforce.'"

4

Wilberforce lived in two worlds. One was the world of Pitt and the politicians and high Society, of Court *levées* and Royal Academy banquets and ministerial dinner-parties. He was tied to it by his friendship for Pitt, by the necessities of his parliamentary career, and by his sense of social vocation. But he could always escape—and, with increasing frequency as time went on, he did escape—into quite another world. He had only to flit from his house at Westminster to his rooms at Clapham; and there, in what he could still describe as a "rural fastness," he found himself among a little *coterie* of more or less intimate friends, all thinking very much alike, all humanitarians, all Evangelicals. History knows them by a not inappropriate name—"the Clapham Sect."

The patriarch of the community was Granville Sharp (1735-1813)—"the abiding guest and bosom friend" of the younger brethren, says one who knew them well; but intimate as he was with them, Sharp seems to have stood on a somewhat different footing from that of the others. He was some twenty years older than most of them: he was shy and diffident: he was relatively poor, too poor for a parliamentary career: he was rather the confidant and counsellor, therefore, than the comrade-in-arms. The next in seniority—and also a little apart from the rest—was Charles Grant (1746-1823), who had entered the service of the East India Company in early life, and after twenty years' honest and lucrative employment had been appointed by Governor-General Cornwallis to the high post of fourth member of the Board of Trade at Calcutta. On his retirement and return to England he joined the Company's Court of Directors, and in 1805 became its chairman. From 1802 to 1818 he sat in Parliament, as member for Inverness-shire. His eldest son was to go far in British politics, as far as the Cabinet and the House of Lords; and it is easy to understand the strength and the weakness of Lord Glenelg's notorious colonial policy when

one remembers that it had its roots in Clapham soil. The rest of
the group—John Shore (1751-1834), William Smith (1756-1835),
James Stephen (1758-1832), Edward Eliot (1759-97), John Venn (1759-
1813), William Wilberforce (1759-1833), Henry Thornton (1760-
1815), and Zachary Macaulay (1768-1838)—were more or less of an
age. Next to Wilberforce, Thornton was the dominant figure. His
father, a successful banker, had been a devoted disciple of John
Newton, helping to support him while he was at Olney and presenting him to the living of St. Mary Woolnoth; and he had left
his son a strong Evangelical and a wealthy man. The great, lofty,
oval-shaped library, designed by no less grandiose an architect than
Chatham, in his house at Clapham was the regular haunt, the club-
room, the meeting-house of the Sect. Between 1792 and 1797
Wilberforce lived in the house, as Pitt had once lived with him at
Wimbledon; and the garden of "Broomfield," which he occupied
for the next ten years, bordered on Thornton's. From 1782 till his
death Thornton held the seat for Southwark. Like Wilberforce he
was an independent-minded Tory; and if Wilberforce turned first
to Stephen for counsel on the Abolition question, he relied most on
Thornton's judgment in general politics. Stephen, who was in the
House between 1808 and 1815, was also more or less a Tory, though
he hated Pitt. Smith, on the other hand, who sat for Sudbury,
Camelford and Norwich, was a Whig. All three, of course, supported
Wilberforce to the end on Abolition; as the gentle Eliot, member
for Liskeard, would have done if he had lived. Macaulay was never
in Parliament, but he was by no means the least active or useful
member of the group. He will presently appear in a leading rôle
in the great adventure of Sierra Leone; and his immense industry
and inexhaustible memory made him a kind of living encyclopædia
for the Abolitionists. If a date, a number, an incident were forgotten, if the authority for some point of evidence were doubtful,
"Look it up in Macaulay," they used to say. None of these men, not
even Wilberforce as yet, was in any sense a great public figure; and
it was not till 1802, when John Shore, recently created Lord Teignmouth, came to live at Clapham, that the Sect obtained its most
distinguished member. Shore, like Grant, had gone early to India
to find there an even greater career than Grant's. He had become
not only a trusted official, but a friend, of Warren Hastings himself,
and had accompanied him on his last voyage to England; but his
reputation had not been overshadowed by the attack upon his chief.

In 1787 he was appointed a member of Cornwallis's Council and became his chief collaborator in framing the historic Permanent Settlement of Bengal. In 1793 he succeeded Cornwallis as Governor-General: and, if his critics, while admitting the value of his five years' work in building up the new system of British administration in India, yet deplore his passivity in affairs beyond its frontiers, his adherence to the doctrine of non-intervention in native disputes, his dangerous acquiescence in the rise of the Marathas and the spread of French intrigue, he has his answer in the strict, explicit orders of Parliament and the Company. Rightly or wrongly, he obeyed them and he was rewarded on retirement with a peerage and a seat on Pitt's new Board of Control. Last but not least, John Venn, vicar of Clapham and shepherd of the flock, at whose parish church, as the tablet on its wall now witnesses, the brethren gathered every Sunday to worship and to listen to his sermons. Add to these the intimates who did not live at Clapham but were constantly its guests—Milner, Gisborne, Babington, Clarkson, young Bowdler, and one or two more—and add the brethren's wives and the Grant and Stephen children as they grew up, and the roll of the Clapham Sect is complete.

It was a remarkable fraternity—remarkable above all else, perhaps, in its closeness, its affinity. It not only lived for the most part in one little village; it had one character, one mind, one way of life. They were mostly rich, living in large roomy houses; but they were all generous givers to the poor. Thornton indeed gave away as much as six-sevenths of his income till he married, and after that at least a third of it. They could mostly have been gentlemen of leisure; but they all devoted their lives to public service. They were all what Wilberforce meant by "true Christians." And, as if to make them still more like a single family, they were interlinked by marriage. Thornton's mother was Wilberforce's aunt. Stephen married Wilberforce's sister, Gisborne Babington's, Babington Macaulay's; and Macaulay did not go far outside the circle when he married an old pupil of Hannah More's. It was doubtless this homogeneity, this unanimity that gave the group its power in public life. They might differ on party issues; but on any question of religion or philanthropy the voice of the "Saints," in Parliament or in the Press, was as the voice of one man. It was, indeed, a unique phenomenon—this brotherhood of Christian politicians. There has never been anything like it since in British public life. "Oh, where are the people," asked the younger Stephen in 1845, when all the original members of the group were dead, "who are at once really religious and really cultivated in heart and understanding—the people with whom we could associate as our fathers used to associate with each other? No 'Clapham Sect' nowadays!"

Naturally Wilberforce was far more at home in this suburban fraternity than in London society; but he liked to take a holiday, even from Clapham, and then, obeying the impulse which in most civilised men rebels from time to time against the gregarious instinct, he would bury himself in some remote part of England, sometimes alone, more often with one chosen friend, most often of all with Gisborne in his Staffordshire village. As has been seen, he regarded occasional solitude as essential to his spiritual welfare. "I wish I could sentence some of my friends to a little solitary imprisonment," he once said. "They might then see things in their true dimensions." But, besides that, he was a lover of the country and a hater of the town. From the first he felt stifled in London. In his earliest days there, before his "conversion," he tells his sister that none of the pleasures and interests of London—not Mrs. Siddons, nor the House of Commons—compensates for "the loss of the good air, pleasant walks, and what Milton calls 'each rural sight, each rural sound.'" "I feel a load off my mind," he says, when he gets to Wimbledon. In the next period, similarly, he lives as much as possible at Clapham and as little as possible at Palace Yard. And finally, he abandons Palace Yard, abandons even Clapham, in favour of a house at Kensington Gore, so that, though Parliament may force him to stay for months in London, at least it shall not rob him of a garden. He took an intimate delight in flowers. "He would hover from bed to bed over his favourites," the *Life* records; "and when he came in, even from his shortest walk, deposited a few that he had gathered safely in his room before he joined the breakfast table." So, in all his homes, it was the garden that mattered most. "I can never get there sufficiently early," he writes, "or stay there in the morning long enough to witness the progress of the spring." His so-called "study" at Kensington was a spreading walnut-tree beneath which he would read and write whenever the weather permitted; and when the nightingales were singing as, *incredible dictu*, they used to sing in Kensington, he would linger out there late at night. But a suburban garden is a makeshift at the best; and whenever Wilberforce got really out into the country, his spirits automatically rose. It was the Lakes, then just coming into vogue with English intellectuals, that called to him most insistently. "I long for the rocks and mountains of Cumberland," he tells Lord Muncaster whom he often visited there; "the very idea refreshes me." The older he grew, the more he longed for this refreshment. "It is not a mere imagination," he writes to Lady Olivia Sparrow from Barmouth in 1823, "that in the case of a cold-blooded creature like myself, a country of lakes and rocks and mountains, like that which I am now inhabiting, appears to call forth all the affections into augmented animation. . . . When I was a very young man (a *very* young man, understand), I was always in danger of falling in love when I was an inhabitant of romantic countries: so even now the same sublime scenery warms my heart with a double measure of friendship." One year he took a house for some months at Lyme Regis and promptly fell in love with that romantic sweep of coast past Golden Cap to Portland. Two of his best-remembered holidays were spent in visits to the wooded valley of the Wye and to the strip of Devon coast where, in rock-strewn steeps and combes, Exmoor falls to the sea. He was perfectly content, however, with nature in her less spectacular garb, never more content, indeed, than in Needwood Forest which, then happily unenclosed, stretched down to Yoxall Lodge. Every day he would go rambling there: and Gisborne would often hear him, far off among the trees, singing away *fortissimo* for mere joy.

It was well that Wilberforce loved nature, for he took little delight in art. Fortunately, he allowed his portrait to be painted several times; and in three cases at least the result was admirable —for his earlier life, the Rising portrait, now in private ownership; and for his later years, the Richmond, now in the Combination Room at St. John's, and the unfinished Lawrence, now in the National Portrait Gallery.[1] But, though Gainsborough was still living when he came to London and though he used to meet Reynolds at any rate in those earlier, freer days, he never seems to have thought or talked about them afterwards. One is tempted to suspect that art and artists, though scarcely banned altogether like the theatre, lay dangerously near the moral pale. And one wonders if his taste in architecture was any better than that of those kindred

[1] Frontispiece.

Methodists who had begun to sprinkle broadcast over England those edifices which, even if allowance be made for the rigours of economy, seem almost to assert a calculated and defiant contrast with the grandeur of the great cathedrals and the loveliness of the mediæval parish-church. One sorry criticism, at any rate, escapes him. "The Pavilion in Chinese style," he notes on the occasion of his encounter with the Prince Regent at Brighton; "*beautiful and tasty*" . . . "though it looks," he adds, at a happier second thought, "very much as if St. Paul's had come down to the sea and left behind a litter of cupolas."[1]

In poetry, too, his taste, though strong, was limited. He used to combat Dr. Johnson's drastic opinion of devotional poetry. "Religion," he would say, "ought to be the very region of poetry." And mainly, doubtless, on that account, his inevitable favourite among the poets was Cowper. During his lifetime, the stars of Keats and Shelley flashed and fell across the sky, but apparently he did not mark them. His one recorded allusion to Byron refers characteristically to his conduct rather than his poetry. When he was an old man, a neighbour read to him Moore's *Life* while he paced up and down the room; and what particularly impressed the reader was "his anxiety to find out anything in Lord Byron's favour." "There now," he would stop and exclaim, "surely there is good feeling there!" Scott's romantic ballads he devoured with a schoolboy's gusto. *Rokeby* "interests him beyond measure." He thinks *Halidon Hill* "very beautiful." But conscience is lurking in the background. Though he reads *The Lady of the Lake* "with delight and wonder," and considers "all that precedes and follows, *And, Saxon, I am Rhoderick Dhu*, quite inimitable," he regrets "there not being so much of a moral as in *Marmion*." And these joys are dangerously intrusive. Of *Rokeby* the diary confesses, "Left off and locked it up during Sunday, and did not read it myself after the general reading, knowing that I could not finish it without sitting up late." About the poet of his beloved Lake Country he can have had no such compunctions, but we only know his judgment of the man—and that in his post-revolutionary period—not of his work. "Wordsworth, the poet," notes the diary, a few weeks before Waterloo, "breakfasted with us and walked garden—and, it being the first time, staid long—much pleased with him." Shortly after he meets him again at a dinner-party, "very manly, sensible, and full

[1] This *mot* has also been attributed to Sydney Smith.

of knowledge, but independent almost to rudeness." Three years later he is entertained by the poet's sister at Grasmere and sees "the moon and a flood of light from Wordsworth's terrace."

The same Puritan spirit broods over his enjoyment of what he calls "light reading." He is as frankly delighted with Scott's novels as with his ballads. A few years before his death he had a sequence of them read to him—*The Fortunes of Nigel*, *Heart of Midlothian*, *Old Mortality*, *Rob Roy* and *Peveril of the Peak*. He listens eagerly to them all. Nigel haunts him "strangely." He is deeply moved by Jeannie Deans's "truly Christian character and beautiful." But he is glad when *Peveril* is finished. Because it bores him? Not at all. "This class of writing" is "too interesting." It makes other books "insipid." He is uneasy, too, over Boswell's *Johnson*. It fascinates him. He leaves it "with reluctance" for more serious things. It detains him "almost the whole evening." And yet, he complains, it is "mere chit-chat." His conscience, in fact, always watching how the hurrying hours are spent, is only really at rest if the book is "improving"; and his Puritanism, it seems, regards no book as "improving" unless it is either directly religious or ethical in purport or adds something concrete and practical to the reader's knowledge. There are, of course, exceptions. He is never uneasy about Shakespeare. He often reads it aloud in the evening with admirable voice and spirit. And he shares the reverence of his age for the Classics. At one time he is vowing to read at least a hundred lines of Virgil every day; at another he is closely annotating Horace's *Satires* or committing an *Ode* to memory. But the great mass of his reading—and he was an insatiable reader all his life—lay in those two "improving" classes, and, of the second class, particularly in history, ancient or modern, from Ferguson and Gibbon to Voltaire. So engrossed were he and Babington once in English history that they took the book with them on their daily walks, "one of them reading aloud whilst his steps were guided by the other."

It was the same with music. "What!" he cried, when invited, after his retirement from active life, to attend an amateur concert at an early hour; "Music in the morning! It would be as bad as dram-drinking." And, when, in the evenings, he often joined, says an intimate, "in singing or chanting," it was something very different, one suspects, from the ballads and love-songs with which the young songster from Yorkshire had once delighted fashionable drawing-rooms. Certainly in music as in poetry, it was the religious theme that moved him most. "Quite overpowered by the Hallelujah Chorus in the Messiah," says the diary in 1828; "a flood of tears ensued, and the impression on my mind remained through the day."

5

With his busy life in London, with the brotherly society at Clapham, with the unfailing companionship of books, above all, perhaps, with his constant sense of communion with another world to which this earth was but a stepping-stone, Wilberforce had so far suffered little from loneliness. Quite early he seems to have discarded the idea of marriage, partly, maybe, in view of his delicate health; and when the war came and continued year after year and the framework of civilised society began to groan and crack beneath the strain, he began to feel that not only the continual preoccupations and anxieties of his political career, but even—strange as it seems now—its personal risks debarred him from sharing his life with another. "I doubt," he wrote to a friend in the autumn of 1796, "if I shall ever change my situation; the state of public affairs concurs with other causes in making me believe 'I must finish my journey alone.' I must differ from you in thinking that a man such as I am has no reason to apprehend some violent death or other. I do assure you that in my own case I think it highly probable. Then consider how extremely I am occupied. What should I have done had I been a family man for the last three weeks, worried from morning to night? But I must not think of such matters now, it makes me feel my solitary state too sensibly." The last words are significant. There were moments now, at any rate, when he did feel lonely. And, for all his protestations, the confession was half-way to a surrender. By the following spring the bachelor of thirty-seven had fallen deeply in love. He had made the acquaintance, at Bath, of Barbara Spooner, the eldest daughter of Mr. Isaac Spooner of Elmdon Hall in Warwickshire. On April 23 he proposed to her. " *Jacta est alea*," cries the joyful diary that night. Not a word now of the dangers and difficulties of the time, though it is only a few days since the mutiny at Spithead. Ten days later, however, the fears and doubts return. He has heard the black news of Austria's separate peace. "Much affected by it for *her* sake," he comments. "Wrote to her and told her that I would not hold her to engagement against her will." Barbara Spooner's reply must have cleared away these hesitations for good and all; for, though nothing could be gloomier than his entry in the diary for May 28—"Daily reports of the soldiery rising. . . . Pitt and the others now convinced that things *in extremis*. . . . I now feel exceedingly hunted and shattered"—yet, while he writes this, he is already on the road to Bath, and two days later he is married.

Mrs. Wilberforce would seem to have attained the Periclean standard of womanly virtue. She did not possess a "dominating personality." She was not one of those "political hostesses" who were better known and more talked of than their husbands. In all the Wilberforce tradition there is very little indeed about her. In the biography of their father the sons seem to have taken their mother for granted. But at any rate we know Wilberforce's own opinion. "I believe her to be a real Christian," he declared on the eve of his marriage; and on his lips no lover's praise could be more fervent. We owe such glimpses as we get of her through other eyes mainly to the holidays she spent with her husband—"Wilby," she called him—and children in the Lakes; for there she was in contact with literary folk who enjoyed writing letters about their friends and what they said and did. Dorothy Wordsworth describes the descent of the Wilberforce family, roughly twenty strong, on Rydal. She admires Mrs. Wilberforce's "goodness and patience and motherliness," but objects to "that slowness and whininess of manner." She makes fun of the queer domestics, particularly the old cook who complained of being unable to get "a drop of beer" nearer than Ambleside. One or two other diverting pictures of the *ménage* are given by Southey. Once he was present at a party to which the Wilberforces had also been invited, and noticed with amusement that Wilberforce had completely failed to realise that it was long past "time to go"—"to the utter despair of his wife, who resigns herself with comical composure to all his comicalities." Another letter describes a visit to Keswick *en famille* in 1818.

> Wilberforce also has been here with all his household, and such a household! The principle of the family seems to be this, provided the servants have faith, good works are not to be expected from them, and the utter disorder which prevails in

consequence is truly farcical. The old coachman would figure
upon the stage. Upon making some complaint about the horses,
he told his master and mistress that, since they had been in this
country, they had been so lake-and-river-and-mountain-and-
valley-mad that they had thought of nothing that they ought
to think of. I have seen nothing in such a pell-mell, topsy-turvy
and chaotic confusion since I used to see a certain breakfast-table
in Skeleton Corner.[1] His wife sits in the midst of it like Patience
on a monument, and he frisks about as if every vein in his body
were filled with quicksilver.

[1] Part of Christ Church, Oxford, in which C. W. W. Wynn, to whom Southey is
writing, had his rooms.

VIII

Persistence

I

MRS. WILBERFORCE was soon to discover that her husband's warnings as to the preoccupations and worries of his political life were not ungrounded. A week was all he could spare for the honeymoon, which was appropriately spent in a visit to Cowslip Green and Hannah More's schools; and then he was back in his place in the House of Commons. Not till the session closed in July could they leave London—first for a few weeks' stay with Wilberforce's mother at Hull, then a round of visits to Babington and other friends, and finally another course of waters at Bath. On November 1, 1797, they were back for the opening of Parliament. "My dearest wife bears my hurrying way of life with great sweetness," wrote Wilberforce to his sister in the following spring, "but it would be a sort of gaol delivery to her no less than to myself to escape from this bustling town."

If the worst strain had passed with the previous summer, the situation was still very critical during those winter months. All hope of peace had been destroyed by the triumph of the militant Jacobins in Paris who were now waiting for Bonaparte's return to launch him on the conquest of England. And in facing this new danger England was thrice handicapped—by the insufficiency of her existing revenue, by the dire need and discontent of her poorer classes, and by the menace of rebellion in Ireland. With the first of these difficulties—the revenue—Pitt promptly grappled with characteristic courage. He astonished Parliament and horrified Society by asking that the Assessed Taxes, which were levied on houses, windows, male servants, horses, carriages, and so forth, should be trebled, and in some cases quadrupled, for all taxpayers whose incomes exceeded £200, graduated abatements being allowed for lower incomes. The Opposition seized their chance with gusto; for it seemed certain this time that Pitt was riding for a fall. "A forced contribution of incomes by forced disclosure," said Sheridan, was "utterly irreconcilable to the spirit of a free and commercial country"; and Fox emerged from his dramatic retirement to denounce Pitt as the author of his country's ruin. "Storm louder and louder," reports the diary during these days: ". . . Anxious in the night about politics. . . . Much discussion with Henry Thornton who sadly worried about assessed taxes. . . . Fox speaking well—much shaken: I think Pitt must give them up." Outside the clamour was no less violent. Mayfair wondered "how people were to live" if the impositions were carried. The City was up in arms: Pitt was told that he would be assaulted if he came there; and, a few weeks later, he was actually hooted on his way to St. Paul's in a state procession. The bulk of his supporters, however, responded to the necessity and patriotism of his appeal, and none more effectively, despite those transient doubts, than Wilberforce. He did not like the Assessed Taxes Bill. "I dread," he said, "the venomous ranklings it will produce." He complained, too, of its pressing more hardly on the middle class than on the rich, and he was "much cut and angry" at Pitt's rejection of certain exemptions for which he asked. But he confessed that he was bound to accept the Bill for the simple reason that there was no adequate alternative. And this support was, as usual, all the more valuable to Pitt because of Wilberforce's reputation for political independence. Naturally, the Whigs were no less irritated on that account. To them, of course, the independence of a man who, ever since that disappointing day when they had prematurely welcomed the pacifist into their fold, had voted steadily with Pitt, seemed an obvious and insufferable sham. And on this occasion Fox himself was goaded into saying so. Wilberforce had certainly tried his temper. He had wandered from the subject of taxation into a strong attack on the famous "Foxite secession" which had lasted now for a year and was to last for three years more—all critical war years for the country. It was a direct assault, he had declared, on the principle of representative government: it was a stimulus to the revolutionary spirit which sought for some other guardians of the public interest than Parliament; and it had inspired the French Government with the belief that the Whigs were allies at heart of France. Fox at once replied, first with a defence of his own conduct, and then with a counter-attack on Wilberforce. "I do not know a man in this House," he said, "who is so ready upon all occasions to lend himself to Ministers, to profess to believe what they profess to believe, to

distrust what they distrust, or to allege for them what he does not
know to be true, or, in short, to lend himself as a tool or instrument
to Ministers upon any occasion on which they may call for his
assistance. I say I know no man more ready to do all this than the
honourable gentleman himself, and this for the most contemptible
party purposes." "I was sadly disturbed," notes Wilberforce, "at
Fox's imputations. . . . But I think I can appeal to God that his
charge was false." He admits a fear, however, that the attack may
have weakened any influence he might have had with the more
moderate members of the Opposition.

Meanwhile he was occupied in an appeal to the patriotism of
London. "Off to the city," he records on December 18, "to try to
move the monied men to exertion." His suggestion was that a body
of business-men should come forward and invite the Government
to propose a levy on property—"one per cent. on the capital or so
much on the income"—and in a few days' time he actually succeeded
in persuading a well-attended City meeting to accept his plan and
to submit it to the Prime Minister. December 23: "Pitt's about
the plan. Found him rational and full of it. Talking with him for
half an hour." In the end, however, the budget, as originally conceived by Pitt, was retained; and early in January the Finance Bill
was passed by large majorities. It marked an important phase in
the education of public opinion to the realities of the long war.
The contest with Napoleon, it was evident now, was not a matter
of active fighting only, of strategy and fleets and armies: it was a
contest also in financial endurance in which the nation as a whole
must play its part.

The new spirit was revealed in the success of the Voluntary
Contribution. Early in the finance debate, Speaker Addington
proposed that men of means and position should show their recognition of the country's needs and so ease the passage of the new
taxation by making free gifts to the State. Wilberforce warmly
applauded. "I have been writing to the Speaker and to Pitt," says
the diary, "confirming one and urging the other to a relinquish-
ment of a portion of their income during the war." Incurably
careless of his private finances, Pitt was always hard up and almost
always heavily in debt; but, as a matter of course, he rose to the
call. He and Dundas and other Ministers followed the Speaker's
lead with £2000 apiece. Wilberforce contributed about an eighth
of his income. The King subscribed £20,000 a year from the privy

purse for the duration of the war. The total was £2,300,000—a not
unworthy gift considering that the givers were also confronted
with the burdens of the new budget.

Wilberforce had had a special reason, and a good one, for
desiring Ministers to take a generous part in this process of self-
taxation. He recognised the justice of the Opposition taunts. A
Government must be very sure its hands are clean before it thrusts
them deep into taxpayers' pockets. And, if Pitt himself was incorruptible, was he keen enough to scent corruption in others? And
had he seen to it that the public revenue was economised to the
utmost before he asked for more?

> It is in the highest degree important [wrote Wilberforce to Hey],
> that Administration should conciliate the good-will, confirm the
> confidence, and animate the spirit of all who are really attached
> to the constitution. This can only be done by reforming any
> manifest abuse, by retrenching needless expenses, and by making
> personal sacrifices. . . . I have been urging these considerations
> in private upon Mr. Pitt, but, unless my hands are strengthened,
> I doubt of my success. He is really—I say it solemnly, appealing
> to Heaven for the truth of my declaration—in my judgment one
> of the most public-spirited and upright, and the most desirous
> of spending the nation's money economically and of making
> sacrifices for the general good, of all the men I ever knew; but
> I have met only with two or three (except truly religious men)
> who have been able to do obnoxious duties and above all to act
> in opposition to the feelings of false honour by resisting the
> improvidence and restraining the weakness of colleagues.

It was an awkward subject even for Wilberforce to raise, and
Pitt was nettled. "Saw very little of Pitt this last week—vexed him
by plain dealing"—so the diary comments, a little coldly, in
November. But the chill was only momentary. The following
week, while the Assessed Taxes debate is on, he sees Pitt almost
daily and finds it not impossible to return to the charge. "Much
serious talk with Pitt, stating the necessity of economy and preventing profusion and jobs."

2

Wilberforce was much less satisfied with the Government's attitude to the problem of destitution. "Much occupied about the scarcity," he notes in February, 1800: "urging Government, which sadly torpid and tardy." And again: "I am much grieved at Pitt's languor about the scarcity. They will do nothing effectual. Great sufferings of the West Riding people." His own proposals were not ideal. He did not see that the most promising policy was the enforcement of a living wage, adjusted to the price of bread. Nor perhaps did he see that the supplementing of wages out of parish poor-rates by the "Speenhamland" plan of 1795 was inevitably and disastrously pauperising the rural population of England. But he did see, at any rate, that this method was inadequate either to cope with the continual fall of wages or to convince the poor that the England they were asked to starve for was not only an England of the rich: and he pressed—both personally on Ministers and in the House of Commons Committee, the daily meeting of which he never missed—for direct assistance from the State for all cases of extreme need, and, at the same time, for some curtailment of luxuries besides the mere rationing of bread. But he could not persuade his colleagues thus "to gain the hearts of our people." "Though thinking their measures too weak," he complains, "I am by far the most urgent in pressing forward those very weaker measures to the execution of which they proceed languidly and lukewarmly. It is really beyond expression vexatious to experience such indifference." And so it goes on, session after session, while the English peasantry grow thin and ragged and desperate. Wilberforce does what little he can do by private charity. In 1801 his gifts to the poor exceed his income by £3000. And he urges his acquaintances to "abridge their luxuries and comforts and superfluities." One Yorkshire friend, he tells Muncaster, has resolved to brew no ale and is striving to prevail on his neighbours to form the same resolution. A year or two later, Dean Milner reports Wilberforce as exhausting his strength on this subject. "And how he does get misrepresented and abused!" he writes. "But you may kick him as long and as much as you please: if he could but fill the bellies of the poor, he would willingly submit to it all."

The abuse came not only from those whose luxuries Wilberforce was fussing to curtail. He was abused, too, by those whose bellies he wanted to fill—and somewhat more justly. For, genuinely anxious as he was that the State should do something to relieve the poor, he would not allow the poor to use the one weapon by which they could relieve themselves. He regarded Trade Unions not only as economically unsound, as tending to force up wages to the detriment of trade in general, but—what was much worse—as politically dangerous. Thus, with his Yorkshire manufacturers at his back (but not the artisans!) he supported the Combination Act of 1799 by which Pitt killed Trade Unionism for a quarter of a century. Indeed, when a smaller measure, dealing with combination in one industry alone, had been introduced earlier in the session, Wilberforce had been the first to ask for a wider Bill, covering every trade. Such a Bill, he declared, "might be of great service to society." He seems to have found no fault with the more glaring defects of the Bill—such as the clause which allowed a single magistrate to convict a man who might be in his own employment —but neither did he oppose the amending Bill of the following year which palliated some of them. But why did he not detect the root injustice of it all? Combination, it is true, among employers to reduce wages was made illegal no less than combination among employees to raise them. But did Wilberforce suppose, did any one suppose, this side of the law would ever be enforced? There is only one explanation, obviously enough. The Combination Acts, passed as they were side by side with an Act to keep the *Habeas Corpus* Act suspended, were part and parcel of the anti-Jacobin reaction. In Wilberforce's mind and Pitt's, the idea of poor men repudiating the salutary discipline of industrial life and coming together in dark places to concoct a common "strike" against their masters was still crimsoned with memories of the Terror. Industrial conspiracy! Was it so long a step from that to Revolution? But there is a further question. If Wilberforce was so desperately eager to relieve the poor, why did he not brave those political risks? Partly, perhaps, because he believed that Trade Unionism would defeat its own ends by increasing the cost of production to the point of falling trade and unemployment. But mainly, surely, because his sympathy for the poor had a curious limitation, had, so to speak, its converse side. Like Hannah More and all his Evangelical friends, he felt that the material hardships of this world were, after all, of secondary importance. We have seen him in the *Practical View* almost con-

gratulating the poor on being saved by their poverty from temptations that might endanger their salvation. It may seem a hard
doctrine—to some, perhaps, an odious doctrine, when they think
how little these good people knew what poverty was—but at least
it was sincere. "I declare my greatest cause of difference with the
democrats," wrote Wilberforce twenty years later, when distress
and discontent were rife again in England, "is their laying, and
causing the people to lay, so great a stress on the concerns of this
world as to occupy their whole minds and hearts and to leave a few
scanty and lukewarm thoughts for the heavenly treasure." It was
as much a cause of difference to the democrats. Nothing that
Wilberforce might achieve for suffering humanity in other lands
could placate the Radicals' hatred of his "other-worldly" attitude
to the English poor. Most of them never forgave him for the
Combination Act.

3

But the worst of England's difficulties in this crisis of the war
was not financial nor economic. From the moment of the collapse
of Fitzwilliam's impulsive effort at conciliation in 1795, Ireland
had drifted first into lawlessness and outrage, then into a bitter
revival of the old religious blood-fued, and finally, after a black
period of repression and reprisals in the North, into the Catholic
Rebellion of 1798.

On April 5 Wilberforce heard the news of the "first blood spilt
in Ireland." He had supported, it will be remembered, Pitt's commercial proposals in 1785; but since then, like too many Englishmen of his own and later days, he had given strangely little thought
to the Irish problem: and when on June 14 Sheridan opened the
Whig attack on the Government's Irish record, he felt unfit to join
in the debate, "not having pondered on the subject." Five days later,
however, he plunged into a hot discussion as to whether the militia
should be allowed to go to Ireland. If suppression were the policy,
he argued, the stronger the force, the shorter and more merciful the
struggle. If concession, it was still more needful to be "unambigu-
ously strong," lest generosity be interpreted as fear. As to the causes
of the rebellion he made no attempt to counter Sheridan's detailed
charges. With that air of impartiality which so galled the Opposi-

tion, he hazarded the opinion that the cause, if carefully investigated, might be found to lie not in anything the present Government had done but in "old and long-standing grievances as to which, according to the course of Providence, we are now suffering the bitter consequences of long-past misconduct and neglect."

Happily, no great military effort was needed. "Rebel camp at Wexford stormed," records the diary for June 28: "all apparently suppressed." But suppression was only the first step. Some constructive settlement had to be attempted if only to prevent this chronic wound in Britain's side from breaking out afresh at some later crisis in the unending war. And, little though he may have studied the Irish problem, Wilberforce, like Pitt, possessed the first essential requisite for its solution. He had, as will be seen more clearly later, a strong anti-Catholic bias; but, belonging as he did to the end of the eighteenth century and not to its beginning, he wholeheartedly accepted the principle of religious toleration. In England, at any rate, he held that the complete civil and political disqualification of Catholics was an anachronism. In 1797 he carried a Bill through the Commons to enable Catholics to serve in the militia, and had confessed himself "too much incensed," when the Bill was thrown out in the Lords. And now he fully shared Pitt's irritation at the opposition of the Ulster Presbyterians to any policy of conciliation. He speaks of Pitt, in a confidential talk at Holwood, "resenting and spurning the bigoted fury of Irish Protestants." He was a witness, too, of Pitt's anger when that hard coercionist, Lord Clare, attempted in the Upper House to palliate and excuse the atrocities committed by the Orangemen in their efforts to disarm the Catholic peasantry on the eve of the Rebellion. "'Well, suppose it were so,' said Clare: 'but surely . . .' I shall never forget Pitt's look. He turned round to me with that high indignant stare which sometimes marked his countenance, and stalked out of the House."

But when it came to concrete proposals for a settlement, Wilberforce was slow to follow Pitt's lead. It has been a common experience of Englishmen who have tried to form an unimpassioned judgment of the Irish question to be buffeted by the naturally fiercer and more personal opinions of their Irish friends; and in Dr. Burgh Wilberforce had a friend who was bitterly opposed to Pitt's plan of Union. It was "only to be done by force," he said. It was clear to Wilberforce from the first, moreover, that Pitt regarded Union as "opening the most promising way by which the Roman Catholics may obtain political power." "Pitt sanguine," says the diary (January 25, 1799), "that after Union Roman Catholics would soon acquire political rights: resolved to give up plan rather than exclude them." And the admission of Catholics, including Irish Catholics recently in rebellion, into the British Parliament seemed to Wilberforce a far graver step than the admission of Catholics in England into the militia. "Would you admit Papists into the Parliament of the English?" he asks his old friend, Hey, and bids him to be sure to answer. But, all the while, he was subjected to Pitt's reasoning and Pitt's optimism. "*Tête-à-tête* with Pitt" is again a constant entry in the diary, and Ireland is the topic. The upshot was almost inevitable. "Poor Burgh wild," he notes in January: "Bankes clear and strong against it. Auckland evidently so secretly"; but he admits to Babington that his own objections to the Union "decrease if anything," though "the preponderance of my judgment is against it on the terms proposed." A fortnight of reflection and much discussion with Bankes, and then "My judgment at length made up for Union." "Burgh is still on fire," he writes, "and I dare scarcely tell him how decidedly I am favourable to the measure."

The passing of the Union Act and its sequel are a familiar story. "I have strange tidings to communicate," wrote Wilberforce to Muncaster on February 7, 1801; "The King and his Cabinet have quarrelled concerning the emancipation (as it is called) of the Irish Roman Catholics—and Pitt, Dundas, Lord Grenville, Windham, and probably Lord Spencer also and Lord Camden are to go out of office. I think you will guess who is to succeed—the Speaker, with Pitt's friendly concurrence. . . . It is strange, and certainly argues great precipitancy and want of foresight, that this was not settled one way or other last year when the Union took place, or at least agreed on so far as to preclude all difference at St. James's . . . I fear the deed is done. The King and Pitt part on affectionate terms—the King saying that it is a struggle between duty and affection, in which duty carries it."

The Union had been crippled almost at its birth. Despite the inauspicious circumstances of its enactment, it is not inconceivable that the unitary form of government might gradually have guided Ireland into the same happy path as it had Scotland, if only it had brought with it—what was even more essential in the Irish case than in the Scottish—complete equality between the national religions. But it was not till Wilberforce's life was near its end that the British Tories reluctantly and imperfectly completed Pitt's design. And then it was too late. Nothing could then avail to lift the curse with which George III's sense of duty had blasted the Union in its cradle.

4

The crowding troubles of these war-years had not diverted Wilberforce from the main purpose of his life. Though almost all his comrades in the cause of Abolition had now resigned themselves to waiting till the war was over, Wilberforce still argued that the very fact that England was at war made it all the more imperative that she should instantly cleanse her shield of its blackest stain. "Is not this a time," he asked the House of Commons, "in which all who believe in the superintending providence of God must feel desirous of averting His displeasure?"

In 1798, therefore, and again in 1799 Wilberforce proposed his regular motion for leave to introduce an Abolition Bill. He was supported on the first occasion by Fox and on both occasions by Pitt. "I always have been," said the latter, "and until my mind shall change its nature, I always shall be a friend to the immediate and unqualified abolition of the Slave Trade." Nor can Pitt's speeches though relatively short, be fairly described as perfunctory; they were closely argued appeals alike to duty and to interest. Dundas, it will be remembered, had once fixed the year 1800 as the limit of his "gradual" Abolition, but only a simpleton would have expected him on that account to support Wilberforce's motion in 1799. Once more he deplored his inability to agree with either side; once more he pursued a middle path; and this time his middle path was to leave it to the colonial Assemblies to bring the Trade to an end by means of regulations in accordance with the Address of 1797. Windham's attitude was more surprising. Hitherto a firm supporter of Abolition, he had suddenly changed sides. He did not, of course—nobody did now—deny or whitewash the atrocities of the Trade. It was, he held, a choice of evils, since instant Abolition would endanger not only the safety and interest of the planters but also the happiness of the slaves. Loyal as ever to his master, he cited Burke as an early exponent of the method of regulation. But if Burke had lived, would he now have been content with regula-

tion? Would he have deserted Pitt and Wilberforce? Would his
hatred of the Revolution have clouded his mind so completely as
to make him forsake the humanitarian field which he had made so
specially his own, just because the Jacobins had run amok in it?
The defection of Windham was partly compensated by the adherence
of a younger and more brilliant Tory. Canning came out decisively
for Abolition in the debate of 1798, and in the following year he
made a long speech on Wilberforce's side—one of those fluent, witty,
incisive speeches which were quickly to set him in the front rank of
British parliamentarians.

From the attendances and the voting it might seem as if Wilberforce was merely wasting time with these annual resolutions. In
1798 he was defeated by 87 votes to 83, in 1799 by 84 to 54. Yet the
debates had not been altogether useless, if only for their revelation
of the collapse of the case for the defence. It was an impressive
fact that nobody now attempted to argue away the horrors of the
Trade. On the moral issue it stood condemned; and each year fresh
revelations rubbed the verdict in. Its advocates were driven back
on such unconvincing pleas as the statement of Mungo Park (who
had recently returned from his first exploration of the interior of
Africa) that, in tribal wars up country, victorious chiefs would
sometimes spare the lives of captives they would otherwise have
slaughtered in order to sell them to the slave traders. More substantial arguments had been met and overthrown. Abolition, said
the Trade, will endanger the islands and the Empire. The truth,
replied Pitt, with unquestionable authority, is exactly the opposite.
Abolition is the *sine qua non* of any improvement in the condition
of the slaves, and this in turn is the only means of checking the
spread of "negro Jacobinism." Well, then, said Dundas, let Abolition
be brought about by the best method—colonial regulation. The
answer to this was even more authoritative; it came from the
colonies themselves. In enacting regulations the Jamaican Assembly
expressly declared that they were "not with any view to the termination of the Slave Trade." And it went farther. It disputed the
right of the Imperial Parliament to carry Abolition against its
will—a defiance which, despite his own argument a few years
earlier, made Dundas (says Wilberforce) "extremely angry with the
Jamaica people." And that was not all. These Jamaica people
finally showed up the *via media* as a blind alley by insisting that the
waste lands of the island must be cultivated, and cultivated by slave-

labour. On the basis of the distribution and supply of slaves in the
past Pitt drily calculated that this would involve the continuance of
the Trade for 240 years.

Assuredly, then, these debates had some effect. The stalwarts of
the Trade in the Commons now numbered only eighty or so. The
rest of its old majority had already reached the stage of abstention.
And since, though they kept away, they could not stop their ears
to the echoes of Wilberforce's moral imperative and Pitt's logic and
Canning's wit, the next stage—conversion to Abolition—was
inevitably drawing nearer every year. And there was a further
value in the debates. They were accustoming public opinion to the
idea that Slavery itself was only less abominable than the Slave
Trade. The Abolitionists had very soon recognised that the assault
on the Trade was only the first phase of a greater campaign. But
they had hesitated to add fuel to the flames of vested interests and
anti-Jacobin prejudices by raising the wider issue. As the case
against the Trade developed, however, the two questions could not
be kept apart. Again and again the argument cropped up that the
Trade should cease, not only because of its inherent evils, but
because it provided new victims for the evils of Slavery. And the
inference was obvious.

At the time, no doubt, it was difficult to realise the silent cumu-
lative effect of these annual debates; and Wilberforce confessed to
the House in 1799 that the prospects of Abolition seemed to him
actually weaker now than they had been when he first raised the
question twelve years before. In 1800, moreover, he consented, for
the first time, to a compromise. Some of the leading members of
the West Indian party told Pitt that they were willing to support a
suspension of the Trade for five years; and to facilitate the introduction of this measure Wilberforce agreed not to move his usual
resolution. But he was reckoning without the "die-hards." A public
meeting was organised and the compromise so vigorously attacked
that it "shook the resolution of our timid converts and all except
Sir William Young turned round." So Wilberforce's concession had
done no good; yet, now that the annual sequence had once been
broken off, he decided to leave it so for a year or two, and it was
not till 1804 that the familiar resolution was again proposed. In
1802, however, in moving for papers, he told the House that he
had not grown cold in the cause and that he would shortly ask them
to reconsider their verdict once more.

Meantime, while he suspended his frontal movement for whole-sale Abolition, Wilberforce was busy with flank attacks upon the Trade. In 1798 he drew Pitt's attention to an Order-in-Council permitting "notwithstanding the war, an intercourse to subsist between our West Indian colonies and those of Spain in which negro slaves are the chief articles for us to supply" and obtained his promise to rescind it. In the same year he averted a more serious menace to the Abolition cause. The conquest of Trinidad and the removal of the Carib tribes from St. Vincent to the mainland after the insurrection of 1796 had provided new areas for cultivation of which the British planters were anxious to avail themselves. Pitt had agreed with the Abolitionists that no new slaves should be imported from Africa for the purpose; but he had almost consented to the planters' proposal that slaves already in their possession might be transferred to the new plantations, though it must surely have been obvious that more slaves would then be bought to fill the gaps on the old plantations, while, on the new plantations, since the cultivation of virgin soil always involved a high death-rate, the planters would soon be raising the old cry—and this time with a better case—that they must import more slaves or be ruined. "Lloyd's Coffee House,"[1] was Stephen's bitter comment, "is in a roar of merriment at the dexterous compromise Mr. Pitt has made between his religious friends and his and Dundas's West India supporters." Wilberforce, however, had still a strong enough hold on Pitt to wreck the scheme. He wrote to him, insisted on an inter-view, and forced him to choose his side. "At last," he says, "got the (proposed) proclamation about slaves rescinded."

There were one or two other small successes. An old Act, which authorised the sale of slaves at the suit of their owners' creditors, was repealed, and a new Act was passed requiring more space between decks in slave-ships and rewarding masters and surgeons for a good bill of health on a voyage. But Wilberforce was not so successful in the matter of the Slave Trade Limitation Bill, a measure brought forward in 1798 and again in 1799 to protect part of the West African coast, especially the neighbourhood of the new colony of Sierra Leone, from the slavers' ravages. On its second reading in 1799 he complains that "Pitt coolly put off the debate when I had manifested a design of answering P.'s speech, and so left misrepresentation without a word"; but he admits, a little

---

[1] The rendezvous of ship-brokers and marine insurance-brokers.

later, that Pitt is "exerting himself" for the Bill; he learns, indeed, that one of the anti-Abolition Ministers has been given "a severe dressing" by his chief before the whole Cabinet. So, in due course, the Bill made its way through the indifferent Commons—the second reading was carried in a tiny House of 60 by a majority of 16—and finally reached the Lords where it was introduced by Grenville, supported eloquently by Bishop Horsley, opposed by Thurlow and the Duke of Clarence, and duly rejected.

5

During these barren years the Clapham Sect had been making, far away from apathetic Westminster, a bold experiment, which, it was hoped, might further the Abolitionist cause more effectively in the end than any amount of hammering at the conscience of Parliament. This experiment had originated in the curious social problem created by the first great act in the British rebellion against Slavery. *Fiat iustitia, ruat coelum*, Lord Mansfield had declared, when, in the course of the Somerset case, allusion was made to the awkward consequences of suddenly freeing the fourteen thousand slaves then estimated to be in England. Justice had been done. The famous judgment had been given. The slaves had been freed in their thousands. And while most of them had remained in the paid service of their masters or found other employment, some hundreds, unwilling or unable to get work, had drifted into idleness and destitution. The negro beggar had soon become a familiar sight in the streets of London; and, some years later, the problem of the black unemployed had been aggravated by the demobilisation of the negroes who had served with the British forces on land and sea in the American war and of whom some had been deposited in Nova Scotia, some in the Bahamas, and some in London. The private charity of the philanthropists had hitherto been the only means of relief; Granville Sharp had himself supported from his slender means a considerable number of regular pensioners; but now it had become evident that more concerted and radical action was required. In 1786, therefore, a "committee for relieving the black poor" was formed; and the result of its discussions was the adoption of a proposal put forward by a certain Dr. Smeathman, an "ingenious and honourable man"—to quote a contemporary—who had lived for three or four years at the foot of the mountains of Sierra Leone. He suggested that the indigent negroes should be transported *en bloc* from London and planted down as a colony in their native Africa. The idea commended itself to the Abolitionists as a means of advancing civilisation in Africa and of proving their repeated assertions that a profitable trade other than that in slaves could be developed there. It also commended itself to Government, who, anxious to rid themselves of the growing nuisance, undertook to provide the cost of transport. What the negroes thought of it is not reported.

In the spring of 1787, then, some few hundred negroes and sixty whites were landed at Sierra Leone. A block of fruitful coastland about twenty miles square, by St. George's Bay, was purchased and in due course formally ceded by King Naimbanna to the British Crown for the use of the settlers, and work was begun on the building of a town. But the little community was soon beset by more than the usual difficulties of an infant colony. Among the negroes were many dissolute idlers who had done no work since they had gained their freedom and, rather than do work now, preferred to wander off into the bush. And among the whites, by some amazing freak or blunder, were several women of easy morals, whose presence was scarcely conducive to the maintenance of health and discipline. Near by, moreover, were slave-depots, French and British, whose agents did all they could to handicap and calumniate the settlement. Finally it had been founded at just the wrong season of the year. The fever-bringing rains set in before the newcomers were acclimatised, and at the end of the first year half of them were dead. The survivors struggled on, their ranks continually thinned still further by desertion, but now keeping disease at bay and cultivating the soil at least enough to meet their immediate needs. And then, in 1789, fell the final blow. One of the inevitable petty conflicts incidental to the Slave Trade had led to the destruction of a neighbouring chief's village by British sailors. In revenge he declared his intention of burning the colonists' little town, and after three days' grace the threat was carried out.

The promoters of the experiment refused to be disheartened by this disastrous start. In 1790 the "St. George's Bay Association" was formed for "opening and establishing a trade in the natural productions of Africa" and in the following year it was invested with a charter and incorporated by Act of Parliament as the Sierra

Leone Company. Sharp was president, Thornton chairman, and Grant and Wilberforce among the first directors. Its meetings at once begin to figure constantly in the diary. In canvassing subscribers Wilberforce is careful to emphasise "the uncertainty of its turning out a profitable concern." The civilisation of Africa and the Abolition of the Slave Trade, not money-making, were its aims. "The design is noble," he wrote to Wyvill, "and I trust it will please God to bless the undertaking." By such honest propaganda substantial capital was quickly raised. And, in the meantime, steps were being taken to save the settlement from extinction. A competent agent was sent out, some sixty of the scattered colonists collected, and a new town begun. In 1792 the negroes who had been demobilised in Nova Scotia requested the Directors to remove them to the more genial climate of Sierra Leone; and, Government having again undertaken to pay for the passage, over 1000 of them were transported to the colony. Public interest in England was increased by this event; more subscriptions came in, till the Company's funds amounted to no less than £240,000; and the colony was well supplied with stores and equipment. A new town, Freetown, was built. A church, a hospital, warehouses were erected. Schools were established and well attended. But, as Clarkson's naval brother, who acted as its Governor for ten months in 1792, soon discovered, the colony's difficulties were not over. Malaria was rife again, and among other visitations of nature, the colony was attacked by "incredible swarms of ants." At another time, a ship laden with African produce for England, worth, £15,000, caught fire and was completely gutted. Many of the recruits from Nova Scotia, moreover, proved far from satisfactory. They clung to the town and refused to cultivate the land. They became insolent and refractory. They demanded a more democratic form of government, sent delegates to state their grievances in England, and, when they returned unsatisfied, broke out in a feeble and short-lived insurrection. It needed a brave and patient man to govern this community; but such a man the Company sent out in 1793, picked from the ranks of the Clapham Sect itself. Yet even Zachary Macaulay's strength was scarcely equal to the task. On him and one colleague the whole life of the place depended—administration, finance, justice, education, even the preaching of sermons and the celebration of marriages. And then there were detailed reports required by the Company and long personal letters demanded, in response to his own, by Wilberforce. Still Macaulay held on, until in 1794, came the crowning disaster. The colony was attacked by a French squadron, piloted by an American slave captain. No resistance was offered; but, despite the Governor's protests, the town was thoroughly pillaged by the Jacobin soldiers and sailors and some of the chief buildings burnt. No wonder that, soon after, Macaulay's health at last broke down; but in 1795, after a short rest in England, he was back at his post. And now the tide began to turn. The French attack, it seems, had done some good. The disaffected Nova Scotians were now more willing to submit to discipline; the damaged town was restored; agriculture and trade increased; in 1798 there were 300 houses and 1200 inhabitants in Freetown, and a profitable business had been established with the surrounding native villages. When Macaulay left in 1799, he could claim that the colony was no longer an experiment but an established institution. In the following year, accordingly, the British Government committed itself yet further. The status of the Company was raised. It became the first of the Chartered Companies, authorised to govern as well as to trade, which were to play their historic part in nineteenth-century Africa—vested with supreme executive and legislative power within the colony and endowed with grants from the British Treasury towards the cost of civil administration and defence. Seven years later the last stage was reached. The Company had done its pioneer work and the Government was ready to relieve it of further responsibility. On January 1, 1808, Sierra Leone became a Crown Colony.

Wilberforce had maintained from the outset the keenest interest in this unique colonial enterprise. He had discussed its early troubles frequently with Pitt and Grenville. He had kept up a steady correspondence with Macaulay. And, despite its chequered fortunes, he could point in the end to the colony as a proof of his old contention that intercourse between Britain and Africa could rest on something better than the Slave Trade. Nor was its example its only service to the cause. When at last the Slave Trade had been made illegal, it was at Sierra Leone that British captains found a home for the rescued victims of piratic slavers; by the end of 1825 it was calculated that nearly 18,000 liberated negroes had been located there. And it was Freetown that became in 1821 the headquarters of British colonial government along the West Coast and the base of the British naval squadrons engaged in hunting trans-Atlantic slavesmugglers. Though the colony to-day is less prosperous and advanced than Nigeria or the Gold Coast, its parents, at any rate, if they could see it, would scarcely recognise what Sharp called "my poor little ill-thriven swarthy daughter, the unfortunate colony of Sierra Leone."

6

Meanwhile the war dragged on into the nineteenth century, and the prospect of a decision seemed no nearer. For a time, indeed, the balance had swung sharply in Britain's favour. In the year after the rupture of Malmesbury's negotiations, Pitt's bold decision to re-enter the Mediterranean, where for more than a year the flag of France had flown unquestioned, had been signally justified. Nelson had missed the French Fleet carrying Napoleon to Egypt, but he had found it again in Aboukir Bay, and in the autumn of 1798 all England had been thrilled by his famous dispatch: "Almighty God has blessed his Majesty's arms by a great victory over the fleet of the enemy who I attacked at sunset on the 1st of August off the mouth of the Nile." ("Are not you almost as delighted with Nelson's letter as with the victory itself?" wrote Wilberforce to Hannah More.) The Continental land-power, moreover, without which no decision was attainable, had been once more added to the British sea-power. The Battle of the Nile, cooping up Napoleon and his army in Egypt, had heartened the Emperors of Austria and Russia to form a Second Coalition, and in 1799 Suvorov and the Austrians had reconquered North Italy, while an Anglo-Russian force had landed in Holland. And then the scales had swung as quickly back again. In the course of the autumn the Austrians had been heavily defeated in Switzerland, the Anglo-Russian army had been compelled to evacuate Holland, and Napoleon, slipping away from Egypt, had returned to Paris and made himself the virtual autocrat of France by the *coup d'état* of Brumaire.

Worse still was to come next year; but before resuming his career of conquest Napoleon made a skilful diplomatic move. On the last Christmas Day of the old century the uncrowned King of France addressed to George III and Francis II a nobly phrased appeal for peace. Ardent Bonapartists have held this act to prove that the greatest war-maker in the history of Europe might have been, had

Fate allowed, its greatest peace-maker. But Pitt and his colleagues did not think so. They believed that Napoleon merely wanted peace in order to consolidate his new hold on France, and, if peace itself were unattainable, hoped, at the least, by these negotiations to break down the only remnant of the Coalition—the Anglo-Austrian alliance. Most critics are agreed, however, that, whether their judgment of the offer was right or wrong, the manner in which they answered it was mistaken. Grenville's reply, with its slighting allusion to the First Consul's status and its suggestion that, if the French wanted peace, they had better restore the legitimate monarchy, may have done some transient good in Vienna; but in Paris it did nothing but harm. It merely made French nationalism more wholeheartedly and more militantly attached to Napoleon and more bitterly averse than ever from the Bourbons.

Not unnaturally, the peace-party in England, who had something yet to learn about Napoleon, were scandalised at this hasty and offensive response to his proposals. The Whig attack on Pitt grew very bitter. And at last Wilberforce began to waver in his support of the Government's conduct of the war. "I am grieved to the heart," he wrote, on hearing of Grenville's dispatch: "fearful that I must differ"; and he braced himself to resume the unpopular part he had played in 1795. But, now as then, he would not commit himself till he had heard Pitt state his case. So yet another of those stern, protracted arguments took place. Once more Pitt recognised the stubbornness and the political influence of Wilberforce's conscience. Once more he tried his hardest to win him to his doctrine of "no peace without security." And this time he succeeded. "Wrote to Pitt, and he sent for me to town," records the diary. "I saw him. Till then I was strongly disposed to condemn the [rejection] of Bonaparte's offer to treat; greatly shocked at it. He shook me." And then, three days later: "Slowly came over to approve of the rejection of Bonaparte's offer, though not of Lord Grenville's letter."

Subsequent events, as in 1795, cemented this agreement. Napoleon's sword was a mightier argument than his pen. In May, 1800, he crossed the Alps. In June he recovered Italy at Marengo. "Pitt's language," wrote Wilberforce to Bankes in July, "is just what we could wish, firm but temperate. He is more sanguine than I am in his expectations, or rather in his opinions, that the Austrians *could* still drive Bonaparte out of the field, if they would exert themselves. But there seems a proper sense of the probable necessity of making peace, with a disposition to assume a firm aspect in order to make it on tolerable terms." But "tolerable terms" were not to be had for the asking; and Pitt's inveterate optimism was soon once more disappointed. In December the Archduke John was heavily defeated at Hohenlinden; and in the following February the Treaty of Lunéville reimposed on Austria roughly the same humiliating conditions as those of the Treaty of Campo Formio four years before. Thus ended the Second Coalition, leaving Britain again with nothing but the mastery of the sea to confront the master of Western Europe.

The fact that this deadlock was as intolerable to Napoleon as to Pitt accounts for the strange interlude of peace which preceded the last, long, finally decisive struggle. The overthrow of British sea-power had become Napoleon's primary object. He sought it first by engineering a combination of the maritime states of the North against England; but the League of the Armed Neutrality was abruptly dissolved by the assassination of its mad leader, the Czar Paul, and the destruction of the Danish fleet by Nelson off Copenhagen. Thus Napoleon was forced back on peace—a peace which would give him time to build an invincible French armada. Circumstances were favourable. In March, 1801, Pitt had resigned; and for more reasons than one the new Ministers were readier than their predecessors to come to terms. "If peace be made," said Wilberforce, "the Government may last." So, on October 1, preliminaries were signed in London, and five months later the Peace of Amiens was concluded.

Wilberforce was with Gisborne at Yoxall when letters from Pitt and Addington told him of the preliminaries. "Fireworks at the Lodge for the Peace," says the diary for October 6: "the children were delighted." Next day he sets out for Bath and notes on his arrival: "The people *intoxicated* with joy here and everywhere. Grand illumination." And he shared himself in the general relief and thanksgiving. "God has of His mercy to this sinful nation," he declared, "allowed a suspension of the work of death and desolation." And he confesses that, if Government had refused the terms, he must have voted with the Opposition. He was rejoiced to find that Pitt approved them, though they were worse for Britain than any he had himself proposed. "We shall have a scene of strange discordance," he writes of the imminent debate: "Lord Grenville is to oppose in the House of Lords and Lord Spencer also; and Windham still more warmly in the House of Commons; but Pitt will support with all his might." Yet, if Pitt admitted that, since the dissolution of the Second Coalition, to make peace was to make the best of a bad job, he denied that he had changed his mind about Napoleon. "I am inclined to hope everything that is good," he said, "but I am bound to act as if I feared otherwise." And Wilberforce, with all his religious hatred of war, could not be more enthusiastic. In reply to Windham's denunciation of Ministers for signing "the death-warrant of their country," he could only urge that, even if the peace should last no longer than three months, it was right, none the less, to conclude it. It would "give Europe a proof of our pacific disposition" and enable us to make "friends who might be of service to us when we should be compelled to enter into a new contest." He guessed, in fact, like most shrewd Englishmen, that the peace was only a truce, only a "suspension," though no one's joy would have been greater than his if indeed the nineteenth century had brought with it the one thing needed to lighten the dreary field of British politics, to ease the hardships of the poor, and, among other accessories of a new age, to ensure the swift triumph of Abolition.

7

Some of Wilberforce's friends had hoped that he might be given a place in a Peace Government; and he confesses himself that, when the news of the change arrived, he "was for a little intoxicated and had risings of ambition." But the following Sunday brought its usual antidote. "Blessed be God," he exclaims in his spiritual journal, "for the day of rest and religious occupation, wherein earthly things assume their true size and comparative insignificance. Ambition is stunted. . . ." In any case, despite his ability, his eloquence, his influence in the country, Wilberforce had no chance of office. For Addington, though he had no great love for the Slave Trade, was not prepared to face the difficulties and discussions which lay in wait for a Prime Minister who pledged his Government to Abolition. A follower of Dundas's "middle way," he was by no means so strong an Abolitionist as Pitt, and, if he had been, he was not the man to dare what Pitt had never dared.

Doubtless, therefore, he had little hesitation in deciding to leave Wilberforce's importunate conscience outside his Cabinet. But he could not altogether escape it. He had not been long at Downing Street before Wilberforce was there with a plan for including in the peace negotiations a proposal for a general Convention of the Powers to consider a joint suppression of the Trade; and the New Year brought him a long, reasoned letter, begging him to take over the leadership of the great crusade and secure its triumph at the Conference of Amiens. "It is not (to a friend I may make the avowal) without emotion," wrote Wilberforce, "that I relinquish the idea of being myself the active and chief agent in terminating this greatest of all human evils; but *you* will readily believe me when I say that any unpleasant sensations on this head vanish at once before the prospect of effecting the desired object far more radically and completely than by any springs I could set in motion." Nothing came of the proposal. It is doubtful whether anything could have come of it. Otto, the French minister in London, had indeed assured Wilberforce that, "if our Government would propose to negotiate for Abolition, then theirs would probably consent to it." But their Government was Napoleon; and Napoleon was already seizing the opportunity of the truce to pursue across the Atlantic the mirage of Empire that had failed him in the East. Undaunted by Pitt's experience he had recently dispatched some 25,000 French troops to fight against Toussaint and the yellow fever for the mastery of St. Domingue; and he was contemplating the transfer of Louisiana from Spain which, could he ever have enforced it against the veto of the United States, would have given France the whole of North America west of the Mississippi and south of the Canadian Lakes. The moment of launching such schemes of imperial expansion was clearly not the moment to abolish the Slave Trade, to antagonise commercial and colonial interests, to cut off the supply of labour for new settlements. Even, then, if Addington had surprisingly accepted Wilberforce's plan and still more surprisingly persuaded Parliament to accept it, the supreme surprise would have been Napoleon's concurrence.

Within a fortnight came another letter. The danger that the unoccupied lands in Trinidad and St. Vincent should be sold without safeguards against the importation of new slaves was again acute. "You perhaps may not know," wrote Wilberforce, "that for several years past Pitt has been assailed by sap and by storm in all

directions and from all quarters.. . . . but he never would give way."
And, on the heels of the letter, came Pitt himself, spurred on by
Wilberforce. "My dear Wilberforce," he wrote next day, "I have
had a long conversation with Addington, and have great reason to
hope from it that he has in no degree committed himself on any
point that can lead to an increased importation of negroes. . . Ever
affectionately yours, W. Pitt." So far, so good; but it was scarcely
safe to leave it at that. "Went after Canning," says the diary a few
days later. He found him "staunch and warm for Abolition" and
persuaded him to raise the question of the unoccupied lands in the
House. The results of this move were more substantial. To a long
and forcible speech from Canning Addington replied by pledging
himself not to authorise the sale of any land in Trinidad without
submitting the conditions to Parliament. He also professed a hope
—but only a hope, as Wilberforce complained—that the policy of
"gradual Abolition," which he had so warmly embraced in 1792
and so coldly neglected ever since, might be reconsidered next year.

But the events of the next year once more thrust the whole
question far into the background. Wilberforce had refrained from
moving his customary resolution in 1801 and again in 1802 in
order that its almost certain defeat should not prejudice his new
proposal for a European Convention. He was about to bring it
forward, however, in the spring of 1803, when Parliament was
informed by royal message of the recall of the British and French
ambassadors and the imminence of war. "You can conceive," he
writes to Babington, "what would be said by Lord Hawkesbury &
Co. if I were to propose the Abolition now." The inevitable indeed
had happened. Addington had spoken of the peace as "a real reconciliation of the two foremost nations in the world." Fox had been
to Paris and come back a warm admirer of Napoleon. But neither
of them had heard Napoleon confessing at the time that "every
treaty of peace means to me no more than a brief armistice." His
deeds, however, had soon proved more eloquent than words. He
had not even had the patience to wait till his great fleet should
emerge from the scaffolding that crowded every dockyard in France.
He had annexed Piedmont and Elba, reinforced his hold on Switzerland, and maintained French garrisons in Italy and Holland. And
he had directly provoked Britain by resuming his designs on the
Levant—discussing the partition of Turkey with the Czar, hinting
at a French occupation of the Peloponnese, and dispatching a mis-

sion to Egypt which publicly reported that its reconquest would be an easy matter. Not unnaturally the British Government had thereupon decided not to evacuate Malta, the strategic safeguard of the Mediterranean, as the terms of peace required. Protests and counter-protests had led to the famous scene in Josephine's drawing-room when Napoleon lost his temper with the British ambassador and railed at him "like a captain of dragoons." "He spoke loud enough," Wilberforce was told, "to be heard by two hundred people, and his countenance was perfectly distorted with passion." Though it was Britain that formally presented the ultimatum, that outburst of Napoleon's was practically a declaration of war. In May hostilities were resumed.

Wilberforce was not exempt from the average Englishman's sentiments. "The news," he notes, of Lord Whitworth's recall from Paris, "had the effect on the sudden of making me feel a sort of intoxicating flush." But, if he did not think, as he had thought ten years before, that war could be avoided, he held that British Ministers had needlessly impaired their moral case by insisting on the retention of Malta as a condition of continued peace, instead of being satisfied with its independence and neutrality. So strongly did he feel on the point that, in the debate on the rupture, as soon as Pitt had finished his defence of Addington's Government and before Grey and Fox had opened the Whig attack, he declared himself in opposition. "Malta," he said, "is indeed a valuable possession, but the most valuable of all the possessions of this country is its good faith. . . . This, then, in my grand objection to the conduct of Ministers, that by claiming the possession of Malta instead of its independence . . . they gave an inveterate enemy an opportunity of mis-stating our real views both to France and to Europe." The House was "very impatient"; "they tried over and over again," says Creevey, "to cough him down"; and when it came to the vote, Wilberforce found himself in a minority of 67 to 398.

Fox knew Wilberforce too well by now to repeat his old mistake. There was no more question in 1803 than there had been in 1795 of his joining the Opposition camp. His conscience obeyed, his one vote of censure registered, Wilberforce was prepared to support Addington's Government no less loyally than Pitt's in its conduct of the war. And soon the rights and wrongs of pre-war diplomacy were driven from all men's minds by the instancy and gravity of the danger which the war itself brought. The domination of Europe,

visions of Empire East or West, everything was now subordinated
in Napoleon's purpose to the conquest of the island people whose
stubborn independence seemed now the only barrier to the limitless
extension of his power. The tents of the "Army of England" soon
stretched along the coast from Ostend to Dieppe; the ports were
crowded with its ferry-boats; while, divided between harbours as
far apart as Brest and Cadiz and Toulon, the French and Spanish
frigates waited for a chance to unite and hold the Channel for the
few days needed to achieve the invasion. In face of such a danger
all Britain was at last "one breath" for war as it had never been
since Chatham's days. But, though party-spirit could be held in
leash, though every one's desire might be to strengthen the Government's hands, the country and its representatives soon began to
chafe at Ministers' seeming inefficiency. "They seem everywhere
in low estimation," notes Wilberforce in the autumn of 1803. In
the Pump-Room at Bath he meets visitors from all parts of England,
and by them all (he says) "they are accused of gross remissness and
incapacity." A little later he complains of the inexplicable delay in
providing arms for his Yorkshire volunteers. "It is shocking work;
yet, not being quite clear that there is much real blame, I do not
like to speak of it in the House." There were more militant critics
who did not control their impatience. "Windham & Co. strong in
opposition," says the diary in December. "Fox manifestly drawing
towards them. . . . 'Tis said that Sheridan tried to frighten him by
saying, ' You will get Pitt in again, if you oppose.' He peevishly
says, ' I can't bear fools, anything but fools.'" It was indeed inevitable that Addington's capacity should be questioned, not so much,
perhaps, on the intrinsic merits or demerits of his case as because he
was standing in the shoes of an indisputably greater man. As even
the Whigs were bound to admit, the country wanted the old "pilot"
back on the bridge. Pitt, however, refused to come out in opposition.
He had pledged himself, when he left office, to support Addington;
and, though he thought his measures dangerously weak, he would
not vote against them. But the tide of genuine, patriotic distrust
and anxiety ran stronger and stronger, and it was swelled by the
lesser current of personal intrigue. Spirits so discordant as Fox
and Grenville were thrown into strange alliance. And at last, in
April, 1804, convinced that the state of the country was now too
critical to justify his holding any longer to his three-year-old
promise, Pitt abandoned the aloofness that had dismayed and

irritated his admirers, and followed Fox in an unequivocal attack on the Government.

Wilberforce had been deeply impressed by Pitt's earlier generosity to Addington, and he observed his gradual change of front uneasily. "He is surrounded by men of party spirit without his integrity and of strong passions." And though Pitt talked long with him and gave him his full confidence, his misgivings were not dissipated. "I fear he has been urged forward by people of less wisdom than himself." What he personally desired and had personally pressed on each of them was a union of Pitt and Addington. He liked Addington despite his lukewarm attitude to Abolition. He liked his peaceableness and his sobriety as much as he disliked Windham's bellicosity or Fox's vehemence. "I cannot help regretting," he says, "that Addington's temperance and conciliation should not be connected with more vigour." And again, "Poor Addington! With all his faults I feel for him."

Had he foreseen the upshot of the crisis, he would have been still more uneasy. It was Pitt's desire, as it was certainly the country's, that in this perilous hour the ablest men in all parties should combine; and he proposed to the King the formation of a Coalition Government including Fox, Grenville and Windham. But George III was scandalised. Make Fox a minister! He was astonished, he told Pitt, that he should "one moment harbour the thought of bringing such a man before his Royal notice." And since, as it happened, the King was once more just recovered from a serious illness, Pitt could not fight him. For over three hours he argued with him as firmly as he dared. With great difficulty he won his consent to the inclusion of the Grenvillites; but, as he had previously confided to Wilberforce, he could not *force* Fox on him. And so it was once more the Minister, though this time the people were more certainly behind him, that submitted, and the wilful man, whom Lord Chancellor Eldon had recently described as "my poor old master," that had his way. It was Pitt's death sentence. Since the Grenville group rejected Fox's patriotic advice and refused to serve unless he were included, Pitt was compelled to form a Government of mainly second-rate men, half Pittites, half Addingtonians, with all a Coalition's drawbacks and none of its advantages. It meant that the enormous burden lay almost wholly on his own shoulders; and presently it broke them.

IX

Victory

I

IN one sense Pitt's return to power was a personal loss to Wilberforce. His relations with the Prime Minister could not be so close and happy as his relations with the private citizen. At times, indeed, towards the close of Pitt's previous tenure of office, their old friendship had been sadly strained. For Wilberforce, as the years went by, had begun to fear that Pitt was not doing all he might do for Abolition. Surely, he kept on thinking, Pitt *could* carry it if only he *would*. Was he not indispensable now to King and country? Could he not compel his colleagues and his party to do almost anything he liked? And when Wilberforce found that even on subordinate Slave Trade questions, such as that of the unoccupied lands, it needed ceaseless watchfulness on his part to combat Pitt's apparent apathy or negligence, he was bitterly disappointed. He knew, too, that his importunity must often worry Pitt, however kindly he concealed it. "Our friendship has starved for want of nutriment," he confessed to a friend in 1798. "I really love him for his public qualities and his private ones. . . . But how can I expect he should love me much, who have been so long rendering myself in various ways vexatious to him."

On one occasion, about this time, Pitt certainly was vexed and did not hide it. The affair of Whit Sunday, 1798, was a queer affair, one of the queerest in the personal annals of British politics. On that day, although it was in the course of a great war and his was the main responsibility for the conduct of it, the Prime Minister fought a duel with pistols against a member of the Opposition. It is true that Tierney's insistent and irresponsible abuse of Pitt and his policy had become wellnigh insupportable; and it is true that, losing his patience at last, Pitt had insulted Tierney by charging him, not altogether falsely, with obstructing the defence of the country. Yet the challenge should neither have been made nor accepted; and it is not surprising that Wilberforce was shocked, "more shocked than almost ever," when he heard of it. It was not only that his friend had risked his life, nor only that both men had set their private feelings before their patriotism. Any duel, under any circumstances, was in Wilberforce's eyes a defiance of God; he had himself on that account evaded Rolleston's challenge; and he was appalled that Pitt of all men should have sanctioned such an impious barbarity by his own example. He at once resolved to do what he could to prevent such a thing happening again, and he hurried up to town to give notice of a motion against duelling. Pitt was angry at this interference—all the angrier, perhaps, if now that the affair was over, his own conscience had begun to prick him. He wrote Wilberforce a rather curt letter. "Your motion," he said, "is one for my removal." Other friends joined their remonstrances to Pitt's; and Wilberforce realising, as he might well have done before, that Pitt's part in the affair must preclude a straight vote on the principle of duelling, withdrew his motion. The incident was closed in an epistolary *réunion*. "I need not tell you," wrote Wilberforce, "that the idea of my being compelled to do anything painful or embarrassing to you has hurt me not a little." "I am, and I trust I ever shall be," he concluded, "your affectionate and faithful friend, W. Wilberforce." "I cannot say to you," replied Pitt, "how much I am relieved by your determination. . . . Much less can I tell you how sincerely I feel your cordial friendship and kindness on all occasions, as well when we differ as when we agree. Every affectionately yours, W. Pitt."

And always, in Wilberforce's heart, was the regretful, almost resentful, feeling that he could never be as truly intimate with Pitt as he could be with Thornton or Stephen or almost any brother of the Sect. Some years earlier, in 1792, he had made an effort to renew that candid conversation of 1786, when he paid a visit to Walmer Castle where Pitt had recently been installed as Warden of the Cinque Ports. "Pitt received me very kindly," says the diary, "and with great warmth of affection." Next day he had his chance. "At night alone with Pitt, but talked politics only—did not find myself equal to better talk. I came here hoping that I might really find an opportunity of talking seriously with Pitt. What am I to do so with any one? O Christ, help me." Next morning he was at it again. "Had some serious talk with Pitt—interrupted or should have had more." It was his last opportunity; and while he confesses, at the close of his visit, his admiration of Pitt's "integrity, public spirit, and magnanimity in despising unpopularity," he cannot give him the highest praise of all: he cannot say he is religious. Indeed even wondered sometimes whether he ought to want so often and so much to be with Pitt and "the old firm." "This is the day," says the diary once, "in which Pitt, Dundas, P. Arden, and Steele are at Hamels. I am disposed to wish myself with them. I find that even here in religious society I can have an earthly mind." And when he is with them, he is not altogether happy. The comments in the diary and journal on a stay at Holwood in 1799 are eloquent enough. "Pitt, Canning, and Pepper Arden came in late to dinner. I attacked Canning on indecency of Anti-Jacobin. Evening he and Pitt reading classics." And next day: "My heart has been moved by the society of my old friends at Pitt's. Alas! alas! how sad to see them thoughtless of their immortal souls; so wise, so acute!" A few days later he attends a party at Dundas's in Pitt's honour. "Pitt's birthday—low-spirited—dined Dundas' great entertainment—Duke and Duchess of Gordon and others. I could not assimilate, and all flat and cold."

So the old friendship had creaked along till the change of Government in 1801 at last freed Wilberforce from the worry of Pitt's shortcomings over Abolition and freed Pitt from the worry of Wilberforce's importunity. And, as it happened, any such sense of disappointment or irritation in that matter as lingered on in the back of Wilberforce's mind was now lost at once in his unbounded admiration of Pitt's conduct in supporting his untried successor. The diary overflows with eulogies. "What wonderful magnanimity!" "Unparalleled in a politician." "I do not wonder if it is misunderstood. . . . Little minds cannot receive the idea; it is too grand for their comprehension. But to any one who fairly considers it in all its bearings . . . it will appear one of the noblest instances of magnanimity that was ever exhibited to the admiration and imitation of mankind." And now the records of meetings and talks became more frequent again as if indeed something like the old familiarity was being at last restored. "Pitt and Rose dined with me quietly to-day. Pitt very pleasant, and we stayed chatting politics." He meets Pitt at a country-house party, walks with him, and talks with him till after midnight, and has another "long discussion" with him after breakfast. On another occasion he and Pitt are talking tête-à-tête all day "from breakfast to dinner." There is real affection, too, in his anxiety at Pitt's taking command of 3000 of the Cinque Port volunteers in the raising and equipment of which the Lord Warden was now spending all his time and much of his money. "I am uneasy at it," he writes. "He does not engage on equal or common terms, and his spirit will lead him to be foremost in the battle"—and so it might have been if, as every one expected, the French had landed on the Kentish coast. Yet his very anxiety forces the truth on Wilberforce. He knows it is not quite what he would have felt ten or fifteen years ago. He knows that the tie between them has gradually weakened, that in their inmost thoughts they have drifted apart. Indeed, as he reflects, he is almost surprised at his anxiety. "For many years," he tells Gisborne, "there has been so little of the *eadem velle et nolle* that there cannot have existed much of what merits the name of friendship for that great man, yet I feel a good deal for him on account of the danger to which he is exposed." That *yet* is significant. There was a gap between them: it might be obscured, it might gradually be narrowed, during the interlude of Pitt's retirement: but it was bound to stand out bleakly again as soon as he returned to office. And unhappily there was time, before the end came, for each of them to widen it.

2

It might be supposed that, since it was merely the King's prejudice that had prevented the formation of a Coalition, the new Government would have been conceded some measure of support or at least of tolerance from a united House of Commons inspired by a single purpose of saving the country from Napoleon. As a matter of fact, the opposition to Pitt, though it could no longer be urged that the safety of the nation required the removal of an incompetent Prime Minister, was no less vivacious than the opposition to Addington. Never, indeed, during his previous term of office had he been exposed to such a weight of attack. Fox and his followers were there as of old: they had returned from their tents before the Peace of Amiens; and now they were reinforced by Grenville and Windham whose criticism of Pitt could scarcely have been more bitter if he had thrust them out of his Ministry with contumely instead of pleading earnestly with the King for their admission. It was a strong combination, and Pitt's colleagues were

w.   Q no match for it. Except for Dundas's experience and Canning's wit they were not a powerful parliamentary team and they worked ill together. Nor were any good recruits available outside. There was only Addington; and his appointment as President of the Council, with the title of Lord Sidmouth, at the end of 1804 betrayed the Government's weakness rather than added to its strength. To make bad worse, Pitt was dogged by a disheartening sense of insecurity. Five physicians were in attendance on the King, watching his aberrations; and every one thought that, if once he crossed the border-line and the Prince came into his own, Pitt would go out and Fox come in.

No lesser man than Pitt could have carried on the King's Government against these domestic odds in time of war—the greatest war in which Britain had ever been engaged and now, moreover, at its most critical stage—and Pitt at forty-five was a very different person from the young Prime Minister of 1783. The physical strain was now evident. Men noted that he was thinner than ever and worried with a cough. But by drawing on his last reserves of strength he succeeded in holding his Government together and his enemies at bay. For nearly a year he maintained his majority in the House of Commons; and then at last came a chance for the Opposition to inflict a blow which shook the credit of his Government, though it did not actually bring about its fall, and shook still more disastrously Pitt's fast-failing health.

In the winter of 1804 the political world was buzzing with rumours of a financial scandal at the Admiralty. The affair was some years old; but since it dated back to Pitt's previous Government and since Dundas, who was now his First Lord of the Admiralty, was the villain of the piece, it was clearly the business of the Opposition not to let the scandal die. And, awkward as it was for him, Pitt, whose views on administrative corruption were notoriously strict, could not attempt to hush the matter up. He had appointed a Commission to inquire into the allegations, and its report on those charges which implicated Melville was published in March, 1805. It happened that Wilberforce was closeted with Pitt, discussing a Slave Trade question, when the first copy of it was delivered. "I shall never forget," he says, "the way in which he seized it, and how eagerly he looked into the leaves without waiting even to cut them open." There was good reason for his anxiety. The report stated that Mr. Trotter, Deputy Treasurer of the Navy, had used £10,000 of public money for private speculation and that Dundas, as Treasurer, could and should have prevented it. Neither then, nor at any time, was it suggested that Dundas had profited himself by such transactions.

The common belief that Pitt took this matter so deeply to heart because of his personal feeling for his old political comrade is exploded by Wilberforce's testimony. He had closely marked Pitt's relations with Dundas. Years ago, as we have seen, he had learned to regard that worldly Scot as Pitt's evil genius: and he was inclined to ascribe to his influence most of Pitt's shortcomings as to Abolition and in other things. So it was probably with some satisfaction that he had observed a rapid cooling of their friendship. A year before this crisis he had noted that "Lord Melville had not the power over Pitt's mind which he had once possessed"; and now he says, "While it was generally thought that Pitt defended Melville out of friendship, I knew that they were scarcely upon speaking terms." And, indeed, a breach is not surprising. For the revelations of the Commission had showed, if Wilberforce is to be believed, that on this very question Dundas had lied to Pitt. "Some years before," to quote Wilberforce's private memorandum on the affair, "Mr. Raikes [Governor of the Bank of England in 1797] had hinted to him that the public money was illegally employed. Dundas soon after coming in, Pitt said to him at once, 'Dundas, here has been Tom Raikes to me with a long story of your way of employing the public money; what does he mean?' Dundas assured him that it was their mistake, and that no money had been drawn except for public service." Under such circumstances Pitt could scarcely have been blamed if he had left Dundas to fight his own battle; and for the credit of his present Government, to adopt an aloof and impartial attitude might well have been to make the best of a bad business. But he determined on a more dangerous course. Was it because he felt his own honour was involved? Or did he shrink from throwing so old a colleague to the wolves, although he had betrayed his trust? Or did he think that, his Government being so weak, an attempt should be made to clear Dundas, however great the risk? That, at any rate, was the course he took. When the Opposition opened its inevitable attack on April 8 with Whitbread's resolutions, some of which directly censured Melville, Pitt at once moved an amendment that the Commission's Report should be referred to a Select Committee of the House for further investigation, on the ground that the complicated Admiralty accounts and especially Melville's share in them had not been adequately examined. Could he secure his amendment, he might hope in the end to carry the same majority with him either to Melville's complete exoneration or at least to some milder reflections on his conduct. But if he lost it, as well he might on such uncertain ground, the defeat would be far more damaging to him and to his Government than if he had held his tongue. It might indeed involve his resignation.

Once before, it will be remembered, in the course of a debate on the conduct of a public servant, Pitt had been influenced by Wilberforce's conscience. This time he could not himself appeal to it. This time, on the contrary, he dreaded its effect on others. For it was just on a personal question of this sort, on a point of official morality, on the behaviour of Melville as on that of Warren Hastings, that Wilberforce's judgment was certain to carry weight; and the very fact that Pitt had not consulted Wilberforce shows that he knew too well what that judgment was likely to be. It was a stormy night in the House. Pitt's own speech had been interrupted by violent outcries from the Opposition, and as the debate dragged on into the early hours and the issue became more and more uncertain, the strain began to tell on him. When at last about 4 o'clock, Wilberforce rose from his seat just behind the Treasury Bench, it was observed that Pitt lent forward and cast him an appealing glance. It reached its mark. "It required no little effort," confessed Wilberforce afterwards, "to resist the fascination of that penetrating eye." But the appeal was too late. Not without a painful struggle, Wilberforce had inexorably made up his mind on the basis of certain simple, undisputed facts contained in the Report. And now, in a short and quiet speech, he judged the case in the way posterity has judged it, in the only possible way.

It seems to me that, if I am willing to admit all which the advocates of Lord Melville argue for, yet I am equally bound to vote for the original motion. If the House were to step out of its way to adjust all the shades of criminality which belong to this case, then indeed it might be necessary to take some proceeding or other similar to that which has been recommended to us by my right honourable friend, the Chancellor of the Exchequer. But here is a plain, broad fact which no subsequent elucidation can possibly explain away. Here is Lord Melville publicly declaring on his oath that he has tolerated his dependent in a gross breach of an Act of Parliament for the purpose of private emolument. . . . If the House were once to suffer a Minister to say that he had connived at a breach of the law by a person who had been his confidential servant for a number of years, and that the superior was to pass uncensured because no personal corruption had been proved against him; if that were once to be admitted as a principle by which the House of Commons is to be directed, it would open a door to every species of corruption, and there would be no security left for the faithful discharge of any public trust.

After dealing, in a similar strain, with the plea that Mr. Trotter's transactions had not actually involved the country in any financial loss, he reminded the House that as the constitutional guardian of the people's purse it was on its trial no less than Lord Melville, and so sat down.

No wonder that, as soon as he had heard the first few sentences of this speech, Pitt sank back in his seat with a gesture of dismay. No wonder that, during the rest of it, his feelings, usually so stonily concealed, were evident to all who watched him. When, shortly after, the division was taken, it was clear that Wilberforce's speech had done its work. Some said he had turned as many as forty votes, but one would have been enough. The figures were 216 for the motion and 216 against. The Speaker's casting-vote was needed and all eyes were turned on the Chair. Abbot went "as white as a sheet." There was a painful silence. For ten minutes he sat still: and then, after a few words of explanation, "I shall give my vote with the ayes," he said; "and so the ayes have it." Instantly the Opposition burst into a roar of triumph. "Resign," "resign," they shouted at Pitt. The hunt was up and one excited country-gentleman uttered a shrill "view holloa" and cried, "We have killed the fox." Other ungallant members crowded round the door to wait for the House to empty and "see how Billy Pitt looked after it." In earlier years there would have been nothing to see. He would have faced worse defeats and deeper humiliation without a change in that stiff, proud demeanour. But now, for the only time on record, he betrayed his emotions in public. He sat still in his place with his little cocked hat pressed down over his forehead to hide the tears of mortification that crept down his cheeks; and presently, with a bodyguard of faithful friends to screen him from those vulgar spies, he was helped out of the House in a state of complete nervous exhaustion.

A year later, when Pitt was dead, a devoted Yorkshire Pittite told Wilberforce he could not vote for him at the election because of what he had done that night. "I believe," he wrote, "that the delinquency of Lord Melville and the desertion of some of his oldest friends inflicted a wound upon his mind [from] which it never recovered, and [which] contributed to his premature death." "It did not injure Pitt's health," is Wilberforce's "docket" on the letter. Maybe it did not, though the contrary seems probable; but even if Pitt, like his father, had gone straight from Parliament to his death-bed, Wilberforce, though he must have been terribly distressed, could have felt no remorse. And surely, when it was all over, Pitt himself must have recognised that he had placed his friend in a dilemma, and that, knowing the man as he did, he ought to have foreseen which choice he was bound to make. In any case he showed no outward sign of resentment. For the little time that was left, his relations with Wilberforce were just as much short of intimacy as they had been before the Melville case—and no more. He would have been scarcely human, however, if the affair had really made no difference to his feelings. He might blame himself in retrospect; but the fact remained that the hand which had dealt him the deepest wound of his political life was Wilberforce's.

And what of Melville? He at once resigned and retired to his Scottish home. But the Opposition continued its attack. It demanded and obtained his impeachment—and this with a bitter and exultant vehemence which soon overreached itself and swung back the tide of public opinion towards Melville as the victim of a factious persecution. From this spirit Wilberforce, of course, was wholly free. He had done his duty, but he took no kind of pleasure in the result. Though he had detested Melville's worldly ways and deplored his influence over Pitt, though it was Melville more than any other politician who had prevented the success of the cause he had most at heart, he had always felt a liking for him. "Must I join the triumph over a fallen friend?" he indignantly replied to one who urged him to join the deputation which carried up the resolutions to St. James's. Inevitably, however, he was regarded by all Melville's partisans as the author of his ruin. Indeed, it was the truth. For, although his impeachment before the Lords in the summer of 1806 resulted in his acquittal on all counts, that earlier vote in the House of Commons had made it impossible for him ever to serve again as a Minister of the Crown. But Melville himself, assuredly no Puritan, possessed virtues which Puritans sometimes lack; and in his attitude to Wilberforce he proved himself bigger-hearted than his friends. A long time passed before the two men saw each other again; but, about a year before Melville's death in 1811, they came suddenly face to face in the narrow passage between the Horse Guards and Downing Street. They recognised each other, as they were bound to do at such close quarters; and for a moment Wilberforce thought Melville was going to pass him by without a word. But he was wrong. "Ah, Wilberforce, how do you do?" cried the genial old Scot and shook him heartily by the hand. "I would have given a thousand pounds for that shake," says Wilberforce, and adds, "I never saw him afterwards."

3

If Pitt's last Government had been stronger, the Melville affair need not have been so painfully important. Nor, if his Government had been stronger, need Pitt, in these last years, have exasperated Wilberforce more grievously than ever before by his conduct in the matter of the Slave Trade.

It might have seemed, at first sight, as if the return of Pitt, who had always professed himself an Abolitionist, in place of Addington, who had always disliked and temporised with Abolition, was the only thing needed to bring about the long-awaited triumph of the cause. For now at last—there could be no mistake this time—the tide was coming in. In a sense, indeed, the Abolitionists had decided the issue by their first crusade. From the moment the British people had been fully and authoritatively informed of the black truth about the Trade, Abolition sooner or later was certain. And it would have come sooner, despite the initial success of Dundas's obstructive strategy, if the first popular impulse had not been confused and checked by the counter-impulses excited by Jacobinism and the Revolutionary War. As it was, though the conviction of sin had been thrust into a corner of the nation's mind during the years of fighting, it had not been eradicated; and, all the while, it had been kept alive by the quiet propaganda of the Abolitionists. The literature about the Trade had steadily increased. The outspoken

opinions of high-minded men all over the country had worked
silently on their neighbours' thoughts. Almost every year men had
read in the newspapers the report of Wilberforce's motion. Gradually, moreover, the anti-Jacobin fury had died down. For many
years yet, it is true, any general advance of liberal ideas was still
to be retarded; vague suspicions of sedition among the working-
classes could still inspire repression; but Englishmen were not quite
so ready as they had been in Robespierre's day to detect a red streak
of Republicanism in every humane crusade. Republicanism, moreover, was dead in France, slain, as Burke had long ago foretold, by
a "popular general's" sword. It mattered less and less, then, that
the cause of Abolition had once been tainted by its Republican
supporters. And so, when the Peace of Amiens lifted for a time the
obsession of war, and nullified for a time the anti-Abolition arguments based on the needs and dangers of war, all the conditions were
favourable for the opening of another active campaign—all but
one. That one, as has been seen, was Addington's dislike of Abolition.

Yet, despite Addington and despite even the renewal of the war,
the hopes of the Abolitionists still rose. In addition to the general
re-awakening of the public conscience, the cause now enjoyed two
tactical advantages. First, the Trade was divided. A majority of
its supporters could still indeed be persuaded by their extremist
leaders to refuse a single inch of compromise; but a strong minority,
alarmed at the probable effect on their profits of the rapid cultivation of sugar in the richer soil of Demerara, Berbice, Essequibo,
and Surinam, lately annexed from the Dutch, were ready to accept
a suspension of the supply of slave-labour for at least a few years.
Secondly, the Act of Union had now brought to the House of
Commons a hundred Irish members, with no local interests in the
Trade nor any special or political connexion therewith, bound too
by no previous votes or pledges, and eager for the most part to
assert their national humanity by supporting Abolition.

Under these happier auspices, the Abolition Committee, strengthened by the inclusion of Stephen, Macaulay, and Brougham, resumed
in the spring of 1804 the activities it had suspended since 1797; and
it was decided that Wilberforce should once more propose in the
Commons that familiar motion he had dropped since 1799. No one,
of course, expected an immediate success. It was too much to hope
that the minority in favour of total Abolition, at once and for all
time, though it was certain to be greatly increased, could be turned

into a positive majority. But before the day for the motion had been fixed Addington fell; and the Committee, hurriedly reconsidering its plans, decided that, though Pitt would never give them all they wanted, he might give them something—something that, at his bidding, would certainly be carried. So, a few days after Pitt's return to Downing Street, Wilberforce was there again, entreating him now to take advantage of the division in the ranks of the West Indian faction and, in concert with the moderates, to propose himself, officially, a suspension of the Trade for a period of years. Somewhat to Wilberforce's surprise, Pitt at once consented; and an interview with Mr. Milligan, one of the moderates, was quickly arranged. But nothing came of it. "My conversation with Milligan," wrote Pitt to Wilberforce, the morning before the debate, "amounted only to this, that he and other sensible West Indians wished for the suppression; but the great majority would oppose it, many from adherence to former opinion, and more from the fear that, if once suspended, the Trade would never be revived. In this state, and having had no time to settle anything with any part of the Cabinet, I see no use in moving the suspension, unless anything arises in the debate to give a favourable opening for it."

It was to be all or nothing then, when, on May 30, Wilberforce rose again to ask the Commons' leave to introduce an Abolition Bill. Whatever their opinions might now be, it was clear at the outset that at any rate members took a deeper interest in the question. The House was by no means full, but the attendance was twice as big as those which had rejected the motion in several previous years. In other respects the debate was like its predecessors. Wilberforce once more outlined the whole case with admirable clarity and studied moderation. Pitt, in a short speech, welcomed the new converts to the cause and declared that the best kind of Abolition was total Abolition, and the best moment for it the earliest possible moment, but promised—with an eye on his divided colleagues—to support a partial or gradual measure if nothing better were attainable. Fox's speech was also short. His main point was that the honour of the country was at stake. It was being "whispered throughout Europe," he said, "that, however we might like lessons of morality, we could not be prevailed upon to give up a profitable branch of commerce very readily." Forty seconds, by Wilberforce's reckoning, was enough for Addington's bald assertion that Abolition was impracticable. Of other old supporters of the Trade, Tarleton and Fuller and Manning stubbornly maintained their opposition, but Barham announced his conversion. The most striking incident was the intervention of the Irish members. They had held that night, to quote the diary, "a great Irish dinner, 33 or 34 dining together," at which Lord De Blaquière, their leader, had proposed the health of Wilberforce for a toast. They had then trooped into the House to vote for him; and, rising last but one in the debate, De Blaquière declared that, though the question was new to Irishmen, they had no difficulty in coming to a unanimous decision on it. A few minutes later, the division was taken. In a House of 173, no less than 124 voted for Wilberforce's motion and only 49 against it.

Success at last!—and far exceeding Wilberforce's hopes. Congratulations again poured in on him—amongst others from Jeremy Bentham, whose friendship he had won some years before by his active, though unavailing, sympathy in the strange affair of the Great Panopticon. And this time the congratulations were better justified. Twice before the House of Commons had voted for an Abolition motion, and nothing at all had come of it. But then the majorities had been slight and not to be depended on: there had been no assurance that the House was ready to proceed beyond the stage of pious resolutions; while now there seemed no reason why it should not see the matter through. And then for the last and grimmest obstacle! "I fear," said Wilberforce, in replying to a cordial message from the aged Newton, "I fear the House of Lords."

No time was lost. On the very night of their triumph, the zealots gathered in Wilberforce's house. Thornton, Grant, Stephen, Macaulay, Brougham and others were there; and, before going late to bed, Wilberforce discussed and settled the main lines of the Bill. Eight days later, on June 7, he moved its second reading. His previous exposition had made it unnecessary for his own part in the opening stage of the debate to be more than curt and formal; but towards the end he rose again to clear Burke's memory from the imputation of unfriendliness to Abolition. Pitt's speech was longer and unequivocally for the Bill. And, though the defenders of the Trade made a desperate effort, brought up the heavy guns of Windham and Castlereagh, pleaded as of old for delay, for time to study the evidence, and stubbornly kept up the fight till 2 a.m., the division went against them almost as heavily as before—Ayes

100, Noes 42. On June 12 the Bill passed through Committee. In
vain the West Indians strove to check its progress at the Report
stage when, says the diary, "they slipped away, and, leaving less
than forty, counted us out." In vain they invoked all the old fears
and prejudices and trotted out the bogey of emancipation—thus,
according to Fuller, the slaves were saying, "Massa King Wilbee
wanted to free them but the Parliament would not let him." The
Bill moved safely over their protests to its final stage. But just
before the last debate there was an anxious moment. Abolition
was not now so new a question to the Irish members, and Wilberforce was dismayed to hear that "they have been persuaded by West
Indians that it is an invasion of private property." Barham's vote,
too, seemed for a time in danger. "Offended by my apparent inat-
tention to him," says the diary for June 23. "I wrote him a letter
of apology, and all healed." But far more disquieting than anything
else was the suspicion that Pitt's support was not whole-hearted.
In one of the debates a back-bench Abolitionist, Mr. Somers-Cocks,
had asserted to Pitt's face that, "if he had employed the fair, honourable influence of office," the object he professed so cordially to desire
would long ago have been attained. More than once Wilberforce
had been tempted to think likewise: he had become more and more
reluctant to recognise the difficulties of Pitt's divided Cabinets; and
now he was disappointed and alarmed because Pitt did not give
more time and more energy to ensure the passage of the Bill. "I
never was so dissatisfied with Pitt as this time," he complains in the
diary. But of time and energy Pitt had little to spare in those days.
His first duty, after all, was to fight Napoleon; and just at this
moment his chief measure for the defence of the country, the
Additional Force Bill, was being bitterly contested in the Commons.
On June 8 his majority had fallen to 40. "The Opposition," notes
Wilberforce himself, "Foxites especially, in high spirits. . . . The
effect of these bad divisions may cause the rats to run, and so pull
him down." Would it have been wise, at that moment, for Pitt to
irritate, perhaps to estrange, the anti-Abolitionists in that weak
majority of his by canvassing the cause of Abolition more personally and provocatively than he did? As it was, his part was by no
means neutral or nugatory. He attended the debates at every stage.
He spoke frequently and always firmly for the Bill. And just before
the end he personally defeated the last attempt at obstruction.
Wilberforce himself had yielded to the Trade's demand that counsel

must be heard; but only one of them had spoken when the old plea for postponement was raised on the ground that members, especially the new Irish members, must have more time to consider the evidence. Pitt was on his feet at once. "Warming in his speech," says the diary, in a very different tone from that of its complaint of Pitt only two days before, "[he] moved against hearing *counsel as well as* evidence, and carried it without a division." It was obvious, indeed, that the question had been thrashed out long ago and that, as Pitt said, "there was no reason to expect that counsel would throw any new light upon it." It was manifest obstruction, in fact. Yet could any one with less authority than Pitt's have swept it so peremptorily aside?

The debate on the third reading took place on June 27. It was short and its result was never in doubt. Pitt's speech, indeed, was more concerned with the results of the measure than with its passage, but he may have won some votes by his tactful and timely handling of the question of compensation. He opposed the insertion of a special clause in the Bill, but he pledged himself to the principle that the State should meet all fair claims for personal losses caused by Abolition. Later on, he interrupted Rose, a close friend and a member of the Government, in the middle of a vigorous speech against the Bill, on a point of order. Two or three old defenders of the Trade, led by its veteran champion, Sir William Young, gloomily paraded the weather-worn scarecrows of massacre and ruin. The bigger men on both sides were silent. Neither Fox nor Windham, neither Canning nor Castlereagh spoke. Towards the end, Addington, speaking as "a warm advocate for Abolition," briefly denounced the Bill—because the negroes would be unable to distinguish between Abolition and Emancipation. Wilberforce followed him with "some rather severe remarks on him and his warm zeal for Abolition"—to quote the diary—which he was glad, being always rather tenderly disposed towards Addington, "did not get into the newspapers." There were no further protestations of national humanity from the Irish members; and their abstention explained the drop in Wilberforce's majority. The figures were 69 for the Bill and 33 against it.

"The Supreme Disposer of all things can turn the hearts of men, and before Him difficulties vanish"—so commented Wilberforce on the conversion of the House of Commons. But only half the victory had been won; and Wilberforce might well pray for more than human agency to convert the House of Lords. As he was "carrying up" his Bill, he was met on the threshold of the House with disappointing news from his old comrade-in-arms, Bishop Porteus. He had discussed the prospects of the Bill with one of his brethren, and they had come to the conclusion that its fate ought not to be hazarded outright. The session was advanced. Most of the bishops were away in their dioceses. Several members of the Government in the Lords were expected to oppose the Bill. Was it not wiser, then, not to risk a positive rejection which would tell against success another year? A visit to Pitt was still more discouraging. The Cabinet, Pitt told him, had agreed that "the subject be hung up till next year." Accustomed now to these swift turns of fortune, Wilberforce at the moment took the disappointment coolly, but the more he reflected, he confesses, the more bitterly he felt it. "I own," he writes to Gisborne, "it quite lowers my spirits to see all my hopes for this year at once blasted, yet I can't help myself." He says nothing of Pitt; but he must have felt again that old unreasoning resentment—unreasoning because Pitt's statement of the case, as clear and logical as ever, had convinced him. The House of Lords, he had explained, "from their habits would not dispense with evidence"; and for evidence there was no time this session. He had argued, further, "that it was best for the cause to be regarded as a new question," for Abolition to be urged *de novo*, mainly on the ground of the increased and increasing danger to the West Indies of permitting further imports of disaffected negroes. Nevertheless, Wilberforce was right to kick against conviction. For Pitt had not mentioned the real argument against immediate action in the Lords. The real argument was the old one—the division in his Cabinet and party. Had Pitt been strong enough to make Abolition a Government measure, to dragoon recalcitrant colleagues, and to press the Bill on the Lords with the united support of ministerial peers behind it, he would not have needed to make any other case for it than that which the Commons had accepted, and he could then have overridden those time-honoured habits in the matter of evidence—the near future was to prove it—as easily as he had crushed obstruction in the Commons.

As it was—it being understood among all parties that the Bill was not to be carried to a division—the debates in the Lords on June 28 and July 2 were a rather bloodless formality. But at least they revealed the weakness of Pitt's position. On both occasions it was a member of the Government, indeed a Secretary of State, Lord Hawkesbury, who opened the debate, not however as the Bill's official "father," but as its firm opponent. He was presently followed by the other Secretary of State, Lord Harrowby, who confessed to friendly feelings for the Bill, but did not presume to urge its merits on the House and supported his colleague's motion for adjournment. And, in between these Secretaries of State, the Lord Privy Seal, Lord Westmorland—"like himself, coarse and bullying," notes Wilberforce, "but without Talent"—boasted his pride, "as a peer of the realm," that the admirable constitution provided one House at any rate in which the interests of the merchants and the colonists would be as carefully attended to as if they themselves were represented there. Finally, Lord Chancellor Eldon judicially admitted that he had never voted on the question, never indeed examined the voluminous evidence, but he advised the House, very gravely, to give "the most mature deliberation" to a measure which, if too suddenly adopted, would bring total ruin to so many individuals. Such was the Government contribution to the progress of the cause which the Prime Minister had so long and so openly supported. The Court, too, was to be reckoned with in the Lords: and four members of the royal family were in their places, prepared to vote with their spokesman, the Duke of Clarence, who, his old antagonism untempered by time, admitted that he chafed against the agreed adjournment and wished for an instant and decisive rejection of the Bill. The poor Bill, in fact, had only three defenders— for Lord Harrowby's speech was scarcely a defence—Horsley, Bishop of St. Asaph, who asked if a British House of Parliament really needed any great length of time to make up its mind on the notorious horrors of the Trade: Lord Stanhope, whose wild tirades and threats were worse than useless and who was only prevented by a timely remonstrance from the watchful Wilberforce from impulsively forcing a disastrous division: and Lord Grenville, who, like Pitt, had supported Abolition in his steady, serious way ever since that day at Holwood when, as Wilberforce now reminded him, Pitt and he had launched the young enthusiast on his long campaign. It was to Grenville, in fact, that Wilberforce had perforce appealed to champion the Bill as its "natural guardian and protector" in the Lords. And it is a final comment on Pitt's position that the man, who in days gone by—when he was a Secretary of State in Pitt's Government, when indeed he had been raised to the Upper House

partly through Pitt's wish to have at least one firm friend of
Abolition among so many of its enemies—would have "fathered"
the Bill as a matter of course, should still, though he was now a
leader of the Opposition, be the only man available to play the part.

In due course the Lords adjourned the Bill by agreement till the
next session. "To be sure," said Wilberforce, "one session in such
a case as this is not much"; and he consoled himself with the
prospect of a final triumph in 1805.

4

A final triumph in 1805? Of all Wilberforce's disappointments,
that of 1805 was to prove the most exasperating. Early in the year
he was given a hint of impending danger, but he does not seem to
have appreciated it. "You will, I know, be glad," Pitt wrote to
him, "independent of politics, that Addington and I have met as
friends; but I hope you will also not be sorry to hear that that
event will lead to political re-union." Wilberforce was pleased at
Pitt communicating this news to him: "it showed me," he says,
"that he understood my real feelings." He was still more pleased
with a talk he had with him as they walked round the Park. "I
am sure," said Pitt, "that you are glad to hear that Addington and
I are at one again." "And then he added with a sweetness of manner
I shall never forget, 'I think they are a little hard upon us in
finding fault with our making it up again, when we have been
friends from our childhood and our fathers were so before us, while
they say nothing to Grenville for uniting with Fox, though they
have been fighting all their lives.'"

It seems strange that Wilberforce should not have guessed why
it was that Pitt went out of his way to appeal to his liking for
Addington and to secure his express approbation of the alliance.
He knew its cause—the necessity for Pitt somehow or other to
strengthen his Government. But did not he also know what one,
at least, of its results must be? Had he forgotten that Addington's
opposition to immediate and wholesale Abolition had markedly
stiffened in the last few years? Could he not foresee that the alliance
would make it harder than ever for Pitt to support it openly and
vigorously? Anyhow, he soon learned the truth. Pitt again sought
his company; but this time it was to lay his dilemma candidly

before him and to beg him to postpone the reintroduction of the Abolition Bill. But Wilberforce had long ago determined never to "make that holy cause subservient to the interest of a party." He was adamant. Providence, it seemed, had at long last set the victory within its grasp. It would be imbecile, it would be impious, not to seize it, however much it might embarrass Pitt. No, he would not delay an instant. Within a week, indeed, of his hearing about Addington he had given notice of his motion. Nine days later, on February 15, he moved for leave to reintroduce the Bill and obtained it without a division. On the 19th it was read a first time; on the 28th it came up for the second reading.

When Wilberforce rose to open the debate, he had every reason to expect that the result of the previous year would be repeated. Opinion in the country at large was, if anything, more interested, more favourable; and nothing had happened at Westminster save the Pitt-Addington alliance, and why should that alter individuals' votes? But as the debate proceeded, he grew more and more uneasy. With the single exception of Barham, the first eight speakers were all against the Bill. Then at last Fox broke the silence of its friends —combative, uncompromising, but not so confident as usual. At the close of a short speech he expressed a "strong hope" that a favourable opinion in the Commons would "make a powerful impression on the public mind." He was followed by Mr. Huddleston, warm for Abolition. And then Pitt got up. On every previous occasion, on the debates on all of Wilberforce's annual motions, at every stage of the Bill in the previous year, Pitt had declared, quite clearly and firmly, that he personally desired immediate Abolition. To declare it again, he may have thought, was a vain repetition; his opinion was notorious. Yet it is surely strange, surely significant, that, on this occasion only, he allowed it to be taken for granted. His brief speech was concerned mainly with the repudiation of an incidental charge which a previous speaker had levelled against the Government—a charge of making an official contract for the purchase of slaves. He said at once that he had not risen "with any intention of entering into the debate," and he sat down without saying a word about the Bill. The chill which seemed to have fallen on the Abolitionist rank and file at the beginning of the evening now sank to freezing-point. Those of them who had usually spoken on previous occasions sat still in their places. It only remained for Wilberforce to wind up the debate. "Though I thought we might be hard run from the face of the House," he said afterwards, "I could not expect defeat." A vigorous effort, however, was obviously needed; and his speech, though he felt, he says, "as if he could not go well," was easily the best of the evening. Boldly—perhaps over-boldly—he met the argument that the end of the Slave Trade would mean the end of Slavery. He would be mad, he said, to look for Emancipation as the instant sequel to Abolition; but he hoped that one day the slaves of the West Indies would be transformed into a free, moral, industrious and happy peasantry. And he closed with the warning which more than once, but not to-night, Pitt himself had uttered. If Parliament did nothing for the negroes, they would be tempted sooner or later to do what they could for themselves. A repetition by Lord Temple of the charge that Government had purchased slaves—another curt denial from Pitt—and then the division. Seventy members voted for the second reading, seventy-seven against it.

As they came away from the division, Mr. Hatsell, the shrewd old ex-clerk of the House, ventured to express his sympathy. "Mr. Wilberforce," he said, "you ought not to expect to *carry* a measure of this kind. . . . You and I have seen enough of life to know that people are not induced to act upon what affects their interests by any abstract arguments." "Mr. Hatsell," Wilberforce replied, "I *do* expect to carry it; and what is more, I feel assured I shall carry it speedily." And certainly there were excuses to be found for the defeat. "All expressed astonishment," says the diary. "The Irish members absent, or even turned against us.[1] . . . Some Scotch, I believe, who last year neutral, voted against us. Great canvassing of our enemies, and several of our friends absent through forget-fulness or accident or engagements preferred from lukewarmness." But explanations of defeat are cold comfort; and, though Wilber-force was very far from despair, though he could even make a show of confidence to kindly pessimists like Hatsell, he was staggered by the unexpected blow. "I never felt so much on any parliamentary occasion," he confesses. "Alas, my dear Muncaster," he wrote a few days later, "from the fatal moment of our defeat on Thursday evening, I have had a damp struck into my heart. I could not sleep either on Thursday or Friday night without dreaming of scenes of depredation and cruelty on the injured shores of Africa. . . . I really have had no spirits to write to you. . . . Still I will do all

---

[1] Nine Irish members were present, and one at least voted for the Bill.

I can. If we cannot stop the whole of this accursed traffic, it is
much to stop half of it; and I am resolved to do what I can, I
repeat it."

5

It was true that a good part of the Slave Trade could be stopped
without a wholesale Abolition Bill. It might be possible to persuade Parliament to accept a partial measure prohibiting the Trade
with foreign countries only. And the Government might take
action, either on its own initiative or under pressure from the
House of Commons, to veto the importation of new slaves into
the old Dutch colonies, recently annexed by Britain, of which the
most important was Guiana. Wilberforce had already taken up the
latter question in 1804, after the adjournment of his Bill in the
Lords. He had told Pitt that he was proposing to ask for a resolution of the Commons; but Pitt had assured him that it was unnecessary. "Called on Pitt (July 3), who positively said he had no doubt
of stopping the Trade by Royal Proclamation. Very strong on this,
and against any vote of Parliament." Wilberforce and his friends
at once submitted. They dropped their plan of a resolution and
waited for the Government to act. But there was prolonged and
inexplicable delay. "Let me beg you, my dear Pitt," writes Wilberforce, ten weeks later, "to have the Proclamation issued. . . . It
will not cost you half an hour to settle this." At last, in November,
came encouraging news. "I am hardly sure," wrote Harrowby,
"that I am not a perjured privy councillor in telling you that the
order about Surinam and all other conquered colonies was actually
on the list of council business on Thursday last." But it was apparently too low on the list. When the opening of the session of 1805
diverted the activities of the Abolitionists to the greater business
of the Bill, nothing more had been heard of the Proclamation.

But the subsequent *débâcle* in Parliament threw Wilberforce
back on to the Guiana question. "I am resolved to do what I can."
And, as the result of his bitter disappointment, there was now
something stiffer, something almost fiercer, in his resolution than
ever before. He did not want to quarrel with Pitt. An entry in the
diary in the previous summer shows how warmly he had still
regarded him—"Appointment with Pitt, who had answered my

last letter in a very friendly way—really affectionate, as I am sure
I felt and acted towards him." But strange things had happened
since then. What was he to think of that extraordinary postponement of the Proclamation? What was he to think of Pitt's share
in that disastrous debate? He notes in the diary that several half-
hearted supporters of Abolition excused themselves to him for not
voting for the Bill "on the ground of Pitt's not meaning it to be
carried." He makes no further comment; but many of his fellow
Abolitionists were not so reticent. They now utterly despaired of
Pitt. They were convinced he had sold his conscience to his Cabinet.
And, though Wilberforce would not go quite so far, though he
still believed that his appeals to Pitt's better mind might ultimately
be successful, he was determined now to be very firm with him.
He would certainly refuse again, as he had refused a month before,
to yield an inch to his personal or party difficulties. He would use
every weapon he had, even if it meant estrangement. He would
go, if need be, to the last extreme of open opposition. If there must
be a quarrel, he could not help it.

   In this mood he wrote Pitt a "strong letter" a few days after
the defeat of the Bill and followed it up in person. That interview
must have been strained. Never before had he actually threatened
Pitt; but now he told him that, unless he promptly dealt with
Guiana himself, he would force the question on Parliament, and
not merely as an independent Abolitionist but in concerted alliance
with Fox and Grenville. Whether or not so stern an ultimatum
was really needed, it quickly had effect. Pitt was not merely as
ready to pledge himself as he had been in the previous year. He
put the matter at once before the Cabinet, and after its next meeting
he wrote to Wilberforce telling him that his colleagues had unanimously agreed to stop the Trade with Guiana and asking him to
draft the requisite regulations.

   Wilberforce was reassured. What he wanted to believe of Pitt
seemed to be coming true. But other Abolitionists, particularly
the Whigs among them, were not so easily satisfied. At the end of
the month a meeting was called by Lord Henry Petty at Lansdowne
House, to consider what steps should be taken to press the question
to an issue independently of Government. It was attended by some
twenty Abolitionists of all parties; but the anti-Pittites, Fox and
Grey among them, were in the majority. Naturally, therefore,
Wilberforce's declaration of confidence in Pitt fell rather flat. "I

saw certain significant winks and shrugs," he told Muncaster, "as
if I was taken in by Pitt and was too credulous and soft." However,
the meeting, in deference to Wilberforce, consented to adjourn for
a few days, while he and Banks attempted, as its authorised agents,
to obtain a further pledge from Pitt. The result was as unequivocal
as ever. Pitt told the envoys to report his answer to the meeting—
that the Government would, by Order-in-Council, stop the Guiana
Trade. It was a pleasant little triumph for Wilberforce. The Prime
Minister's explicit promise, given not merely to a private friend
but officially to the Lansdowne House group, could scarcely be
winked and shrugged aside. So the meeting passed on from the
Guiana question to that of the Foreign Slave Trade and commissioned Lord Henry Petty to give notice of a Bill for its abolition.
It was afterwards decided, however, not to press for this second
object till the first was attained. They would wait for Pitt to carry
out his promise.

They waited for days . . . and weeks . . . and months.

There can be only one explanation of this seemingly astounding
conduct. Notorious among all contemporary politicians for his
personal honesty, Pitt was incapable of a mean deceit at the expense
of Wilberforce and his collaborators. The re-opening of the Slave
Trade issue in Parliament, as his attitude in the last debate had
shown, would certainly have embarrassed him. But this at least is
incontestable—he did not divert the Abolitionists from their purpose by giving them a promise with the deliberate intention of
delaying his fulfilment of it as long as he possibly could. Nor, in
this affair at any rate, was it a question of slowly overcoming the
susceptibilities of Sidmouth and his other anti-Abolitionist colleagues. They had already given in; they had unanimously agreed
to stop the Guiana Trade. The true, the only possible, cause of the
delay was a complex of two connected factors—the condition of
Europe and the condition of Pitt's health.

If the one thought in Wilberforce's mind most of this time was
Abolition, the one thought in Pitt's mind all this time was Napoleon.
The menace of invasion, though custom and calculation of its difficulties had dulled its edge, still hung overhead. And the old
dominant problem of the whole war—how to defeat Napoleon
without Napoleonic armies—remained unsolved. In December
1804, Spain, with her important fleet, joined France; but Britain
still stood alone. Month after month Pitt laboured in vain to create

yet another Continental Coalition. The capricious Romanov vacillated and bargained. The timid Hapsburg preferred a dangerous peace to a still more dangerous war. The inept Hohenzollern waited with greedy eyes on the bait of Hanover which Napoleon, but never Pitt, could offer him. None of them applied to his policy Pitt's single test—"Will it save the liberty of Europe or not?" Meanwhile Napoleon's power was rising to its zenith. Directly or indirectly he was ruler now of all the West of Europe. In May he crowned himself King of Italy at Milan. In June he annexed the Genoese Republic. And thereby he succeeded where Pitt had failed. He had torn up the Treaty of Lunéville; he had destroyed the Balance of Power; and Alexander and Francis were at last goaded into war. The Third Coalition was formed. In the autumn the Austrian and Russian armies took the field, on the understanding, of course, that Britain as usual paid for them. With a selfishness fatal to herself as well as to the rest of Europe Prussia held aloof.

At length, then, with Napoleon's help, Pitt's long and anxious diplomatic campaign had proved, in part at least, successful; but its very success brought new burdens with it. It intensified the violence of the Opposition; for Fox and the Whigs repudiated on principle a policy which had twice failed in practice and was, as a matter of fact, to fail again. Further, it meant an increase of taxation to provide the subsidies, and that, in turn, meant fiercer enemies and cooler friends. And in face of this new crisis Pitt's parliamentary position grew even weaker in 1805 than it had been before. His initial defeat on the Melville affair in April was followed by endless and irritating debates on the question of his impeachment. In the course of them the Addingtonians began to break away, and in July Sidmouth himself resigned. A weaker man than Pitt might now have told his master that he had served him to the limit of his power, that he could no longer bear alone the intolerable load. And Pitt, in his desperate need, went so far as to entreat George III once more to form a National Government by admitting members of the Fox-Grenville alliance to office, especially in view of the next budget. But the King was quite comfortably satisfied as to Pitt's capacity to carry on as before; and the idea of Foxites in the Government inflamed his unstable mind almost as much as that of Fox himself. He talked wildly, it was said, about keeping Fox from his counsels at the cost of civil war. So there was no change.

And, all this time, Pitt was obsessed with innumerable other cares than those of diplomacy and Parliament. He was taking a considerable part himself in the actual conduct of the war. He read and wrote countless dispatches. He personally dealt with much of the departmental business both of the Foreign Office and of the War Office. He was in constant consultation with the Lords of the Admiralty and with the Commander-in-Chief. The crucial decisions, for example, on the naval strategy which triumphed at Trafalgar were his as well as Barham's. An endless string of callers at No. 10—generals, admirals, officials, politicians—was always waiting to fill the corners of his day with interviews—the most famous is his fine farewell to Nelson—and at night his sleep was often broken by the arrival of news that could not wait. The scale of his activities may seem small beside those demanded by the Great Wars of this present age, but then as now there were only twenty-four hours in the day; and Pitt, unlike more fortunate War Ministers, no longer possessed an even passably good physique. Indeed, as his last year drew on, surely he must himself have suspected now and then that his strength was nearing its end.

Set in that perspective, Pitt's failure to redeem his promise in the matter of the Guiana Slave Trade no longer seems astounding. Is it to be wondered at that he began to lose his old swift efficiency in every detail of government? Is it surprising that, when so many questions demanded instant settlement because they bore directly on the war, he allowed other questions to drift on unsettled from week to week? But Wilberforce could not understand this strange, this ominous lethargy; and his disappointment and vexation grew. The pledge had been given in March. By May Ministers had got so far as to consider the draft of the Order-in-Council; but Wilberforce's discussions of it with Lord Camden, Pitt's War Secretary, and with Attorney-General Perceval are constantly interrupted and postponed. He feels there is no driving force behind them, and besides his almost daily calls at Whitehall, he is frequently importuning Pitt by letter or in person. At last the Order is framed, but "so framed," he thinks, "as to be worse than none," and he is off with it to Pitt to insist on emendations. Otherwise, he declares, "I really think we had better run the risk of losing all by trying to carry the measure in Parliament." Pitt asks him to draft his alterations. He drafts them. But, ten days later—it is now June 4—the diary complains: "Pitt has not yet settled it—too bad—though he

authorised Bankes and me to assure the meeting at Lord Lansdowne's that he would do it. Sad work! I write and call again and
again." "Procrastination," he tells Muncaster, "in one whom you
used to call 'The General,' has increased to such a degree as to have
become absolutely predominant." And when, at last, on September
13, the Order-in-Council is issued, Wilberforce cannot ascribe it to
Pitt's awakened conscience. It is chiefly due, he says, to the business-
like methods of an anti-Abolitionist, Castlereagh, who had succeeded
Camden at the War Office.

6

Public men have often been permanently estranged by more
negligible grievances than those which Pitt and Wilberforce inflicted
on each other in 1805. Wilberforce's speech had swayed the House
of Commons to deal Pitt the hardest blow of his career. Pitt's
apathy and inaction as to the Slave Trade must have seemed to
Wilberforce almost a betrayal of the cause he cared for most in
life. But, even so, the friendship was too old, too strongly founded
in mutual respect, to be more than temporarily clouded. Throughout that difficult time they frequently met; but if there was any
unspoken resentment, any latent irritation, on either side, there
was never anything like a quarrel. And in the autumn the cloud
passed over. When at last the Order-in-Council had been issued,
there was no longer any need for those persistent, importunate
calls at No. 10; and, if Wilberforce was constantly dropping in, it
was, as in earlier days, just on the chance of finding Pitt free for a
tête-à-tête about less prickly things than Abolition. Entries like the
following again recur in the diary: "Drove into town to see Pitt
—had much talk with him upon political topics, finding him very
open and kind."

In November came the double-edged tidings of Trafalgar. "So
overcome," notes Wilberforce, "that I could not go on reading for
tears." When Pitt was awakened with the news in the early hours,
he could not resume as usual his interrupted sleep; and the dawn
found him busy with the day's work. Had victory on sea been
followed by victory on land, his life might have been saved. But
Napoleon had discounted Trafalgar. Denied sea-power, he could
still show himself the master of the Continent. Already the "Army

of England" had been flung across Europe from the Channel to the Danube; and on the day before Trafalgar 25,000 Austrians had surrendered at Ulm. A few weeks later, on December 2, the joint armies of Austria and Russia were crushed at Austerlitz. Napoleon had destroyed Pitt's Third Coalition almost as soon as it was made. And he had destroyed Pitt too. The tremendous blow gave a fatal turn to what had seemed at first a transient attack of gout. On January 23 Pitt died.

Wilberforce was staying with Babington in the country and it was not till he returned to London on the 21st that he heard how ill Pitt was. Next morning, he was "too unsettled and uneasy about Pitt" to stop at Clapham. He drove up to town and called on various friends. All gave him a "bad account." Rose, who had come from the patient's house at Putney, told him that the doctors had given up hope. On the 23rd he heard from Bishop Tomline that the end had come about half-past four in the morning. When he set himself, that night, to record the final item in the diary wherein, for twenty-five years past, with the candour of the confessional, he had chronicled so much that was good and so little that was bad of his famous friend, his first thought was that his patriot *par excellence* had died as he had lived for his country, and his mind flew back to Trafalgar. "Pitt killed by the enemy as much as Nelson," he writes. But there is something solemn in Pitt's death that curbs the quick emotion he had felt at the news of Nelson's. "Deeply," he says, "rather than pathetically affected." "This late event," he writes to Muncaster two days later, "saddens rather than softens my heart. There is something weighing down the spirits." And in the same letter he reveals wherein the sadness lay. He had once described Pitt as more genuinely patriotic and more pure-minded than "any man, *not under the influence of Christian principles*, I ever knew." He had never, of course, regarded him as positively un-Christian, an infidel like Hume or Gibbon. He was to learn presently, indeed, that the dying man had allowed Bishop Tomline to pray with him, murmured the responses, asserted his faith, and declared that he had tried, with many errors and failures, to serve God and mankind. But Wilberforce, as we know, had wanted more than that; he had wanted Pitt to share in the fuller revelation which had transfigured his own life; and he had dreamed of Pitt —years afterwards, as we shall see, he confessed it—his great virtues thus supplemented and illumined, his great powers reinforced, playing the part of the ideal statesman of the *Practical View*, transfiguring the life of England. He had never ceased to desire that, one day, he might be permitted to be the instrument of such a change in Pitt, to make him see the logic of his faith as he saw it. Once, at least, during that visit to Walmer, he had tried, and failed. And now it was too late. "I own," confessed Wilberforce, "I have a thousand times (aye, times without number) wished and hoped that a quiet interval would be afforded him, perhaps in the evening of his life, in which he and I might confer freely on the most important of all subjects. But the scene is closed—for ever."

The last duties of his friendship were still to be fulfilled. On January 27 a motion was proposed for a public funeral and for the erection of a monument "in the Collegiate Church of St. Peter, Westminster, to the memory of that excellent statesman." To a later generation it seems, at first thought, astonishing that the motion should have been opposed; but it is not easy in the middle of a war to take a generous view of a statesman whose conduct of it has been unsuccessful. And this was the morrow of Austerlitz. Neither Windham nor Fox, in truth, was merely factious in his opposition. Neither denied Pitt's great abilities; but Windham maintained that the greatest national honours should not be bestowed for merit, however high, unless it were united with success, and Fox refused to subscribe to the "excellence" of a statesman whose system of government had been, in his opinion, disastrous to the country. It was one of those rare occasions when parliamentary warfare is ennobled by the sincerity of the disputants and the solemnity of their theme. Pitt's friends and enemies could speak of the dead man, as they never could of the living, without a touch of personal bitterness, without a thought of votes to be won or lost, but in simple loyalty to their convictions. Castlereagh's reply was temperate and dignified; and Wilberforce, who followed him, warmly acknowledged the honest motives of Pitt's critics. But he declared that it was neither just nor wise to make success the criterion of honour; and then, venturing on more contentious ground, he claimed that at least in one outstanding achievement Pitt had been successful—he had saved England from "the revolutionary spirit that had convulsed France and alarmed the whole civilised world." "I feel this motion," he said at the close of his brief speech, "to be but a small tribute of deference to the memory of a man who was ever the object of my esteem and admiration, who was equally distinguished for great talents, for exalted character, for enlarged views, for personal purity, and for indefatigable patriotism. . . . To whatever regarded his own interest he was perfectly indifferent. He was always forgetting himself but always remembering his country."

The motion was carried by a large majority, but, a few days later, came another on which Wilberforce's views were shared by few. Always incorrigibly careless of his private finances, Pitt had left some £40,000 of tradesmen's debts behind him, and Wilberforce was one of those who did not wish them to be paid by vote of Parliament, partly on the principle that private debts should never be made a public charge and partly for fear lest at a time of increased taxation this extra burden, relatively slight as it was, should be resented by the taxpayers and "create a feeling very injurious to Pitt's memory." For three days, therefore, he was busy canvassing his friends and the City for private subscriptions; but, with the exception of Perceval who was "warm and generous as ever" and, though not a man of large means, promptly offered £1000, he met with practically no support. The diary bears witness to his disappointment; yet, strongly as he felt about it, he could not bring himself to oppose the motion for public payment which was now proposed in Parliament. Nor, of course, could he support it, as Fox and Windham did. He left the House, therefore, before the debate on it began.

The funeral was held on February 22. In the procession, at Lord Chatham's request, Wilberforce was one of those who carried the banner before the coffin, and his place in the Abbey was in the forefront of the mourners. Pitt's grave had been prepared close to his father's; and as he stood beside it, it seemed to Wilberforce as if Chatham's adjacent statue was "looking down with consternation into the grave which was opened for his favourite son."

Fifteen years later, Wilberforce wrote down his mature impressions of Pitt's character and career. It is a document of the first historical importance; annotations and corrections reveal the pains its author took with it; and its publication in 1897 was eagerly welcomed by students of the period. But for present purposes it is enough to draw attention to one remarkable fact. The document shows that in 1821 Wilberforce's opinion of Pitt was, in all essentials, precisely the same as in 1806. Fifteen years of experience and reflection, fifteen years under other Governments with other policies than Pitt's in war and peace, had only deepened and clarified his earlier convictions. His admiration is still the same, still only clouded by the one regret that so great a man should not have been greater still. If only, at the outset of his career, he had resolved "to govern his country by *principle* rather than by *influence*!"

"All his faculties then possessed the bloom of youthful beauty as well as the full vigour of maturer age; his mind was ardent, his principles were pure, his patriotism warm, his mind as yet altogether unsullied by habitually associating with men of worldly ways of thinking and acting, in short, with a class which may be not unfitly termed ' trading politicians.' . . . No one who had not been an eye-witness could conceive the ascendancy which Mr. Pitt then possessed over the House of Commons." If only he had tried to "govern by principle," he would have succeeded. And then the whole English body politic would have been cleansed and strengthened. Even so great a cataclysm as the French Revolution would have left it unshaken. "Such a spirit of patriotism would have been kindled, such a generous confidence in the King's Government would have been diffused throughout all classes, that the very idea of the danger of our being infected with the principles of French licentiousness . . . would have been an apprehension not to be admitted within the bosom of the most timid politician; while the various reforms which would have taken place and the manifest independence of Parliament would have generated and ensured in the minds of all reasonable men a continually increasing gratitude and affection for the constitution and laws of our country. On the other hand, the French, infatuated as they were . . . could never have been so blind to their own manifest interest as to have engaged their people in a war with Great Britain from any idea of our confederating with the Crowned Heads of Europe to crush the rising spirit of liberty in France. Hence we should have escaped that long and bloody war. . . ."

It is as old as politics, as old as the vision of the βασιλεὺς φιλόσοφος —this idea of a favourite statesman rising clean above the bounds of circumstance; and there have been others besides Wilberforce

who believed that Pitt could have done it, could have cut away all
the oblique supports of the old régime, dispensed with the votes he
won by the distribution of innumerable "places" and with the votes
the King won for him by the "influence" of the Crown, and rested
his authority on his "principles" alone. It is, indeed, conceivable—
though the speculation is idle enough—that, if Pitt had adopted and
improved on his father's rôle, if he had set himself, a second Great
Commoner, at the head of a real democratic movement in England,
in temperate alliance with the new ideas in France, he might have
made himself an almost omnipotent dictator. But Wilberforce is
not thinking of anything like that. He does not even presuppose
some drastic measure of parliamentary Reform, something more
than the suppression of bribery and corruption. No: he would
have us believe that, working within the structure, more or less
unchanged, of the old eighteenth-century political system, Pitt,
single-handed, could have moralised English politics. Almost a
miracle ? Well, it was as something in the nature of a miracle that
Wilberforce regarded it, as something, at any rate, beyond the
unaided power of man. For, when he speaks of "government by
principle," he means much more than the government of a good
man. Before his eyes, all the time, is his vision of the "true Christian," and just as Pitt was in his mind, years before, when he wrote
the passage on the ideal statesman in the *Practical View*, so now he
is imagining Pitt as more than the bold reformer, as the ideal
statesman himself. And what a vista opens at the thought! Consider, he says, the effect on Pitt himself and those about him, on
his use of his brain and his faculties, on his choice of friends, on
his official appointments in Church and State. And consider how
these men, in turn, in their appointments would have followed the
same rules of choice, and so on throughout the descending sequence
of the public service. "Who can say what would have been the effect
of those religious and moral secretions, if they may be so termed,
which throughout the whole political body would have been
gradually producing their blessed effects in augmenting its fulness,
symmetry and strength!" It was not the least of Wilberforce's
tributes to Pitt's greatness to conceive him thus, if once his eyes
had been opened to the truth, initiating and directing that one
experiment in aristocracy which mankind has never cared or dared
to try—a government of saints—and bringing down to English
earth the heavenly pattern of a Christian State.

And there, as before, the deeper criticism ends. Wilberforce touches on a few minor foibles of Pitt's—his shyness amounting sometimes almost to *gaucherie* ("He was one of the shyest men I ever knew," is a pencil comment in the margin); a touch of pride, but none of arrogance; his occasional fretfulness in his later days; an oversanguine judgment of men and things. But these are trivialities beside his virtues—his honour, his truthfulness, his open mind, his incorruptibility, above all his selfless love of England. Long ago, in the first days of their friendship, the strength and purity of Pitt's patriotism had been impressed indelibly on Wilberforce's heart. Time might cool a little the warmth of his regard, blemishes might be detected in other aspects of the man, but that picture, at least, was safe from disillusion. It flashes instantly before him at the news of his death. And now, forty years after its first impress, it remains unchanged. "No man ever loved his country with a warmer or more sincere affection."

7

It is sometimes said that Pitt's death was a necessary preliminary to the Abolition of the Slave Trade; and under all the circumstances it is probably true. But the censure implicit in the statement should fall on George III rather than on Pitt. Had Pitt been allowed to form a national administration, had he needed no longer to defer to inflexible colleagues and uncertain followers, had he been granted, in fact, a new lease of strength and freedom, there is no reason whatever to suppose that, as soon as it was clearly in his power, he would have hesitated to do what he had described, times out of number, as demanding instant doing. Nor does it detract in the least from the credit due to Fox to say that in this matter he was more fortunate than Pitt. When at last he was accepted perforce by George III as a Secretary of State in a Government composed of Foxites, Grenvillites and Addingtonians, if he was obliged to assuage the royal fears of Catholic Emancipation, there was no need to compromise on Abolition. It could not, indeed, even now, be brought forward as a Government measure by a Cabinet which included Windham and Sidmouth; but now, at any rate, for the first time, a decisive majority of Ministers, headed by Grenville, their chief, were ready to support or at least to accept it. Meantime the reawakened public interest had not only been maintained, it had been strengthened. In the winter of 1805-6 Clarkson had emerged from his retirement, resumed after nine years' absence his seat on the Abolition Committee, and straightway, a giant refreshed, set off on another tour of propaganda. "This journey," he declares, "I performed with extraordinary success." What particularly heartened him was to find that the younger generation, who had grown up during the years of silence and inaction, embraced the cause with all the ardour of their elders in old days. So now, for the first time since 1792, there was something better than appearances to justify the hopes of the Abolitionists. Public opinion and political opportunity really coincided. The stars at last were in conjunction.

However deep his personal regrets, Wilberforce, too, must have realised at once that Pitt's death had opened a new prospect for his cause; and he had lost no time in showing that, whatever might be the new alignments of political forces, the immediate advocacy of Abolition would be the supreme test of his allegiance. Once, during Pitt's lifetime, Fox had let fly a rather venomous shaft of wit at his professions of independence. "If Wilberforce were compelled," queried somebody at Sydney Smith's hilarious dinner-table, "to desert either the cause of the slaves or the party of Mr. Pitt, to which would he adhere?" "Oh," said Fox, "he would be for Barabbas." But if Wilberforce, as was true enough, had always shrunk from opposing Pitt, it had been mainly on personal grounds; and, before Pitt was in his grave, he startled his friends by pledging his support to one of Pitt's warmest Whig opponents in the imminent by-election for the vacant seat at Cambridge University. "My suddenly promising Lord Henry Petty," records the diary for February 13, "(which done too hastily from wishing to show Lord Henry how much both I and the cause felt indebted to him) has produced a sad degree of rufflement. Dear Dean [Milner] much hurt about it for my sake. I am accused of changing sides." Pitt's friends might have been still more scandalised if they had known that Wilberforce was now frequently closeted with Fox. And to Wilberforce himself it seemed a strange turn of the wheel that had brought him, on the same old quest, to Fox's door instead of Pitt's. "Though intimate with Pitt," he muses, "for all my life since earliest manhood, and he most warm for Abolition, and really honest; yet now my whole human dependence is placed on Fox, to whom [all] his life [I have been] opposed, and on Grenville, to whom [I was] always

rather hostile till of late years, when I heard he was more religious."
He found Fox "quite rampant and playful as he was twenty-two
years ago, when not under any awe of his opponents. . . . Talked
as if we might certainly carry our question in the House of Commons, but should certainly lose it in the House of Lords." This
last confession took Wilberforce aback. From Fox of all men this
submissiveness, this scarcely rampant attitude, towards an obstinate
House of Lords was not what he expected; and he even wondered
whether Fox had been "got at" by the Court. But the suspicion
proved unfounded. Fox had an *entrée* denied to Pitt; and Wilberforce soon learned that "the Prince had given his honour to Fox
not to stir adversely." Meantime he was conferring also with the
new Prime Minister and even with Sidmouth; and it was presently
decided that, before a wholesale Abolition Bill was launched, soundings should be taken, so to speak, by the introduction of a partial
measure, taking up and completing the work of Pitt's Order-in-
Council. On March 31, accordingly, Attorney-General Pigott moved
for leave to introduce a Bill to prohibit the importation of slaves
in British ships into the colonies annexed by Britain during the
war or into the colonies of a foreign state and to prohibit also the
outfitting of foreign slave ships in British ports or the employment
of British capital or labour therein. "How wonderful are the ways
of Providence!" exclaims Wilberforce a little later: "the Foreign
Slave Bill is going quietly on." On April 18 it was read a second
time—very quietly indeed; the West Indians did not even divide
the House. Very quiet, too, was the final stage on May 1; only a
handful of members troubled to attend, and the third reading was
carried by 35 votes to 13. In the House of Lords the Bill was once
more "fathered" by Grenville; but Grenville was now Prime
Minister, the first to sit in the Upper House since the beginning of
the Abolition movement; and, partly, no doubt, on that account,
the Bill had a far smoother passage than any of its predecessors, far
smoother than Fox might have supposed. The opposition obtained
indeed a hearing for counsel on behalf of certain London merchants
and shipowners who had petitioned against the Bill; the Duke of
Clarence bluntly attacked it on the second reading, and Westmorland and Hawkesbury promised opposition at a later stage. But
there was no division. On the third reading the attack stiffened.
Eldon, from the Woolsack, pronounced against the Bill. Lengthy
speeches were made against it by Hawkesbury, Westmorland, Sussex,

and that old campaigner, Sheffield. On the other hand there were favourable surprises. A rift appeared in the hitherto united opposition of the Royal Family. The Duke of Clarence was answered by his cousin of Gloucester in a maiden speech, condemning "that shocking traffic in human blood" and warmly supporting the Bill. And Sidmouth, as the outcome possibly of Wilberforce's pleading, declared that the Bill, as an instrument of "gradual and progressive Abolition," was entitled to his consistent vote. At the end of a long debate the third reading was carried by 43 votes to 13.

The result of these debates was even more auspicious than might appear. For though Sidmouth might choose to ignore it, both Fox and Grenville had boldly shown the whole of their hand. Fox had made it clear that this Bill would soon be followed by another; that it was total Abolition he meant to have, and quickly. "The passing of it," he declared, speaking not only for himself but for several of his colleagues, "however unfortunate this Administration might be in other respects . . . would bestow more true glory upon it and more honour upon our country than any other transaction on which we could be engaged." And Grenville had denied that the Bill was, as its enemies had said, "Abolition in disguise." It was Abolition, or a step to Abolition; but there was no disguise. "I saw our strength," he told Wilberforce afterwards, "and thought the occasion was favourable for launching out a little beyond what the measure itself actually required." And it was certainly remarkable that such candour had provoked no desperate rally of the Trade, no stampede for safety and the rights of property, among the rank and file in either House. The omens, indeed, were so propitious that the three protagonists held "anxious consultations" as to the desirability of attempting the final measure at once. "It was almost decided to try," said Wilberforce. He was for it himself, and so it seemed was Fox; but Grenville's cool reason prevailed. They would have no chance that session, he argued, in the Lords, with the bishops leaving town and so forth. One preparatory stroke, however, could be dealt before the iron cooled. It was agreed that a resolution for total Abolition should straightway be proposed in both Houses.

There was no delay. Procrastination, in this affair at any rate, had disappeared with Pitt. At the beginning of June the new proposal was discussed in the Cabinet. On the 10th Fox moved a resolution in the Commons—its language a deliberate echo of the resolution which Wilberforce had moved, year after year, in vain. And once more Fox took occasion to lift the cause to a pedestal above all others. "So fully am I impressed," he said at the outset, "with the vast importance and necessity of attaining what will be the object of my motion this day that, if during the almost forty years that I have now had the honour of a seat in Parliament, I had been so fortunate as to accomplish that and that only, I should think I had done enough and could retire from public life with comfort and the conscious satisfaction that I had done my duty." This time there was a fuller House and the debate was more even and protracted. The resolution was ably supported by Romilly, the new Solicitor-General, Lord Henry Petty, Canning and Wilberforce. It was opposed by the Old Guard of the Trade—Tarleton, Gascoyne, Young, Manning—and by Windham, Castlereagh and Rose. But the result was even more decisive—114 to 15. A fortnight later the same resolution was moved by Grenville in the Lords. Sidmouth, it seems, had now taken alarm; and he opposed it on the curious pretext of not wishing to have it put upon the Journals of the House that any long-established custom of the country was inhuman and unjust until some definite mode was adopted for its abolition. Only Hawkesbury and Westmorland spoke with him. Erskine, the new Chancellor, the Bishops of London and St. Asaph, and all the other speakers were on Grenville's side. The resolution was carried by 41 to 30.

Wilberforce, of course, was jubilant at this unbroken series of successes. "If it please God to spare the health of Fox," he says, "and to keep him and Grenville together, I hope we shall see next year the termination of all our labours." But there was still one more thing to be done this year, one more point to be gained in that amazing session. He feared, and Stephen agreed, that the passing of the resolution, foreshadowing as it did the triumph of total Abolition, would spur the Trade to a hurried extension of the traffic in the hope of securing such extra profit as it could before the end. The remedy was obvious—a preventive Act of Parliament—and in those strenuous days there could be no difficulty about a little thing like that! Wilberforce hastened to headquarters. "With Fox for one hour and a half. He very rational and unaffected." Seven weeks later the session ended, but there had been time to rush through both Houses a Bill to prohibit the employment in the Slave Trade of any ships not hitherto employed therein.

w.   s

It was, as has been seen, a concurrence of favourable circumstances that had made it possible for so much to be done towards
Abolition in the session of 1806; but that it actually was done and
done so quickly was mainly due to Fox's ardour for the cause. His
brief tenure of office, after twenty-two years in opposition, was not
marked by any great achievements in the field of domestic or foreign
affairs. He soon found that he could do no more than Pitt to stop
the war, to relieve the burdens of the poor, to appease and rein-
vigorate Ireland. But into the channel of Abolition the pent-up
stream of his passion for freedom and his hate of cruelty could flow
with an overwhelming rush. And no one can help wishing that
he had lived to see the end of it. As it was, he was put out of action
even before that one session closed. At the end of June Wilberforce
was dismayed to hear that he was dangerously ill with dropsy,
almost as dismayed as he had been six months before by the similar
news of Pitt. Yet it was only since then that he had really seen
Fox at close quarters. Now and again, in earlier years, he had been
brought into casual contact with him on Abolition business; but,
quite apart from the special obstacle of Wilberforce's intimacy with
Pitt, there had never been any question of frequent or friendly intercourse between them. The respect which Wilberforce's genuine
philanthropy had won from Fox in the days before 1793 had been
steadily overclouded by disgust at his servility—as it seemed to
him—to Pitt and Pitt's policy. And to Wilberforce after 1785, Fox's
morals, his *amours*, his gambling, his boisterous, indecorous, irreligious humour must have seemed no less than horrible. Add to
that his sympathy with France in the days of the Terror, and who
can wonder if the Saint regarded him as almost an embodiment of
the vices and blasphemies of Jacobinism? And though years had
passed, though Fox's violence had mellowed, though he had become
indeed in these latter days almost "respectable," a Pharisee would
still have shrunk from him. But it was not so with our Puritan.
Now at last he really saw the man and knew him; and in a twinkling
he had succumbed—as who did not?—to the magic of his simple,
human personality. "I quite love Fox," he confesses, on hearing
the bad news, "for his generous and warm fidelity to the Slave
Trade cause." And then the familiar note of regret—"Poor fellow,
how melancholy his case! He has not one religious friend or one
who knows anything about it." The end was not far off. He was
already strictly confined to his room, though he longed, he said,

" to go down to the House once more to say something on the Slave Trade"; and in three months' time he died—how differently from Pitt—a happy man.

8

It is eloquent of its altered fortunes that the Abolition cause was not set back by Fox's death. Whatever his earlier anxieties, there is no note of alarm in Wilberforce's comment on it. The old feeling that, year after year, his life is going by and the goal still unattainable no longer haunts his mind; and this time no regrets for a wasted session could cloud the joy with which, when Parliament rose, he fled from London and "slipped into the snug and retired harbour of Lyme for the purpose of careening and refitting." He was soon busily at work there, preparing for publication a final statement of the case for Abolition. " A pamphlet," he says, "thrown in just in such circumstances, may be like a shot which hits between wind and water." But in the middle of October his quiet labours were interrupted by a letter from the Prime Minister announcing the dissolution of Parliament. "Sadly unsettled by the news," he comments; for he knew that bad times and discontent, especially in the cloth industry, had strengthened the hands of his Whig opponents, and the last thing he desired at the moment was to divert his energies to an exhausting electoral contest. Very reluctantly, therefore, he posted off to Yorkshire, and was instantly engulfed in the dust and clamour of a hot election—speaking to "scores of faces"—dragged wildly about in his carriage ("several run over, but not much hurt")—escorted on his way from one town to another by "sixty gentlemen on horseback"—chaired through the streets amid cheers and groans and missiles, one of which hit him on the forehead ("happily not hard, and I kept watching afterwards")—until the last day came and set him once more at the head of the poll, though the opposition had succeeded in unseating his colleague, Lascelles. All this was precious time lost for the pamphlet; and succinctness was not Wilberforce's literary *forte*. The pamphlet grew into a booklet of nearly 400 pages, and, when at length it was published under the title of *A Letter on the Abolition of the Slave Trade addressed to the Freeholders and other inhabitants of Yorkshire*, the opening move had already been made in the last fight for Abolition.

It was evident, once again, at the very outset, under what different auspices the Abolitionists were now engaged: for Grenville, in consultation with Wilberforce, had decided to start the Bill in the House of Lords, and to make it, moreover, the first important business of the session. The new Parliament met on December 15, and the week before Christmas was devoted to the usual formalities. Then, on the second day of the New Year, on the Prime Minister's motion, "A Bill for the Abolition of the Slave Trade" was read a first time in the House of Lords. It was a simple, straightforward measure. After a reference in the preamble to the resolution of the preceding year, the first clause enacted that after May 1, 1807, the African Slave Trade and "all manner of dealing and trading" in the purchase of slaves in Africa or in their transport from Africa to the West Indies or "any other island, country, territory or place whatever" is hereby "utterly abolished, prohibited, and declared to be unlawful"; and that any of His Majesty's subjects acting to the contrary shall pay £100 for every slave so purchased, sold, or transported. Clause II declared that any British ship thereafter employed in the Trade shall be forfeited to the Crown. Further clauses were inserted at a later stage providing for the penalisation of insurance contracts for safeguarding the Trade; for the payment of bounties for all slaves captured from British ships, or from enemy ships in war-time, to the officers and men engaged therein; and for the placing of such captured slaves at the disposal of the Crown either for service in the army or navy or for a limited and regulated apprenticeship to private persons.

Before the Bill came up for second reading the little group of unrepentant champions of the Trade, headed by the Duke of Clarence and Lords Westmorland and Hawkesbury, made a last attempt to revive the obstructive tactics by which the Lords had killed Dundas's "gradual" Abolition Bill in 1792. Up to a point Grenville patiently gave way. The obstruction, he knew, could not last long since this time the general feeling of the House was not behind it. So the papers asked for were duly laid on the table; petitions were accepted; and counsel heard for the petitioners. But that was enough. The further demand, the old demand, that evidence should be called at the bar was resisted by Grenville and successfully resisted without a division. Thus a month, but no more, had been wasted when, on February 5, the crucial stage was reached. The debate was opened by Grenville in a speech which

Wilberforce enthusiastically described as "one of the most states-
manlike I ever heard"; and certainly in its breadth, clarity and
logical arrangement it reads like a speech of Pitt's. There is no
need to recapitulate its arguments: they rested mainly on the two
principles which Pitt had so often expounded—justice to Africa and
security for the West Indies. But the peroration was unusual. It
was not the familiar appeal to the honour of the nation and the
conscience of the House, but a personal eulogy.

> This Bill will be supported in another place by a person to whom
> the country is deeply indebted for having originally proposed
> the measure and for having followed up that proposition by
> every exertion from which a chance could be derived of success.
> I cannot conceive any consciousness being more truly gratifying
> than must be enjoyed by that person on finding a measure to
> which he has devoted the labour of his life carried into effect—
> a measure so truly benevolent, so admirably conducive to the
> virtuous prosperity of this country and the welfare of mankind
> —a measure which will diffuse happiness amongst millions now
> in existence and for which his memory will be blessed by millions
> yet unborn.

It may have been this tribute to Wilberforce which goaded
Westmorland into an equally personal peroration. At the close of
a fighting speech on the losses to British property and the gains to
foreign traders involved in a surrender of the traffic by Britain
only, he declared that he would never yield to popular declamation.
"Though I should see the Presbyterian and the prelate, the Methodist and the field-preacher, the Jacobin and the murderer unite in
support of it, in this House I will raise my voice against it." "Westmorland bespattered me," reported Wilberforce to Muncaster; "but
really it was a double pleasure to be praised by Lord Grenville and
abused by Lord Westmorland." The noble earl was not holding the
last ditch single-handed. Beside him stood a Prince of the Blood,
an ex-Prime Minister, an ex-Secretary of State, a great sailor, and
a great lawyer. The Duke of Clarence was as sturdily downright
as ever, but "worse (says Wilberforce) in point of execution than
usual." "Sidmouth," to quote again that eager listener, "fretted
and hurt me"—naturally enough; for Sidmouth, who had nearly
slipped off the old, crumbling *via media* in the previous year, had

now recovered his footing, and, like an echo from Dundas's best days, insisted, as an ardent and consistent seeker after Abolition, that it must not be attained by an Abolition Bill but rather by the imposition of a rising tax on slaves. The Jenkinson of 1792, similarly, showed himself still alive and little changed in Hawkesbury, while St. Vincent, with his heart in the mercantile marine, was Rodney reincarnate—"the West Indian islands," he declared of his own knowledge, "are paradise itself to the negroes in comparison with their native country." Eldon, lastly, went back still farther, dragging from a century's dust the memories of John Locke and Somers to remind a feebler generation that the Trade in their day had been sanctioned by the wise and good. Lord Morton brought the speeches for the Trade to a total of seven. Ten, including Grenville's, were made against it—by the Duke of Gloucester, the Bishop of Durham, and Lords Selkirk, Rosslyn, King, Northesk, Moira, Holland and Suffolk. Wilberforce was particularly pleased with Holland and Moira, the latter of whom curtly referred his fellow peers to the Old Testament and also, with better judgment, to the New. When the division was finally taken, the second reading was carried by 100 votes, including 28 proxies, to 36, including 8 proxies—a majority of 64. Next day the Bill passed through Committee, the opposition only pleading that the words "inconsistent with the principles of justice and humanity" should be cut out from the resolution quoted in the preamble. Of those who had not spoken on the previous day, Lord Redesdale supported the amendment, and the Lord Chancellor, the Duke of Montrose and Lords Carnarvon, Lauderdale and Stanhope opposed it. It was lost by 33 votes to 10; and this was the last time the Upper House divided on the Bill. The final stages brought out two more supporters, the Bishop of London and the Duke of Norfolk. On February 10, after a very brief discussion, the Bill was read a third time.

Wilberforce had been a watchful visitor at all these debates; and on more than one occasion members of the House had sought him out at the close of the evening to proffer their congratulations. "Several peers," the diary quaintly notes, "now speak with quite new civility." "How striking to observe," it goes on, "Pitt and Fox both dead before Abolition effected, and now Lord Grenville, without any particular deference from Court, carries it so triumphantly. But let us not be too sure." And indeed when the Abolition Committee met to consider the prospects in the House of Commons and scrutinised the roll of members, their minds were by no means easy. Grenville himself shook his head when he saw the "terrific list of doubtfuls." But the time for calculating chances had gone by. Battle had been already joined. On February 10, the very day on which the third reading was carried in the Lords, the first reading was moved in the Commons. It was not Wilberforce who moved it, but, properly and significantly, the Minister who had succeeded Fox as Foreign Secretary. For Grey, now Lord Howick and one day to be "Earl Grey of the Reform Bill," was in most things, and not least in the matter of the Slave Trade, the political heir of the man he had followed through the wilderness for so many dreary years. But in this initial skirmish, of course, there was little fighting to be done; and Howick closed a brief debate by conceding the enemy's request that the second reading should be taken in a fort-night rather than a week. Brief as it was, however, the debate had roughly shown how the forces were divided; and Wilberforce's spirits mounted at the evident strength of the Abolitionists. "Our prospects brighten," he records; and throughout the fortnight of suspense his hopes continued steadily to rise. On the morning of February 23 he muffled his excitement in working hard to perfect Howick's equipment—then dined with a few friends—and so to the House.

It was clear at once that it was to be a "great night." The House was unusually full and it betrayed, says Wilberforce, an "astonishing eagerness." The days of doubt and discomfort and compromise were clean forgotten. The country gentlemen of Britain, free at last to lighten consciences which had never been quite easy since the grim tale of crime and cruelty had first been told them, strove with one another for the chance to strike a blow at the dying Trade. A speech was hardly finished before six or eight of them were on their feet to catch the Speaker's eye. If the choice fell on an opponent of the Bill, they sat in frosty silence. Of the old stalwarts of the Trade, indeed, only Gascoyne and Manning cared to face it: and not one of its friends amongst the first-rank politicians said a word. Windham silently carried his convictions into the lobby, but Castlereagh and Rose did not even vote. Very different was the swift response accorded to Abolition speakers—to Howick when he challenged the appeal to seventeenth-century wisdom and declared that "the names of Pitt and Fox are not inferior to any other"; to Roscoe, when he said that, though

Liverpool itself was his home, he had never ceased to condemn the Trade for thirty years; to Fawkes, the new member for Yorkshire, when he expressed his pleasure at being privileged to speak in unison with his respected colleague for the county. All the time the enthusiasm was steadily rising and it reached its climax at the close of the Solicitor-General's speech. Almost every speaker for the Bill had followed Grenville's precedent and ended with a compliment to Wilberforce. But Romilly's was the most eloquent, the most daring of them all.

> When I look [he said] to the man at the head of the French monarchy, surrounded as he is with all the pomp of power and all the pride of victory, distributing kingdoms to his family and principalities to his followers, seeming when he sits upon his throne to have reached the summit of human ambition and the pinnacle of earthly happiness—and when I follow that man into his closet or to his bed, and consider the pangs with which his solitude must be tortured and his repose banished, by the recollection of the blood he has spilled and the oppressions he has committed—and when I compare with those pangs of remorse the feelings which must accompany my honourable friend from this House to his home, after the vote of this night shall have confirmed the object of his humane and unceasing labours; when he retires into the bosom of his happy and delighted family, when he lays himself down on his bed, reflecting on the innumerable voices that will be raised in every quarter of the world to bless him, how much more pure and perfect felicity must he enjoy, in the consciousness of having preserved so many millions of his fellow-creatures, than——

The startling comparison in that tense atmosphere was like a spark on gunpowder. The House was on its feet, giving Wilberforce an ovation such as it had given to no other living man. Round after round they cheered him, till the tumult echoed in the ancient roof that had looked down on every scene of Wilberforce's parliamentary career, but never on such a scene as this. It was the supreme moment of Wilberforce's life, yet Wilberforce himself was scarcely conscious of it. In the middle of Romilly's noble tribute, when he spoke of his happy welcome home that night, his emotions overwhelmed him. He hardly knew when Romilly had finished or what that storm of cheering meant. Insensible, as he afterwards confessed, to all that was passing around him, he sat bent in his seat, his head in his hands, and the tears streaming down his face.

When presently he came to himself, a prolonged attack was being made upon the Bill by a Mr. Hibbert who had been connected with the Trade for many years but had only recently entered Parliament. At its close he rose to deliver his last Abolition speech. It was not in scope or form or substance one of his best. But indeed no great effort of argument or eloquence was needed; and his main concern was to applaud the lofty and liberal feeling which the younger members of the House especially had shown that night, and to deprecate once more any bitter or exaggerated charges against their beaten enemies. The West Indian planters (he reminded the House) unlike their critics, had lived all their lives in the deadening atmosphere of slavery. . . . It was now late; and after one or two more short speeches, the question was loudly called for. So the House divided: and when at last the figures were read out, it was found that the second reading had been carried by the tremendous majority of 283 to 16.

The victory was final. It was useless for the Trade to oppose the further stages of the Bill with such a majority behind it. On February 27 it passed into committee without a division. The penal provisions were now inserted, and an amendment to postpone the operation of the Bill for five years was defeated by 175 votes to 17, Canning speaking against it. On the other hand a concession was made to the opposition on a point of sentiment. Howick suggested to Wilberforce that the obnoxious phrase about "justice and humanity" might be dropped from the preamble. "The whole merit of the great victory is yours," he wrote, "and . . . I should be most unwilling to set up my judgment in contradiction to yours." But Wilberforce at once agreed. It was politic and it cost nothing. "The preamble," he said, "has not suffered in its substantial force." On March 16 Lord Henry Petty moved the third reading. Hibbert again opposed it, at still greater length. And this time Windham, who had voted among the sixteen opponents of the second reading, broke silence with a speech of scornful scepticism. "It is not true," he said, "that Parliament is about to abolish the Slave Trade. We are only abolishing our share in it. And it is even doubtful if, after all, this measure will in any degree diminish the traffic in slaves on the coast of 'Africa." Castlereagh, too, was pessimistic. The only results of the Bill, he thought, would be that the attachment of the West Indian colonies to the mother-country would be shaken, that they would smuggle in the slaves they were forbidden to import, and that the mortality would therefore increase. There was too much truth, it will soon be seen, in these cold forecasts, but to both of them Wilberforce made a confident reply; and since Windham had appealed, as usual, to the great authority of Burke, he took occasion once more to correct him. Burke, he told the House, had often declared, both publicly and privately to himself and his friends, that he fully shared their views on Abolition. Francis, Sheridan, Henry Thornton, and Barham also spoke for the Bill. But there was no life in the debate. The opposition had recognised defeat and did not even press for a division. So the Bill was read a third time, without a dissentient vote; and on March 23 it returned to the Lords.

And then, at this eleventh hour, Wilberforce feared for a moment that the prize was after all to be dashed from his hands. For some weeks past the Government had been tottering, and now it was rumoured that it had actually fallen. What if the Bill should be lost in the chasm between two Administrations? But Wilberforce was quickly reassured. Perceval, who was marked out as the next leader of the Commons and was himself a loyal Abolitionist, told him that Eldon, Hawkesbury, and Castlereagh, the Bill's most powerful foes, had all accepted Parliament's decision and would themselves do anything that was needed to carry the Bill into effect without delay. Nor, indeed, was it true that Grenville had yet resigned. He had been given notice, so to speak; the King had declared his intention of finding other servants; but no other Government had been formed when, with one last protest from Westmorland, the Lords confirmed the Commons' amendments. Two days later, on March 25, the King's assent was given and the Bill became law.

"Well, Henry," said Wilberforce to Thornton, when the brethren of the Clapham Sect gathered at his house immediately after the second reading, "Well, Henry, what shall we abolish next?" And never had the Saints been so triumphant, so light-hearted, as on that night. "Let us make out the names of those sixteen mis-

creants," cried William Smith. "Never mind the miserable sixteen,"
replied Wilberforce, looking up from a note he was writing as he
knelt by the crowded table, "let us think of our glorious 283!" But,
when the jubilant company had gone and Wilberforce was left
alone, his thoughts turned wholly to humility and gratitude before
"the Giver of all good." "God will bless this country," he said.

X

Sequel

I

AT the passing of the Abolition Act, Wilberforce reached the zenith of his career. He was now only 48; he was to live till he was nearly 74; but he was never to achieve another personal triumph equal to that of 1807. It would be quite false, however, to suppose that the rest of his life was a protracted anti-climax. His triumph over the Slave Trade had finally confirmed his unique position in the political and social life of England. High Tories might still shudder at his Evangelicalism and discover something of the old Jacobinical taint in his aberrations from the straight and narrow path on such questions as Parliamentary Reform and Catholic Emancipation. Radicals might come to hate the man who could cover the attempt to suppress the rising forces of democracy with a smoke-screen of pietism. But all the world between, the great mass of moderate men, the dominant opinion of the governing class—in Parliament, in Society, in the rank and file of the Evangelical body now growing to its fullest girth, and among his faithful Yorkshiremen—all this world accepted Wilberforce as the authentic keeper of the nation's conscience. Henceforth, till the end, for good or ill, his moral authority was almost pontifical.

It meant, of course, a still busier life for him. No organisation of "good works" was complete without his patronage. At any philanthropic meeting his presence on the platform was almost a matter of course and always warmly recognised by the audience. On one occasion an emotional friend of his burst into tears "at seeing him so applauded." His house was more thickly thronged with visitors than ever. All sorts and conditions of men, from Cabinet Ministers to impoverished parsons, were always coming in. Absolute strangers, of either sex, called to ask his advice. Once, he records, "a young female of twenty came into my library, whose first words when we were alone were, 'I have run away, Mr. Wilberforce!' And a long piece of business have I had with this young fugitive, whose companion, however, I am assured, is of

her own sex—her maid-servant." "You can scarcely conceive," he
complains a few years later, "the prodigious amount of inconvenience which I sustain from not thinking it right to allow my
servants to say, when I am within, that I am not at home." The
importunate besiegers might be told that he was engaged or that
he only saw visitors by appointment. But it was not the least use.
"People will force their way in . . . and you can little conceive
how difficult it often is for me to force my way out of my own
house." So much fame and so much rectitude combined indeed to
drive him to a quaint expedient. He bought a small house close
by his home, and to this refuge, nicknamed "The Nuisance," he
would fly for privacy. "Even there," he says, "I should be no more
safe, if it were known that I had such a lurking-hole, than a fox
would be next Mr. Meynell's kennel." His correspondence, similarly,
grew to immense proportions. "They are become an unspeakable
plague to me," he says of his letters; "they form my chief occupation"; and his new colleague, Fawkes, exclaimed, when he saw
the day's tray-full, "If this is to be member for Yorkshire, the sooner
I am rid of it the better!" Once, indeed, the faithful, and always
candid, Stephen had told him that he could not accept these minor
preoccupations as an excuse for neglect of the greater cause. He
firmly bade him "*make* time" for Abolition business. "If you are
to be only a battering-ram to be pushed forward," he writes, with
an anxious profusion of metaphor, "instead of a fore-horse in the
team to pull as well as guide the rest, the Abolition is undone. It
will sink under the weight of your daily epistles. Your post-
privilege will be the bondage of Africa, and your covers the funereal
pyre of her new-born hopes. Millions will sigh in hopeless wretched-
ness that Wilberforce's correspondents may not think him uncivil
or unkind."

But Wilberforce, being what he was, had to be civil and kind.
And it was not only the interviews and the letters that stole his
time. The calls of Society, too, now pressed more hardly on him
than before. The most exclusive hostesses were anxious to parade
the hero of the day; and it needed all his resolution to refuse and
refuse again. Yet refuse he had to; otherwise, as he said, it would
"lead to an endless round of dinners." But there was one particular
star of the fashionable world who would not endure refusal. When
Wilberforce was in Paris in 1785, it had been discreetly hinted to
him that a match between Mademoiselle Necker and Pitt might

not be inappropriate. Whether the girl saw Wilberforce in those days is not recorded; but the famous Madame de Staël was determined to see him now, and as a guest at her own table. The assault was skilfully conceived. She told Romilly that she wished to make Wilberforce's acquaintance more than that of any other man, and Romilly duly passed it on. She told the Duke of Gloucester that Wilberforce did not know "how really religious she was" and bade him ask the great man and herself to dinner. The invitation of the Abolitionist prince even Wilberforce could scarcely refuse. He came, and was overwhelmed with her compliments on Abolition. "All Europe," she told him, was thrilled. She "almost asked" for copies of his books. And before they parted, she insisted on his dining with her in company with Harrowby and Mackintosh, both Abolitionists, of course. "I could not well refuse," is the diary's naïve complaint. But in cold blood he could not face it. He wrote to excuse himself; and though he said he might come in after dinner, when the time came he shied even from that. But he was not to escape so easily. Madame de Staël was on her mettle. Bets were made among her friends as to the issue. And Wilberforce, when he heard it, suffered "much unpleasant doubting." But when he heard also—and this was her master-stroke—that Madame de Staël was "sure I should come *because I had said I would*," the game was up. He went, and enjoyed it vastly. "A cheerful pleasant dinner —she talking of the final cause of creation—not utility but beauty —did not like Paley—wrote about Rousseau at fifteen, and thought differently at fifty." And, after dinner, a *salon*—"a brilliant assembly of rank and talent." "The whole scene," confessed Wilberforce next morning, "was intoxicating even to me. The fever arising from it is not yet gone off." "I am sure," he adds, "I durst not often venture into those scenes. The seasoning is so high that it would render all quiet domestic pleasures insipid." Indeed the old Adam had been dangerously happy and in most vivacious form. "Mr. Wilberforce," his hostess told Mackintosh afterwards, "is the best converser I have met with in this country. I have always heard that he was the most religious, but I now find that he is the wittiest man in England." She was even tempted to read his books. At any rate she praised them. *C'est l'aurore de l'immortalité*, was her comment to a friend of Wilberforce's on the *Practical View*.

A little later, Wilberforce made the acquaintance of another celebrated lady, who also knew something of France; and Madame d'Arblay was no less delighted with him, though Fanny Burney's style is not quite so exuberant as Madame de Staël's.

Let me steal a moment [she writes to her father from Sandgate] to relate a singular gratification, and, in truth, a real and great honour I have had to rejoice in. You know, my *Padre*, probably, that Marianne Francis was commissioned by Mr. Wilberforce to bring about an acquaintance with your F. d'A. . . . *Eh bien*, at church at Sandgate, the day after my arrival, I saw this justly celebrated man, and was introduced to him in the churchyard after the service by Charles. The ramparts and martellos around us became naturally our theme, and Mr. Wilberforce proposed showing them to me. I readily accepted the offer, and Charles and Sarah, and Mrs. Wilberforce and Mrs. Barrett, went away in their several carriages, while Mr. Barrett alone remained, and Mr. Wilberforce gave me his arm, and, in short, we walked the round from one to five o'clock. Four hours of the best conversation I have, nearly, ever enjoyed! He was anxious for a full and true account of Paris, and particularly of religion and infidelity, and of Bonaparte and the wars, and of all and everything that had occurred during my ten years' seclusion in France; and I had so much to communicate, and his drawing out and comments and episodes were all so judicious, so spirited, so full of information, yet so unassuming, that my shyness all flew away and I felt to be his confidential friend, opening to him upon every occurrence and every sentiment, with the frankness that is usually won by years of intercourse. I was really and truly delighted and enlightened by him; I desired nothing more than to renew the acquaintance, and cultivate it to intimacy. But, alas! he was going away next morning. That his discourse should be edifying, could not, certainly, surprise me; I expected from him all that was elevated in instruction; but there was a mixture of simplicity and vivacity in his manner that I had not expected, and found really captivating. In contemplating the opposite and alas, hostile shore which, to our fancy's eye, at least, was visible, I could not forbear wafting over to it a partial blessing, nor refuse myself beseeching one from Mr. Wilberforce; and the smiling benevolence with which he complied has won my heart for ever. *Addio, Padre mio.*

F. d'A.

But a deeper tribute than any that Fashion or Letters could pay to Wilberforce was paid by the freeholders of Yorkshire. Their allegiance had been tested, as has been seen, in the autumn of 1806; six months later it was tested again; for in April, 1807, the new Government decided on a dissolution. And the result, this time, was a Yorkshire election scarcely less famous in political annals than the historic contests for Middlesex or Westminster. Both parties had at once determined to fight, and, what was more, to spend, to the last limit, in order to win those two cardinal seats. Huge sums were promised on both sides; one peer, indeed, was ready to sacrifice the whole of his property in Barbados. Even for the whole-hearted party candidate the prospect was alarming; and Fawkes, brief as had been his taste of the joys or toils of Parliament and large as was his fortune, refused to face the cost. His place on the Whig side was taken by Wilberforce's old opponent, Lord Milton, and Lascelles stood again for the Tories. What chance, it might well be asked, had a man who had always declared, and continued stoutly to declare, his independence of both parties—unless indeed he were a millionaire? And Wilberforce, who was quite well-off but not immensely rich, was advised by his friends to withdraw from what must prove a hopeless struggle. He was tempted to agree with them. He hated the violence, he dreaded the physical fatigues, of an election. He was no longer young enough to delight in battle with the influence and wealth of the great Yorkshire families on either side. "What greater enjoyment can there be in life," asked the Duke of Norfolk, "than to stand a contested election for Yorkshire and to win it by one?" Wilberforce could have given him several answers. As he confessed to Muncaster, he "sickened at a contest." And yet how could he skulk away from his old supporters on the very morrow of his triumph? How could he, with the cheers of the Commons still ringing in his ears, confess by his withdrawal that Yorkshire was bound to vote for money rather than for merit? It was impossible. Immediately after the dissolution he posted off for York.

He found that Lascelles and Milton had "already engaged canvassing agents, houses of entertainment, and every species of conveyance in every considerable town." It was evident, indeed, in every way that the party organisations were far more efficient and compact than anything an independent candidate could improvise. But, if he could not appeal to the spirit of party, he could appeal to the spirit of independence; and there were Yorkshiremen who could put the second before the first. "We cannot desert Mr. Wilberforce," said a member of his audience on nomination day, and promptly put down £500. Others caught fire from his example, no less than £18,000 was immediately subscribed, and, as the contest drew on, the flow of money steadily increased. His opponents, however, had still the longer purse as they had had the better start; and when, on May 20, the polling began, it was evident at once that Wilberforce must suffer heavily from lack of transport for his supporters—so evident, in fact, that his legal adviser from London declared, when the first day's poll had closed, that he "had obviously no chance, and the sooner he resigned, the better." But if Yorkshiremen wanted to vote for Wilberforce, they were not going to be prevented by the fact that nearly all "the barouches, curricles, gigs, flying wagons, and military cars" (to quote the *York Herald*) that crowded the roads round York for fifteen days belonged to Milton or to Lascelles. "No carriages are to be procured," reports a friend from Hull; "but boats are proceeding up the river heavily laden with voters; farmers lend their wagons; even donkeys have the honour of carrying voters for Wilberforce; and hundreds are proceeding on foot." One such party was met by a member of his committee on the road from Wensleydale. "For what parties, gentlemen, do you come?" he asked. "Wilberforce to a man" was the reply. One freeholder from near Rotherham had refused to be deterred by lack of transport or the means to purchase it. He had come all the way, he boasted, behind Lord Milton's carriage.

Ill organised though it was, this enthusiasm quickly told. By the end of the fourth day, Wilberforce was 111 ahead of Milton and 375 ahead of Lascelles. Every time-honoured device was tried by his opponents. Palpable lies were whispered about or openly printed on handbills. What the diary calls "the mob-directing system" was put in force. "Twenty bruisers sent for, Firby the young ruffian, Gully and others." And when these were "directed" into the storm that raged all day about the hustings, it was often impossible for hours together for Wilberforce to gain a hearing. But still, each night, he continued, though not by much, to head the poll. On the twelfth day he fell ill and could not leave his room. At once the word went round that he was dead. But his victory was now secure; and at the final count the figures read—Wilberforce, 11,806; Milton, 11,177; Lascelles, 10,989.

W.   T

It was said that the combined expenditure of his two opponents amounted to £200,000. The subscriptions which poured in for Wilberforce, not only from Yorkshire but from all over the country, reached in the end a total of £70,000. But more than half of it was returned; his actual expenses were less than £30,000. These are significant figures. Even in those halcyon days of Old Corruption it was possible for a great and scattered constituency to return the better, though the poorer, man; and even in an election which was notorious for the strength of the party spirit it evoked, it was possible for such politically minded electors as the Yorkshiremen to set at the head of the poll a politician who had voted in his day for Fox as well as for Pitt, who had censured Melville no less than Hastings, and whose one great political achievement had been carried through from first to last outside the ring of party warfare.

2

After their brief share of office the Whigs returned to the wilderness for another twenty-three years; so that, till almost the end of his life, and as long as he remained in politics, Wilberforce had to deal with a succession of Tory Governments, backed by fairly consistent majorities. His independence, therefore, was much the same kind of independence as that which Fox had jeered at in the old days. When Wilberforce declared he could bind himself to no party, it did not mean that he had no principles. "Independents" in the House of Commons have never been, can never be, absolute neutrals. And Wilberforce's principles were, in their general colour, Tory principles. Now as before, he sat on the Tory side of the House. His friends among its leading members were mostly Tories. He was never intimate with Grey. He could never really like Brougham. But his heart went out to Perceval, partly because he was, as he says, "a most generous creature" and "sweet-tempered," partly for the same reason which made him always friendly to Addington, because he was religious; he has been called, indeed, "our first really devout Prime Minister." Canning, too, for other reasons, he liked and admired; and his sentiments were so far reciprocated that Canning at one time made him his confidant in his queer, unhappy feud with Castlereagh and wrote him long letters, subscribed "very sincerely and affectionately," to justify his refusal ever to stand second to his rival. But this, of course, did not prevent Wilberforce from being almost as shocked at their duel as he had been at Pitt's and from wishing "the King would declare that neither of them should ever serve him again in a public station." Of Lord Wellesley, too, he thought highly, and he came to regard even Hawkesbury, soon to be Liverpool, as "a really sensible man." His political *milieu* had been, in fact, decided for good and all when he entered Parliament at Pitt's side in 1780. His place was among the Pittites; it could never be among the disciples and heirs of Fox.

His attitude to the fall of Grenville's Government betrays at once his Tory outlook. It had been practically dismissed by George III on the old Irish question. Grenville himself told Wilberforce that, when he refused an absolute promise never to propose any extension of power to Roman Catholics, "Then," said the King, "I must look about me." And Wilberforce was too satisfied with the result to think twice about the means. "It is in one grand particular," he said, "the same question as in 1784. My then principles, to which I still adhere, would govern my vote, even if I did not think so favourably of Perceval as I do." What principles? Was it only because the Ministry of All the Talents, like the Fox-North Government, was a coalition? "Coalitions," said Wilberforce, when one seemed likely to be formed again in 1809, "are odious things, and lead to the dissolution of all principle and the loss of all credit in public men." But there was another significant point of similarity between 1807 and 1784. On both occasions George III had used his prerogative to dismiss a Government he did not like and to replace it with a pure Tory Government, willing to work in unison with his personal policy. And Wilberforce's attitude to the prerogative was not the attitude of a Whig.

So he resumed, naturally enough, the kind of independence he had practised under Pitt. He publicly admitted his debt of gratitude to those who had carried Abolition; but he denied that he had any right to repay it by parliamentary support. And most of his Abolitionist intimates took the same line. "I am glad to find," he writes, "that Bankes, Babington, and I, and Grant, and Henry Thornton too, all settle down into trying the new Ministry and treating them as their measures deserve." And on the most vital question of all it was easier for Wilberforce to treat their measures kindly than it had sometimes been in Pitt's day. The war had entered on its final phase. It was now, in a far more direct and generally

accepted sense, a defensive war. There was no occasion now for
Wilberforce to be torn between his allegiance to Government in
war-time and his love of peace. Even he could not share in the
renewal of pacifist agitation in 1807-8. For no man of any common
sense could any longer believe in the possibility of peace till Napoleon
abandoned his attempt to force Britain into sharing the subjection
of the rest of Europe. But, if the primary issue between peace and
war could not now be raised at Westminster, there was material
enough for party strife, as bitter as of old, about the methods by
which the war was prosecuted; and in the course of the next few
years Wilberforce was obliged to make up his mind on four outstanding controversial questions.

Far the most important of these was the question of the Peninsular Campaign. There was no party flavour in the universal
enthusiasm with which the news of the Spanish Rising of 1808 was
received in England. Since Austerlitz and the death of Pitt, Englishmen had "rolled up the map of Europe"; they had abandoned, once
for all, the heart-breaking policy of stimulating and subsidizing
monarchical coalitions; they had stood grimly aloof while Napoleon,
having come to terms with the Czar at Tilsit, began to organise
the whole Continent as a single subservient instrument for the
economic destruction of England. And now, against all hope, a rift
had suddenly appeared in that close-drawn net. Regardless of
Spanish pride, the Corsican had coolly planted his brother Joseph
on the throne of Spain; and the Spaniards had risen, not at the
bidding of an autocrat nor bribed by English pay, but aflame with
the new spirit of nationality which was presently to kindle in other
parts of Europe and to burn through the foundations of the
Napoleonic Empire. Naturally there was no doubt in either English
party as to the necessity of fastening on this breach in the wall,
of directing through it the pent-up stream of British trade, of
assisting the Spanish Juntas with troops and arms and funds.
"Every head and heart," writes Wilberforce to Muncaster, "are full
of schemes and sympathies for the poor Spaniards"—Whig heads
and hearts as well as Tory. Sheridan, indeed, prepared a speech
which was meant, says the diary, to "electrify the country." But
"the opportunity being delayed, he, going upstairs, got so drunk"
that, when he spoke, "he was like a man catching through a thick
medium at the objects before him." Wilberforce himself pressed
for a Joint Address from both Houses, committing the country to

the Spanish cause. But this general enthusiasm and this concord of parties did not last long. The new attempt at military intervention on the Continent soon seemed as disappointing as the old. Wellesley's victory at Vimiero in August, 1808, was robbed of its fruits by the senior generals who took over his command and signed the unfortunate Convention of Cintra. In the winter Napoleon himself appeared in Spain with a quarter of a million men to smash this impertinent Spanish revolt; and Moore's retreat to Corunna, though it brilliantly saved his little army from the enemy's grasp, was none the less a retreat. It was all certainly disheartening. The rising seemed doomed. And, remembering the wretched series of fiascos in Flanders, the Whigs for the most part turned round and denounced the Spanish adventure. They were supported by a strong body of public opinion, but not by Wilberforce. The "Independent" voted, indeed, against the Government in 1810 on the inquiry into the Walcheren *débâcle*; but, when Ministers refused to jettison the Spanish patriots, when in 1809, having taken Wellesley's measure, they sent the unpopular general back to Portugal with a British army, to win, before the year was out, the victories of Douro and Talavera and the title of Lord Wellington, and when thenceforward they made Wellington's policy in the Peninsula their own, they could count on Wilberforce's vote.

On the three other controversial questions arising in this final period of the war—the seizure of the Danish fleet in 1807, the quarrel with the United States in 1812, and the coercion of Norway in 1814 —it was not so easy for Wilberforce to agree with the Government. The seizure of the Danish fleet could only in fact be defended by the casuistry of war. We know now—what Canning, then Foreign Secretary, half knew from his secret service and half guessed—that by the secret clauses of the Treaty of Tilsit Napoleon and Alexander had agreed to persuade or, if need be, to compel the Scandinavian Powers to join the Continental System and to place their fleets at the disposal of the anti-British alliance. Canning promptly countered this threat by dispatching a strong force of ships and troops to demand the surrender of the Danish fleet, though Denmark was still neutral. The Danes refused; whereupon Copenhagen was bombarded, and the fleet carried off by force. Was Canning justified in thus anticipating Napoleon's plans and methods? It was certainly a poser for Wilberforce's conscience. He discussed it at length with

Sidmouth who condemned the *coup*, mainly because he believed the
Danes were preparing to fight the French, and with Admiral
Gambier who was "quite satisfied of the rectitude and extreme
utility" of it, and spoke "in high terms of the Divine goodness and
of the protection of Providence." "After much (I trust impartial)
reflection," writes Wilberforce to Hey, "I am convinced that, under
all the circumstances of the case, the Danish expedition was just.
. . . It was absolutely essential to deprive the Danes of a fleet
which, combined with that of Russia, would otherwise have soon
conveyed a French army to Ireland or Scotland." He confesses to
Babington, however, that he could scarcely have dared to advise
the expedition if he had been a member of the Cabinet; and he
insists that the captured fleet should not be used by Britain, but
should be "kept as a sacred deposit, to be restored on the termination
of the war." Such are the compromises to which, as long as war
continues, all but the most cantankerous consciences must needs be
driven.

The Norway case was similarly a product of war morals. As
the struggle with Napoleon neared its end, Prince Bernadotte of
Sweden was urged by the Czar Alexander to join the Allies and
create a diversion with a Swedish force in Prussia. He agreed, but
at a substantial price. He insisted, and the Czar promised, that in
the event of the final triumph of the Allies, Norway should be
severed from Denmark, with which it had been united for nearly
400 years, and annexed to Sweden. The fact that such a transaction
would be undoubtedly repugnant to the majority of the Norwegian
people was simply ignored. The compact was signed in 1812, and
in 1813 it was confirmed by Britain in the separate Treaty of Stockholm with Sweden. In the autumn of that year, the Swedish Prince
and his army took their part in the decisive battle of Leipzig.
Napoleon's power was broken, and Bernadotte claimed his reward.
The Danes submitted; they surrendered Norway by the Treaty of
Kiel; their garrisons and officials evacuated the country. But the
Norwegians did not submit; they refused to yield to the hated
Swedes. Force was therefore needed; the treaty of 1813 became
operative; and the British fleet was ordered to reduce the Norwegians to obedience by a strict blockade of their coast. The result
was mercifully quick. Confronted with famine and starvation, as
well as Bernadotte's invading army, the Norwegians came to terms
in a fortnight. But, at the time the blockade was begun, there was

no saying how long they might have held out, and by many
Englishmen the whole business was regarded with deep aversion.
In a debate in the House of Commons in the spring of 1814—interesting, among other reasons, as the occasion of the maiden speech
of the young Whig who was one day to be Earl of Durham—the
Opposition violently criticised the use of the British navy for so
objectionable a purpose. The Norwegians will say, declared Sir
James Mackintosh, "Here are those boasted advocates of human
liberty, those deliverers of mankind, come to starve our infants,
because our countrymen will not submit to slavery." There could
only be one answer, and Canning gave it. He wished the treaty had
never been made. He had himself urged the House not to sanction
it. He would pay any price to be relieved of its obligations. But it
had been sanctioned; it could not be evaded; and honour required
its fulfilment. It was an inexorable argument, and Wilberforce
perforce accepted it. "The idea of starving these poor people is
shocking," he writes in his diary the night before the debate. "Oh,
how hideous are war's features when closely viewed!" But with a
touch of practical shrewdness he adds: "The truth is Norway would
not starve. She would submit, if she knew she must." That night,
however, he "slept but ill, from uneasiness about the approaching
Norway question." And next day it was only with reluctance, and
late in the debate, that he spoke in support of Canning's case. The
whole treatment of Norway, he declared, was a piece of flagrant
injustice. "I consider the partitioning of states against their will
a most despotic sacrifice of public rights." But the execution of
the treaty was a matter of good faith; and he only hoped that the
Government, who had not, it appeared, originated the policy of
the cession, would do all it could, in carrying out its unpleasant
duty, to minimise the sufferings of the Norwegian people.

If Wilberforce's "independence" had been flavoured with Whig
rather than Tory principles, he might perhaps have taken sides
with the Opposition over Norway. He would almost certainly have
done so over Denmark. And on the third question—the quarrel
with the United States—the conflict between his natural instincts
and his political friendships was no less obvious. High Tory circles
had never forgotten, still less forgiven, the American Revolution.
The enthusiasm of Jefferson and his party for the Jacobins and
their unconcealed antagonism to Britain had confirmed them in
their opinion that Americans in the mass were dangerous and

rather disreputable Radicals, cloaking a spirit of sheer licence with fine phrases about freedom. They forgot the ties of common blood. They ignored the marked British sympathies of New England. And they intensely disliked having to treat this upstart nation as a fellow member with Great Britain in the society of states. It is now admitted, on the other hand, by all impartial students that, when the quarrel came to a head, the attitude of the American Government was mistaken. They should have seen that Napoleon's Continental System was just as derogatory to the rights of neutrals as the Orders-in-Council with which Britain countered it, and that British interference with their trade was only more palpable than French because Britain commanded the sea. They should have realised, too, galling as the British claim to search for deserters and to impress British subjects on American ships might be, that Napoleon's contempt for other people's rights and feelings was far more cynical and sweeping. But it is also admitted that, though British Ministers did not in the least desire war with the United States—with a white population a third the size of Britain's and twelve times the size of Canada's—at the climax of the struggle with Napoleon, and though, indeed, their policy was by no means unconciliatory, yet in the exposition of it, in the able dispatches they penned for American perusal, they failed utterly in tact. It may be that President Madison and his followers would have had their fling at the kingdom of George III in any case; but the cold, formal, superior tone of even the best-intentioned approaches from the Foreign Office was little calculated to placate their animosity. It was no new thing, unhappily, in 1812. Ten years earlier, the American Minister in London, then Mr. King, had begged Wilberforce to use his influence with Addington and his Foreign Secretary to do what was most needed to promote an Anglo-American *entente*. "I don't mean to insinuate," he had written, "that Ministers are deaf to justice and that they adopt measures of which we may justly complain. No, it is the omission of minor offices, which, like an omitted visit, produces more coldness and finally dislike than a downright injury." And Wilberforce had understood what he meant. He was one of the few Englishmen of the time who detected this half-unconscious failure in tact and appreciated its pernicious effects on American opinion. He was not handicapped by any political prejudice against the United States. He had entered Parliament in 1780 as a declared opponent of the American War, and his first and closest political comrade had been Chatham's son. When the crusade for Abolition absorbed his mind, he was drawn closer to America by the knowledge that one of the first assaults upon the Slave Trade had been made by American Quakers; and despite the special difficulty of Slavery in the Southern States—or rather because of it—he felt that the cause of Abolition should appeal to America above all other countries. Shortly after the triumph of 1807 he had written to Jefferson, urging an Anglo-American compact for the final suppression of the Trade. He took a liking, moreover, to the Americans he met in London. They might not be— and who was?—all that he would have wished on the cardinal point —"I fear there is little spirit of religion in America," he once said— but he admired their directness, their simplicity of manners, their common sense. "Dined at Hampstead to meet Jay, the American envoy, his son, etc.," records the diary, "quite Americans—sensible —very pleasing, well-informed men."

Wilberforce, therefore, was more dismayed than most Englishmen when the quarrel began to drift towards an open rupture in the winter of 1811-12. He speaks of "the grief and pain with which the very thought of a war with America fills my heart." And if it should come, "I cannot look forward," he says, "to the idea of victory in any war between Great Britain and America." When the question was raised in the House of Commons on February 13 by Whitbread's motion for the publication of the official correspondence, he was only just convalescent from an illness of some weeks' duration; but he insisted ("much sooner, perhaps, than was prudent," he confesses) on attending and taking part in the debate. He opposed the motion, and thereby angered Whitbread who was "very rough and rude." But in this case his attitude was not governed by Ministerial sympathies. He argued very sensibly that the publication of the dispatches, just at this moment, was far more likely to inflame opinion on both sides of the Atlantic than to soothe it. And that led him to the root of the trouble on the British side—the insular aloofness and insensitiveness of the British official mind towards the outer world. "I confess," he said, "that there is not at all times a sufficient attention in this country to the spirit of conciliation towards other countries and especially towards America. It would be well if persons in high situations of government had been more abundant in their civilities to that nation which, being a new one, is naturally more jealous of etiquette, possibly from feeling that it does not stand on as high ground as other and older states." This was precisely what needed saying and it was well said. Three weeks later, on March 3, he supported Brougham's demand for an inquiry into the effects of the Government's main instrument of economic warfare with Napoleon, the Orders-in-Council. They might or might not, he said, be a primary cause of the distress of the mercantile middle-class, for which Brougham was the spokesman; but they were certainly one of the causes of our quarrel with America. "I never was a warm friend to those measures," he writes of the Orders-in-Council, "or rather no friend at all but an enemy to parts of them. I am sick at heart from the sad prospect of a war with America."

The Government was shaken by this general revolt. It conceded the inquiry; it made up its mind to abandon the Orders; it began the awkward business of climbing down. An instant declaration might conceivably have forestalled the war, but unhappily, at this decisive moment, the whole machine of Government was temporarily put out of operation by the Prime Minister's sudden death. On May 11 Perceval was assassinated by a lunatic. It was a great personal blow to Wilberforce. "Perceval had the sweetest of all possible tempers," he sadly comments in his diary, "and was one of the most conscientious men I ever knew." His grief would have been deeper still if he had realised the public disaster which the private tragedy had involved. The formation of the Liverpool Ministry meant delay; and it was not till June 16 that Castlereagh announced that the Orders-in-Council were immediately to be suspended. The sands had run out. Three days later, long before the news of the British concession could reach the other side of the Atlantic, President Madison declared that the United States were at war with Great Britain. On July 19, little knowing that the tidings of the actual rupture were already far on their way across the ocean, Wilberforce declared, in the closing debate of the session, the sentiments which all Englishmen ought to have felt. "I most earnestly trust," he said, "that we are not to be involved in the misfortune of a new war, aggravated by possessing almost the character of civil strife—a war between two nations who are children of the same family and brothers in the same inheritance of common liberty."

3

On the Government's war-policy, then, Wilberforce did not oppose his Tory friends. He was disquieted at their conduct towards Denmark and Norway, he criticised their American diplomacy, but he felt that in the main their case was justified; and on the supreme question of the Peninsular campaign he was wholly with them. In domestic policy, on the other hand, he could make a better claim to independence. On the two leading issues of Roman Catholic Emancipation and Parliamentary Reform he moved steadily away, during these years, from the orthodox Government faith. On neither of them could he ever be described as a Whig. But on both of them he was, or became, at least a Tory of the Left.

Most of the few Tories who had swallowed Pitt's moderate proposals for Reform in the 'eighties had long since succumbed to the anti-Jacobin reaction and joined with Pitt in driving the whole Reform movement underground. At the beginning of the nineteenth century it seemed as if Reform was dead; and when presently it began to show signs of life and even to creep back timidly into parliamentary politics, the Tory rank and file had no doubts as to the propriety of killing it and this time really killing it. Not so Wilberforce. He had indeed supported Pitt's system of repression, but he realised now that times had changed. True, he was as much afraid of Trade Unionism as ever. In 1806 he had been the leading member of a House of Commons Committee on the Woollen Manufacture and had drafted its able Report—chiefly memorable for the support it gave to the "domestic system" of production in the clothiers' village houses, which naturally appealed to Wilberforce's love of rustic life and faith in rustic morals and which he rightly believed could be carried on successfully side by side with the "factory system" in the towns—and in the course of this Report he had repeated his case for the Combination Laws: not only the risk of wages being forced so high as to ruin "the whole commercial greatness of our country," but also the political dangers of any organised society of workmen. But this did not mean that Wilberforce, in these years at any rate, was an alarmist. Jacobinism was now a very old story. Progressive opinion in the country, though far from contented with the operation of the constitutional machine, was not so high-strung as in those hysterical days. Now, surely, thought Wilberforce, was the moment for attempting Reform without the risk of its becoming Revolution. And so in 1809, when Curwen introduced his Bill for making the sale of seats in Parliament illegal, he supported it. He stood, he said, where Pitt had stood at the outset of his career. If a moderate measure of Reform was desirable then, it was no less desirable now. "Let us not be called upon to stand still, nor let us libel the constitution so far as to say that it is necessary to its preservation that we should cherish its radical defects." At a later stage, he outspokenly attacked corruption in the bestowal of offices, titles and contracts. But he was not yet ready to tackle the basic question of representation, and he neither spoke nor voted for Burdett's drastic motion in the same session. Next year, however, a significant entry appears in the diary for May 5—"Wyvill breakfasted with me about Parliamentary Reform." And on May 21 he votes for Brand's motion for a Committee to consider the means of making the representative system "more complete." A month later he presents a temperate Address from the inhabitants of Sheffield; and while dissociating himself from "wild measures" and eulogising the constitution, he pleads again for the removal of the anomalies that blemish it.

It was but a moderate line he took, but it was really independent. His Government friends, though they could not resist the attack on positive corruption and accepted Curwen's Bill, set their faces against any tampering with the "rotten boroughs," and they resented Wilberforce's revivification of the younger and more liberal Pitt. Even Canning let fall one of his barbed sarcasms. And some of Wilberforce's Tory constituents in Yorkshire were up in arms. Letters of protest were addressed to their recalcitrant member, reminding him of "the general disinclination of reflecting men to any change in the representation." But he maintained his independence. "All seems quiet now," he notes; "but how little are men aware of the real dangers of the country! How little do they look forward to our probable state fifteen or twenty years hence!" This was written in 1810. By 1830 the continued refusal of Reform had brought the country to the most acute political crisis it had known since the days of the English Revolution.

Similarly moderate, similarly independent was Wilberforce's attitude to Catholic Emancipation. He was not, it has been seen, a bigot about Popery. Nor was he by any means a Gallio. He was a zealous English Protestant: the historic antipathy to Rome was in his bones. "When I recollect the history of past times," he once said in the House of Commons, "I cannot but be jealous of the Roman Catholic religion." While, therefore, he accepted the principle of toleration and utterly condemned the injustice and futility of trying, as the system of the Penal Laws had tried, to stamp out Romanism in Ireland by pains and penalties, he was not prepared to move an inch beyond passive tolerance. He did not realise the tenacity with which the national spirit of the Irish clung to its creed nor the responsibilities which the Union had imposed on the Government of the United Kingdom. To his mind one of the fruits —the happiest, perhaps—of the Union should be the gradual conversion of the Irish to Protestantism. "So long as the bulk of the Irish are Roman Catholics," he once remarked to Grenville, "the Protestants and the friends of Great Britain will be in truth a garrison in an enemy's country; and our great endeavour ought to be to enlighten and thereby, I trust, to convert the Roman Catholics. Much, I verily believe, might be done in that way in twenty or thirty years." It is this strange idea that supplies the key to his policy throughout. On that ground he repeatedly opposed grants, whether by the Grenville Government or its successors, to the college of Maynooth for the education of a Catholic priesthood —a "most pernicious measure," a "very dangerous" development. And on that ground he defended the maintenance of the Established Church in Ireland, mainly supported though it was by compulsory Catholic contributions. He admitted the anomaly; but, like most Englishmen of his day who thought about it at all, he saw only one way to its removal—the way of "enlightenment." More than half a century was to pass before Gladstone dared to take the other way—the way of disestablishment. To Wilberforce and most of his contemporaries such a surrender was inconceivable. They would have regarded it as nothing short of a betrayal of their faith, a cynical compact with wrong, a dooming of the Irish people to the dark for ever. As it was, Wilberforce was shocked at the sympathetic references to Catholicism in Parliament. "It is grievous to see," he says to Stephen after a debate in 1808, "that we are only nominally a Protestant people." "I am not one of those men," he had himself declared in the previous year, "who entertain the large and liberal views on religious subjects, insisted on with so much energy by the honourable gentlemen on the other side. I am not so much like a certain ruler of whom it has been so happily said that he was an honorary member of all religions."

The same motive—the avoidance of anything that would strengthen the Catholic Church in Ireland—inspired his attitude to the political issue. It has been seen how long he hesitated over the Union, how he only succumbed at last to Pitt's personal pressure, and how uneasy he felt at Pitt's intention to complete his Irish settlement by the political enfranchisement of the Catholics. And when Pitt was dead, the fear of Catholics in Parliament took a stronger hold on him. Was it not enough that Catholics now could vote? Should they also be allowed to sit? It was on this point chiefly that he differed from Grenville and the Whigs at the very moment he was so closely tied to them by the cause of Abolition. It was largely because they were pressing for Catholic Emancipation that, once Abolition had been carried, he was not altogether distressed at their fall. "I feel deeply impressed," says a letter of that time, "with the sense of the importance of not embarking on a Roman Catholic bottom (if I may so term it) the interest and well-being of our Protestant empire." But he could not fold his hands on that. The peculiar standing in politics which the triumph of Abolition had given him forced him into closer quarters with the problem. He had been lifted above all personalities and parties as the friend of the oppressed; and there were some who thought that he must therefore be a friend of the Irish Catholics. Letters flowed in, entreating him to add Emancipation to Abolition. "I hope," wrote Sydney Smith, "now you have done with Africa, you will do something for Ireland. There is no man in England who from activity, understanding, character, and neutrality could do it so effectually as Mr. Wilberforce." These challenging compliments could not be run away from, and Wilberforce applied himself to a new and fuller study of the available literature on the question. The result was scarcely what Sydney Smith and his friends had hoped, but it was something. Guided always by that dominant religious motive, Wilberforce gradually came to the conclusion that it weakened the Protestant cause in Ireland to keep Catholics out of Parliament when once they had been given the parliamentary vote. "The Catholic hierarchy," as he put it a few years later to a friend, Hey, "can do just as well through the medium of members of Parliament *called* Protestants, but who, being elected by Roman Catholic voters and having little or no real religion

themselves, are implicitly subservient to their constituents' purposes." They can indeed do better, since such representatives "do
not call into action the Protestant spirit in the same degree." The
Catholic Church, meantime, increases its hold on its members by
agitating the grievance of their exclusion from Parliament. Inclusion, on the other hand, will "connect them to the Protestant system
by the various ties which unite men who act together in Parliament
and which would render it improbable that they would join a
foreign enemy in separating Ireland from Great Britain." "Where
can be the wisdom," he sums up, "of retaining the prison dress when
you have set the men at liberty?"

Wilberforce did not reach this position at one bound. As early
as 1808, it is true, the diary admits, "I strongly incline to their
coming into Parliament, though not to their seeing with other
men's [priests'] eyes." But in a debate of that year he declares he
must still resist the Catholic claim on the ground that public opinion
in England is overwhelmingly against it. It can only raise vain
hopes and make grievances more bitter. "Alas!" he complains, "they
are driving the Roman Catholics to rebellion. How mad to be thus
stimulating them by telling them they are enslaved and oppressed!"
But, year by year, he moves farther away from the intransigeant
attitude of almost all his ministerial friends save Canning, farther
away, too, from the prejudices of his own familiar circle. Nor does
his argument as to the anti-Popish instincts of the British public
lose any of its force. When the question becomes a burning issue
in 1813, the Protestants sweep the country, "Meetings against
Roman Catholics in all parts of England." But it is characteristic
of Wilberforce that the unpopularity of a cause stiffens him in his
adherence to it. Slowly, somewhat anxiously, but steadily, he comes
to conviction. "I am very doubtful which way right." "Lord direct
me; all the religious people are on the other side." "It grieves me
to separate from the Dean and all my religious friends; but conscience must be obeyed." And so, in the course of the great debates
of 1813, though public opinion is at least as hostile as it was in
1808, he declares himself converted to Emancipation. It is absurd,
he argues again, to keep Catholics from the House when you have
already given them the vote. And, forgetting his own alarms at
the dangerous effect of Whig speeches a few years back, he tells the
House that it cannot expect the Catholics to be satisfied and tranquil.
"Light and knowledge are spreading in Ireland; and the more they

extend, the more will the Catholics of Ireland desire to enjoy all
the privileges of freemen. . . . We are now suffering from the
follies and vices of our forefathers. Ireland has been treated as a
conquered country; and the remaining links of her ancient chains
press more severely on her because she has been admitted to a part
of the blessings of the British constitution." He begs the House,
therefore, to see the wisdom of concession. "This is a golden opportunity which may never return if we now lose it."

The speech made a profound impression. As Canning said,
Wilberforce's opinion was peculiarly powerful because it was known
to be conscientious and had been so deliberately formed. And it
produced almost a sensation in the religious world outside. The
Evangelicals, fiery Protestants as they were and largely responsible
for keeping alive the hate of Rome among the general public, were
astounded. Even Hannah More and her kinsfolk were within an
ace of quarrelling with Wilberforce about it. But there was no call
for these alarms. Emancipation had no chance in 1813. The House
of Commons might accept Grattan's resolutions, as it did the one
which Wilberforce supported; but that was all. The Government
was not prepared to frame a Bill, nor Parliament to pass it. Nor
was Wilberforce prepared to follow to the end the path to which
Sydney Smith had pointed. He could not do for Ireland what he
had done for Africa. Deeply conscious of the public influence he
now possessed, he would labour to form a true opinion on each
outstanding issue: he would fearlessly declare it and vote for it;
but, if, as in this case of Catholic Emancipation, popular prejudice
was against him, he would not devote all his time and strength to
fighting it. He was not, it may be said again, an "all-round"
statesman: he could only go crusading in one cause.

4

Wilberforce, indeed, had begun to feel that the demands of
general politics, which as member for so important a constituency
as Yorkshire he felt bound to meet, were absorbing too much of
his time. How conscientiously he performed his duties in the House
of Commons has already been observed. "There is scarcely any
member of Parliament," he writes to one of his constituents in
1811, "who has much, or I might almost say any, private business,

who attends the discussions on public questions with anything like the same degree of regularity as myself or who takes part so much in them. . . . I have stayed till the very end of the session, I believe, every year of the last twenty-three or twenty-four." Nor is there any other member, he adds, who is so consistently asked to serve on Committees of the House. And the innumerable hours he spent at Westminster were not the only time he gave to his parliamentary duties. They pursued him home. Yorkshiremen, eager for a word with their member, increased the crowd that packed his waiting-room at Kensington; and letters from constituents swelled the appalling bundle on his table. The strain of fulfilling conscientiously all these responsibilities weighed on him more and more. How long, he began to ask himself, could he endure it? His first political obligation, after all, was to hold and extend the ground won by the Abolition Act; and this, as will presently be seen, meant constant watchfulness and work. Was he not in danger of being cramped and crippled for that service by the business of general politics? If he could not scamp his manifold duties, as Stephen wished, shut the door in strangers' faces, consign their letters to the waste-paper basket, ought he not to reduce his public obligations—even, perhaps, to resign the Yorkshire seat?

And there were other considerations moving him in that direction. He was only fifty-two, but his constitutional frailty had always forbidden him to count on a long life. Though he had never again been so near death as he was in 1788, he had once or twice been dangerously ill; and he was frequently ailing and often confined to his room for a week or more at a time. He was beginning, too, to detect, or to imagine he detected, the first advances of old age. His eyesight was not much worse than it had always been, but "I am much impressed," he notes, "with finding my memory more decayed than I had conceived. . . . This is surely a strong argument for retiring. . . . I may forget engagements, declarations, and things which I have said." But what weighed most of all with him was the fact that he now possessed a growing family and had far too little leisure to do a father's duty as he believed it should be done. Writing in 1810 from a country house at Hurstmonceux which a friend had lent him for a summer holiday, "I have had an opportunity," he says, "of becoming acquainted with my own children who, it is no exaggeration to declare, seldom get a quiet minute with me during the sitting of Parliament." There

W.   U

were six of them—four sons and two daughters—and at this date
the eldest, William, was already twelve years old. He was never
happier than in their company, nor they than in his. In his own
unfading youthfulness of spirit he held the key to children's hearts.
An historian of the Clapham Sect has recorded how its grave
deliberations in Chatham's library were sometimes interrupted by
a burst of merriment from the garden outside. It marked the
approach of Wilberforce, striding across the lawn with a laughing
boy clinging to each hand. He loved to read aloud to them on
Sundays or to make them read aloud to him. And when he could
snatch an hour or two from his London week-days he would carry
them off to the British Museum or, better still, "to see the great
fish, and to toy-shops" or "to see some jugglers." At home, too,
for all his years, the little man could be very strenuous—"running
races with them in the garden" or "playing blind-man's buff for
two hours" on Twelfth Night. But this casual intercourse, these
jolly interludes, were not enough. More and more, as they grew
up, Wilberforce's mind was troubled by the question of their education and his parental part in it. It seemed to him a very grave
matter—perhaps too grave a matter. For he was always wondering
whether, when the time came, they would get their supreme chance
of felicity and take it, as he had been led by divine accident to take
it thirty years ago. "I humbly trust," he wrote about this time,
"that I can say with truth that the spiritual interests of my children
are my first object. I mean that I wish to see them become real
Christians rather than great scholars or eminent in any other way."
And we know how much he meant by "real Christians." He was
wise enough, indeed, not to try to force on them what, as he believed,
could only come by Grace. He was dismayed, for instance, and not
unnaturally, when an Evangelical friend of his told one of his boys,
who had just brought home a good report, that it was "God's work
on the heart." "I fear above all," he says, "his being led to affect
more than he really feels." But, none the less, few fathers of those
days can have seasoned their intercourse with their children with
so much of the moralities. Were they reading a poem of Scott's,
it was the moral of the tale, not its romance, he fastened on. Were
they studying history together, it was the moral conduct of its
characters on which he tried to fix their minds. When the bell for
family prayers cut short their reading of Robertson's *History of
America*, he made its heavy tones chime with the vices of the Spanish

conquerors—a whimsical but very effective aid to memory. "To this hour," confessed one of his sons long afterwards, "the sound of a bell insensibly reminds me of his exclamation: 'There it is again! *Cruel* Cortes! *Perfidious* Pizarro!'" And often in the merriest hours of a country holiday the children would be reminded, in that simple unaffected way their father had of mingling grave and gay, of the author of all their pleasures. "Mr. Wilberforce made us all very happy," writes a friend at a family picnic-party. "He read, and talked, and carved, and reminded us of the benevolence of God." And, of course, there were also more direct methods of moral education. The children were taken to church at an early age. They listened to a multitude of sermons. And their father, with that rare capacity again for frank and easy talk on those intimate matters about which parents usually find it very hard to speak, would discuss and criticise their conduct with them and especially their conduct towards one another. When two of the boys were at school together, he provided each of them with a paper of "Hints," "to be often read over," bidding the elder to guard against his disposition to dragoon the younger and bidding the younger not to resent the elder's commanding ways. "Often reflect," he tells them both, "that you are both children of the same father and mother; how you have knelt together in prayer; have played together as children, and have sat round the same table on a Sunday in peace and love. Place the scene before your mind's eye, and recollect how happy mamma and I have been to see you all around us good and happy."

To a father so devoted to his children, so anxiously watchful of their little foibles, feeling so acutely his responsibility, it seemed increasingly regrettable, as they drew near their 'teens and the difficult age, that in London, at any rate, and while Parliament was sitting, he should be able to see so little of them. It was this, indeed, more than any other argument, that influenced him when in the session of 1812 he came to the decision to resign his seat. It was not lightly come to. The seat for Yorkshire was one of peculiar prestige and authority in the unreformed House of Commons; the man who held it, though he might never be a Minister, was always a parliamentary personage. Ties, too, that time has tightened and familiarised are hard to break; and how strongly the majority of his constituents desired to maintain them had been very plainly shown by their energy and enthusiasm in the great fight of 1807.

Nor could Wilberforce obtain any unanimous counsel from his friends. Grant and Henry Thornton were against his leaving Yorkshire, and so, too, was the Speaker when he called to ask his advice. Stephen and others were for his migration from Yorkshire to some small seat which would involve him in little, if any, local obligations and would not necessitate his continual attendance at Westminster. Babington advised a clean-cut retirement from Parliament altogether. Between these choices he wavered long, but at last he settled on the middle course. It was hard enough to abandon the great county, to step aside from the regular daily march of politics, to become, so to speak, an intermittent politician. "I feel very deeply," the diary confesses, "the loss of my high situation, and being out of the *dramatis personæ* whilst my friends are acting their parts." To go farther, to win entire freedom, to leave Parliament altogether—that was impossible! "It is like closing my account," he wrote to Babington; "and I seem to have done so little, and there seem some things which it would be so desirable to try to do before I quit Parliament, that I shrink from retirement as from extinction." It only remained, then, to find a quiet seat ; and there was little difficulty about that in those days. Lord Calthorpe had exactly the thing in his pocket—the ancient borough of Bramber, now a tiny out-of-the-world village near the Sussex coast. And Lord Calthorpe was Wilberforce's wife's cousin. No need, then, for Wilberforce to fight an election for the seat, no need to spend a fortune on it. Lord Calthorpe would simply give it him. And so, in the autumn of 1812, on the eve of a General Election, his "resigning advertisement" was published in the newspapers. The Castle Yard at York, with its crowd of cheering freeholders, knew him no more. Without any fuss or bustle whatever—by the mere transaction of a few formalities—he was duly "elected" for Bramber. Lord Calthorpe begged him "in the kindest manner possible . . . to consider it quite as my own."

The migration was widely lamented in Yorkshire. A meeting of the electors passed a unanimous resolution of gratitude for "his unremitting and impartial attention to the private business of the county, and for his independent and honest performance of his trust on every possible occasion." From his birthplace came a more diffuse and dithyrambic message. "As freeholders of Yorkshire resident in or near Hull," runs one of its paragraphs, "we indulge in the grateful feelings of an honest pride; we exult in the reflection that the illustrious names of those incorruptible patriots, Marvell and Wilberforce, adorn our records and shed a lustre on this the place of their nativity." And, of course, there came innumerable private letters of regret from his constituents, one of whom expressed the fear that Wilberforce's retirement would "throw the county into the permanent possession of the two noble Earls who alone possess length of purse sufficient to command it." Other admirers, unaware of his acceptance of Bramber, pressed him to stand for a variety of seats—for Westminster, for Lewes, for Dover. "Would you believe it," he writes, "R. really and gravely asked me to stand for Warwickshire, in the Birmingham interest, and to be the business member. I am not yet quite insane." But of all the tributes perhaps the pleasantest came from an unexpected quarter. Soon after the Election, Wilberforce was approaching the House of Commons one day when Sheridan accosted him. When he heard of his resignation of his Yorkshire seat (he told him), he had been on the point of writing to him to urge him to reconsider his decision, under the impression that it meant complete retirement. "Though you and I have not much agreed in our votes in the House of Commons, yet I thought the independent part you acted would render your retirement from Parliament a public loss."

5

Wilberforce's retreat from Yorkshire is not to be wondered at. It is astonishing, rather, that he should have held on so long, considering the multitude and variety of his activities. Besides the main preoccupation of the Slave Trade (which must be dealt with presently), besides the unceasing routine work for the local interests of Yorkshire, besides his careful studies and speeches on the main political issues of the day, besides the innumerable visitors and letters and the elaborate organisation of his private charities— besides all this, he was an unfailing attendant at almost every kind of meeting for the promotion of religion and philanthropy. The diary for four consecutive days in the "May Meeting" period of 1813 contains the following items: "May 4th. Annual sermon and meeting of Church Missionary Society for Africa and the East. . . . Meeting afterwards, and spoke. Late to Asiatic Society when took the chair. . . . 5th. British and Foreign Bible Society anniversary—full meeting—I spoke and well received. . . . 6th. Prayer Book and Homily Society—spoke, after a sermon. . . . 7th. Jewish Meeting anniversary. . . . I spoke."

Of these Societies—and there were others—two may be singled out as the special objects of Wilberforce's busy devotion. The British and Foreign Bible Society was largely his creation. No one felt more keenly the handicap imposed on the cause of Christianity at home and abroad by the difficulty of providing a sufficiency of Bibles. Now and again he had himself given money for the purchase of them to poor parsons in country districts; and he had warmly supported such spasmodic efforts as had hitherto been made to secure a more widespread distribution. But the need could not be fully met without some regular and permanent organisation: and early in 1803—in the days of the truce and the invasion-scare—the diary records a breakfast-party with three friends "on Bible Society formation." A few days later the discussion was resumed at the counting-house of Mr. Hardcastle, a city friend, near Swan Stairs on Thames-side; and by the light of candles—so dark was that April morning—the little group decided on the inauguration of the Society, with Lord Teignmouth as its first president. It was destined to do much more and go much farther than its founders ever dreamed; yet to some religious minds it started on its career with a sinister defect. It included Nonconformists as well as Anglicans. Indeed, Wilberforce's filial, but by no means Evangelical, biographers are at pains to defend their father's "holy daring." To Wilberforce himself, however, this feature of the Society seemed one of its greatest merits. In earlier life, it is true, he had taken alarm at the growth of Nonconformity. In 1790 he had voted with the majority against the repeal of the Test Acts, but only after long hesitation and reflection, and the "satisfaction" the result gave him was, he confessed to Hey, "by no means unalloyed." By 1797 he had become definitely more liberal. So far from showing any bitterness or jealousy towards the "Sects," the *Practical View* appealed for the co-operation of all Christians who were agreed on "the grand fundamentals." In 1800 it was his personal intervention which prevented Pitt and his colleagues from tampering with the Toleration Act in order to suppress itinerant preachers. "That they should think of attacking the Dissenters and Methodists!" he exclaimed. And he spent some hours with Pitt, "at a *tête-à-tête* supper," convincing him that that "class of clergy" were not posi-

tively immoral. With the Methodists, indeed, as was natural
enough, he had become actively friendly; and his admiration for
"that great and good man, Charles Wesley," was so deep that for
many years, together with two friends he asked to join him, he
provided an annuity for his widow. In 1812 the Methodist body
passed a public vote of thanks to him for his service to the principle
of toleration. All this, of course, was looked askance at by Anglicans
of the stricter school. Wilberforce was half a Methodist, they said,
and it was actually one of the minor reasons he put to himself in
favour of retirement from the House of Commons that the work
he could do there might be better done "by persons not labouring
under the stigma of Methodism." Nor was it unnatural, perhaps,
in those days, that he should be suspect, devotedly loyal though he
was and remained to the Established Church: for he stood quite
frankly on its left wing, and there were plenty of Anglicans at that
time who conceived collaboration with Nonconformists to be
something akin to treason, and could never have regarded the Bible
Society as a fine opportunity for the united labour of all Christians.
So it seemed, however, to Wilberforce. It was a "grand" sight, he
says of its sixth anniversary meeting—"five or six hundred people
of all sects and parties, with one heart and face and tongue."

Wilberforce was also one of the fathers of the Church Missionary
Society, first discussed in his room at Battersea in the winter of
1796, and founded in 1799, largely owing to his exertions. He was
keenly interested, too, in the London Missionary Society, founded
in 1794. Every one knows how great a work these and kindred
bodies were to do, not only in their own religious field but also in
maintaining a tradition of humane and honest conduct towards the
native races with which Englishmen on the advancing fringes of
the British Empire were now to come increasingly in contact. It
was inevitable that their missionaries should sometimes be ill
suited to their difficult task: that some of them should be feckless
or fanatical, arrogant or even self-seeking. It was inevitable, too,
that their supporters in London should sometimes show more zeal
than knowledge and should be tempted—and use their influence to
tempt the Government—to form hasty and unfair opinions. A
time was to come when "Exeter Hall" was to be regarded with mild
irritation or cynical amusement in some quarters at home as the
shrine of impractical and goody-goody humanitarianism, and with
something akin to hatred in some quarters in the colonies as the

home of a lot of ignorant and prejudiced busybodies, avowedly
hostile to the colonists and all their ways. And there were periods,
it must be confessed, when missionary circles in London seemed
obsessed with the belief that, if white men and black were in conflict, the white men were necessarily and entirely in the wrong, and
the black necessarily and entirely in the right—a belief that, in so
far as it affected policy, was as injurious in the long run to the
interests of the weaker race as to those of the stronger.

   The most famous, and in the end the most mischievous, example
of this one-sidedness belongs to South African history. The Great
Trek is the national epic of the Boers—a romantic story of adventure
on the open *veld*, of danger and death, of stubborn courage and
achievement—but it was a great disaster to South Africa. It severed
the political unity which the nature and circumstances of the
country demanded; it doomed it, over and above the troubles
between whites and blacks, to seventy years of friction and strife
between the two European peoples which had made it their home.
And in the complex of causes which brought about the Trek, the
strongest and most insistent thread is the cleavage in principle
between the Boers on the frontiers of Cape Colony and the British
Government in London as to the manner in which the native races
should be treated. Disagreement, tension, there must have been in
any event: for, while the new humanitarianism had so swiftly
assailed and captured public opinion in England, those remote,
hard-headed pioneers were still living in the atmosphere of the Old
Testament, still believing themselves authorised to deal with the
savage Kaffirs as the Chosen People dealt with the Amalekites. In
any event, therefore, the abolition of Slavery throughout the British
Colonies in 1834 must have produced a serious crisis in South Africa.
But it might not have resulted in the actual secession of the recalcitrant Boers if it had not been followed by Lord Glenelg's retrocession
to the Kaffirs of the province of Queen Adelaide in 1835. And Lord
Glenelg, of course, was none other than the son of Wilberforce's
intimate of the Clapham Sect, Charles Grant. But even the retrocession, again, might not have proved decisive if it had not been
regarded by the Boers as the culmination of a deliberate policy of
friendship to the natives and enmity to themselves, inspired for
years past by the malignant slanders of the missionaries. This was,
of course, a prejudiced, an exaggerated view, but it was not entirely
unfounded; and for such grounds as there were, Wilberforce and

his friends were, in part at least, responsible. They were biased—
perhaps inevitably biased. In dealing with the Slave Trade they had
been at closer quarters with the abuses they attacked. They saw
the slave-ships; they examined the slave-captains; the bulk of their
evidence came from people engaged in the Trade and very little of
it from missionaries; Newton himself had been in it up to the
eyes. The opposition, moreover, the champions of the Trade, were
on the spot; and the case against them had to be sustained under
their watchful criticism and powerful counter-attacks. It was
possible, therefore, for Wilberforce to form fair and well-balanced
opinions on the Slave Trade without going himself to the Guinea
Coast or taking himself the Middle Passage. But it was quite otherwise with regard to the sweeping charges of inhumanity levelled
against the Boers. Wilberforce never met a Boer. He knew nothing
of the realities of life on the Karoo or by the Kei. Almost his only
source of first-hand information was the statements of the plaintiffs
in the case—the missionaries. And for a man of Wilberforce's
prepossessions this was fatal to fair judgment. Secular evidence he
would have weighed and winnowed; but these were ardent, active
Christians, sacrificing themselves to their faith, witnesses to the
eternal truth; and he was ready to believe almost anything these
men of God might say.

To what lengths this enthusiasm could carry him is illustrated
by the famous Vanderkemp controversy. Dr. Vanderkemp was a
single-minded zealot in charge of the London Society's Mission at
Bethelsdorp. He was particularly obnoxious to the Boer farmers of
the district, partly because he maintained in happy security—or, as
they held, in demoralising idleness—a number of Hottentots who
might otherwise have been obliged to work on their farms, still
more because his were the most vehement and vociferous attacks
on their humanity. And it intensified their chagrin that he could
reach the ears of Government. "If Mr. Wilberforce," wrote Vanderkemp's colleague, Mr. Read, to London in 1811, "the friend of
injured Africa, had a fair statement of this business, he would surely
exert himself." And so he did. He took the matter straight to the
Prime Minister, Perceval, and thence to Liverpool at the Colonial
Office; and the upshot was a prompt request from the Secretary of
State to the Governor of the Cape to give the charges his "most
serious attention." A full inquiry was accordingly instituted by
four judges on what became known in South African tradition as

"the Black Circuit." The results of it were interesting. Instead of
the murders by the score they had spoken of, the missionaries could
only formulate seventeen specific charges of the capital offence. Of
these all failed. One of the accused was convicted of assault. Of
fifteen persons accused of violence, six were acquitted. Vanker-
kemp's accusations were thus shown to have been by no means all
the outcome of fanatical imagination. Undoubtedly there were
Boers who were often cruel to their slaves and native labourers;
and it was all to the good that some of them had been detected,
proved guilty, and punished. Wilberforce, so far, had been justified
in his exertions. But there was another side to it. The acquittals
had been more numerous than the convictions. And bitter was the
talk that ran from farm to farm up-country. Had not the missionaries been shown to be reckless and undiscriminating slanderers
of innocent folk? Had not their high-placed friends in London
unhesitatingly supported them? And was life tolerable under an
alien and distant Government, the strings of which such men as
these could pull? In a long view, indeed, the harm done perhaps
outweighed the good; and Wilberforce, in his degree, must be held
accountable for both. When he was discussing the matter with
Liverpool and "Lord N.," "Vanderkemp," said the latter, "is a
worthy man, but an enthusiast." "Poor Lord N.," is the diary's
amazing comment; "Was not then St. Paul an enthusiast?"

It is easy to smile at such extravagances, easy to deride the
lop-sided dogmatism that sprang from too catholic a trust in the
divine inspiration of missionary evidence. Certainly Wilberforce
and his friends were sometimes over-ready to believe evil; but it
should not be forgotten that they had been face to face with the
unquestioned horrors of the Slave Trade. These were the things
that white men had done to black, and, outside the scope of British
Abolition, were still doing. And though the farmers of South
Africa were of a wholly different type from that of the West Coast
slavers, it was not quite unreasonable to suspect that they might
not maintain, at least without "interference" from Downing Street,
a wholly different standard of conduct towards their uncivilised
neighbours. And this, too, should be remembered. With all their
limitations and mistakes those pioneers of the British philanthropic
school were on the right side. It was they who planted in the public
conscience of their countrymen not merely a sensitiveness to wrong,
but a positive sense of obligation towards the backward peoples of

the world. And in so far as the conduct of British Government towards the native races in their charge was to be inspired throughout the coming century by the ideals of trusteeship, the honour of creating that tradition lay with them.

6

The Church Missionary Society dealt with the East as well as Africa; and the field in which Wilberforce was more keenly interested than in any other was India. At the outset of his political career he had been brought face to face with India and the problem of its government. He had listened in those early days to Burke's doctrine of trusteeship. He had wholeheartedly accepted it. He had played his part in securing the impeachment of Warren Hastings. But, as the effects of his "conversion" took a deeper and deeper hold on all his life and thought, he had begun to diverge from Burke's path. Burke's opinions about India were dominated by his respect for antiquity. The whole complex structure of Indian life, with all its innumerable differences from our own, with all, too, that European critics must needs regard as defects or abuses, was too ancient, too venerable, to be rashly interfered with. He was not greatly concerned by the fact that its myriad inhabitants were not Christians. Religion, above all else, was a matter of old tradition; above all else, an intimate, personal thing. It was not, he held, one of the duties of British statesmen to question or dictate the religious opinions of their fellow subjects in any part of the Empire—not even in Ireland, nor yet in Canada. "I would have us govern Canada," he said, in his plea for the toleration of Roman Catholicism among the French Canadians, "in the same manner as the all-wise disposition of Providence would govern it. We know that He suffers the sun to shine upon the righteous and the unrighteous; and we ought to suffer all classes, without distinction, to enjoy equally the right of worshipping God according to the light He has been pleased to give them." And in the same spirit he conceived it to be no business of the British Government to combat Hinduism or Islam in India. So thought most Englishmen then and since, but not Wilberforce. For Wilberforce, while he could tolerate Nonconformity and, with an effort, Romanism, drew the line at "heathen" creeds. To him the notion of the British Government fulfilling a trust for the welfare of the Indian people seemed almost farcical if it did nothing whatever to raise them from ignorance and idolatry and to save them—so indeed he saw it—from eternal damnation.

A member of Parliament in Wilberforce's time had an excellent opportunity, at regular, if somewhat distant, intervals, of airing his views on India. For, though by Pitt's Act the British Government was now, so to speak, a partner in the government of India, the active agent on the spot was still the East India Company; and every twenty years the Company's Charter had to be renewed by Act of Parliament. Twice, therefore, during Wilberforce's tenure of a seat—in 1793 and in 1813—the whole Indian question was fully discussed, not merely in one night's debate, but at all the stages of the requisite Charter Bill. And already in 1793 Wilberforce was convinced that it was an essential, nay, *the* essential, function of the Government not merely to permit but actively to foster Christian propaganda throughout the area of its Indian administration. Accordingly, when the debate came on, he proposed a series of resolutions, to be transmuted on acceptance into clauses of the Bill, declaring the "religious improvement" of the Indians "by all just and prudent means" to be our "peculiar and bounden duty" and calling for the provision of chaplains and schoolmasters throughout British India. At the outset he was not without allies. He found Pitt, indeed, indifferent; but he obtained Archbishop Moore's blessing; and, still more useful, he won a promise of support from the Minister in charge of the Bill, Dundas. It was mainly due to this last potent factor that the House accepted the resolutions without demur. Wilberforce was deeply moved. "The hand of Providence," he exclaims in his religious journal, "was never more visible than in this East Indian affair." But his confidence was premature. Like a giant roused from sleep, the India House began to stir. The Company had always set its face against missionary effort. It had even refused, with one or two exceptions, to carry missionaries to India on its ships. It was a cardinal point of its policy to abstain from any kind of tampering with Indian beliefs and customs. "East Indian directors met," says the diary, "and strongly reprobated my clauses." It was the opening move of a swift and vigorous campaign. Anglo-Indian opinion was solidly mobilised. Influence was brought to bear in Society and Parliament. And when the debate was resumed, Dundas, with his eye on the storm-clouds, trimmed his sails. Wilberforce was to suffer many such sudden changes of fortune in the course of his career; but this was one of the first of them and it hit him hard. In vain he strove to disarm the opposition. "It is not meant," he said, "to break up by violence existing institutions and force our faith upon the natives of India, but gravely, silently and systematically to prepare the way for the gradual diffusion of religious truth." It was no use. "The East India directors and proprietors have triumphed," he writes to Gisborne, "all my clauses were last night struck out on the third reading of the Bill (with Dundas's consent!! this is *honour*), and our territories in Hindustan, twenty millions of people included, are left in the undisturbed and peaceable possession, and committed to the providential protection of—Brama." "How mysterious, how humbling," he meditates in the journal, "are the dispensations of God's providence! . . . May not this have been because one so unworthy as I undertook this hallowed cause?"

Twenty years later he returned to the charge with undiminished zeal. All that he heard, all that he read, in the interval had intensified his horror at the abysmal depths of Indian paganism. At times the thought of so many million fellow men and fellow subjects blinded and doomed seems almost to have got on his nerves: there is an almost ranting note in some of his attacks on Hinduism and on the lethargy of Government. "To me," he writes to a clergyman in 1807, ". . . our suffering our East India subjects . . . to remain, without an effort to the contrary, under the most depraved and cruel system of superstition which ever enslaved a people, is . . . the greatest by far, now that the Slave Trade has ceased, of all the national crimes by which we are provoking the vengeance and suffering the chastisement of Heaven." And in the following year he is moved to a queer outburst on hearing the rumour that Napoleon was resuming on a grand scale his preparations for the conquest of the East. He can scarcely have supposed that Napoleon of all men would deliberately concern himself with Christian propaganda in India; but he could imagine his cynical ambitions to be the instrument of a higher will. "Should this country," he writes to Hey, "use the powers of its government for the avowed purpose of shutting the Scriptures out of our Indian empire, how could we hope that God would not employ the French army in breaking down the barriers we had vainly and wickedly been rearing and thus open a passage by which Christian light might shine upon that darkened land." All the time, too, his work with the Church Missionary Society, which largely owed its existence to the failure to secure Government action in 1793, was feeding his resentment at the discouragement and frustration of missionary efforts in the East. One case made a specially sharp impression. An unfortunate missionary, refused a passage by the Company, had made his way out to India, as other zealots had done, by a circuitous route. On his arrival he was promptly ordered to depart—not unnaturally, since he was without the requisite official licence. "On his stating that he had no money," to quote Wilberforce's account, "he was told he might go before the mast. The poor fellow—chiefly from grief—sickened and died."

It was with growing impatience, therefore, that Wilberforce awaited the expiry of the Charter; and this time he was determined not to fail from over-confidence or lack of preparation. Early in 1812 he began to plan his campaign. "It will be necessary," he says, "to call into action the whole force of the religious world." Sundry bishops were accordingly canvassed, and a meeting was held at Bartlett's Buildings with the Archbishop of Canterbury (now Manners-Sutton) in the chair. The fact that Perceval was still Prime Minister was of good omen. He told Wilberforce that he approved his object but "saw great difficulties in the way." What, he asked him, were his positive proposals? At the least, replied Wilberforce, the insertion in the forthcoming Charter Act of the same declarations of principle which had been embodied in his resolutions in 1793 and also some provision for opening the doors of India to the missionaries. That their entry should be regulated, that a licence-system of some kind must be maintained, he was ready to admit; but he had formed no opinion yet as to who should control it. Obviously not the Company. Indeed he was fast moving towards agreement with the Company's commercial rivals. He was contemplating the abolition not only of the monopoly but of the Company itself, "rather than not insure the passage for the entrance of light . . . into that benighted and degraded region."

But he found that the benighted and degraded condition of Indians did not sting men's consciences so acutely as the barbarities of British slave traders. "I am sadly disappointed," he confesses, "in finding even religious people so cold about the East Indian instruction." And about this time he received a warning which might well have revealed to him the peculiar difficulties and dangers of the dubious ground he was so confidently treading. He heard from private sources a "most alarming" report that the Maharaja of Gwalior had written to the Secretary to Government "resenting our measures for proselytising India." "Surely this is the evil spirit's stirring up," cries Wilberforce in dismay. But Burke would have known better than that. While Burke would not have palliated the survivals of primitive barbarism which still figured among Hindu religious customs, he would have understood, none the less, the natural indignation of an Indian prince at the charge that all his countrymen were living in a pit of mire and shame. No wonder that Wilberforce's extremism should have stiffened the opposition of those whose knowledge of India and its problems was wider than his. And there were extremists on that side too, who held not only that Government should itself have nothing to do with mission work in India but that unofficial Christian propaganda of any kind—even the circulation of the Bible—should be prohibited. By the time the Bill was ready for discussion, the Anglo-Indian party as a whole had hardened in the opinion that the licensing of missionaries should be reserved in the new Charter as in the old for the Court of Directors of the Company—in other words, that the question should stand for twenty years to come as it had stood for twenty years past.

The power of the India House, however, was not all that it had been in 1793. The financial position of the Company was suffering from one of its periodic crises owing to the cost of Lord Wellesley's "forward" policy; and the clamour of its rivals in the British business world for admission to the Indian trade was the louder now that Napoleon had shut them out from European ports. The Company itself, moreover, was not unaffected by the new ideas about the purposes of British rule in India. The old assumption that the British were only in India in order to trade there had disappeared. Nor could those negative duties of maintaining peace and justice, which had been almost automatically created by the development of trade, long suffice for a Government inspired by a sense, however new and callow, of trusteeship. Already the idea was in the air that something positive should be done in India to advance the general well-being of the people, and not merely their material well-being. It was in the Charter Act of 1813, accordingly, that the first small step was taken in the gigantic task of Indian education. It was provided that one lac of rupees (about £10,000) should every year be "set apart and applied to the revival and improvement of literature and the encouragement of the learned natives of India, and for the introduction and promotion of a knowledge of the sciences among the inhabitants of the British territories in India." With this proposal Wilberforce, of course, agreed. "Knowledge of all sorts" should certainly be disseminated throughout India. But, if once the door were opened to Western science, could it be shut to Western religion? The dilemma was vehemently pressed by Wilberforce. "Is Christianity the only thing," he asked, "we refuse to offer to our Indian fellow-subjects?" And he was supported by at least one notable Anglo-Indian. His colleague of the Clapham Sect, Lord Teignmouth, spoke with the authority of an ex-Governor-General when he declared himself in favour of mission work in India provided that Government was only concerned to authorise and regulate it. Ministers, too, were sympathetic. Perceval was dead, but Castlereagh agreed with Wilberforce that it was no longer possible to reject the principles expressed in the resolutions of 1793: and on the crucial question of missionaries' licences he proposed that, since it was impossible to exclude the Company from all authority in the matter, applications for licences should be made to the Court of Directors as before, but that, in the event of a refusal, the applicant could appeal to the Board of Control, i.e. the British Government. This was more than a compromise: it was giving all that Wilberforce could ask; and it was hotly opposed by the Anglo-Indian body. But Castlereagh himself introduced it in the House of Commons, and after warm debates it was duly incorporated in the Bill by safe majorities.

Wilberforce had not ventured, this time, to expect success. "We carried it," he says, "beyond all hope. I heard afterwards that many good men had been praying for us all night." But in truth he was fighting a winning battle; and the two long speeches he delivered in the course of the debates and afterwards published, though they rank high among his parliamentary efforts, were not really needed to turn the scale. Their value lies in their frank recognition of the inhabitants of British India as fellow subjects with Britons at home, no less entitled to enjoy, as far as might be, the benefits of British civilisation. Sixty million Indians, he told the House, had been incorporated in one body politic with themselves; but its cohesion could only be secured by the goodwill of both its parts. "No government can be really secure which does not rest on the affec-

tions of the governed or at least on their persuasion that its maintenance and preservation are in some degree connected with their
own well-being." And how was this frame of mind to be induced?
By extending to Indians the blessings of British laws and institutions, and above all by letting in "the genial influence of Christian
light and truth." Opinions may differ as to the application of this
doctrine of mutual goodwill, but in principle it is incontestable,
and it was the doctrine by which British statesmanship in India
was to be governed throughout the coming century. But it is
almost lost in the denunciations of Indian morals to which far the
greater part of Wilberforce's speeches were devoted. His specific
charges were not untrue. With his usual industry he had patiently
built them up from the books or oral evidence of men who had been
in India. And it was well, perhaps, that Parliament should not
overlook the dark side of the picture—the primitive and indecent
character of many Hindu rites, the savage custom of infanticide
or that which doomed the widow to immolation on her husband's
pyre, and the prevalence of murder, rape, fraud, perjury and all
the crimes. But that was the only side that Wilberforce painted.
He said not a word about the higher traditions of Indian life, about
its poets and philosophers and saints, about that ancient literature
and learning which the very Bill before him was concerned to
revive and foster. The incandescence of his faith had blinded him.
He could see no good at all in paganism.

7

It was as well, perhaps, that Wilberforce could not give all his
mind and time to vindicating the veracity of the apostolic Vanderkemp or to elaborating his indictment of Indian morals. These
were but excursions from the field that he had made his own and
trod with surer steps. Throughout these years the cause of Abolition was still his supreme interest and occupation. For the passing
of the Act had done much, but not all that needed to be done. It
had done much because it was an Act of the British Parliament
and Britain was mistress of the sea. Without the British navy it
might, indeed, have been almost a dead letter, but in 1807 the British
navy began its long task of driving the Slave Trade off the water.
It patrolled the Gulf of Guinea. It nosed round the West Indies.

w.   x

Many a thick-skinned smuggler saw a British cruiser on his track
and knew that the tables were turned—that the law had gripped
him and his slaves were free. But, so long as the war lasted, there
were far too few ships available for the complete suppression of
illicit trade. In 1811 the diary records a visit of Wilberforce's to
the First Lord to urge him "to clear the coast by a thorough sweep,"
and another in 1812 for "getting more naval force on the African
coast." Not yet, therefore, could the natives of the Guinea Coast
feel quite secure from the raider and the kidnapper; and even their
protectors were still viewed with uneasy suspicion. One day, for
example, a negro came out in a canoe, loaded with fruit for sale
to H.M.S. *Assistance* which was lying near shore at anchor. Finding
the Commodore on the quarter-deck, he asked him: "What ship
is this?" "King George ship," replied the Commodore (who tells
the tale), "man-of-war ship." But the negro doubted. "No," he
said, "you Bristol ship." Assurances to the contrary were useless.
The man became more and more alarmed. "Dom your heart, you
Bristol ship," he cried at last; and, leaping overboard and aban-
doning his canoe, struck out desperately for shore.

Nor was it only a question of British slave-smuggling. When,
indeed, the Act of 1807 was reinforced by the Act of 1811 which
made slave trading a felony punishable by transportation, the
British share in the Trade was practically eliminated. But, if
Windham's scornful prediction had been a poor argument against
the Abolition Bill, it was palpably true. Of course the Trade did
not come to an end just because Britain had abolished it. Denmark
had fulfilled her undertaking in 1803, and in 1807, three weeks
before the passing of the British Abolition Act, the American Congress had passed an Act prohibiting "the importation of slaves
into any part or place within the jurisdiction of the United States";
but all the other sea-powers were still engaged in the Trade. France,
it was true, to whom the second largest share had once belonged,
was temporarily shut out from it; her ships could only venture on
it, if at all, at the risk of falling prizes to their British enemies.
But how could it be ensured that France would not return to it
when once the war was over? The same applied to Holland and
Spain and Portugal, whose slave-ships were exposed to capture so
long as they were in Napoleon's control. And the trade of neutral
Powers, like Sweden, could only be abolished by the free choice of
their own Governments. Thus, until, on the one hand, the British

and American Acts were rigidly enforced and until, on the other hand, other Governments could be persuaded to follow the Abolitionist lead, the triumph of 1807 meant something much less than the total abolition of the Slave Trade.

To Wilberforce, moreover, the cessation of the Trade was but the first step in transforming the relations between white and black in Africa. He had always held—and Pitt had warmly agreed with him—that the Trade had inflicted a terrible injury on Africa, that it was not enough to stop inflicting it, that Britain must do what good she could to make amends. Pitt's greatest speech on Abolition had closed, it will be remembered, with a vision of a civilised and enlightened Africa. The same idea had inspired the bold experiment of Sierra Leone, which was now about to be transferred to Government. And it was with this object, as well as for the purpose of securing and extending the ground won for Abolition, that, a few weeks after the passing of the Act, the African Institution was founded, with the Duke of Gloucester as president, and Wilberforce, the aged Granville Sharp, and other Clapham brethren among its first directors. It was, so to speak, the heir of the old Abolition Committee and the Sierra Leone Company, and it carried on and widened the work they had done to inform and stimulate public opinion. Grenville, Howick and Perceval were original members; and among those who attended its first anniversary meeting—"a magnificent day," says the diary—were some fifty or sixty members of Parliament.

But, as before, Wilberforce's main labours for the cause were personal and behind the scenes. His letters on the subject formed the chief ingredient in that vast correspondence—letters to President Jefferson proposing that the British and American Governments should agree to allow the seizure by either navy of the slave-ships of either country; letters to Consul Gambier at Rio, urging him to take measures "to detect any British ships or men bringing slaves into Brazil"; letters to Perceval and Canning, pleading that special instructions should be sent to the revenue officials in Trinidad and Demerara to "stimulate their exertions"; letters to Lord Liverpool about the welfare of the West Indian slaves; letters to Brougham and Lord Holland suggesting a tactful assault on the Spanish deputies visiting London; letters to Castlereagh on the Swedish treaty. And there were innumerable interviews with people of all sorts and countries—strange, interesting people some of them, like Miranda (an unscrupulous Venezuelan adventurer who plotted with the British Government "to insurge South America"), whose exotic figure flits across the pages of the diary, "talking till half-past eleven and still untired," bringing a Mexican friend to dine at Kensington Gore, appearing suddenly on the veranda in the middle of family prayers with two deputies from Carácas, triumphantly announcing the abolition of the Trade in Venezuela. Before long, too, the old parliamentary canvassing and wire-pulling were again required. For Wilberforce and his colleagues were forced to the conclusion that smuggling could never be effectively suppressed unless all the slaves in the British West Indies were officially registered, so that any illicit importation could be at once detected and the planter compelled "to trust to the increase of his actual stock." He began boldly with a direct assault on the Prime Minister, and after some months he succeeded in persuading Perceval to make the experiment in Trinidad. There was some hesitation and delay in the Cabinet. The Law Officers shrank from overriding the colonial authorities. But finally in 1812 the order for registration was duly made. Meantime, in concert with Romilly and Brougham, Wilberforce had begun to move for an Act of Parliament imposing a register on all the British West Indies. But this needed long and careful preparation; and when they were ready to launch their Bill, they found the whole aspect of the world had changed. Napoleon at last was falling. New vistas of peace and international concord were opening up. And the minor question of registration was temporarily shelved in order that the Abolitionists might be free to concentrate on working for a general international agreement for the suppression of the Trade.

Some progress had already been made since 1807. Some of the South American communities, severed from Spain by the war, had followed in the footsteps of the United States. Abolition had been carried in Venezuela in 1810, in Chili in 1811, in Buenos Ayres in 1812. Europe, too, was moving in the same direction. At the time of the ill-famed Treaty of 1813, the Swedish Government, pressed by Castlereagh who in turn had been pressed by Wilberforce, disavowed the Trade and promised never to take part in it. But similar attempts to persuade the Spaniards and the Portuguese, when the Rising and the Peninsular War brought them into close contact with the British Government, had not been so successful. When their deputies first came to England in 1808, Wilberforce

promptly set himself to get them "well impregnated with Aboli-
tionism." The leaders of both political parties were pricked on to
the assault, while he busied himself with the question of trans-
lating English propaganda into Spanish. Later on, he collaborated
privately with Castlereagh in bringing pressure on the Government of Portugal. But Spain had refused to commit herself, and
Portugal had tried to drive a bargain—"audacious and even
atrocious," Wilberforce called it—which would guarantee her in
the uncontrolled extension of the Slave Trade south of Cape Palmas
if she abstained from operating north of it.

Meantime the question of action by individual states was being
merged into that of united action by all Europe. The end of the
twenty years of fighting was in sight. Loyally supported by the
Government, Wellington had stuck grimly to his task in the
Peninsula. In 1812, by the captures of Ciudad Rodrigo and Badajos
and the victory of Salamanca, he had opened his path to Madrid
and permanently freed the south of Spain. Forced back for the
moment into Portugal, he broke out again in the spring of 1813
and within six weeks he had driven King Joseph and the bulk of
his forces over the Pyrenees. He was checked for a time on the
frontier by the necessity of reducing San Sebastian and Pampeluna;
but in the autumn came his last magnificent struggle with Soult
in the Pyrenees, and before Christmas the British army was en-
camped on the plains of France. In March, 1814, they entered
Bordeaux. Meanwhile Napoleon's fate had been determined at the
other end of Europe. The phantom of world-dominion had lured
him at last to disaster in the Russian snows. Yet even now, even
after the Retreat from Moscow, he might still have saved himself
if the 300,000 veterans, cooped up in Spain by Wellington, had been
available. As it was, he raised incredible new forces with incredible
speed. But, on the news of the Russian catastrophe, Central Europe
was up in arms. In 1813 German nationalism, once betrayed to
Napoleon by Prussia, was led by Prussia to deliverance. Russia once
more moved West. Sweden came down from the North. Austria
rose again in the South. On October 17, Napoleon, with 180,000
men, faced the circle of his enemies, 300,000 strong, at Leipzig.
For three days he stood at bay, and then with half his army fled
back across the Rhine. There were still anxious moments. Victory
sets a strain on all alliances; and the three great Continental Powers,
each with a single eye to its own interests, wrangled and vacillated.

The Rhine frontier was feebly offered to Napoleon and insanely refused. But when at length the Allies, reunited under Castlereagh's firm lead, began to converge on Paris, the last inimitable efforts of Napoleon's soldiership could only postpone for a moment the inevitable end. "How wonderful," writes Wilberforce on April 9, "are the events of the last few days! After hearing that Bonaparte had dashed into the rear of the Allies, it seemed doubtful what would happen, when suddenly we heard on Tuesday that they were marching on Paris. Then we hoped for the best, but how little expected that to-day, Saturday, we should hear of Bonaparte's accepting the Emperor of Russia's offer, renouncing the throne, and agreeing to retire to Elba!" "My wife and children went out to see the illuminations," records the diary, "and stayed till late."

Two thoughts came instantly into Wilberforce's mind when he heard the great news. "How can I but wish," he says in a letter he wrote that day to Hannah More, "that my poor old friend Pitt were still alive to witness this catastrophe of the twenty-five years' drama?" And his private pæan of triumph closes with the cry: "Oh, for the general abolition of the Slave Trade!" The age of war was over, a new age of peace had begun, and of all its promised fruits none seemed to Wilberforce so desirable as this or so certain of attainment. It was incredible that liberated Europe should reimpose on Africa the chains and torments of the Trade. "It would be too shocking," he writes to Gisborne, "to restore to Europe the blessings of peace with professions of our principles, justice and humanity, and at the same moment to be creating —for so it would really be doing wherever the Slave Trade is extinct —this traffic in the persons of our fellow-creatures." To this plank he clung steadily in the whirlpool of diplomacy in which the statesmen of Europe were now for many months involved. From the outset nothing else, except the blockade of Norway, in all that complex of interests and ideals really gripped his mind. Nor was he content merely to act, as hitherto, by personal pressure on British ministers. He took a hand in the game himself. "I am about to correspond with a real live emperor," he tells Gisborne, "not merely such a sort of Birmingham emperor as Bonaparte"; and within three weeks of Napoleon's abdication he had dispatched to Alexander a voluminous epistle, detailing the history and the horrors of the Trade and the measures so far taken for its abolition and praying that the Czar might prove to be God's "chief agent" in delivering Africa as well as Europe. The rôle appealed to Alexander, but neither he nor any one else could forcibly override the primary obstacle—the opposition of France. "Their merchants," reports the diary, "are intent on gain anyhow. Grégoire and all the old *amis des noirs* men are in exceedingly bad odour. No respectable persons will have anything to do with them." But Wilberforce refused to despair. He wrote a series of letters to Talleyrand, one of which was printed as a pamphlet. He wrote to the Archbishop of Rheims and to Lafayette. He talked to Humboldt, who came to see him with Lafayette's introduction. He even contemplated a personal attack on Paris; but he was persuaded that his presence might embarrass the efforts which Castlereagh and his colleagues were sincerely making to achieve what he desired; and the less notorious Macaulay was sent instead. But Macaulay was no more successful than Clarkson had been in earlier days. It is not surprising. Frenchmen could scarcely be expected to subscribe upon the instant to British doctrines of philanthropy, which, after all, had taken many years to win their way in Britain. Nor, perhaps, was a zealot of the Clapham Sect the best-qualified of Englishmen to expound them to Parisians. A little more sensibility, a quicker tact, and the French Colonial Minister, Malouet, for example, might not have been stung to the *brusquerie* with which he met Macaulay's arguments. "Do you English mean," he asked, "to bind all the world?" Talleyrand was too old an artist to be so blunt, but his replies to Wilberforce were no less negative. He rained compliments on him and on his country. "Cette lettre, Monsieur," he writes, "a été pour moi l'occasion de renouveller toute mon admiration pour un pays dans lequel les plus grands hommes d'état non seulement conçoivent les projets les plus utiles au monde, mais en poursuivent l'exécution avec cette prudence, cette sagesse et cette persévérance qui en assurent le succès. . . . Combien est heureuse l'Angleterre de posséder des hommes qui savent mettre vingt ans à établir une belle institution! La méthode des mesures violentes et précipitées a failli perdre la France. . . . J'ai souvent tremblé pour la civilisation européenne. Je me rassurais en contemplant la sagesse, la raison, la prudence et les manières de vos hommes d'état." How typically dexterous!— for all this, of course, is but a preface to a plea for delay. The writer himself—*ça va sans dire*—had long been a convinced Abolitionist; but the majority of Frenchmen are still prejudiced. "Vous conaissez la nature des préjugés: ce n'est point en les heurtant qu'on peut en triompher. Il faut des ménagements. Il faut surtout de la patience et du temps." Talleyrand was saying, in fact, with his silken tongue what Malouet had said. France was not going to abolish the Slave Trade instantly at England's bidding; and it was impossible either for Alexander or for Castlereagh to force her. Wilberforce had urged that no West Indian island conquered from Napoleon should be returned to Louis XVIII without immediate Abolition; and the British Government tried to bargain with islands and with money. But negotiations could not be broken off on that point only. Nor would such intransigeance really serve the cause; for, as Liverpool explained to Wilberforce, to alienate France on that issue would stiffen the resistance of Spain and Portugal to Abolition. Could more indeed have been done than Castlereagh did? Was it, under the circumstances, a grievous failure of diplomacy to obtain nothing but France's promise to Abolish the Trade in five years' time, and in the interval to support Britain in urging the principle of Abolition on the rest of Europe? Wilberforce, at any rate, thought so. Amid the storm of applause that greeted Castlereagh as he entered the House of Commons on his return from Paris, he sat silent; and as soon as the Treaty had been laid on the table and the renewed cheers had died away, he was on his feet and in open opposition. "I can assure my noble friend," he said, "that, if I had not been able to concur in the salutations with which he has been welcomed on his return, it is not from any want of personal cordiality, but because, seeing him come up to the House bearing the French Treaty and calling to mind the arrangements made in it respecting the Slave Trade, I cannot but conceive that I beheld in his hand the death-warrant of a multitude of innocent victims—men, women and children—whom I had fondly indulged the hope of having myself rescued from destruction."

8

But to lose the first trick was not to lose the game. The Paris negotiations were but a preliminary to the Congress at Vienna; and Wilberforce's initial disappointment only intensified his eagerness to secure a general European Charter of Abolition. When, therefore, the Czar, who had come to London, expressed a desire to see him, he leaped at the chance. "Got up by half-past six," says the diary of June 12, "that I might pray to God for a blessing on my interview." So far as it went, the interview was a success. Alexander was very affable, very sympathetic. When Wilberforce spoke of his fears that the French might not keep their promise at the end of five years, "We must make them," he cried impetuously; and then, correcting himself, "We must keep them to it." That the delay had been allowed at all was not his fault. "What could be done," he said, "when your own ambassador gave way?" It was clear, indeed, that the Czar would prove but a broken reed unless Castlereagh were firmer at Vienna than he had been at Paris; and Wilberforce promptly threw himself into a lightning campaign to rouse the public opinion of the country. Once more the crusader's call was heard all over England, and once more the response was prompt and overwhelming. The triumph of 1807 had been no transient phenomenon; the conscience of the British people had been permanently awakened; the humanitarian tradition had begun. Within a few weeks 800 petitions, bearing nearly a million signatures, had reached the House of Commons, demanding that Parliament should, somehow or other, prevent the revival of the French Slave Trade. And this time Parliament itself needed no spur from outside. On July 27 Wilberforce moved an Address to the Prince Regent, regretting that so little had been done for Abolition at Paris and calling for more drastic action at Vienna; and, since Castlereagh accepted it in principle, it was carried without a division. Two days later, an amendment to the Address upon the Peace, similar in content and also moved by Wilberforce, again found no opponents. These portents were not lost on Ministers. Whatever Jenkinson and Hawkesbury might have thought about it in the old days, there was now no warmer Abolitionist than Liverpool. "If I were not anxious for the Abolition of the Slave Trade on principle," he wrote to Wilberforce, "I must be aware of the embarrassment to which any Government must be exposed from the present state of that question in this country." No clearer mandate has ever been given by public opinion to a diplomat than that which Castlereagh took with him to Vienna. It was indeed so clear to all the world as to handicap the British plenipotentiaries. "The display of popular impatience" on this one subject in Britain —so Castlereagh grumbled to Liverpool—would be used by the foreign diplomats as an instrument for wringing concessions out of us in other fields. And, in any case, it can scarcely have seemed

a grateful task—to urge idealism on Metternich and Talleyrand.
What angry mutterings there would be in that jealous international
congregation! What resentment at the idea of Britain trying to
dictate to Europe! What sneers at the shopkeepers of the *Ile Mar-
chande*, for whom "leur économie politique est leur raison d'État,"
who had given up the Trade because they thought it did not pay
and were now terrified lest their commercial rivals should prove,
in keeping to it, that they had been mistaken! Still, there was the
mandate—an unequivocal, national mandate, only to be disregarded
at the cost of losing office.

Castlereagh did not disregard it. He pressed obstinately for a
convention. But the crux of the matter was not at Vienna, it was
at Paris, and Paris was apparently immovable. Not only had the
Government set its face implacably against immediate Abolition;
it was contemplating the reconquest of St. Domingue from the
negroes and its forcible return to the plantation system. The
appeal to humanity seemed wholly useless, and Wilberforce fell back
on the appeal to the pocket. Might not France give in, he asked,
if England made further sacrifices, if she surrendered Mauritius,
St. Lucia, or any other islands? He was quickly undeceived. "Elle
n'est point ici," wrote Humboldt, "comme elle l'étoit en Angleterre,
une affaire d'argent; elle est liée uniquement à des passions nation-
ales." The worst, in fact, had happened. The maintenance of the
Trade had become a point of national honour. Nor was that all.
The triumphant Royalists had not forgotten that the cause of
Abolition had been linked with the beginnings of the Revolution.
As in England twenty years before, so now in France it stank of
Jacobinism. "French Royalists," wrote Lord Holland to Wilberforce, "make no difference between you and me or between me and
Tom Paine." Even the institution of a new Abolitionist society in
France was on that account impracticable. It would fatally recall
the *Amis des Noirs*. "Tout le monde," said Humboldt, "se gendar-
mera contre cette Société." It was even impossible to persuade any
publisher in Paris to face the financial risk of printing a translation
of Wilberforce's public letter to Talleyrand. It was impossible,
too, to get Abolitionist articles into the French newspapers. The
Trade, on the other hand, could command what space it pleased;
and the French public, its national pride thoroughly on edge,
read with gusto the affirmations of French independence and the
innuendoes against Albion, and furiously clapped the allusions to

the burning question which authors or actors inserted in the current drama.

But Wilberforce did not abandon hope. The cause, after all, had been almost as desperate in England not so long ago. And there were Frenchmen, as he knew—some of them, indeed, were his personal friends—who stood above the current of popular passion and who thought, as he did, that France had no excuse for the revival of an abuse which at the moment, as the result of the war, was quite extinct. He persisted, therefore, with his campaign. Leaflets and pamphlets in French and German were spread abroad by the African Institution. An essay by Sismondi and a reprint of that treatise on the impolicy of the Trade which Clarkson, who was now again in Paris, had once presented to Louis XVI, swelled the stream of propaganda. But all his operations might have proved unavailing if Wilberforce had not found two powerful allies. The first of them was the King of France. Louis XVIII had been as keenly interested in the question as his ill-starred brother; it was said, with pardonable exaggeration, that the only genuine Abolitionist in France was the King. "That he is so," wrote Lord Bathurst to Wilberforce in October, "his letter to the Regent, a copy of which I enclose, will, I am sure, convince you." The second ally was the Duke of Wellington, now British ambassador at Paris. To Wellington the suppression of the Slave Trade was a simple matter of clean humanity. Assured of the King's support, he was not inclined to make diplomatic allowances for national pride or Royalist prejudice; and he fought as stubbornly at Paris as Castlereagh at Vienna, supplied, like Castlereagh, with copious ammunition from Wilberforce, Stephen and Macaulay. When the French publishers refused, Wellington personally undertook to get the Letter to Talleyrand widely distributed; and he persuaded Madame de Staël to provide a translation of Wilberforce's booklet of 1807, which, in an abridged form, he similarly circulated. Meanwhile he was using all his popularity at the Tuileries to stiffen the King's convictions and to bring pressure on his Ministers; and presently, as the abandonment of the St. Domingue expedition showed, the mood of blank negation began to soften. At last, in November, came a surprising, if only partial, surrender. An *ordonnance* was issued forbidding French subjects to engage in the Slave Trade north of Cape Formosa at the mouth of the Niger. Thus the whole of the Upper Guinea Coast was officially secured from a revisitation by French slavers. The Duke promptly reported the good news to Wilberforce. "C'est vous et Lord Wellington," wrote Madame de Staël, "qui aurez gagné cette grande bataille pour l'humanité. Soyez sûre que votre nom et votre persévérance ont tout fait. . . . Vous avez inspiré à votre héros Wellington autant d'ardeur pour faire du bien qu'il en avoit eu pour emporter les victoires. . . . Je me mets à vos pieds de tout mon cœur."

There the matter rested for a few months longer; and then the decision was suddenly taken out of the hands of the kings and diplomatists at Paris and Vienna. In the last week of February, 1815, the imperial exile broke from his prison in Elba. On March 1 he landed at Cannes. On March 20 he entered the Tuileries, vacated a few hours earlier by his Bourbon rival. But Napoleon knew well enough that Europe would not let him stay there without a struggle. He instantly began to prepare for it; and, while he extorted yet another army from exhausted France, he strove to disarm his opponents by fair words and to weaken them by intrigue. He informed the Allied Sovereigns, still gathered at Vienna, that "his dearest wish was to make the Imperial Throne of France a bulwark for the peace of Europe." He requested Marie-Louise to return with her child to Paris for the impending coronation. He strove to reawaken jealousy and discord between Russia and the Central Powers. He tried to re-establish contact with Talleyrand. And what of England? He had not forgotten his most tenacious enemy. With instant understanding of the question which had troubled Anglo-French relations all the months of his exile, he struck boldly for the favour of the British Government and people by proclaiming the total and immediate abolition of the Slave Trade. It was Napoleon's first move in the campaign which closed at Waterloo.

And when the Hundred Days were over, when Louis was back on the throne, when Wellington had become a still more commanding figure in the public opinion of Europe, it was impossible for the most stubborn Royalists to force the reversal of Napoleon's coup in direct antagonism to England. Louis himself during his flight from Paris had promised instant Abolition; and, when Castlereagh on behalf of the four Powers formally insisted that French slave-trading must not be revived, Talleyrand acquiesced, and the usurper's act was duly repeated. "I have the gratification of acquainting you," wrote Castlereagh to Wilberforce on the last day of July, "that the long desired object is accomplished and that

the present messenger carries to Lord Liverpool the unqualified
and total Abolition of the Slave Trade throughout the dominions
of France."

Meanwhile Castlereagh had been faithful to his mandate at
Vienna. From the outset of the Congress there was nothing for
which he and his colleagues pressed so resolutely. Alexander, too,
had kept his word and assumed the rôle which Wilberforce had
urged on him. Talleyrand, likewise, kept the French promise to
support the cause in principle; and it·was he who moved on
December 10, 1814, for a committee of plenipotentiaries to prepare
a general convention. On the part of Austria and Prussia there
could be no difficulty; they were purely continental Powers, with
no colonies or sea-borne trade. It was from Spain and Portugal that
the opposition came. They had to consider, they argued, the welfare
of their colonies, though, as matter of fact, their colonies were
already practically lost to them. They could not at once suppress
the Trade. They would need, they said, at least eight years' grace.
An agreement on the principle, however, could be and was obtained.
On February 8, 1815, the representatives of the Eight Powers adopted
a joint declaration condemning the Slave Trade and declaring their
intention, without any precise commitment as to dates, to secure
its universal abolition as quickly and effectively as possible. The
text of this declaration was one of the documents annexed to the
Final Act which was signed on June 9, and nine days later sealed at
Waterloo.

In 1815, therefore, of all the European peoples who had ever
had a hand in the Slave Trade, only the Spaniards and the Portuguese
were still engaged in it; for liberated Holland had renounced it
early in 1814. And Spain and Portugal, it was manifest, could not
long resist the explicit moral judgment of all Europe to which
they had themselves subscribed. To have secured that explicit moral
judgment did not mean, as will presently appear, that the Trade
had been destroyed; but at least it was a long step towards its
destruction. And unquestionably the dominant factors in this
achievement were the lead which the greatest slaving Power had
given in 1807 and the remarkable exhibition of the strength and
unanimity of British public opinion in 1814. Nor can it be questioned
that for both these factors Wilberforce had been primarily responsible. A crowded Abolitionist meeting in London in 1814 had
addressed him as "the father of our great cause." And now he had

added to his fame among his countrymen a fame throughout all
Europe. As the Slave Trade became a leading issue in the general
politics of civilised society, so he took rank among the world's
great men. In every capital his name was known: in every enlightened circle he had his readers and disciples. The Sovereigns
and Princes of the great Alliance, gathered in London, each paid
his tribute. His conversation with the Czar was the first of many;
for the vein of mysticism in Alexander had found something kindred
and attractive in the pious Englishman's conviction of the providential ordering of the world. The Duchess of Oldenburg insisted
on an interview. The King of Prussia presented him with a set
of Dresden china—"the only thing," he said, "I ever got by spout-
ing." Prince Blücher dispatched his *aide-de-camp* from the field of
Waterloo to tell the story of the battle to the Prince Regent—and
to Wilberforce. But all these tokens of his fame left his simplicity
quite unspoiled. It touched him far more deeply than did any of
these gilded compliments when, during his holiday that autumn,
he came to a secluded village in North Devon and, it being known
that Wilberforce was there, the bells of the little church were set
ringing.

XI

The Shadow

I

ALREADY before Waterloo was fought, there were signs that, as far as the internal condition of England was concerned, the end of the war was not to mean the beginning of an age of prosperity and contentment. The one boon above all others which the mass of the English people had expected peace to bring them was cheaper bread: and at first it seemed that peace had brought it. In 1814 the price of corn fell with a rush. But the effect on agriculture, abnormally diverted to corn-growing during the war, was naturally disastrous. Farmers by the score threw up their farms in despair. Many of them became absolute paupers. And the landlords, with derelict farms on their hands and rents falling, their new enclosures and developments no longer profitable, easy mortgages converted into crushing burdens, watched with dismay the rapid fading of their dreams of permanent war-prices and high rents. Only one thing, it was thought, could save English agriculture—to shut out the corn which foreign producers, freed from the trammels of the war, were now ready to pour into England—and this thing a Parliament practically monopolised by the landlords was quite prepared to do. Nor was this class-interest the only interest. The war, as every war in which these islands are engaged must do, had planted in many men's minds the desire to make the country self-supporting in the necessaries of life. So, in the spring of 1815, the notorious Corn Law was passed, prohibiting the import of corn unless the price of wheat were more than eighty shillings a quarter. At a stroke the one supreme boon of peace for the masses was snatched away. The hungry poor were to go hungry still. No wonder that the patience, which had endured so much and so long because the war, it seemed, necessitated it, should now at last begin to break. "Public discontent running high, Corn Bill *causa*," notes Wilberforce early in March. "Corn Bill in Committee—sad rioting at night. Both doors of the carriage which set down members

opened, and member pulled out. None much injured." "Report on
Corn Bill. . . . Some mobbing, and people savage and inveterate
—alas! alas! Charles Grant and Mr. Arthur Young, the agricul-
turist, slept with us for security." "Sir Joseph Banks' house sadly
treated; all his papers burnt."

If Wilberforce's house could still be regarded as a refuge from
the mob, it was only because he had not yet spoken on the Bill;
and before the debates were over, he felt obliged to speak. "At my
prayers this morning," says the diary for March 10, "I reflected
seriously if it was not my duty to declare my opinions in favour of
the Corn Bill. . . . I decided to do it. I see people wonder I do not
speak one way or the other. It will be said, he professes to trust in
God's protection, but he would not venture anything. . . . Besides,
it is only fair to the Government, when I really think them right,
to say so, as an independent man, not liable to the imputation of
party bias, corrupt agreement with landed interest, etc." Nor was
the idea of "log-rolling" quite absent from his mind. He had
already, indeed, when pressed to speak, told Huskisson that he
would do so if the Government would support his Slave Registration Bill; and, though he could not drive this particular bargain,
he felt, as he wrote to his eldest son, that to back the Government
now would render it more disposed to help him on missionary and
religious questions. So, on the afternoon of the 10th, he spoke.

> There was a general impression [he said] that the opening of our
> ports freely for the importation of foreign corn would prevent
> agriculturists from supplying our home-market and would
> occasion a general decline and decrease of our agriculture. If
> that were true, it was necessary for the general weal of the
> Empire that the legislature should adopt proper remedies before
> it was too late. . . . If the whole of Europe were under one
> government—if it were one great family—if all countries were
> as much disposed to dispense happiness as they were often found
> inclined to injure one another, he should then say, Let every
> country produce that which the nature of its soil and other
> circumstances may render beneficial, and let it supply other
> nations with its superabundance. . . . But it was worthy of the
> most serious consideration that those very countries from which
> we might derive supplies were countries which, at no great
> length of time, might be united against this nation. . . . No,

there could not be any truth more certain than this—that a
great country like England should be independent of foreign
nations with regard to the supply of food. . . . Manufacturers
were protected: why not agriculture too? To save agriculture
was to save the workers on the land. . . . The House should
consider the situation of the peasantry who could not attend to
plead their cause. They should consider them as calling on
Parliament with ten thousand tongues to protect them and their
families. As to the cost of bread, he had not heard one single
argument to show that, because the restricting price was fixed
at 80 shillings, the price of corn must necessarily be raised to
that extent. At the same time he was personally in favour of
the lower limit of 76 shillings.

This speech did not go unmarked. Early next morning, an old
servant of Wilberforce's, who had set up as a greengrocer, went as
usual to Covent Garden market to buy vegetables for his shop. "So
your old master has spoken for the Corn Bill," he was told, "but
his house shall pay for it." And, though the threat never materialised, it was thought prudent to station a sergeant, four soldiers and
a "peace-officer" in Wilberforce's house. "Were you to enter the
dining-room at family prayer time," he wrote to his son, "you
would probably begin to think that we were expecting a visit from
the ex-Emperor." The following characteristic comment appears in
the diary a few days later: "The soldiers (Scotch) behave extremely
well; they come into prayers and pleased to do so."

These incidents of 1815 are a significant introduction to the
next seven years—the last years—of Wilberforce's active political
life. What he did about the Corn Bill he felt it his duty to do about
all the primary issues of that time. The welfare of his "negro
clients" might still be the dominant interest of his life; but the
Member for Bramber could no more be silent about other leading
questions than the Member for Yorkshire. In a sense all England
was his constituency now. He was regarded by a large part of his
countrymen as the nation's moral oracle. Writing in 1817, the poet
Southey went so far as to say that "the weight with which his
opinion comes to the public" was "far greater than of any other
individual." And that opinion he was bound to give; for silence
would be as easily misunderstood as an old Delphic riddle. On

W.   Y

behalf of his dominant interest, moreover, it was but common
sense to acquire merit in the Government's eyes by honestly supporting its measures when he honestly agreed with them. So he
spoke—and his reputation suffered. For the "Independent" was
still, of course, a Tory: his speeches in this period were mainly
Tory speeches, and it is doubtful whether the members of any party
since Cromwell's have been so ferociously abused, in life and in
their graves, as the Tories who ruled England for seven years after
Waterloo.

Students of those days, whose hearts are not tutored by their
heads, may find it difficult not to join in the chorus of vituperation
when they read of the bitter sufferings of the poor, of the ill-
concerted and, under the circumstances, strangely temperate agitation of half-fed, desperate men, and of its blind and sometimes cruel
suppression by a narrow oligarchy of the landed rich. But the
historian who, at the risk of seeming smugly callous, tries to understand before condemning, who asks himself why those oligarchs,
who after all were average Englishmen, acted as they did, will find
two or three things to say in their defence. Some of those men, he
will admit, who voted for the Corn Bill were prompted by sheer
class-selfishness, but not all. There were some who genuinely
agreed with Wilberforce that to save the landed interest was to
save the country too. And one of these was Huskisson, who, mistaken as he was on the Corn Laws, was soon to prove himself a not
illiberal statesman and a sound economist. It is only fair, moreover,
to remember that the most unselfish, the most philanthropic
patriots could not have averted, and could not have done very much
to ameliorate, the distresses of the poor. The forces of the Economic
Revolution, industrial and agrarian together, were beyond the
control of any Government or any party. Adjustment to so swift
and drastic a change was only possible with time and with suffering.
And meanwhile the most well-meaning Englishmen had nothing
authoritative to guide them but the almost sacrosanct economic
principle of *laissez-faire*. To improve the conditions or lessen the
hours of labour, to protect the poor from their masters or from
themselves—all such interferences with the natural operation of
economic laws were likely, the professors told them, to do more
harm than good. And, if one is tempted to think that men so
hated in their day must have given good cause for hate, it is only
fair again to remember—and it is easy for the present generation

to understand—the effects of the disillusionment that came with peace. So long as the war lasted, the wretched poor, overwhelmed through no fault of their own by inexorable economic forces far beyond their comprehension, could find at least the cold comfort of something to explain it all and somebody to blame. They cursed the war and endured it: they cursed Napoleon and beat him. But when the war was over, when bread was dearer, trade slacker, everything worse instead of better, they looked, with the added bitterness of disappointment, for something and somebody else to blame. It scarcely needed the Corn Law to expose the criminals. They turned and cursed the Tories, all the more savagely because those tyrants were their countrymen; and as their misery dragged on and deepened, they cursed the whole of the political and social order which the Tories typified and dominated.

The Tories were aware of this; and it explains, if it does not excuse, their hard and barren policy. The significance of those Corn Bill incidents is not exhausted. Those soldiers at family-prayers in Wilberforce's house give a true touch of high colour, an authentic hint of melodrama, to the picture of the time. If the poor detected their enemies in the debates on the Bill, the rich detected theirs in the riot and arson that ensued. The English governing class, it has been seen, had never quite abandoned their belief in the possibility of revolution, and now it gripped them again as firmly as in the blackest period of Pitt's repression. The alarm this time could hardly be called a panic. Nerves had been hardened since the days of the Terror. An English mob was scarcely so terrifying as Napoleon at Boulogne. But, if Sidmouth and his kind were neither neurasthenics nor cowards, they were certainly afraid. They saw, and saw rightly, that the mass of the people were more actively discontented with the existing order than they had ever been. They failed to see that Jacobinism had never taken root in England and was now quite withered up. They failed to appreciate the striking fact that, in so far as this discontent was vocal, it called for no Gallic cataclysm but only for a quiet and a not so very sweeping change in the English Constitution. They failed to realise that the one thing that could drive those slow Englishmen to revolution was an absolute, permanent refusal of any measure of reform—the rigid maintenance of a system which gave to a small minority of rich men, mostly landowners, an almost complete monopoly of political power. To be so afraid and to be so blind—those were the Tories' cardinal sins. Afraid and blind, they set themselves, tragic patriots, to saving their country by the one means most likely to destroy it. And if ever they wanted to strengthen their resolution by appealing to some indisputable authority, if ever they wanted a name to conjure with, they recalled the memory of Pitt. Dark over all those frosty years—the great years of the Pitt Clubs, where full-blooded young Tories of the Right exuberantly toasted the hero of repression—lies the shadow of Pitt: but it was the old Pitt of the war-period, not the young Pitt in his first decade of office.

It is against this background of anxiety and negation that the conduct of Pitt's old friend through the seven years of reaction must be viewed. No one nowadays can deny that Wilberforce was one of the best of his class—really disinterested, really trying to act on principle rather than on prejudice. But he, too, was afraid. It was unfortunate, perhaps, for his judgment that he should have been appointed a member of the Secret Committee of the House of Commons which, together with a similar Committee of the Lords, was appointed early in 1817 to examine the papers in the Government's hands "respecting certain practices, meetings and combinations in the metropolis and different parts of the kingdom, *evidently calculated* to endanger the public tranquillity . . . and to bring into hatred and contempt the whole system of our laws and constitution." There was thus set out before him a terrifying array of evidence, some of it true and quite innocuous, some of it honestly mistaken, and some of it actually manufactured by "Oliver," the Government spy and *agent provocateur*. He read of the agitation and unrest which had grown with the growth of want and misery since the trouble began over the Corn Law—of great mobs harangued in violent language by demagogues like Hunt and Thistlewood, of intermittent rioting and arson, of the distribution in one or two cases of arms, of Luddist outbreaks for the destruction of machinery, of people waiting in provincial towns for the arrival of the mail-coach to bring them the expected news that London had risen and "the Tower and the Bank were in the hands of the insurgents," of the Radical Cartwright and his Hampden Reform Clubs, of Spence's Societies for the nationalisation of land. Some of it at least was alarming, and all of it was one-sided. Wilberforce and his colleagues had no personal contact with the poor, no direct knowledge of their real desires, and there were no "go-betweens" to bridge the gulf of class and to tell them that the mass of the English people were not out for revolution. Almost inevitably, therefore, Wilberforce's alarm increased. Three days after the appointment of the Secret Committees he writes to his family at Hastings: "We are here in the midst of accounts of plots, etc., but a gracious Providence, I trust, watches over us. Remember to pray in earnest against sedition, privy conspiracy, and rebellion." Already it is as bad as that. "We are not to divulge," he writes again from the Committee-room a little later; "but thus much I may say . . . that the seizing of the ringleaders on Monday last prevented blood-shed from the Spa Fields mob on Monday." So already repression is the remedy. It is clear, too, already that Wilberforce has made the fatal blunder of regarding bitter denunciation of the unreformed constitution as tantamount to sedition. His attitude to Cobbett betrays it. "Hunt," he writes, "is a foolish, mischief-making fellow, but no conspirator, though the tool of worse and deeper villains. Cobbett is the most pernicious of all." Now Cobbett's power in creating and mobilising Radical opinion was unquestionably tremendous. The *Political Register*, especially when its price dropped to twopence in 1816, sold at the rate of 50,000 copies a week and was eagerly devoured by the discontented throughout the country. And Cobbett's language was immoderately bitter, often grossly unfair, sometimes quite inaccurate. But the most important fact about Cobbett was that he pleaded definitely for constitutional action and definitely discouraged violence. Yet against Cobbett Wilberforce's whole being revolted. He could not give him his due. He could not help conceiving him as a Paine, if not a Robespierre. And the cause of this almost instinctive repugnance was the cause of most of his prejudices. The man was irreligious. When the Prince Regent, of all men, in his talk with Wilberforce at Brighton in 1815, "spoke strongly of the blasphemy " of Cobbett's writings, the diary adds, "and most justly," with amazingly unconscious irony. So far as saints can hate, Wilberforce hated Cobbett: and Cobbett, without any qualification, returned his hatred.

The result of the Secret Committees was a foregone conclusion—the question indeed had been frankly begged in the terms of their reference. Their almost identical reports declared that a widespread conspiracy was afoot, organised by secret societies, for the subversion of the constitution and the spoilation of property. Armed with the weapon it had asked for, the Government promptly intro-

duced a Bill for the suspension of the Habeas Corpus Act till the
end of the session together with two other instruments from Pitt's
armoury—a Seditious Meetings Bill, which prohibited all un-
licensed assemblies and for such as aimed at changes in Church or
State prescribed the death-penalty for a refusal to disperse, and a
Bill to punish attempts to tamper with the allegiance of soldiers
and sailors. All these measures were duly passed by big majorities.
The Secret Committees, meantime, were too useful to be dispensed
with. They continued to investigate the stream of alarmist evidence
and to report their belief in the existence of a "traitorous conspiracy." And indeed, once this belief had entered men's minds,
there was enough happening in England that spring and summer,
not merely in spies' note-books but in the light of day, to give it
firm root. Fires were still strangely frequent in rural areas. Riots
continued in towns, sometimes with loss of life. The march of the
Manchester Blanketeers on London terminated, it is true, in a
pitiful fiasco; only twenty of them got as far as Staffordshire; but
at the moment of its initiation it had seemed a serious business.
Ten thousand men had gathered for the send-off; and several
hundreds had taken the road. A little later there were outbreaks
in Yorkshire and the Midlands, which, feeble and futile as they were,
seemed ominous enough to those who did not know that they had
actually been provoked by "Oliver." At any rate the Secret Committees were more than ever convinced of the reality of the danger;
and in June the Government asked for and obtained an Act to prolong the suspension of the Habeas Corpus Act till March 1, 1818.

Ministerialists and Grenvillites alike stood solidly behind the
Government throughout the session, and Wilberforce was with
them. "Seditious Meetings Bill. I spoke first opportunity, strongly
defending the Bill." He took no part in the debate on the first
Habeas Corpus Suspension Bill, but he supported the first reading
of the second. The disaffection, he argued, which unquestionably
existed, was mainly due to deliberate corruption of the ignorant.
The object of the Bill was to enable the Government "to take away
those who infused the poison." Would the power be abused? "He
could not easily believe that the noble lord (Sidmouth) would so
far forget the character he had always sustained as to employ the
authority entrusted to him for wicked or oppressive purposes.
Although Parliament might not be sitting, no case of cruelty or
hardship could remain unknown in the present state of the Press,

and every such case would most certainly be canvassed whenever Parliament should be reassembled. . . . When Ministers pledged themselves that this measure was necessary, he felt himself, however reluctantly, compelled to yield to such necessity. He certainly thought it an evil: at the same time he hoped that the natural good sense of the people of England would at length restore to them their ancient rights. Till then, he must, for the sake of the patient poor, for the sake even of the turbulent themselves, consent to the passing of the Bill." Romilly and Brougham protested in vain. The bulk of the Tories, not so reluctant as Wilberforce to tamper with the English traditions of personal liberty, nor so anxious as Canning to prove justification, waited impatiently for the division and carried it by more than two to one.

Wilberforce's attitude had quickly become notorious; and, as in Fox's day, it was all the more irritating to the outvoted Opposition because of the additional weight which his reputed independence gave it. In the debate on the third reading, Sir Francis Burdett vented the bitter feelings of most Radicals in a personal attack. "I confess," he said, "I am astonished at the concurrence in this measure of an honourable and religious gentleman who lays claim to a superior piety. . . . Nothing could be more anti-Christian than to shut up persons in solitary confinement. . . . The honourable and religious gentleman recollects, no doubt, the denunciation of Jesus against the wicked: ' I was hungry, and ye gave me no meat. . . . I was sick and in prison, and ye visited me not.' . . . The honourable and religious member was shocked the other day at the description of Africans chained and carried into slavery. How happened it that the honourable and religious member was not shocked at Englishmen being taken up under this Act and treated like African slaves?" As the speaker harped on his refrain, loud cries of "Order" were raised, and not from the Tory side of the House alone. But Wilberforce could look after himself. When Burdett had done, he rose at once in response to "the sort of call made upon him by the honourable baronet." In a short speech, none the worse for being unprepared, he reiterated his conviction of the danger of leaving at large "those who had long been employed in spreading a poison that had already attacked the vitals of the constitution." Then, turning towards Burdett, "How," he asked, "can the honourable baronet talk as he does of those religious principles on which the welfare of the community depends? I would fain believe that he desires as sincerely as I do myself to perpetuate to this country the blessings she enjoys. But if I could be base enough to seek the destruction of those institutions which we both profess to revere, I will tell him what instrument I should choose. I would take a man of great wealth, of patrician family, of personal popularity, aye, and of respectable talents. I am satisfied that such a one, while he scattered abroad the firebrands of sedition under pretence that he went all lengths for the people, would be the best agent for the malevolent purpose of destroying their liberties and happiness." "Never in my parliamentary life," said a member afterwards, presumably no Radical, "did I hear a speech which carried its audience more completely with it or was listened to with such breathless attention."

Next session a similar but less offensive attack on Wilberforce was made by Tierney, now the Leader of the Opposition. The occasion was the second of the two fiery debates in the spring of 1818, in which the odious machinations of "Oliver the Spy" were thrust into the light. Ministers were in an unenviable position. No one now believes that Sidmouth deliberately employed "Oliver" as an *agent provocateur*; but, unwilling to confess the lesser crime of employing him at all in such life-and-death matters without sufficient knowledge of his character, they decided to brazen it out and trust to their majority. What, then, was Wilberforce to do? One cannot help regretting that he did not do what Romilly expected of him—that he did not forget for once his personal respect for Sidmouth and insist at least on an inquiry. But in the first debate—on a motion for referring the question to the Secret Committee—while he reprobated the use of spies at all as "equally repugnant to honour or morality or to the feelings of a gentleman and almost as objectionable on the grounds of political expediency," he gave his vote against the motion. And in the second debate— on a motion for instituting an inquiry *de novo*—he spoke and voted in the same way. But the House, it seems, had not been sure of it. Charges of "trying to catch the member for Bramber's vote" were bandied across the floor. And it was this that gave Tierney his cue.

I do not wish [he said] to speak disrespectfully of the honourable member for Bramber; and certainly there is no individual more capable of giving effective support to Ministers and their measures when he chooses to turn out (*cheers and laughter*).

What his vote will be on the present occasion it is not, perhaps, easy to prophesy. . . . Generally, his phraseology is happily adapted to suit either party; and if, now and then, he loses the balance of his argument and bends a little to one side, he quickly recovers himself and deviates as much in an opposite direction as will make a fair division of his speech on both sides of the question (*continued cheers*).

The taunt brought Wilberforce to his feet. The last speaker and himself, he said, were old soldiers in parliamentary warfare; and he quite understood that the Leader of the Opposition had to say what was expected of him.

But to what length must party-feeling have reached in this House, when it is asserted that, because a person is not systematically opposed to every motion of Government, he cannot form an honest opinion on any subject presented to him in Parliament. (*Cries of No, No, from the Opposition.*) Well, if gentlemen are anxious to disclaim such an injustice, I hope that I and an honourable friend of mine [William Smith] will in future be treated with somewhat more respect.

"Wished not to speak," he notes that night; ". . . Tierney gave the last prick which forced me to rise; though not at all ill-naturedly, I am glad to say. Nor was I ill-natured, I hope: thank God, I did not feel so."

2

In the latter part of 1817 and throughout the following year trade steadily improved. Unemployment decreased. The poorest classes climbed for a moment above starvation level. And, immediate and significant result, the spasmodic turbulence ceased: the "traitorous conspiracy" faded into the background. But the relief was transient. The reputation of the Tories—and of Wilberforce—was yet to receive its darkest stain. To meet the new demand from the Continent the manufacturers overproduced, just as they had done at the close of the war. Continental purchasing power was quickly exhausted: employers were left with big unmarketable stocks: slump succeeded boom: and in 1819 unemployment and want were as bad as ever. Immediately and significantly the political agitation revived. But its character was still scarcely Jacobinical. The organisation of nocturnal drilling was alarming, and doubtless intended to alarm. But that was the worst. Popular discontent no longer showed itself in violent outbreaks, in riots and burnings, but in relatively orderly mass-meetings for the single object of demanding Parliamentary Reform. It was one of those gatherings, however, that set the stage for tragedy. The crowd which assembled on August 16 in St. Peter's Field on the outskirts of Manchester to listen to Hunt and other orators was neither armed nor bent on violence; but it was enormous—it numbered between 50,000 and 60,000 men, women and children. And the Government can hardly be blamed for holding a small force of cavalry in readiness. The responsibility for what occurred lies almost wholly with the local magistrates. They allowed the meeting to begin and then, suddenly losing their heads, they ordered the Yeomanry, ill-trained for such a task and ill-suited for it by their political sympathies, to make their way through the throng and arrest Hunt; and finally, when the Yeomanry were entangled and hustled in the crowd, they ordered the colonel in command of the Hussars to charge. The result was the "Massacre of Peterloo." Eleven were killed or died of their hurts, and several hundred were injured by sword-cuts or horses' hoofs, or crushed in the panic rush for safety. It was not the tragedy itself so much as the Government's subsequent conduct that blackened its record. Without pausing to investigate the facts, Ministers thanked the magistrates; declared, on very dubious ground, that the meeting had been illegal; and committed Hunt and some of his colleagues to trial for "a conspiracy to alter the law by force and threats." Lastly, as if to justify this hasty pre-judgment of the case, they pleaded once more, when Parliament met in October, that measures of general repression were impera-tive. This time they did not move the suspension of the Habeas Corpus Act: it has never been suspended in Britain since 1818; but they moved and carried the "Six Acts," the kernel of which was the prohibition of unofficial public meetings and an attempt to tax the Radical Press out of existence. The agitation for Reform was to be silenced.

Wilberforce came up to this stormy session with the fear of revolution more firmly fixed than ever in his mind. "Seldom has a boy returned on a black Monday," he writes to a friend, "with more reluctance than I to St. Stephen's. I dare not be too confident that we may not witness scenes of something nearer to civil war than this land has exhibited since 1646." However groundless it may seem to cool students at the safe distance of a century, however reassuring the fact, admitted even in the Secret Committees' Reports, that the people at large showed little sympathy with rioters and incendiaries, this fear was now shared by almost all the members of Wilberforce's class, by Whigs as well as Tories, by business-men as well as landlords. Robert Southey, for example, told Wilberforce that, "if the licentiousness of the press were not effectually curbed, we should both be sent to the scaffold." "He will not forget this," Southey observes, "and I shall take care to deepen the impression." It scarcely needed deepening. When Wilberforce asked his correspondents in the country for first-hand information as to the conditions in their neighbourhood, their replies were uniformly sombre. A Yorkshire friend tells him, for example, in October, "that the West Riding of our county is in an alarming fermentation—the lower orders generally corrupted and the merchants and higher manufacturers scarcely daring to resist the tide of blasphemy and sedition." "You may remember," writes Wilberforce, passing the news on to Stephen, "the assassination of a merchant three or four years ago near Huddersfield, when it was said that, at the time the fatal shot was fired, there was a general shout of triumph from the tops of the houses, hay-stacks, and other elevated situations." In Leicester, again, so he heard, "the lower orders are in the habit of meeting by night in parties of twenty-five to practise the pike-exercise." But what most alarmed and repelled him—what spurred him to repression more than all else—was the agitators' open defiance of religion. "Heretofore they inveighed against the inequality of property," runs a private memorandum of this period, "and used every artifice to alienate the people from the constitution of their country. But now they are sapping the foundations of the social edifice more effectually by attacking Christianity."

And so, on Peterloo as on "Oliver," his voice and vote were Sidmouth's. It was not, of course, a blind, automatic conformity: he could scarcely give Sidmouth what he had never given Pitt. And on Peterloo he was certainly influenced in some degree by an opinion given him by a "very sensible and dispassionate man (no partisan

of Ministers) who halted at that place a short time after the tumult."
The colour of this opinion is suggested by Wilberforce's comment—
"I think the magistrates have been unjust to themselves in not
publishing what may be called their *case*." And so, when Tierney
moved a moderate amendment to the Address, asking for a parliamentary inquiry, Wilberforce opposed it, partly on the ground that
the law-courts were the proper place for ascertaining the truth of
criminal charges and not the House of Commons, where evidence
could not be tendered on oath, and partly because an inquiry would
cast a slur on the whole body of magistrates on whose loyal service
the local administration of the country rested. But he committed
himself no farther than that. When an angry opponent charged
him with "warmly defending" the magistrates' conduct, "I am not
prepared," he replied, "to defend any more than to attack them."
Still less, it goes without saying, could he be accused of any lack
of sympathy with the victims of the "massacre." "Can there be
one man here," he asked, "who does not from his soul lament these
transactions? If there be, it must be one who has learned to look
to slaughter and civil war for the regeneration of his country."
No less firm was his support of the "Six Acts." Opposition to them,
he believed and said, could only be inspired either by reckless
coquetry with revolution or by blindness to the reality of the
danger. "It is one of the peculiar excellences of the British Constitution," he declared when he urged that the Seditious Meetings
Bill should be passed, but should run for three years only, "to be
able in times of popular commotion to strengthen the hands of the
executive government, and afterwards, when the danger is past, to
revert to our former state of liberty and freedom."

Towards the end of that angry session the following entry
occurs in the diary: "Dec. 16th.—Took my place, as for some little
time past, the last seat on the Opposition bench. Finding that
Opposition complained of it, I named it this evening to Tierney who
behaved very kindly about it." All things considered, the complaint
was not unreasonable.

3

Certainly there were Radicals who hated Wilberforce. Francis
Place, the stubborn champion of Trade Unionism and the backstairs architect of Reform, described him in his analysis of the

Peterloo debate as "an ugly epitome of the devil." Cobbett's hatred dated back to his unregenerate days, when, in strange contradiction to his later self, he was the close ally and constant correspondent of so stiff an oligarch as Windham. There are one or two angry thrusts at the uncongenial "saint" in his letters about the odious Peace of Amiens. Fox, he declares, in his attacks on Windham's war-party, "is most insidiously and malignantly aided by Wilberforce"; and alluding to a speech of Wilberforce's in Yorkshire he begs Windham to obtain for him "these precious morsels of eloquence." Wilberforce, too, it appears, is at the back of the mischievous attacks on the manlier sports, especially bull-baiting, which Windham so queerly loved and the popularity of which in Staffordshire and Lancashire Cobbett associated with the peculiar bravery of the troops enlisted in those counties. So it was with the gusto of an old feud that Cobbett in later days assailed the preposterous "Independent." Above all the other victims of the *Political Register* he enjoyed putting Wilberforce in the pillory; and when he used his frequent and very effective device of a Public Letter, he reiterated that too-widely respected name with special zest—"Well, Wilberforce. . . . Now you will observe, Wilberforce. . . . Mark it, Wilberforce; note it down. . . ." Still more pointed is the climax of the final crescendo in his often-quoted letter to Orator Hunt, written after his flight to the United States on the suspension of the Habeas Corpus Act in 1818.

> Think of it. A hundred brace of wood-cocks a day. Think of *that*! And never to see the hang-dog face of a tax-gatherer. Think of *that*! No Alien Acts here. No long-sworded and whiskered Captains. No Judges escorted from town to town and sitting under the guard of dragoons. No packed juries of tenants. No Crosses. No Bolton Fletchers. No hangings and rippings up. No Castleses and Olivers. No Stewarts and Perries. No Cannings, Liverpools, Castlereaghs, Eldons, Ellenboroughs or Sidmouths. No Bankers. No squeaking Wynnes. No Wilberforces. Think of *that*! No Wilberforces!

The Radical dead-set against Wilberforce is nowhere better illustrated than in Hazlitt's *Spirit of the Age*, published in 1825. Those lively "studies in contemporary biography" are admirable reading; but drab history must regard them primarily as a warning against a too easy acceptance of contemporary judgments. Hazlitt pokes fun, though not unkindly, at Jeremy Bentham; he makes him out an industrious, benevolent, amusingly childish pedant; and he denies that the man, whose influence was to do more in the long run for the better government of England than that of any other of his day, "has given any new or decided impulse to the human mind." Coleridge, "by dissipating his intellect and dallying with every subject by turns," has done little or nothing to justify the high opinion of his friends. Two pages of venom are devoted to the Tory politics of Scott—his unworthy acts of adulation; his littleness, pique, resentment, bigotry, and intolerance; his forgetfulness of all that was due to the pride of intellect and the sense of manhood, the moment his own interest or the prejudices of others interfered, and so forth. Sir Francis Burdett, on the other hand, whom a sober-minded historian of by no means illiberal views has described as "superficial and self-advertising," is pictured as "a plain, unaffected, unsophisticated English gentleman"; "one of the few remaining examples of the old English understanding and old English character"; "never violent or in extremes except when the people or the Parliament happen to be out of their senses, and then he seems to regret the necessity of plainly telling them he thinks so." After that it is no surprise to find Lord Eldon and Wilberforce classed and limned together on the Plutarchian plan. But it is a little surprising to find Hazlitt painting Wilberforce blacker than Lord Eldon. He depicts Eldon and the Tories of his type as spoiled children, fractious and selfish, all urbanity and good-humour until their interests are threatened. It is a bitter enough picture, but not so malignant as that which follows.

Mr. Wilberforce is a less perfect character in his way. He acts from mixed motives. He would willingly serve two masters, God and Mammon. . . . We can readily believe that Mr. Wilberforce's first object and principle of action is to do what he thinks right; his next (and that we fear is of almost equal weight with the first) is to do what will be thought so by other people. . . . His "conscience will not budge," unless the world goes with it. He does not seem greatly to dread the denunciation in Scripture —"Woe unto you, when all men shall speak well of you." We suspect that he is not quite easy in his mind, because West-India planters and Guinea traders do not join in his praise. [This is hard hitting, but worse is to come.] Mr. Wilberforce's humanity will go all lengths that it can with safety and discretion; but it is not to be supposed that it should lose him his seat for Yorkshire, the smile of Majesty, or the countenance of the loyal and pious. He is anxious to do all the good he can without hurting himself or his fair fame. His conscience and his character compound matters very amicably. He rather patronises honesty than is a martyr to it. His patriotism and philanthropy are not so ill-bred as to quarrel with his loyalty or to banish him from the first circles. . . . He has had two strings to his bow—he by no means neglects his worldly interests while he expects a bright reversion in the skies. Mr. Wilberforce is far from being a hypocrite; but he is, we think, as fine a specimen of *moral equivocation* as can well be conceived. . . . He carefully chooses his ground to fight the battles of loyalty, religion and humanity; and it is such as is always safe and advantageous to himself. . . . He has all the air of the most perfect independence, and gains a character for impartiality and candour when he is only striking a balance in his mind between the *éclat* of differing from a Minister on some vantage-ground and the risk of odium that may attend it.

And so on, till, at the close of the essay which is certainly the most vindictive of the set (for Hazlitt mingles his abuse of Scott with some kindly praise of his novels), Wilberforce is robbed even of the credit which Fox and Grey and Romilly and Mackintosh, nay, all but the most spiteful opponents accorded him.

Something of this fluctuating, time-serving principle [runs the final paragraph] was visible even in the great question of the Abolition of the Slave Trade. He was, at one time, half inclined to surrender it into Mr. Pitt's dilatory hands, and seemed to think the gloss of novelty was gone from it and the gaudy colouring of popularity sunk into the *sable* ground from which it rose. It was, however, persisted in and carried to a triumphant conclusion. Mr. Wilberforce said too little on that occasion of one compared with whom he was but the frontispiece to that great chapter in the history of the world—the mask, the varnishing, and painting. The man that affected it by Herculean labours of body and equally gigantic labours of mind was Clarkson, the true Apostle of human Redemption on that occasion, and who, it is remarkable, resembles in his person and lineaments more than one of the Apostles in the *Cartoons* of Raphael. He deserves to be added to the Twelve!

These caustic pages have been quoted at some length because so many good opinions of Wilberforce have been recorded in this book. It is needless to check the string of epigrams or to reopen the Clarkson controversy. Readers of the foregoing chapters can form their own opinions. Nor will they find it difficult to understand why anti-Tory rancour was thus concentrated on Wilberforce's head. When party feeling runs high, the man who tells you he is neutral and seems always to side with your opponents is more provoking than a down-right inveterate enemy, especially when his profession of neutrality is so far believed in by a great part of the public as to give unusual weight to his opinions. That this palpable Tory, this man of wealth and property, as stiffly bound to the interests of his class as any landlord, should pose as an impartial arbiter above the heat and dust of party conflict—it was intolerable. Still more galling, the pontiff was a pietist. A frankly cynical tyrant is more endurable than one who crushes his victims in the name of God; and to men like Hazlitt and Cobbett the "other-worldliness" of the rich and comfortable Wilberforce's religion seemed positively nauseating. They gnashed their teeth at his genteel tributes to the "patient poor." And his Puritanical activities outside politics, his campaigns for stricter morals and a sterner Sabbath—what were they but one more symptom of class-tyranny, an attempt to rob the poor of their harmless sports and to deaden their meagre leisure-hours while the profligacy and idleness and irreligion of the rich went unrebuked? Wilberforce, in fact, was the obvious target for the hostility with which many Radicals then regarded the Churches—and not without reason. For organised religion in England as a whole was on the classes' side, not the masses'. The sudden revival of zeal for the Established Church in the days of the French Revolution was largely due to the belief that Jacobinism and Atheism were inseparable twins, that the rights of property would be remembered as long as Christianity were not forgotten. The agitation for the building of more churches needed no ulterior motive when the fast-growing towns had only "church-room" for one in seven of their population and when at Manchester, for example, the vicar had to read the banns for at least 120 couples every Sunday; and Arthur Young was right, when he took a lead in this agitation in 1798, to insist that new churches were particularly needed for the poor. But the ulterior motive was always there. "Where are they [the poor]," asked Arthur Young, "to learn the doctrines of that truly excellent religion which exhorts to content and to submission to the higher powers?" And when the agitation at last bore fruit, when, in 1818, Parliament voted no less than a million pounds for church-building, there was no concealing—there was little attempt, indeed, to conceal—the conviction that the Church was the natural ally of the State in the conflict with Reform. As Liverpool, the Prime Minister, told the House of Lords, the political aspect of the matter, the prevalence of dangerous influences in crowded centres of industry, was one of his reasons for regarding the New Churches Bill as actually "the most important measure he had ever submitted to their lordships' consideration."

Take account of such facts as these and of the ease with which party spirit exaggerates and generalises, and it is easy to see why Wilberforce was anathema to the Radicals; why the blood rushed to Cobbett's head when the Saint inveighed against the profanation of the Sabbath or bestowed the benediction of his faith on the existing political and social order; why those vigorous haters would have hated him more, not less, if they had known that his decision to support the Corn Bill was made at his prayers.

4

Party feeling cannot be bothered with fine distinctions. It can only sustain itself by digging the dividing ditch as deep as possible and making the best of everything on one side of it and the worst of everything on the other. Since, therefore, Wilberforce's neutrality was merely nominal on the main issue, since he supported Sidmouth's general system of repression as consistently as Pitt's, he was classified by the fiercer Radicals as an uncompromising reactionary with nothing to offer to the discontented but a policy of blank negation. And this was unjust. For, while he spoke and voted for repressing agitation, he pleaded also for positive measures to remedy the ills on which agitation fed—the destitution and the ignorance of the masses. In one of his speeches on Peterloo he declared that it was everybody's duty "to do all that was possible

w. z

for relieving the distresses of the laborious poor." He drew attention, very rightly, to the bad effect on character of the disastrous
"Speenhamland" system of parish aid; and suggested that the
Government should find some means of providing paid employment. Later in the session he emphatically supported the proposal
of Bennet, the Whig, for public relief work on roads and canals.
"Every possible plan," he said, "should be tried." And when, in a
debate on a petition on behalf of the Scottish poor, Castlereagh
argued that Scottish landowners should tax themselves for poor-
relief as heavily as their English *confrères* before England could be
fairly asked to share Scotland's burden, Wilberforce insisted that,
whatever the unfairness, it would be inhuman to allow these long-
suffering Scots to suffer absolute want. Of this debate the diary
notes: "I am told, and I fear justly . . . that I was extremely harsh
against Castlereagh." In the same session he pleaded for the education of the poor. "Have you reflected," he wrote to Dr. Chalmers,
"on the effects produced in this country by the newspapers? They
are almost incalculably great, and on the whole, I fear, very
injurious. It is my persuasion that our safety will henceforth be to
educate our people up to the newspapers, if I may so express myself.
We must so much enlighten them that they may be armed against
those delusions." In the same strain he told the House of Commons
that, until it made amends for its long neglect in this matter, he
saw no prospect of tranquillity or prosperity in England. Education could not be left to evolve itself. If people were destined to be
free, they must be made fit to enjoy their freedom. . . . Flat platitudes, no doubt, to-day; but not platitudes in 1819. To many
Tories of the Right, in fact, such arguments must have seemed
mischievously false.

One could scarcely expect, however, that these mild suggestions
would tell in Wilberforce's favour with the Radicals. He did not
press them far—never so far as to embarrass the Government. He
started no great campaign for relief works or for education. That
was not his vocation. And so the critics, if they marked these little
signs of grace at all, merely added them to their sum of the paste-
board saint's hypocrisies. It is rather more surprising that Cobbett
and his friends gave Wilberforce no credit for his opposition to the
full Tory doctrine on minor issues. It was dishonest of Hazlitt to
mock at Wilberforce's humanity where white men were concerned
and to say not a word of his fight against the increased severities

of the Penal Code and especially the Game Laws by which the more ruthless section of the propertied class strove to deter the destitute from stealing that they might not starve. Over seventy offences were made capital during the reign of George III. At the date of Peterloo death was the penalty for stealing five shillings from a shop or two pounds from a dwelling-house, for damaging an embankment or a hop-plantation or cutting down a tree, for stealing a sheep or linen from a bleaching-green or destroying a machine, for being found disguised on a highroad or for impersonating a Greenwich pensioner. Still more outrageous and still more senseless were the Game Laws. For, as the results proved, no fear of penalties, however barbarous, could keep the hardy English peasant from trying to catch a rabbit on the squire's land so long as he had no food or even so long as the London poulterers were never punished for buying and selling the game he poached. In 1816 the landlords passed an Act enabling two magistrates to order the transportation for seven years of a person found at night in an enclosure with any instrument for killing or trapping game; and all Romilly's protests could not persuade Parliament to go farther than to limit the penalty in the following year to persons found with any weapon of offence. Even to threaten an assault with intent to prevent a poacher's arrest was a capital crime. As far as the death-penalty was concerned this savage code defeated its end. For nineteen trivial capital offences out of twenty, "injured persons would not prosecute; judges laboured to procure an acquittal; juries perjured themselves rather than convict." But the twentieth cases were numerous enough. And the convict who was not hanged was condemned to transportation to Botany Bay—which sometimes proved worse than a death-sentence—or to the foul and degrading conditions of English prisons.

The severities of the Penal Code, like those of the Slave Trade, could not long survive the appeal to ordinary humanity and common sense. But in the one case as in the other, vigorous and pertinacious spokesmen were required to make it heard; and as in the one case Wilberforce could rely on the support of Romilly and Mackintosh, so in the other Romilly and Mackintosh could rely on the support of Wilberforce. It will be remembered that, as early as 1786, inspired by Romilly's first protests, he had carried a small ameliorative measure through the Commons.[1] "The barbarous

---

[1] See p. 49 above.

custom of hanging," he had then declared to Wyvill, "has been tried too long and with the success which might have been expected of it." In a letter to Stephen in 1810 he deplores his being prevented by an attack of fever from hearing Romilly's speech in the House on capital punishment. And his heart was not hardened, as the heart of Eldon and others of his class, by the arguments of the era of repression. Shortly after the Corn Bill riots—the soldiers had only left his house within the fortnight—he notes in his diary a typical instance of what he baldly calls "our bloody laws": "An affecting visit from Mrs. B., the wife of an attorney of respectable station and character, near thirty years in Leeds, convicted of forgery on stamps and deeds, and to be hanged this day week." Again, he notes in 1818: "Mrs. Fry called early about a poor woman under sentence of death for forgery"; and once more he inveighs against "our murderous laws." In 1819 he presented to the House of Commons a petition on the subject from the Society of Friends. In the course of his speech—a speech which reminded the Whig chronicler, Greville, of "the better days of the House of Commons" —he recalled the devotion of the Quakers to all humane causes and not least to that of Abolition; and, amid general cheers, he paid an eloquent tribute to Romilly whose tragic suicide had occurred a few months before. That he should assume himself the task of revising the "hanging laws" was, as he told a friend who urged it on him, utterly impossible. "I can write but little," he pleaded, "I can scarcely read at all." And in his speech he called for "some individual of competent knowledge, industry, and ability" to undertake the task. It was clear enough to whom he was pointing as Romilly's successor; and when, a few weeks later, Mackintosh moved for a Select Committee to consider the laws prescribing the death penalty for felonies, Wilberforce vigorously supported him. "I have never heard," he said, "a more able address, a more splendid display of profound knowledge of the subject with such forcible reasoning of the facts." "He spoke admirably," notes the diary, "I very middling." But Wilberforce's opinion, however he expressed it, carried votes. The Committee was obtained by 147 to 128, and Wilberforce was appointed on it. Its work procured in the following year the repeal of several of the more flagrant laws; and in 1821 Mackintosh, supported again by Wilberforce with voice and vote, carried further measures, dealing with horse-stealing and forgery, through the Commons. But the pace had become too fast for the

Lords, particularly for Lord Eldon; and further progress was barred till Peel succeeded Sidmouth at the Home Office and himself took up the cause.

On the Game Laws Wilberforce was equally vocal and persistent. In 1817 he supported Romilly's one successful attack—on the sweeping application of the penalty imposed in 1816. It was unjust, he said, to punish so severely "an act, which it was contrary to the natural feeling of mankind to say was, in itself, a crime and which men could never be brought to think a crime merely because there were legislative provisions against it." "It was not right to make up in severity for a defect of power." And he went farther. "I strongly object," he said, "to game being put on the same footing as other property." "It is not considered any crime," he said later in the session, "to purchase this sort of luxury for a gentleman's table, while the poor wretch who purloined it may suffer the loss of his liberty and perhaps be led to the gallows." In 1819 he declared the Game Laws to be "so opposite to every principle of personal liberty, so contrary to all our notions of private right, so injurious and so arbitrary in their operation that the sense of the greater part of mankind is in determined hostility to them." But on this question Wilberforce had to vote with minorities. Stealing five shillings or masquerading on the highway—such felonies as these might be more leniently regarded by the landlords' Parliament; but poaching was the unforgivable sin. And Wilberforce had retired for some years from politics before, in 1831, a Bill promoted by Althorp, himself a landlord and a sportsman, and carried through both Houses amid all the turmoil of the Reform Bill, swept the whole bad business of the Game Laws into limbo.

Nor was Wilberforce silent on other abuses in the penal system. He frequently referred in the House to the evils of transportation; and in 1819 he supported Bennet's motion for a committee of inquiry in a long speech which closed with an appeal to Castlereagh to reconsider his opposition to it. With the scandal of the prisons he had been brought into touch some twenty years earlier through his friendship with Bentham. He had then tried to secure more effective support from Pitt and Dundas for Bentham's Utopian penitentiary, the "Panopticon"; and had angrily deplored the distress and loss of money in which the failure of the scheme involved its creator. "Bentham cruelly used" is a recurrent note in the diary of those days. And Bentham deluged him with characteristic letters.

"Kind sir," runs one of them, "the next time you happen on Mr. Attorney-General [one day to be Lord Eldon] in the House or elsewhere, be pleased to take a spike, the longer and cheaper the better, and apply it to him by way of a memento that the Penitentiary Contract Bill has, for I know not what length of time, been sticking in his hands." A few years later Wilberforce was again involved in the question of prison reform, but not this time on the side of the reformers. The shocking management of the Cold Bath Fields jail might possibly have received impartial treatment in Parliament in 1798 if it had not been a party issue. But it happened that many of the suspected Jacobins, arrested after the suspension of the Habeas Corpus Act, had been imprisoned there; and it was Sheridan and the Whigs who pressed the case for an inquiry. Pitt refused it, and Wilberforce supported Pitt. Finally, in 1818, Wilberforce was introduced to the heroic work of Mrs. Fry among the female prisoners in London. One day in February the diary records a Quaker dinner-party in his house—"Mr. and Mrs. Buxton, Mr. S. Hoare, jun., Mrs. Fry, Miss Priscilla Gurney—very interesting talk indeed, and agreed to meet to-morrow at Newgate." So next day, "Went with our party to meet Mrs. Fry at Newgate. The order she has produced is wonderful—a very interesting visit—much talk with the governor and chaplain—Mrs. Fry prayed in recitative—the place from its construction bad." "Much impressed," he notes a few weeks later, "by Mr. Buxton's book on our prisons and the account of Newgate reform. What lessons are taught by Mrs. Fry's success! I am still warmed by the account. Were I young, I should instantly give notice of the business, if no one else did." And in the following year, when Alderman Wood presented a petition from the City Corporation complaining of the crowded state of Newgate, Wilberforce joined with Brougham in its support.

There was one more field of Wilberforce's interests in which the champions of the poor might have found, if they had wanted to find, something to mitigate their sweeping condemnation. These years saw the first symptoms of the reaction against industrial *laissez-faire*. Men were beginning to feel that the heartless logic of the "dismal science" would no longer justify the State in allowing the wholesale sacrifice of children to the Moloch of British trade. More than a decade had passed since Sir Robert Peel, the elder, had proposed and carried in 1802 the first of the great series of Factory Acts, forbidding apprentices in cotton or woollen mills to work before six in the morning or after nine at night or for more than twelve hours a day, excluding time for meals. Wilberforce had warmly backed this measure; and his ardour had been heightened by a personal appeal he had received from "an honest and hard-working couple whose child was barbarously torn from them and sent down to a distant cotton-mill." "I have since conversed with these people," he wrote, "and seldom have heard a more artless, affecting tale." This was doubtless one of the influences which led him to press for the extension of the Bill to cover "free-labour children" as well as apprentices; but Sir Robert opposed the proposal and it failed. This extension, however, was precisely what Sir Robert himself brought forward in 1815 and again in 1818. For the progress of the Industrial Revolution and the growing concentration of cotton-spinning in the towns had involved the increasing employment of children who were not apprentices and so unprotected by the Act of 1802. That Act, in fact, as its author admitted in the House, had quickly become "almost a dead letter." Ten times the number of children were now employed and most of them were worked for at least fourteen hours out of the twenty-four. He now proposed, therefore, that no child under nine should work in cotton mills or factories and none under sixteen should work more than $12\frac{1}{2}$ hours, including one hour and a half for meals. Together with Huskisson and the younger Peel, Wilberforce heartily commended the Bill: but he asked for a further limitation. "It is cruel to imagine," he declared, "that children of nine years of age are able to sustain labour as long as those of fifteen or sixteen years"; and he suggested that children from nine to twelve should be allotted shorter hours than those of twelve to sixteen. It mattered little, in the upshot, that this suggestion was not adopted : for the Bill, having passed the Commons, was slaughtered in the Lords. Next year, however, the Lords themselves initiated, and the Commons duly accepted, a virtually identical measure except for the significant extension of the work from $12\frac{1}{2}$ to $13\frac{1}{2}$.

Wilberforce's humanity was likewise engaged in the cause of the chimney-sweeps. It is now almost forgotten that, a hundred years ago, the chimneys of the rich were swept by little boys—about five hundred of them in London, it is reckoned, and as many more in the provincial towns—who were forced to climb the flues, spurred up by their masters, if need be, with fire or pin-pricks or the whip; scraping the skin from knees and elbows; incurring malformations and diseases in bodies often left unwashed year in, year out; suffocated sometimes in a mass of soot at some far corner in a labyrinth of ancient flues or burned to death when ordered to extinguish a "chimney on fire" or when crawling by mistake into a lighted flue. But so it was; and it remains one of the grimmest puzzles of that age that, despite persistent ventilation of it, the scandal was permitted to go on. One mild Act of Parliament alone was passed to deal with it, in 1788, and that was not enforced. Societies for superseding Climbing Boys, founded in London and in Yorkshire towns in 1803 and onwards, laboured in vain. At last in 1817 a concerted move was made in Parliament. Petitions were presented, a Committee was appointed, and it presented a sensational report. Thereupon Bennet brought in a Bill to prohibit boys from climbing chimneys in the future, with the exception of existing apprentices over fourteen years old: and as in his campaign against the Criminal Laws and the Game Laws, so in this Bennet found a sturdy ally in Wilberforce who assisted him to prepare the Bill and seconded his motion for leave to introduce it. On this occasion Wilberforce read a letter from a clergyman in a county town, reporting that within the last few months "two children had stuck fast in chimnies and perished in that shocking state from suffocation." The Bill passed safely through the Commons, but was held up in the Lords; and next year the Lords threw out a second Bill. In 1819 Bennet proposed a third Bill; and this time the Commons proved more restive. But Wilberforce rose to the occasion with a fighting speech. He met the argument that the masters could be trusted in their own interest to protect their boys with the conclusive example of the Slave Trade. And he met the argument that a life-saving device, like the new sweeping machines, would quickly overcome custom and prejudice and come into general use without interference by the State with the equally telling example of vaccination. "In a long course of years, machines may get the better of old habits; but what numbers of wretched boys will suffer in the meantime!" The speech told. The Bill was carried. But the Lords once more destroyed it. Then Bennet made his final effort. He moved and carried a Bill, not to prohibit climbing—for that was clearly useless—but to limit the age of employment and otherwise to improve its conditions, just as Wilberforce, when the Abolition of the Slave Trade had seemed hopeless, had pressed at least for limitation. The result was no better. To the tune of Lauderdale's economic dogmas and Eldon's flippant sarcasms, even this mild measure of amelioration was rejected by the Lords.

5

On all those issues Wilberforce was on the liberal side, and there was one other issue on which he showed a genuine independence—an issue which, in the course of 1820, set all other political issues in the background and which in the result did more than anything else, more than Peterloo and the Six Acts, to discredit the Old Tories. The affair of Queen Caroline was a very controversial and a very sordid business. It was precipitated, it will be remembered, by the death of George III at the beginning of the year. The new King's official wife, who for some years past had been living a life on the Continent, which, to say the least, was indecorous and indiscreet, was determined to assert her rights as Queen of England. George IV was equally determined to refuse them, at the price, if need be, of instituting proceedings for divorce on the charge of adultery, despite the notorious looseness of his own domestic life. Ministers were in an odious dilemma. They must have recognised the arbitrary egoism of the King's attitude. They must have known that it would heighten his unpopularity with the mass of the people. But they knew too that the King was obstinate and was even capable of recklessly dismissing the Government if it refused to carry out his will. They therefore attempted a compromise. They agreed to his demand that Caroline's name should be omitted from the prayer in the Liturgy for the King and Queen, on the understanding that any attempt to prosecute her should be abandoned. But such a compromise was not at all acceptable to Caroline. She set out from Italy for England. At Montbard she was met by her staunchest champion, Alderman Wood, and at St. Omer by Brougham whom she chose for her chief legal adviser. Nothing—or nothing at least that George was prepared to offer—could now stop her from finishing her journey. On June 5 she landed at Dover and proceeded to Canterbury. Next day she drove through welcoming crowds to London.

"She arrived about six in London—crowds greeting her," records the diary. "She approaches wisely, because boldly. Fixes at Alderman Wood's. Brougham in the house. How deeply interested all are, indeed I feel it myself, about her! One can't help admiring her spirit, though I fear she has been very profligate." But more was required of Wilberforce than an onlooker's interest. Public opinion had turned instinctively to him, a few years before, on a question in which party politics and royal morals had been similarly interwoven—the question of the sale of official secrets by the mistress of the Duke of York. And now, in this far graver crisis, the call was clearer still. Justice and morality, the prestige of the Crown and indeed of the whole system of government it represented, were already drifting into the whirlpool of party faction. Now, if ever, was the time for the Independent to intervene, for the Keeper of the Nation's Conscience to give the lead. But it was not a storm that could be stilled by some fine moral gesture. King and Queen were at open strife. Behind the obstinate man stood the Government and the Tories of the Right. The obstinate woman could count on Brougham's eloquence and Denman's character, on the votes of other Whigs, if not their friendship—the Whig ladies did not call on her till the crisis was over—and on the almost passionate adherence of the English people at large. With the principals in such a temper, their forces aligned, and public feeling running high, all Wilberforce's adroitness, all his humanity and tact, might well prove unavailing to prevent the horrid battle being fought to a finish. He did not underestimate the difficulty himself. Discarding all visionary ideas of reconciliation, he set himself to postpone any official proceedings and gain time for a compromise. What followed may be learned from his own notes.

I resolved, if possible, to prevent the inquiry; an object which could only be attained by such an amicable adjustment as should give neither party cause for triumph. When Lord Castlereagh had made a motion to refer the papers to a Secret Committee, I endeavoured to interpose a pause during which the two parties might have an opportunity of contemplating coolly the prospect before them. Accordingly I sounded the House (June 7); my proposition was immediately adopted and a pause was made with the declaration that its purpose was to give opportunity for a final settlement. What followed is before the world—the correspondence, and subsequently the conferences which took place between the King's servants and the Queen's law-officers. The concessions made by the King's servants, as Mr. Brougham afterwards declared in the House of Commons, were various and great. The name and rights of a Queen were granted to Her Majesty without reserve, any recognition of which had formerly been avoided. A royal yacht, a frigate, etc., were offered. It was agreed that her name and rank should be notified at the court either of Rome or Milan—the capitals of the countries in which she had expressed her intention to reside; and that an Address should be presented to the Queen, no less than another to the King, to thank her Majesty for having acceded to the wishes of the House of Commons.

The one concession omitted from this list was the restoration of Caroline's name to the Liturgy; and on this point the King refused to retract the step he had compelled his Ministers to take. Wilberforce himself wrote to him, earnestly praying for this act of grace and frankly warning him of the dangerous feeling in the country. But the King made no move. Nor did the Queen. "I fear," laments the diary on the following Sunday, "lest it should please God to scourge the nation through the medium of this rupture between the King and Queen. If the soldiery should take up her cause, who knows what may happen—and is it very improbable? O Lord, deliver us!" Wilberforce's only hope was that the Queen would yield on the Liturgy point, if entreated so to do, not of course by the King, but by the House of Commons. Accordingly, on June 20, he gave notice of a motion for an Address. But there were soon signs that this hope was scarcely justified. That very night "just as I was going up to bed," relates the diary, "I heard a knocking at the door announcing a letter from the Queen. . . . Alderman Wood had given her a mistaken account of my notice, and she wrote a warm, expostulatory letter—her own ebullition." Next day, "Brougham brought me a second letter from the Queen, more moderate." On the 22nd, the day fixed for his motion, he received a communication from the Queen's chief agent which once more raised his hopes, and not without reason. "She will accede to your Address," wrote Brougham, "*I pledge myself.*"[1] It was in a confident mood, therefore, that he introduced his motion in a crowded House. Members were "very noisy and impatient; would not hear Acland or even my own reply quietly"; but the great majority were with him. The motion was carried by 391

[1] Italics not in the original.

votes to 124; and Wilberforce and three other members were appointed to present the Address to the Queen. On the morning of the 24th they donned their Court dress and proceeded to Wood's house in Portman Street. "There was a great mob about the door," wrote Wilberforce to his wife, "which, if it had been night, would have been very dangerous." As it was, they were hissed and booed; but no stones were thrown. When they reached the presence they soon found that their mission was a failure. The Queen had never really trusted Brougham. "If my head is on Temple Bar," she had said, "it will be Brougham's doing." And now she had listened to other counsellors who had made it their business to fan that distrust. Two days after she reached London, Cobbett had written to bid her "beware of insidious and perfidious advice." On the 10th he had told her that it is the universal hope that she will not suffer herself to be induced to accept *any compromise.* On the 12th he warned her that her enemies were now proscratinating in the hope of dealing with her when the public enthusiasm had died down. Finally, on the 23rd, the day before her audience with Wilberforce, he had told her, not indeed untruly, that the people would be with her if she rejected the Address. "Mr. Wilberforce's motion is clearly seen through by the public," he wrote, "who have no doubt that it is intended to effect by supplication that which it is perceived cannot be effected by threats. . . . The writer of this paper presumes humbly to express an opinion that the Answer to this Address should *explicitly reject the advice* contained in it. . . . An Answer of this description would, it is believed, put a stop to the efforts of Mr. Wilberforce." So Wilberforce found the Queen steeled against compromise. "Her manner," he says, "was extremely dignified, but very stern and haughty." He read the Address. "Alas! the answer most decidedly rejected our mediation."

Cobbett had certainly scored. Wilberforce's efforts had been put a stop to. He was angrily accused, indeed, of having misled and humiliated the House of Commons through his absurd illusion that the Queen would listen to its counsel: and the King's partisans denounced him as a feckless busybody who ought never to have interfered. He could easily have rebutted these charges. He had only to make public Brougham's explicit pledge. But this he refused to do—"a political forbearance," confessed Brougham himself, "which I never knew equalled."

Public battle was now inevitable. Since Caroline had refused a

compromise, George was determined to get rid of her; and his
Ministers obediently prepared a Bill of Pains and Penalties as an
instrument of divorce. But there were still some who believed that
Wilberforce, if he had failed with the wife, might yet succeed with
the husband. He was pressed to return to town in August, amongst
others, by William Lamb (later Lord Melbourne) who thought there
was "great danger of serious popular tumult and insurrection."
"If anything is to be done," he wrote, "your presence and influence
will do it." "Mr. Wilberforce is looked up to," wrote Madame
d'Arblay to a friend, "as the only man in the dominions to whom
an arbitration should belong." And Wilberforce himself had
thoughts of urging the King "to go to the House of Lords and
declare he gives up his own wishes to the gratifying of his people."
But such hopes as he had were weakened by the open letter which
Lord John Russell published in *The Times*. "Although I generally
differ from you in politics," it ran, "I warmly admire your generous
efforts for the welfare of mankind, and I believe you capable of
doing a great benefit to the country. You, sir, and some others
whose support is the sole strength of Administration, are bound to
interfere. . . . In your hands is, perhaps, the fate of this country."
"How could he hope," was Wilberforce's comment, "that I should
prevail on the King to accept my mediation as that of a neutral
man, when publicly called upon to come forward by one of the
strongest partisans of the Opposition." Whether Lord John's letter
made much difference or not, the King himself soon settled the
matter. An impulsive go-between sent a messenger to fetch Wilberforce post-haste from Weymouth to Salt Hill to see the King who
was informed that he was expected. George's reply showed that
Wilberforce was right not to set out on such a hasty errand. He
said that, if he conferred with Mr. Wilberforce it must be on
some political business, and that he never talked on political
subjects with any but his Ministers.

So what has been justly called "The Queen's Trial" proceeded
on its course. "It will be long, painful, and disgusting," Wilberforce
had prophesied in the House, "and what in my mind aggravates
the evil, Parliament is not clear in the matter. We marry our Kings
and Queens contrary to the laws of God and of nature, and from
this source proceed the evils which I am now anxious to avoid."
And he had taken occasion to make clear his sense of the hardships
which the ill-used, if foolish, Caroline had endured. "I am strongly

impressed," he had said, "with a feeling for the Queen's situation in early life, and in what I lately proposed, her advantage was especially intended." No one can doubt nowadays that Wilberforce's intervention *was* to her advantage. Outwardly, it is true, she won the battle. The Bill of Pains and Penalties passed the Lords by such slight and falling majorities that Ministers ultimately abandoned it. "This morning," says the diary for November 11, "the early coaches from London came in, men and horses covered with white favours—emblematic, I suppose, of her innocence—for the rejection of the Bill against the Queen or rather for Lord Liverpool's giving it up when carried only by nine." Caroline had won the battle, but at a heavy price. Day after day she had sat in the crowded Chamber, respondent in a divorce-case, while the Crown Lawyers paraded their wretched Italian innkeepers and chambermaids to try to prove her adultery. One black day the strain had been too much. When the notorious Majocchi was produced, she rose in agitation, crying "Teodoro![1] No! No!" and hurried from the House. And when it was all over, "I do indeed feel thankful," she wrote, "*mais hélas*, it comes too late. . . . No one in fact care for me; and this business has been more cared for as a political affair dan as de cause of a poor forlorn woman. . . . I feel very unwell, fatigued, and *ébayé*." Some months later she had recovered enough of her strength to renew the fight. The King refused to allow her the share she claimed in his Coronation. The Privy Council decided against her claim. The Primate told her that he could only officiate by "orders from the Sovereign." Undaunted, she drove to Westminster Abbey on the day of the ceremony and asked to be admitted. She might have got in, alone and unattended, but at the last moment she turned back. The watching crowd, once so mad for her, broke into laughter. "Shame!" they cried, and "Off!" So she drove away, and within a fortnight she died. Her official husband continued to live his customary life for nine more years.

It was pathetically true that most of her champions had cared for her cause "as a political affair." Was Brougham thinking only of the "poor, forlorn woman?" Was Cobbett? She had better have trusted Wilberforce. For, if he too had another motive than mere chivalry or justice, at least it was not partisan: it was not to truckle to the King nor yet to discredit him, not to serve the Government

[1] Or "Traditore."

nor yet the Opposition, but simply to terminate the scandal and save the country from a disgraceful and demoralising exhibition.

6

The Queen's Trial marks the turn of the political tide. In 1820 the septennium of reaction was nearing its end. When Castlereagh committed suicide in 1822, Canning, who had resigned in 1820 from loyalty to his friendship with Queen Caroline in earlier days, became, in the teeth of the King's enmity, Foreign Secretary and Leader of the House of Commons; and he soon secured a place in the Government for his comrade, Huskisson, with his Pittite tendencies towards Free Trade. Peel, meantime, had succeeded Sidmouth at the Home Office and set himself to sweep away the whole dirty system of *espionage* and intrigue, to resume Mackintosh's campaign against the Penal Code, and to establish law and order on the firm basis of an efficient police force. In two years' time, through the remarkable alliance of Hume and Huskisson, the Combination Acts were repealed. The positive repression of the poor had ceased.

But nobody was yet prepared to take up the Radical cry for Parliamentary Reform. If the young Tories had been converted to it, the Government and the party would have instantly split in two. And on this fundamental question the Whigs were still divided. Young Lambton had already begun to lose his temper with his father-in-law, Lord Grey, who told him in 1820 that he had no reasonable hope of Reform being carried in either of their lifetimes, and with other pundits of the party, like Lord Holland, who had said, a year before, that, if it were carried, "it would be as bad as a revolution." It was not strange, therefore, if Wilberforce did not move in this decade beyond the point he had reached in 1810. "I continue friendly," he tells a Yorkshire friend in 1817, "to the moderate, gradual, and almost insensibly operating Parliamentary Reform which was last brought forward by Mr. Pitt"; but, "I am firmly persuaded," he adds, "that at present a prodigious majority of the more intelligent people of this country are adverse to the measure." A year or two later, the fact that the Radical demagogues were preaching Reform—a fact which should really have been reassuring—frightened him off the whole question, just as it frightened Grey who at this time detested the Radicals and had no doubts of "the wickedness of their intentions." So, in the course of a speech in 1819, Wilberforce confessed that he had once favoured "a moderate reform of the system of representation in that House," but "now," he declared, "nothing like a moderate reform will satisfy the discontented. No! Nothing will now satisfy them but the utter destruction of the Constitution." With the subsidence of agitation and the end of the Sidmouth period, he became again a moderate Reformer, but with a little more stress now on the "moderate." He was shyer than before of altering the representative system. He intended to speak on Lord John Russell's motion for Reform in 1822 and he voted for it; but next day he regrets in the diary that he did not explain "the principles of my vote," i.e. "that it was to put an end to the moral corruption of elections in the smaller towns where drunkenness and bribery gain the day." Those are the evils, he writes a little later, "which call by far the loudest for reform. I verily believe, and have long believed, the constituent body to be more corrupt than the representative." Very moderate sentiments indeed! Still he never barred his mind, like many Tories and some Whigs, against real Reform: and in 1831 when the old man in his retirement heard the news of Russell's introduction of the first Reform Bill, while he confessed to his son that he "almost trembled" at the thought of its consequences, nevertheless, in another letter, he admitted that "on the whole I think I should have been favourable to it."

There was nothing so hesitating and half-hearted in Wilberforce's attitude to the Irish question. Time only strengthened his adherence to the liberal view. In April, 1819, the diary betrays him closeted at Grattan's house with Plunket, Tierney, Brougham, Mackintosh and other Whigs, and agreeing with them on the terms of a motion for Roman Catholic relief. When Grattan died in the following year, he joined with Grant in echoing Mackintosh's noble tribute in the Commons. And in 1821 he made a fine speech for the second reading of Plunket's Roman Catholic Disability Removal Bill. "Persecution for religious opinions," he declared, "is not only one of the wickedest, but one of the most foolish things in the world"; and he confessed that England's treatment of Ireland was "enough to awaken every generous sympathy in the human mind." He recalled the days when Ireland was called "The Mother of the Saints" and "possessed more pure religion than any other country in Europe." He reminded the House that the Glorious Revolution had brought liberty to England but not to Ireland; that England had treated Ireland as a stepmother her step-child. "Can it be wondered at," he asked, "that she has struggled to shake off the yoke of her oppressors?" Passing to the Union, he repeated his previous assertions that, of his personal knowledge, Pitt had considered the emancipation of the Catholics as the essential complement to Union. He was not alarmed by those critics of the present Bill who thought no Catholic would be satisfied with any concession short of a seat in Parliament. Was that so great an evil? If Catholics are hostile to this country, if they are subservient to their priests, all the more reason for bringing them into the British Legislature where their prejudices can be softened by a closer knowledge of this country and its Constitution. If the Irish were supposed to be ill qualified for orderly politics, whose fault was it? Has good treatment ever made a generous and high-minded people into rebels? The difference between the English and the Irish was significant. The Englishman's peculiar characteristic was his willingness to submit his conduct to the law of the country. The Irishman's was directly the reverse—a natural impatience at the restraints of law. From what could that difference spring but from the Irish being denied the enjoyment of the British Constitution? To give the Catholics the vote and go no farther was to let them out of prison and keep them in their convicts' dress. It was an effective speech— "I was complimented," says the diary—and it was followed by a more elaborate effort by Canning. But the day of Catholic Emancipation, though a little nearer than the day of Reform, had not yet come. The Bill passed the Commons by small majorities and was rejected in the Lords by 159 votes to 120.

In foreign policy, likewise, Wilberforce was on the liberal side. He entirely approved of Castlereagh's attempt to disentangle England from the coils of the Holy Alliance; but he was prepared to go farther than Castlereagh, to proceed with Canning from a negative aloofness from Reaction in Europe to a positive alliance with Liberalism. Hazlitt's venom was never more reckless than when he wrote of Wilberforce: "Not a word has he to say, not a whisper does he breathe, against the claim set up by the Despots of the Earth over their Continental subjects, but does everything in his power to confirm and sanction it." Yet in 1821—four years before Hazlitt published his essay—in the debate on the imposition of a constitution on Naples by the Holy Alliance, Wilberforce had denounced the conduct of the three great military Powers as unjust, abominable, and hostile to every idea of liberty. Castlereagh's guarded language, he said, was not enough for him; and in answer to his argument that the Powers would be deterred by their mutual jealousy from any territorial aggrandisement, he told the House to remember the fate of Poland and that "each monarch has a way of taking a slice." Again, in the following year, he came out in opposition to Castlereagh on the Greek question. "It is a disgrace to all the Powers of Europe," he said, "that, long ere now, they have not made a simultaneous effort and driven back a nation of barbarians, the inveterate enemies of Christianity and freedom, into Asia. . . . I know of no case in which the power of a mighty country like England could be more nobly, more generously, or more justifiably exerted than in rescuing the Greeks from bondage and destruction."

Manifestly, then, Wilberforce's place was on the left, not on the right of the Tory party. His political friends were not Castlereagh nor Sidmouth in those days, still less Eldon, but Canning and Huskisson. He was a welcome guest in the latter's country house, and with Canning he became so intimate that one night, as they walked away together from a late sitting of the House, he spoke to him of the serious things that lay nearest his heart. "He had neither father nor mother to train him up," comments the diary. "I always wondered he was so pure." Indeed, if Wilberforce had continued in Parliament after 1823, he would certainly have failed to maintain the last vestiges of a claim to "independence"; for he would have found himself in close accord, on every dominant issue, with the party which Canning and Huskisson led. If Wilberforce was Pitt's political brother, these were his political sons. All three had felt the shadow of Pitt's war-period and accepted a second era of repression in his name. But Canning and Huskisson had not forgotten the sanguine, liberal, unwarped Pitt of the days before the war; and it was this Pitt, and no other, that Wilberforce had really loved. "A vile picture," he commented on seeing, about this time, Hoppner's striking portrait of Pitt as he was in his later days; "a vile picture—his face anxious, diseased, reddened with wine, and soured and irritated by disappointment. Poor fellow, how unlike my youthful Pitt!"

XII

Second Crusade

I

SINGLENESS of purpose is the crusader's characteristic virtue and the secret of his power; and throughout those clouded and restless years after the war, though Wilberforce was obliged, as has been seen, to play his part in current British politics, his mind was still mainly engaged in the fortunes of the negroes oversea. The sovereigns and statesmen at Vienna had only willed, they had not carried out, the general Abolition of the Slave Trade, and, with one exception, the will of the British delegates alone was ardent and sincere. The exception was the Czar of Russia, and Russia was not a sea-power. So, if anything was to be done towards converting the resolutions of Vienna into realities, it was soon evident that the British Government would have to do it virtually single-handed. And since its mandate in the matter from Parliament and public opinion was as clear and vehement as ever, it did not shrink from the task. Pressure on Spain and Portugal, the only two Powers which had not yet agreed to Abolition, was vigorously resumed. In 1815 the Portuguese Government agreed, not without a grant of £300,000 from the British Treasury and the remission of £450,000 of debt, to limit its share in the Trade to the transport of slaves from Africa south of the Equator to her trans-Atlantic "possessions," and made fair promises of total Abolition in the near future. The Spanish Government was more backward. It pleaded that its colonies were not so well stocked with slaves as the British colonies had been in 1807. It complained of the economic loss involved and the difficulty of compensating its traders. It rubbed in the fact that Britain had already seized sundry Spanish slave-ships and refused to restore them. But it did not close the door to any settlement: it hinted at a bargain after the Portuguese model. "With unfeigned joy I state to you," wrote Wilberforce to Stephen in 1816, "that I have just heard from Lord Castlereagh that the Council of the Indies, to which the whole question of the

Abolition had been referred by the Spanish Government, has
reported in favour of total and immediate Abolition. But a
minority of seven, of whom one has large property in Cuba, has
protested against the others and made a separate report. Even they,
however, have recommended abolishing north of the Line immediately and totally in five years. But all the Council seems to wish
to make it a condition that we should give them money or at least
give up their captured ships." These were the lines on which
negotiations somewhat haltingly developed. "April 30, 1817.
Almost immediately after breakfast forced to town to Castlereagh
on Spanish Abolition—with him for above an hour. He really takes
much pains for the cause. He says he has written more on this head
than any other. The Spaniards are pressing hard for £600,000 and
a loan." The upshot was the signature of a treaty in Madrid in
September, 1817, under which Spain undertook to abolish the Trade
straightway north of the Equator and totally in 1820, and Britain
undertook to pay £400,000 to compensate for the captured slave-
ships and "for the losses which are a necessary consequence of the
Abolition of the said traffic." So the Spaniards secured their bargain,
because the cause of Abolition had taken so strong a hold on
Englishmen that they were willing to pay other peoples to follow
their example. In ordinary times £400,000 might not have seemed
a very large sum. As Castlereagh confessed, when he commended
the Treaty to the Commons in February, 1818, the Spanish merchants at Havana had offered five times that amount for the
privilege of continuing the Trade. But these were not ordinary
times. Britain was in the trough of post-war financial depression.
"If the coffers of the country were full," protested Sir Gilbert
Heathcote, "I should be willing enough to give the noble lord even
a million of money if he wanted it; but, now the coffers are empty,
we cannot afford unnecessary expenditure, and I am averse to
granting 400 pence to any potentate in Europe." This protest
brought Wilberforce up. If the country were really determined, he
said, to bring about a universal Abolition of the Slave Trade—and
Heathcote had admitted that—the method of bargain was cheaper
than the method of force. The removal, moreover, of this obstacle
to friendly relations with Spain might well lead to an increase in
our commerce with that country. And in any case it was right for
England, treading this new and difficult diplomatic path, to be
generous. "Generosity is only justice. Considering the many

blessings which the Almighty has showered on this country, it would be shameful to refuse such a sum for so great a purpose." Mackintosh and Grant supported Wilberforce. There was practically no further opposition, even from those who felt most acutely the effect of bad times and heavy taxes on the condition of the poor. "I believe," said Bennet, "that, if you went from house to house, you would have no difficulty in raising a contribution for the purpose of putting down this traffic." In a small House of 60, only four votes were cast against the grant.

Thus, by 1818, all the leading countries of the Western world had made the Slave Trade illegal or pledged themselves to do so in a few years' time. But this did not mean, even when those few years were up, the cessation of the Trade. As a matter of fact it actually increased. And the reason was quite plain. Of all the states which had enacted an Abolition law, only Britain made any serious effort to enforce it. Under strict orders from a Government sincerely bent on executing the almost passionate determination of the British people, the British Navy made it virtually impossible for the Trade to be carried on in British ships. But foreign Governments were not so zealous. They had passed their noble resolution at Vienna; and then, relieved of the tiresome philanthropy of Castlereagh and Alexander, they had done nothing at all. True to her undertaking France abolished the Trade by law in 1818; but the penalties for its infringement—fine and confiscation—were not enforced; and for years afterwards slavers, French and other, continued to sail under the French flag. Spain and Portugal likewise fulfilled their promises and enacted total Abolition under relatively mild penalties—Spain in 1820, Portugal, after some procrastination, in 1830. Yet, as late as 1836, the British officials at Sierra Leone reported that "there is nothing in the experience of the past year to show that the Slave Trade with Spain has in any degree diminished." And, as late as 1838, Palmerston brusquely told the Portuguese Minister, "that the Portuguese flag is lent, with the connivance of Portuguese authorities, to serve as a protection for all the miscreants of every other nation in the world who may choose to engage in such base pursuits." The United States had prohibited the importation of slaves in 1807; and the Anglo-American Treaty of Ghent in 1815, in tune with the Treaty of Vienna, had denounced the Trade and pledged the two signatories to use their best endeavours for its universal Abolition. In 1820 Congress proved the earnestness of its intentions by making direct participation in the Trade an act of piracy, punishable with death; and in 1821 Wilberforce paid a warm tribute to the zealous co-operation of American cruisers with British off the African coast. Nevertheless, as time went on, the Stars and Stripes were more and more misused, till it became a literal truth that of all the flags of the Atlantic nations the Union Jack alone was no protection to a slaver.

In the face of these disquieting facts there was only one means by which the British purpose could be realised. Somehow or other, the other maritime states must be persuaded either to co-operate with Britain in joint police-work or to allow Britain to do their share of it by giving her permission to inspect suspicious vessels flying their flags and, if found to be slave-ships, to arrest them. It was on this object, therefore, that Castlereagh concentrated his diplomacy; and he succeeded in including in the Treaty with Spain clauses permitting a reciprocal right of search and detention and instituting two mixed Anglo-Spanish Commissions to decide the fate of ships so captured. Similar arrangements were made in 1817 with Portugal and in 1818 with Holland. But, though British diplomacy continued stubbornly to press the point, it was years before any further success could be attained. There need have been no lack of opportunity for a general discussion and an international accord. The Powers at Vienna had agreed to hold annual conferences for the furtherance of their declared desire for universal Abolition. But it was not till 1818 that the first of such congresses assembled at Aix-la-Chapelle; and then Castlereagh's proposal that a reciprocal right of search should be conceded, to be carried out by special warships named by the several Powers, was decisively turned down. For the Powers—always, and intelligibly, jealous of British sea-power—felt that the right of search, however, reciprocal and however guarded, would give the British Navy something like a licence to interfere, at pleasure, with all their sea-going trade. An alternative proposal by the Czar for the establishment of an international Board of Control on the African coast with an international fleet under its direction was no less decisively rejected. In 1822 a second Conference was held for the same purpose at Verona. Castlereagh had recently committed suicide; but the British case for Abolition was safe in Wellington's hands, and Wilberforce again appealed to Alexander's better self, both in a public and in a private letter. The latter, he confessed, "though civil in terms, was frank

in matter: and it plainly intimated that we should have no favourable opinion of his religious or moral character if he did not
honestly exert his powers on our behalf.". But neither Duke nor
Czar could dictate to Europe. Verona was as fruitless as Aix.

No less stubborn and more lasting was the opposition of the
United States. By 1841 all the other unpledged Powers—France,
Austria, Russia, Prussia and Denmark—had agreed to the reciprocal
right; but the American Government and Congress still resisted it,
mainly because the right of search was precisely the question on
which American opinion was most sensitive, especially where
Britain was concerned. Again and again, therefore, the advances of
British diplomatists were courteously, but very firmly, repelled.
And the case became still more intractable when it was entangled
in the domestic American controversy over slavery itself. The
Governor of Liberia reported in 1839 that "the chief obstacle to the
success of the very active measures pursued by the British Govern-
ment for the suppression of the Slave Trade on the coast is the
American flag." There were Abolitionists, of course, in the United
States, no less ardent and sincere than those in England. Protests
were constantly made. Leading American statesmen demanded
action. But the law remained unenforced, and when in 1842 the
Treaty of Washington provided for joint operations by British and
American cruisers off the African coast, the American side of the
bargain was never effectively nor consistently executed. So, by the
middle of the nineteenth century, the great bulk of the Slave Trade,
now grown to proportions far greater than when Wilberforce first
took up the cause of Abolition, was still safeguarded from suppression by the simple device of hoisting the Stars and Stripes. Not till
the quarrel over Slavery had come to an issue, not till Lincoln was
in power and the Civil War had actually broken out, could the
scandal be swept away. In 1862 an Anglo-American Treaty was at
last concluded, conceding a mutual limited right of search and
establishing mixed courts on the African and American coasts.

Wilberforce, happily, could not see so far ahead. But already
between 1815 and 1823 the obstacles to making Abolition a reality
were distressingly plain. The lessons of Aix-la-Chapelle and Verona
sank into his mind. He could not explain away the failure by any
lack of sincerity or effort on the part of the British representatives.
It is true that he had concurred with the other Abolitionists in
sending Clarkson to Aix to watch their case. But, as he said at the

time, he had "no suspicion of Castlereagh"; and when the Foreign
Secretary returned from the Congress and in a long interview told
him "all that had passed between him and the other Powers," he
did not question that everything possible had been done. At the
Congress of Verona, similarly, he was more than satisfied with
the Duke of Wellington's "admirable zeal, perseverance, judgment
and temper." "*Dieu défend le droit*," he wrote to Macaulay; "I shall
love all generals the better for it as long as I live." No; Britain
was not to blame; and what hope was there of overcoming the
indifference and jealousy of foreign Powers? Could the Slave Trade,
Wilberforce began to ask himself, ever really be abolished as long
as slaves existed? Could that branch of evil ever be destroyed
unless the whole tree from which it sprang were dug up by the
roots ?

2

There was another train of events which was turning Wilberforce's thoughts in the same direction and with greater force. One
of his chief arguments against the Trade had been that the cessation
of the importation of fresh slaves into the islands would compel
the West Indian planters, in their own material interests, to treat
the slaves they already possessed with greater care for their health
and strength and to introduce any such improvements in their
social and moral conditions as would permit an increase in the
birth-rate. But, year after year, the Abolitionists waited in vain
for the realisation of these hopes. New slaves were still smuggled
in, contrary to the law, under foreign flags. There were just as
many charges of ill-treatment and moral degradation. And they
were just as difficult to bring home to the culprits. "I am quite,
quite sick of the West Indies as a field of labour in our cause,"
Stephen confessed to Wilberforce. "To load the shelves of a Minister
with laboured memorials, to haunt him with conferences for years,
and at last to be turned round by the whisper that a Governor
stands well with great men and must not have his toes trod upon,
is beyond all patience. . . . I really think we shall do nothing
effectual to check colonial crimes till we blazon them to the English
public and arm ourselves with popular indignation." Wilberforce's
patience, too, was strained; but he clung to the idea that the

planters would still accept reform if only smuggling could be stopped, and he believed it could be stopped by the passing of an Act of Parliament requiring all slaves in the British islands to be registered. He had begun to work for this measure (it will be remembered) before 1814 and had only dropped it in order to concentrate on his campaign for an international repudiation of the Trade. But early in 1815 he took it up again. "Meeting on West India conduct at the Duke of Gloucester's," records the diary for February 15: "long discussion—Lords Grenville and Lansdowne there, Babington, James Stephen, sen. and jun., and Harrison. Resolved on pushing Registry Bill immediately." "March 1st. An interview with Liverpool, Bathurst, and Vansittart, when they told us they could not support the Registry Bill for want of proof of actual smuggling of slaves." When Napoleon broke out of Elba, Wilberforce was inclined to postpone the Bill once more, but he was overruled at another Abolitionist meeting at the Duke of Gloucester's house, attended by Grenville, Lansdowne and Romilly amongst others. "I against bringing on the measure this year. But Grenville strongly for it, and all the rest gave way." Accordingly, five days before Waterloo was fought, Wilberforce introduced the Bill to the Commons in a speech of nearly two hours. "Got through pretty well," he notes. Romilly backed him, while Marryatt opposed for the planters. Barham, supported the Bill in principle but called for a preliminary inquiry into the condition of the slaves. Castlereagh admitted that the Government was bound by its pledges to favour any measure that would facilitate Abolition; but he asked Wilberforce not to press the Bill forward with undue haste, if only to give the colonies time to understand it. The best thing, he suggested, would be for the colonies to carry such a measure through their own legislatures. In his reply, Wilberforce acknowledged that the Bill could not be pressed to its conclusion in that session; and "leave to introduce" was granted without a division. The result of the first reading debate, three weeks later, was the same; but Wilberforce took the opportunity of nipping Castlereagh's suggestion in the bud. "I have heard enough of the West Indian legislatures," he said, "not to have any very sanguine expectations from that quarter. It is melancholy to reflect that, notwithstanding all the admonitions which they have received on the subject of mitigating the state of slavery, so little has been done by them." To compare them, he went on, with Parliament was ridiculous. "What

sort of British constitution is it when nine-tenths of the people are
not even virtually represented in the legislature?"

No more could be done that session; but the campaign had
been opened and the "West Indians" were hurriedly taking down
the weapons that had lain on the shelf since their great defeat in
1807. "I am assured," Wilberforce tells Macaulay, "that they are
mustering all their forces and all their natural allies against us.
. . . The British merchants are joining the general body of our
opponents." And of all the planters' weapons none was seized again
more heartily than the stabbing-knife that was stained with
Ramsay's blood. "If all that was published about me were true,"
said Wilberforce in 1816, in a debate on a petition from the Bristol
merchants against the Registry Bill, "nothing but a special Providence can have prevented my being hanged thirty years ago." A
few weeks later, the slaves themselves made a present to their
masters of a stick to beat their friends with. Like the troubles in
St. Domingue in 1791 and in Jamaica in 1795, so now the slave
revolt in Barbados was ascribed to the criminal folly of the Abolitionists. The slaves had broken out on the night of Easter Sunday,
and with drums beating and horns blowing had set to work to fire
their masters' sugar-canes and destroy the overseers' houses and
sugar-works. Some sixty estates were more or less damaged. No
European was killed. And the rebels, wandering about with a vague
purpose of destruction and no military organisation at all, were
easily suppressed by the troops. Several hundreds were shot in
action, and many of the prisoners were tried and executed. From
the uncouth banners they had carried—one of them representing
the King of England bestowing a crown upon a negro—and from
their own confessions, it was clear that they believed themselves
to have been freed from slavery by the British Parliament and only
retained in it by their masters. They seem, indeed, to have been
surprised at the intervention of British troops in a quarrel which
did not concern them. It was not such a very serious affair, then,
but enough for the planters, with a little exaggeration and a little
titillation of the baser race-instincts to fashion into a savage indictment of the Abolitionists. "If anything happens to our island,"
Lady Malmesbury had said in 1791, "I should certainly, if I was a
planter, insist on Mr. Wilberforce being punished capitally." And
if English gentlewomen were not quite so savage now, the rancour
of the planters was fiercer than it had ever been. Wilberforce met

their charges as he had met them before. In the debate of June 19 he reminded the House that from the very outset of the movement the West Indian party had accused the Abolitionists of aiming at wholesale and immediate emancipation. "Nor have they confined their assertions to this House or to this country. They have actually printed and published in the West Indies that the design of the friends of Abolition was to make all slaves instantly free. . . . Though unable to read, the domestic slaves could obtain and promulgate the notion that their friends in Great Britain were labouring to give them liberty while their masters were the only persons that opposed it. I beg leave, therefore, to say distinctly that I and my friends are clear of the blood so unhappily shed." And he went on to review some of the other "grand arguments" used against him in the course of his long campaign for the betterment of the negroes' lives. "They charge me with fanaticism. If to be feelingly alive to the sufferings of my fellow-creatures is to be a fanatic, I am one of the most incurable fanatics ever permitted to be at large." All these weapons had been used before, he said, and he had beaten them and would beat them again. And why was he so confident? "Because the people of England are religious and moral, loving justice and hating iniquity. . . . I rely upon the religion of the people of this country."

A trust so complacent, so unctuous, and, as they knew in their hearts, so well-grounded could only intensify the planters' anger. They felt, as the frontier-farmers in South Africa felt, that this insufferably pious busybody was making infinitely more difficult the difficult task of keeping a black race in due subordination to the white. They felt, too—and the future was to prove them right— that the freer the negroes became, the less work their masters would get out of them. So they redoubled their efforts; they even laid a voluntary tax on the export of their sugar to finance their propaganda; and their invective became more virulent than ever. "A more scandalous attack I have seldom seen," wrote Wilberforce to Stephen of an article in a West Indian newspaper, "but I am rather animated than discouraged by it. . . . I get more and more to disrelish these brawlings and to be less and less touchy as to my character." This unconcern for slander has come, he thinks, from advancing years and "the decay of natural spirits" and "some little, I hope, from a growing indifference to human estimation." But not all his collaborators were so hard-skinned; and there was one who was almost as sensitive as the unhappy Ramsay. "He is in so nervous a state," Wilberforce tells his wife, "that there is great cause for serious alarm about him. It is anxiety and, even still more, vexation at himself for being anxious that so harasses him. A cheerful temper is a great blessing."

Certainly the cheerful Wilberforce was not to be hindered by calumny from pressing on the Registration Bill, nor yet by the caution or apathy of Ministers. If the Government were against the Bill, he told Liverpool in 1816, he would fight it, painful as it might be: and he would win, because, in the long run, "the religious and moral part of the community will never sit quiet and leave six or seven hundred thousand human beings in a state of studiously preserved darkness and degradation." What did, however, give him pause was the increasing gravity of the situation in England. All through 1816 the clouds of popular discontent were banking up; and Wilberforce began to wonder whether it was wise to urge the grievances of the West Indian negroes in competition, so to speak, with the grievances of the English poor. At the end of that dark year he entered the following quaintly characteristic note in a manuscript-book devoted to West Indian materials: "Against precipitancy—Moses 80, Aaron 83 years old, when God sent them to lead out the Israelites from Egypt. Abraham 100 years old when Isaac born." A little later his mind is made up for delay. "I have for some time," he tells Macaulay in January, 1817, "been unwillingly yielding to a secret suggestion that it would be better perhaps to lie upon our oars in the Registry Bill and West Indian cause. When Parliament meets, the whole nation, depend upon it, will be looking up for relief from its own burthens; and it would betray an ignorance of all tact to talk to them in such circumstances of the sufferings of the slaves in the West Indies. We should specially guard against appearing to have a world of our own and to have little sympathy with the sufferings of our countrymen." This letter would have been grist for Cobbett's mill. For, when Parliament met, it was not so much the sufferings of the poor as their supposed sedition that it fastened on. Before the end of a month Wilberforce was engulfed in the Select Committee. And from that moment, for five years to come, all legislative proposals on the slaves' behalf were shelved as the Revolution and the War had shelved them from 1793 to 1804.

It did not mean, of course, that the cause had lost its sovereign place in Wilberforce's mind. He had decided not to press it on a distracted Parliament and public; but he would not let it be forgotten. Just as in that earlier interlude of waiting he had moved his annual resolutions for Abolition, so now from time to time he moved, with full-length speeches, Addresses to the Regent deploring the continuance of the Trade under foreign flags and reiterating the obligation laid specially on Britain by her previous share in it to leave nothing undone to protect and enlighten the injured Africans. But there was now this difference. The resolutions had been lost. The addresses were carried *nem. con.* And during these years, again as in that previous interlude, the cause of the slaves was being steadily strengthened by the accumulation of evidence as to their condition and by its regular submission to Parliament. Thus, on April 22, 1818, two motions were made for papers respecting the treatment of slaves in the West Indies—one by Wilberforce, the other by Romilly; and the latter's speech was devoted to an *exposé* of things, which, by official admission, had happened in Dominica and St. Nevis. One planter, for instance, had assaulted one of his female slaves, bound her neck and limbs in an iron chain, and fractured her arm. He had been duly charged for these offences by the Attorney-General; but the local grand jury had thrown out the bill and had thought fit to remark on the dangerous consequences of this and similar indictments. Another planter had ordered two slave boys, accused of receiving a stolen pair of stockings, a hundred lashes apiece, and a sister of one of them thirty lashes for shedding tears when she saw them beaten. Again the Attorney-General had been satisfied that the evidence justified a prosecution and again the grand jury had rejected it. Moving on another occasion for papers on St. Christopher, Romilly described the case of the Rev. Mr. Rawlins, manager of an estate in that island. A runaway slave had been caught and brought back to the plantation in an exhausted state. Next day he was severely flogged, and, the day after, was set to work chained to another slave. He complained of pain and hunger and tried to lie down, but was beaten to his feet, Mr. Rawlins being present. In the course of the day he died, still chained to his comrade. This time the law could not be wholly evaded. The coroner's jury did their best for Rawlins: their verdict was "Died by the visitation of God." But at the trial Rawlins was found guilty of manslaughter and sent to prison for three months with a fine of £200. By colonial standards, as Marryatt

indeed admitted to the House, this punishment was regarded as
very severe, but not by British standards. The Colonial Secretary,
Lord Bathurst, frankly told the Governor that "Mr. Rawlins could
not have been guilty of manslaughter: it must have been murder
or an acquittal."

These were not isolated cases. It was clear, in fact, that while
Governors and Law Officers, vigorously supported no doubt by
the Colonial Office, might try to enforce the laws against the mal-
treatment of slaves, they could do little or nothing without the
co-operation of the planters. And the planters as a body, it was
increasingly evident, had stopped their ears to all humanitarian
appeals from England. It is not to be supposed that as a body they
were cruel to their slaves; but interference had hardened their
hearts and closed their ranks. They would tolerate cruelty rather
than allow the conviction of any member of their little community
to be hailed as a triumph by those sanctimonious busybodies in
London. They would do their best to evade and nullify such laws
and regulations as were thrust upon them from outside. And, if a
sop must be thrown to the "Saints," they would themselves pass
laws and regulations—and leave them unobserved. "As to those
laws," said Romilly in the House, "which look so well on paper,
which appear so well calculated to benefit the slave population, they
not only are not executed, but were never intended to be executed."
And he quoted the following passage from a dispatch from Governor
Prevost: "The Act for encouraging the better government of slaves
lately passed in Dominica appears to have been considered, from the
day it was passed till this hour, as a political measure—to prevent
the interference of the mother-country in the management of the
slaves."

In eliciting and publishing such facts as these Wilberforce and
his allies were really doing more for the slaves than in pressing any
legislative measures. They were convincing themselves—and taking
the first steps to convince Parliament—that the slaves could not be
protected from cruelty and degradation by a Registration Bill or
any other measure which depended for its ultimate effects on a
"change of heart" among the planters. In 1822, the year which
marked the liberal renascence in the internal politics of Britain, a
liberal movement began which was to determine the destiny of
hundreds of thousands of human beings living on British soil
oversea. By 1822 the Abolitionists had decided to undertake a second

and a greater crusade. And this time they leagued themselves not merely against this or that monstrous product of the slave-system. They were going out to transform the very basis of the relations between Englishman and African in the tropics. They were going out to abolish Slavery itself throughout the British Colonies.

3

The anti-Slavery crusaders were accused, not always without justice, of painting the results of emancipation in too gorgeous colours. But Wilberforce's idealism was not altogether untempered by common sense. He certainly believed that the freed slaves would become an industrious, prosperous, and relatively civilised peasantry. Doubtless he underestimated the time this transition would take. But the present backward condition of the British West Indies is no proof of negro incapacity: it is due to far wider economic factors and the failure (till the last few years) of the British Government to grapple with them. British Tropical Africa, moreover, has furnished striking evidence of the ability of negroes, unstunted by slavery and protected from European adventurers, to cultivate with energy and profit the produce of their own lands. But what of other human faculties? To what point could their civilisation rise? How far, how deep could their education go? Could they develop the business-like qualities on which the white race prides itself— orderliness, efficiency, organisation? Had they any capacity for politics? . . . The world still awaits a final answer to these questions. In the annals of mankind, so long and yet so short, the day when Africa emerged from the unknown and joined the common stream of human life is still as yesterday. In Wilberforce's time it was almost literally yesterday. Yet to all those questions he was already inclined to give an optimistic answer. It was mainly his religion, of course, that made him sanguine, his faith in the providential progress of the human family; but there was one practical experience, one curious yet very characteristic episode in his life, that served to confirm his trust. This episode was his "mentorship" of the King of Hayti.

Christophe was a negro, born in slavery at St. Kitts. His capacity and honesty had already raised him above the dead level of manual labour when he became involved in the revolution in

Hayti (or St. Domingue). It gave his natural gifts a chance to be proved; he became one of Toussaint's chief lieutenants and under his rule he gained a rough-and-ready knowledge of administration. He took a leading part in the successful rising against Toussaint's sanguinary successor, Dessalines, in 1806; and thereupon he assumed the government of the north part of the island, the south part falling to his fellow officer, Pétion, a mulatto. In 1807 he promulgated a Napoleonic constitution under which, as President and Commander-in-Chief for life, he virtually perpetuated his own military autocracy. A few years later he converted the Presidency into an hereditary Kingship. The coronation was held on the Champ de Mars at Cape François, in great state, with the whole army in attendance; and, still true to the Napoleonic model, King Henry the First of Hayti himself assumed the crown before he was crowned again by his archbishop. But it was not to Napoleon that his political sympathies turned. The French were his natural enemies. He and his people lived in constant fear of French attempts to reconquer the old French colony and to force the free citizens of the new kingdom back to their old slavery. Such a reconquest had indeed been attempted by Napoleon in 1802-3 and contemplated by the restored Royalists in 1814; and to avert this danger it was to England that Christophe looked. On the night of his coronation, at an official banquet to which the resident British and American merchants were invited, the King himself gave the toast—"My dear brother, George! May his life be preserved by the Great Ruler of the Universe, and may he oppose an invincible obstacle to the unbridled ambition of Napoleon and remain always the constant friend of Hayti!" Christophe was far too shrewd, indeed, not to realise that in British support lay his best chance of maintaining an independent negro state. He had a remarkably well-disciplined army and a little fleet of one 44-gun frigate, nine sloops, eleven brigs, and sundry small craft; but what was that against the power of France? This, however, was not the only motive that led Christophe to invoke the sympathy and help of Wilberforce and his group. Security had to come first; but when he had done all he could, by instituting a system of conscription, by enforcing laborious military training, and by building forts, to make himself secure, he turned with no less zeal to improve the civil condition of his people. The royal treasury was full; and he determined to spend lavishly on education. Schools and colleges were to be established and staffed, so far as might be, by qualified Englishmen. For the spirit and method of the system were to be English. His people must learn to speak good English instead of bad French; and they must be changed, if possible, from Roman Catholics into Protestants. "They wish to annihilate every trace of a Frenchman," a visitor reported.

In 1817, accordingly, Wilberforce received a personal appeal from King Henry. It interested and attracted him enormously; and after satisfying himself in an interview with Liverpool that the Government had no objection to his corresponding with a foreign potentate, he warmly responded. A voluminous and protracted correspondence ensued. "He has requested me," wrote Wilberforce to Stephen, "to get for him seven schoolmasters, a tutor for his son, and seven different professors for a Royal College he desires to found. Amongst these are a classical professor, a medical, a surgical, a mathematical, and a pharmaceutical chemist." He was given wide powers. Not only the choice of individuals, but the amount of their salaries, within limits, was left to his discretion; and over £6000 was transmitted to him for making advances to the men he might appoint. It was no light charge. It meant yet more fatiguing letters. It meant a great many interviews with candidates and the most careful consideration of each case. "Much harassed," the diary confesses, "by applications for recommendations to Hayti by people of whom I know nothing." And, of course, as soon as the rumour of this benevolent and wealthy monarch of the Caribbean got abroad, it was not only men of missionary spirit or an enthusiasm for educational experiment that pricked up their ears. "Rely on it," wrote Stephen, who had lived there himself, "that in general there are only two motives strong enough to keep any man or woman, without necessity, six months in the West Indies— religious zeal and *auri sacra fames.*" It was certainly a harassing task and it put a heavy strain on Wilberforce's none too abundant strength. "Never have I worked harder," he tells Babington, "than at my Haytian letters, and yet at last the ship went away without much that she was to have carried. But we shall have another opportunity, D.V., in about a fortnight." At one time he invites two rival candidates to his house "that they might stay with me a few days and enable me the better to take their dimensions"—an austere ordeal for them. "I have succeeded in finding a physician," he writes to Hey, "but I still want a surgeon, and much more a

W.

2 B

divine. Oh, what would I give for a clergyman who should be just such as I could approve!" And his friends and allies shared his enthusiasm. "Were I five and twenty," wrote Joseph Banks, "as I was when I embarked with Captain Cook, I am very sure I should not lose a day in embarking for Hayti. To see a set of human beings emerging from slavery and making most rapid strides towards the perfection of civilisation, must I think be the most delightful of all food for contemplation." Wilberforce felt just the same. "How I wish I was not too old, and you not too busy, to go!" he exclaims in a letter to Macaulay.

Yet all this enthusiasm and all this hard work could not achieve the impossible. At first there were encouraging reports. One of the schoolmasters Wilberforce appointed wrote that "the youths applied to their work with almost unexampled zeal and that their progress was really greater than he had ever witnessed in the same time." But not all the Englishmen sent out to Hayti were so keen or so successful. It was not that the salaries offered were insufficient to tempt good men. Christophe engaged a Court Painter from England at 5000 dollars a year; and he declared his intention of sending home two of his best schoolmasters, when their time came to retire, possessed of independent means. Nor was Wilberforce's judgment quite unpractical. Writing to a friend to ask his assistance in finding a good tutor for the King's son, "I should prefer," he says, "a man of sound sense and of some knowledge of the world, provided he was really a practical Christian . . . to any man of great religious zeal who might be likely to push matters further than the state of the King's mind or the circumstances and disposition of the population in general would probably bear"—sound enough missionary doctrine from Vanderkemp's admirer. The difficulty was to find sufficient good men to face so great an adventure, a climate to which the lives of so many British soldiers had notoriously been sacrificed in the war, and conditions so uncertain, so seemingly contingent on Christophe's single personality, that their new careers might well be brought to an end before they had well begun. So the men found were not all good men; and the strain of tropical life is quick to expose the weak streaks in any white man's character. Some of the professors quarrelled with each other or took to drink and vice; and even the best of them, the men who could bear the strain, began presently to write desponding letters home. No wonder Wilberforce was anxious. No wonder he had misgivings, for example, about some simple ploughmen whom the unflinching Christophe requisitioned, ploughs and all, to teach his people English methods of agriculture. "My heart quite fails me," he told Macaulay, "at the idea of sending those four raw creatures into so distant and to them so strange a clime, without preparing them more for what they have to expect." And, in truth, one wonders what became of them!

But if the results of the experiment were disappointing, it was not Christophe's fault—unless it was a fault to try at all to civilise his people. He was held up to ridicule or detestation by his enemies in Europe—and he had plenty of them in France and in West Indian circles in England—as a grotesque black military despot and a monster of depravity and cruelty. "You know, I doubt not, enough of the case," wrote Wilberforce to Archdeacon Wrangham, "to prevent your being misled by the scandalous falsehoods which are so shamefully propagated against King Henry's character." And there is at least one piece of substantial evidence to show that Wilberforce was right in the main. In 1814 a British naval officer of repute was sent to Hayti by his admiral to examine the conditions of trade. He reported that the principal resident European merchants, some of whom had been there ever since Christophe's accession, were unanimous on the most vital point. "We conceive our persons and property under the protection of the King," they told him, "to be as safe as in Kingston unless the French land an expedition." "Nor could I hear," adds the officer, "of one act of injustice that could fairly be attributed to the King. He is sharp in his dealings and in making them fulfil their contracts. But it is almost needless to mention how far a merchant adventurer will go for gain and how necessary it is to watch them." In 1818 the same officer paid a second visit to the island and wrote a long account of it which carries on its face the stamp of impartiality. The following are extracts:

> The King is in his person what in England you would call a fine portly looking man. . . . He is now growing stout; and on horseback, where he certainly looks his best, has much the appearance of old George. . . . He is quite black, with a manner and countenance, when in good humour (and I have never seen him in any other) very intelligent, pleasant, and expressive. . . . I am told by those who have seen him in one of his gusts

of passion that it can only be compared to a hurricane for its
fury; but fortunately the fit now comes very seldom and does
not last long. . . . None but the Queen dare go near him in
these paroxysms. . . .

His avowed intention is a religious, moral and political
change. How far he is sincere and how far he possesses talents
capable of bringing about so great a change, time will best
show. . . . It is *his* mind and his alone that governs all; he
has the ablest men of his kingdom employed about his person,
but they are mere executors of his will. One proof of his being
neither a very changeable nor cruel man is that almost all the
great officers of the palace, who were there four years ago, are
there now; and they bear, generally speaking, the characters of
good and just men.

The rest of the account is mainly concerned with the details
of Christophe's educational schemes, especially the "four schools
under Englishmen on the Lancasterian system." Two of the young
Englishmen in charge—one had been a monitor in a London school
in the City Road, the other was "a young Aberdeen collegian"—
had already made good. But the two others had already failed.
One was dead "and an excellent riddance"; the other had been
found by the King "drunk at 12 o'clock in the day amongst his
scholars" and was "certain of dying this season by all accounts."
There is a special tribute, further, to the hospitals. "Dr. Stuart,[1]
the Professor of Anatomy, is come out with Mrs. Stuart—he appears
a man of about twenty-eight and very clever—he has taken charge
of the hospitals, and no one, not even the Governor, dare ask him
a question—he orders what he likes and it is immediately given
him—in short, he says that there is nowhere in Europe a more
liberally endowed hospital." Finally, before he left, our witness
had an audience of the King.

He was in high good humour and received me as an old
friend. . . . We conversed a great deal upon the changes that
had taken place since my last visit. In answer to something
complimentary which I had said of his schools, he said, "My
wish is that my fellow-citizens may be made capable by education of enjoying the constitution I intend for them; and if I

[1] The right spelling seems to be "Stewart".

live long enough, the world will see that this has always been nearest my heart and occupied all my thoughts. But I must have time." . . . He has offered, through England, twenty millions of dollars to France to make an independent peace guaranteed by England, but without the guarantee he would not give 20 dollars. . . . He certainly is bringing that great question to a fair trial—whether the negroes possess sufficient reasoning powers to govern themselves or, in short, whether they have the same capacities as white men. And he is the only man, I think, in the world who could have given it so bold a trial.

That question needed a longer trial than Christophe or any other man could give it in the normal span of life. And Christophe was denied even that. In 1820, only two years after the above account was written, a group of officers, resenting the continued maintenance of Christophe's rigid discipline, mutinied; they were backed, it seemed, by most of the army; and Christophe, deserted and desperate, committed suicide. The news was a shock, but not altogether a surprise, to Wilberforce. He had heard of Christophe's stern military system and he had been uneasy. "I know not that a day has passed," he said, "that I have not prayed for him." But he recognised that this militarism was enforced on Christophe by the insecurity of the international status of his kingdom and particularly by the danger of attack from France. Wilberforce, indeed, had hoped against hope to secure an acknowledgment of Haytian independence from the Congress of Aix-la-Chapelle, though he knew that Castlereagh, however firm on Abolition, was scarcely likely—being, as he remarked, "a fish of the cold-blooded kind"— to venture on this thorny side-issue. Nor, even if Castlereagh had been willing to press the claims of Christophe, would the Continental Powers have conceded them in the face of an indignant France. So Wilberforce was not far beside the mark in thinking that the character of Europe was at least as much to blame as the character of Christophe for the tragedy that destroyed him and his dreams.

For his dreams died with him. The educational system quickly collapsed. "Every day something transpires," wrote Dr. Stewart from Hayti six months later, "to show the importance of King Henry to the Haytians. His greatest enemies now acknowledge that they never had a chief whose powers of mind and body were so fitted for command." And perhaps the mere demonstration of his capacity, pointing a moral which Wilberforce and other philanthropists in Europe could not miss, had been Christophe's greatest service to his race. For fourteen years he had kept in discipline and order an uncivilised people, degraded by slavery and barbarised by the horrors of a servile war. He had recognised their moral and mental backwardness, and had devised and begun to construct the machinery for their enlightenment. He had corresponded closely and lengthily with one of the most famous men in Europe. And he had been born a slave.

4

And so, one motive interlacing with another, the abolition of British Slavery was determined on by the men who had abolished the British Slave Trade. But, as the years passed in which they stiffened to their purpose, it became increasingly apparent that the leader of the first crusade would be unable to lead the second. In 1821 Wilberforce was only sixty-two, and many statesmen over sixty have fought and won great battles; but the infirmity which had dogged him all his days was now beginning to get the upper hand. It was not only the increasing failure of his eyesight—and there were times when he could not read or write at all—nor only his permanent gastric weakness. He had also developed a tendency to lung trouble which made the close atmosphere of the House of Commons on a damp or chilly night peculiarly dangerous. In more than one winter he was kept away from the House by repeated illnesses. "I fear that I shall do little more good," he confesses in the diary, when the complaint first takes hold of him. "Alas that I have not laboured more to make the best use of my faculties! . . . It is a stroke which I own I feel." But he faced the inevitable with his usual temper. "It is suitable," he said, "for an aged Christian to show himself willing to retire and let others take the more leading stations." Moses, he had told himself, was an old man when he started on the march from Egypt; but he had not led his people into Canaan. "And the Lord said unto Moses, Behold, thy days approach that thou must die: call Joshua."

After consultation with Stephen and other intimates, his choice of a successor fell on Thomas Fowell Buxton, whose acquaintance

he had made through his friendship with the Norfolk community
of Quakers. Buxton was born in 1786 and as a young man he had
become keenly interested in the question of the criminal law and
the management of prisons. In 1817 he had published a pamphlet on
prison discipline which was warmly praised by Wilberforce and
Mackintosh, and in 1818 he had entered Parliament as member for
Weymouth. Wilberforce had taken to him from the first. He was
a serious man. "He never was a child," said a friend: "he was a
man when in petticoats." And he was profoundly religious. Wilberforce was impressed, too, by the solid capacity he showed in the
House—the capacity of one "who could hew a statue out of a rock,"
he once remarked, "but not cut out faces upon cherry stones."
Moreover, he was, like himself, an "independent" in politics; and
it was, in Wilberforce's eyes, the "old honourable distinction" of
the cause in which Pitt and Fox, Grenville and Grey, had worked
together that it transcended parties. So, on May 24, 1821, having
been particularly impressed with a speech of Buxton's on the
Criminal Laws on the previous night, he made him a definite
proposal.

He reminded him that, thirty-three years ago, when about to
begin his campaign against the Slave Trade, he had been smitten
by an almost desperate illness and had begged Mr. Pitt to promise to undertake it in his place. "I thank God, I am now free
from any indisposition; but from my time of life and much
more from the state of my constitution . . . I ought not to
look confidently to my being able to carry through any business
of importance in the House of Commons. Now for many, many
years I have been longing to bring forward that great subject,
the condition of the negro slaves in our Trans-Atlantic colonies
and the best means of providing for their moral and social
improvement and ultimately for their advancement to the rank
of a free peasantry. . . . I have for some time been viewing you
in this connection; and after what passed last night, I can no
longer forbear resorting to you, as I formerly did to Pitt, and
earnestly conjuring you to take most seriously into consideration the expedience of devoting yourself to this blessed service.
. . . Your assurance to this effect would give me the greatest
pleasure—pleasure is a bad term—let me rather say peace and
consolation."

This appeal from scarred and laurelled 62 to unblooded 35, from one, too, who was regarded by all Buxton's circle as the best, if not the greatest, man in public life, was not to be resisted. Buxton had not hitherto paid close attention to the details of the Negro Question; but he had joined the African Institution, his heart and his vote had been always with Wilberforce, and he recalled how his Quaker mother had impressed the iniquity of slavery on his child's mind, how his sister's refusal to eat slave-grown sugar had made him think while he laughed at her, and how his first speech at Trinity College, Dublin, and his first public pronouncement at a meeting at Tower Hamlets had each been concerned with the Slave Trade. To devote himself henceforth to the overthrow of Slavery was no break with his past. Nothing indeed could better accord with the traditions of his social *milieu* and the promptings of his own serious ambition. He accepted the proposal. An alliance, which as Wilberforce put it, "may truly be termed holy," was struck up.

For a year or two it could still be an alliance. Wilberforce could not banish altogether the odious thought of retirement, but now that he had secured the succession, he was determined to hold it at bay as long as he could; and, provided he could keep his health, his parliamentary powers were not yet by any means exhausted. It was the veteran, therefore, who opened the campaign against Slavery by attacking it in one particular field. Slavery had been customary among Europeans in South Africa since the old days of the Dutch occupation of the Cape; but a new situation had been created in 1820-1 by the introduction into the eastern part of Cape Colony of some five thousand British settlers. This "Albany Settlement" had been organised and executed by the Government as a minor palliative for unemployment in Britain; and it had been made a condition of the grant of lands that predial or farm slavery should not be practised. But to Wilberforce slavery in the house was as bad as, in some respects it was worse than, slavery in the field; and on July 25, 1822, he moved an Address, urging that all slavery, domestic as well as predial, should be prohibited in the new settlement by a "fundamental law," as it had been from the first in the colony of Sierra Leone. Perhaps the most interesting passage in his speech was one in which he showed that he had grasped what statesmen have often failed to grasp—the essential singleness of Africa. "Let me earnestly conjure the House," he said, "to estimate this motion at its just importance. The countries which we are now beginning to settle are of very vast extent; but, still more, by imperceptible boundaries they communicate with the almost interminable regions of the African continent. And my object is to secure, throughout that vast extent, the prevalence of true British liberty instead of that deadly and destructive evil which would poison the whole body of the soil and render that prodigious area one wide scene of injustice, cruelty and misery." But still more important for the future was the affirmation—or the pointed reaffirmation—of his general purpose. "Not I only," he said, "but all the chief advocates of the Abolition of the Slave Trade—Mr. Pitt, Mr. Fox, Lord Grenville, Lord Grey and every other—scrupled not to declare from the very first that their object was, by ameliorating regulations and more especially by stopping that influx of uninstructed savages . . . to be surely though slowly advancing towards the period when these unhappy beings might exchange their degraded state of slavery for that of a free and industrious peasantry." There was a miserably thin House to listen to this declaration, but among the few members present, of course, was the new "ally" and he was well rewarded. "This was the best speech," said Buxton in after years, "that I ever heard him make."

But this Address was only a "local operation." Something more was needed to launch a general attack all along the line. That winter the Abolitionists met in what Wilberforce called "a secret Cabinet Council," and it was decided that a definite call to the new crusade should be issued to the country. And the voice, it was agreed, must still be Wilberforce's. So, early in the year, he shut himself up in his new country house at Marden Park and worked away at a public statement. Stephen had thought of helping him as Babington had helped him in preparing the case against the Slave Trade in earlier days. But on the whole, he writes, "you would do better without me." "My province would be that of the driver only . . . and then Mrs. Wilberforce will flog the driver every day if she thinks we do too much (she gave me fair warning of it on Sunday), and I shall flog myself if we do too little." So Wilberforce toiled on alone, and he found the strain far heavier than he had in 1790. "At work on my Manifesto," says the diary for January 26, 1823, "but I cannot please myself." "I am become heavy and lumbering," he confesses to his old collaborator, Babington, "and not able at once to start into a canter, as I could twenty years

ago. Happily it is a good road and in the right direction." "I get
on slowly," he complains a few days later. "Music in the evening.
To have friends in the house sadly consumes time, though no one
loves music better than I do; yet the time is short with me and I
must husband it." Meanwhile he was encouraged by news from
Macaulay of the activities of the "conspirators" in London. "I have
had two long talks with Brougham," he wrote, "and have gradually
opened to him our feelings and views. I cannot help hoping that
we have gained him." In the middle of February Wilberforce
returned to town with "a good deal of my piece" ready for press,
but "sadly out of heart about it." Early in March it was published.
It is a pamphlet of fifty-odd pages, entitled *An Appeal to the Religion,
Justice, and Humanity of the Inhabitants of the British Empire in
behalf of the Negro Slaves in the West Indies.* It gains by its relative
brevity. It is well packed with facts and well argued. The tone is
not in the least fanatical. Indeed Wilberforce is careful, more than
once, to insist that his charges must not be construed too sweepingly,
that not all slave-owners regard or treat their slaves in the same
way. And the presentation is simple and effective—first, an analysis
of the conditions of slavery; secondly, a rebuttal of the old argument that the colonial legislatures should be left to improve those
conditions and prepare the way for emancipation by themselves;
lastly—and here, perhaps, confidence has to take the place of proof—
an assurance that the negroes will not only be more moral and
more Christian as freemen than as slaves but will also work harder.
On the whole, a very serviceable piece of work, and Wilberforce
need not have been so diffident about it; for it produced a quick
effect on public opinion—all the quicker because this second appeal
was not a novelty like the first. The campaign against the Slave
Trade had prepared the ground. It had revealed the horrors of
Slavery itself as an essential part of its case. It had galvanised the
public conscience and created a new and very sensitive humanitarian tradition. Opinion, therefore, responded at once. Again the
letters of congratulation and approval poured in from all quarters,
the most remarkable, perhaps, being one from a West Indian planter
who declared that he hoped the Appeal would achieve its purpose—
so moved was he by reading it—even at the cost of all his property.
And again the Quakers were to the fore. They drew up a petition
entreating Parliament to follow up the good work it had done, and
was still doing, for the destruction of the Slave Trade by taking

measures to redeem the hundreds of thousands of their fellow human beings now in bondage in the British colonies. And again the presentation of it in March, 1823, was entrusted to Wilberforce. He reminded the House that it was the Society of Friends who had first petitioned Parliament against the Slave Trade—quiet, retiring people, only obtruding themselves on the public at the imperative call of justice and humanity. "It certainly is an extraordinary anomaly," he went on, "that the freest nation that ever existed on the face of the earth . . . should be chargeable with the guilt and inconsistency of allowing slavery in any place under its control. . . . Never, perhaps, since the world began has there been such a strange instance of the sufferance of an evil in consequence of its being removed out of sight." He regretted now that he and his friends had not attacked Slavery itself from the first; but they had felt that to press for the greater object might weaken their chance of achieving the less. They had always looked forward, however, to emancipation as their ultimate goal. Even Mr. Dundas had proposed that Slavery and the Trade should end together. "I am fully aware," he concluded, "of the feelings entertained and the difficulties I had to encounter when I first brought the question of the African Slave Trade before Parliament between thirty and forty years ago. I well remember that those who were neutral as well as several who were friendly repeatedly told me that it was impossible I should ever succeed. I determined, however, to persevere; for I felt quite sure that, in England, such a cause must be finally successful. I say the same now." Directly Wilberforce had finished, Canning rose. "Is it my honourable friend's intention," he asked, "to found any motion on the petition?" "It is not," replied Wilberforce, but referred to "an honourable and esteemed friend of his"; whereupon Buxton gave notice of a motion, to be submitted a month hence, that the House should take into consideration the state of slavery in the British colonies.

Wilberforce had taken the lead for the last time, and he was thoroughly dissatisfied with his performance. "Fatigue rather stupefied me," he complains, "and I forgot the most important points. But Canning's generalship admirable." He had expected, it seems, a full debate; and Canning's precipitate question had taken him aback. He had been "thinking over the topics to be ready for reply," he says, "and was quite confounded. All of us *abattus*. Never almost in my life was I so vexed by a parliamentary pro-

ceeding. I felt as if God had forsaken me. . . . I could scarcely get
to sleep and was ashamed to see my friends, though they tell me
the effort was better than I had.conceived." So much distress at
so slight a set-back—he had suffered many far worse reverses in the
old days—suggests overstrain.

Wilberforce was more contented with the part he took in the
debate on Buxton's motion on May 15. Public opinion had had
time in the interval to make itself further heard. "The country
takes up our cause surprisingly," comments the diary: "the petitions, considering the little effort, very numerous." It was therefore
with a sense that the electorate was awake and watching and in
something like the exciting atmosphere of 1791-2 that the House
listened to Buxton's introductory speech. To Wilberforce it must
soon have seemed that he had chosen his successor well. It was an
admirable speech, full of substance, point and interest. And it was
a bold speech; for it did not evade, it quickly and frankly faced,
the oldest and, for timid minds, the most effective of all the Opposition's arguments. He admitted, at the outset, the danger of a negro
insurrection.

"Wherever there is oppression there is danger. . . . The
question is how that danger can be avoided. I assume that it is
to be avoided by giving liberty for slavery, happiness for misery."
And he effectively quoted Pitt's assertion that "it was impossible
to increase the happiness or enlarge the freedom of the negro
without adding in an equal degree to the security of the colonies."
"But even supposing the danger of giving to be as great as the
danger of withholding—there may be danger in moving and
danger in standing still, danger in proceeding and danger in
doing nothing—then I ask the House whether it be not better
for us to incur peril for justice and humanity, for freedom and
for the sake of giving happiness to millions hitherto oppressed
than for slavery, cruelty, and injustice." So much for the appeal
to fear; next, the appeal to the sanctity of property. The Abolitionist proposal was to declare the freedom of all children born
of slaves after a certain day. This plan of progressive abolition
had already been applied successfully in the northern part of the
United States; and under its operation slavery was already
dying out quite peacefully in the British Empire itself. General
Brownrigg and Sir Alexander Johnston had introduced it in

Ceylon, Sir Stamford Raffles at Bencoolen, and Sir Hudson Lowe at St. Helena. But the public had not marked these things, even in St. Helena about which a veritable library of books had recently been written. "Generations yet unborn shall know that on such a day in July Sir Hudson Lowe pronounced that the weather was warm; and, that, on such a day in the following December, Bonaparte uttered a conjecture that it would rain in the course of the week. Nothing has escaped the researches of the historian—nothing has been overlooked by the hungry curiosity of the public. Yes! one thing has been; that Sir Hudson Lowe gave the death-blow to slavery in St. Helena." The plan then had been tried; it was actually in operation on British soil; but none the less the West Indian planters would resist its application to themselves. "I know the answer that will be given. 'The father is mine; the mother is mine; and therefore the child is mine.' But is that justice? You have made it a crime to go to Africa and enslave a full-grown man there. How is it less a crime to make a new-born Creole a slave? . . . It is a crime to murder a man; is it no less a crime to murder a child? It is a crime to enslave a man, is it no crime to enslave a child?" The claim, moreover, to a right of property in the man-slave was not unimpeachable. The planter, say, had inherited him from his father who had bought him from a neighbour who had bought him at Kingston slave-market from a trader who had bought him from a man-merchant in Africa. "So far you are quite safe. But how did the man-merchant acquire him? He stole him: he kidnapped him. . . ." A daring attack this, on the citadel of property; and Buxton very wisely followed it up with a hint at compensation. "When I say that the planter has no claim against the slave, I do not say that he has no claim against the British nation. If slavery be an injustice, it is an injustice which has been licensed by British law." Finally he enumerated his definite proposals—the emancipation of all children born in slavery after a certain date and the amelioration of the lot of existing slaves by attaching them to the soil, by giving them a higher status than that of chattels in the eyes of the law, by removing all obstructions to manumission, by providing religious instruction, enforcing marriage and making Sunday a day of rest, and by restraining the master's authority to punish—and on this basis moved the general

motion, "That the state of Slavery is repugnant to the principles
of the British Constitution and of the Christian Religion; and
that it ought to be gradually abolished throughout the British
Colonies, with as much expedition as may be found consistent
with a due regard to the well-being of the parties concerned."

This time a full debate could not be avoided. But the Government was not yet prepared to go all the way with the Abolitionists;
and when Canning followed Buxton, his denunciation of the evils
of slavery was scarcely less vigorous, but he did not commit himself so definitely to its extinction. He moved a group of resolutions,
as amendments to Buxton's motion, emphasising first the need for
"effectual and decisive measures" for improving the conditions of
the existing slaves, and looking forward to ultimate emancipation
when, as the result of a "determined and persevering, but at the
same time judicious and temperate enforcement of such measures,"
the time should be ripe for it. It had been arranged that Wilberforce
should answer Canning; but again Canning's tactics had taken
him aback. He had watered Buxton's wine and yet not robbed it
altogether of its body. To make the right reply to this move, to
accept the offer as it stood or insist on more, to make the choice
on the instant—it was certainly, as the diary says, "an awkward
situation." "I could not learn what our friends thought and I never
got up so utterly unprepared, but D. G. I believe hit the point." He
began by reinforcing Buxton's case that Slavery was inconsistent
with British political and religious ideals. This was familiar
ground; and as he covered it with easy eloquence, he came to his
decision not to break with Canning. "I thanked God I judged
rightly," he afterwards wrote to one of his sons, "that it would
not be wise to press for more on that night." So he expressed agreement with Canning's desire that emancipation should come gradually with the growth of moral improvement in the slaves—and
had not Buxton himself admitted that they were not ready for it
yet?—rather than by the sudden stroke of Parliament. "But when
we consider," he said, "the claims of these unhappy people and the
time that has been already lost in accomplishing this great and
high duty, we ought not to prolong their slavery an hour more
than is absolutely necessary." And, in any case, the task of improvement must not be left to the colonial legislatures; it must be taken
in hand by Parliament itself. "After all that my right honourable

friend [Canning] has conceded," he concluded, "we stand in a new situation. . . . We have now an acknowledgment on the part of Government that the grievances of which we complain do exist. We have also the assurance that a remedy shall be applied. . . . I will no longer detain the House than by expressing my confidence that we shall this night lay the foundation of what will ultimately prove a great and glorious superstructure."

It was certainly no more than a foundation. Slavery was to be prolonged for a good many hours more—for over ten years. But it is easy to understand, and not so easy to condemn, Canning's desire to evade a rapid forcing of so big an issue. Wilberforce's speech, at any rate, secured it for him. It muzzled the "Saints," and the other side, the planters' representatives, could not venture to quarrel with any policy that postponed their doom. It will be remembered how scornfully they had met the first attack upon the Slave Trade—with what wholesale denials of its inhumanity and assertions of the falsehood of the Abolitionists' case, with what confident appeals to commercial and national interests as necessitating the indefinite continuance of the Trade. But now it was clearer than ever that the first crusade had achieved more than its own deliberately limited purpose. In eliciting the truth and educating the British people for the destruction of the Trade, it had cut away the supports of Slavery. So, when Charles Ellis rose to put the planters' case, he could not defend Slavery; he could only describe it as an unfortunate system in which the unhappy planters, through no fault of their own, had been involved. He could not plead for its continuance; he was bound to promise his support to Canning's resolutions. All he could do was to put his own interpretation on them, to suggest that their purpose could best be realised (in words that Abolitionists themselves, he pointed out, had once used) "by a benign, though insensible, revolution in opinions and manners, by the encouragement of particular manumissions and the progressive amelioration of the condition of the slaves, till it should slide insensibly into general freedom . . . in short, an emancipation of which not the slaves but the masters should be willing instruments or authors." There was no necessity for Canning to accept or to reject this interpretation of his policy; and the long debate ran smoothly on. Only Brougham, who came out definitely for Abolition with a full-dress speech, ventured to doubt the efficacy of the amending resolutions, though he did not question their sincerity. But at the very end the Abolitionists tried to pin Canning down. At the close of Buxton's reply, Canning declared, by way of making his position perfectly clear, that he did not accept the principle that the children of slaves must always be slaves. "Then one day," said Buxton promptly, "every child shall be free. When will that day come?" "I say," replied Canning, "I abjure the principle of perpetual slavery; but I am not prepared now to state in what way I would set about its abolition." With that Buxton had to profess himself content; and Canning's amendment was carried without opposition.

5

The cause was now formally launched, and the Abolition Cabinet held constant meetings, some of them in the early morning at Wilberforce's house, reminding him "of the old bustle of a Kensington Gore breakfast." But for the moment, having tied their hands by accepting Canning's pledges, they could do nothing but await their execution. And for Wilberforce at any rate it was anxious waiting. "I wish," he tells Macaulay, "I could be as easy about insurrections as you and Stephen." His fears were quickly justified. The Government's first step, while it went to prove its sincerity, revealed the practical difficulty of the policy of gradual amelioration leading up to freedom. Canning's resolutions were sent out to the Governors of the West Indian colonies together with a letter from Bathurst, the Colonial Secretary, urging, as an immediate measure in compliance with the wishes of Parliament, the abolition of the flogging of females and of the use of the whip in the field. The news of this positive interference instead of mere pious declarations from Westminster and Downing Street produced a storm of indignation among the planters. An Address was moved in the Jamaica Assembly for the removal of Bathurst from the Government. Other speakers declared that Jamaica should sever herself from the British Crown. And the Assembly unanimously carried a protest against a "decree," "whereby the inhabitants of this once valuable colony (hitherto esteemed the brightest jewel in the British Crown) are destined to be offered a propitiatory sacrifice at the altar of fanaticism." Worse was to happen in other colonies. The planters of Barbados, suspecting that one of the local missionaries had sent home bad reports on the condition of their slaves, destroyed his meeting-house, and drove him from the island. When the Governor offered £100 reward for the detection and conviction of the rioters, they issued a counter-proclamation that "the good people of Barbados would take care fitly to punish such person or persons as should make any discovery." There was a still graver outburst in Demerara. Governor Murray, alarmed at the "feverish anxiety" displayed by the planters when he communicated Bathurst's dispatch to them, decided to conceal its contents from the negroes. But the planters did not conceal their angry talk, and there were slaves who overheard it. From plantation to plantation ran the rumour that the King of England had set them free and that their masters had suppressed the edict. One night (August 18, 1823) some 13,000 of them rose, demanding immediate emancipation. They did not loot or burn, but they imprisoned the white men on their estates and ransacked their houses for arms. Two overseers, resisting them, were killed. The troops were called out and the "insurrection" was easily and quickly suppressed. Over a hundred slaves were killed. One soldier was wounded. On the whole the "insurgents" had shown great self-restraint, but their punishment was savage. Within the next three weeks fifty-seven were hanged. Martial law was kept in force for over five months. As late as January, 1824, three slaves received the ghastly penalty of 1000 lashes each. If they survived it, they were to be worked in chains, two of them for life, the third for seven years.

The news from Demerara reached London in an inevitably distorted form. The slaves had risen *en masse*, said rumour; and white men had been murdered. "What!" cried Wilberforce on hearing of it: " have they given such an order without preparation, and without explaining their purpose to the slaves—why, it is positive madness!" "The whip is the grand badge of slavery," he said again; "they should have begun with all those reforms which would have had a wonderful influence without seeming directly and suddenly to weaken the master's authority." But such reasonable protests were of little use. They could not save Wilberforce and his friends from the old recriminations. Government had blundered, and they were the obvious scapegoats. Even Canning's private secretary, the gossip ran, had declared that the insurrection "had been *instigated* by Wilberforce, Buxton and Co." Once more the hunt was up. The West Indians redoubled their abuse of the old arch-hypocrite who had dyed his hands with British blood; and British journalists, led by Theodore Hook, joined in the hue and cry. But Wilberforce was quite inured to calumny. "*John Bull*, for three or four weeks past," he writes, "has been abusing me grossly. . . . One of his paragraphs was sent me the other day, with only these three words, 'Thou vile hypocrite!' . . . My judgment is clearly that it will be best to let him go on; to give him rope, according to the common saying."

Far more important—the cause had received a set-back. Canning was not the man to drop the fiery business altogether because he had burned his fingers. But his performance in 1824 was not up to his promise in 1823. On March 16 he laid before Parliament a full statement of the Government's policy in the form of a draft Order-in-Council for ameliorating the condition of the slaves in Trinidad, accompanied by a draft Proclamation to be issued in all the West Indian colonies, referring to the erroneous belief that emancipation had been carried and to the acts of insubordination it had caused and declaring that the slaves "will be undeserving of our protection if they fail to render entire submission to the laws as well as dutiful obedience to their masters." The Order-in-Council was a lengthy document. It established a new Government official, the "Protector and Guardian of Slaves," charged, in the first instance, with the duty of acting on a slave's behalf in all major legal proceedings in which he might be involved. It prohibited the use of the whip or any other instrument for enforcing labour. It limited the number of lashes that could be inflicted for any offence on any one occasion and forbade any whipping at all if the effects of a previous punishment were still uncured. It abolished the whipping of female slaves entirely. It prescribed that a record book should be kept on every plantation in which exact particulars of every punishment, exceeding three stripes, must be recorded, together with the nature and place of the offence; and that a literal transcript of the entries in this book should be presented by the owner or manager of the plantation every quarter to the commandant of the district and an oath taken that the entries were complete and the transcript exact; and that all these returns should be forwarded by the commandant to the Protector and Guardian of Slaves. It made provision for the issue of licences authorising any clergyman or priest or public teacher of religion to solemnise the marriage of slaves; and it forbade the separation of husband from wife or parent from child by sale. It endowed slaves with the full right of acquiring, holding, and disposing of property. It established saving-banks for slaves. It forbade the levy of any tax on manumission beyond a registration fee of twenty shillings. It removed all obstacles to a slave's purchase of his freedom at a price to be fixed, if necessary, by a process of official arbitration. It prescribed that any slave should be admitted to give evidence on oath if he was certified as fit to do so by any religious minister or teacher. It required the submission of an annual report by the Protector and Guardian of Slaves to the Governor on the performance of his duties and the detailed operation of the various clauses of the Order, and the transmission of this report to the Secretary of State. Finally, it laid heavy penalties on infringements of the foregoing clauses and in particular provided that any owner, manager or overseer, twice convicted of cruel or unlawful punishment, should, in addition to the penalties, be disqualified from acting in such capacity in future, and that, in the case of an owner so convicted, his slaves should be confiscated to the Crown.

This thorough-going Order, Canning explained, was to be applied to Trinidad and also to St. Lucia and Demerara, which likewise possessed no legislatures of their own and in which, as he said, the power of the Crown was unshackled. He hoped the results of it would quickly lead to the enactment of similar legislation by the Assemblies in Jamaica and the rest of the West Indies. But, when he sat down, he can scarcely have believed that he had satisfied the Abolitionists. The Order-in-Council itself was patently sincere; and it was a far more detailed and drastic interference in the handling of the slave-question than any Government had yet attempted since the abolition of the Trade. But that was all that could be said of it: and Buxton was quick to point out how far it was from fulfilling the pledge contained in Canning's own resolutions of the previous year. He had promised amelioration for all the slaves in the West Indies. The Order only dealt with the 35,000 slaves in Trinidad and a few more in the other subject colonies, and left the welfare of the rest of the 700,000 slaves in the West Indies to the proved indifference of the island legislatures. He had promised, further, that this general amelioration should lead in the fulness of time to general liberation. The Order only dealt with individual manumission. It said not a word to suggest, that, even in Trinidad alone, slavery was not to last for ever. "Canning opened

in a very guarded speech," was Wilberforce's disappointed comment.
"Buxton strong, above concert pitch. I was better voiced and better
heard than usual." And certainly this speech—his last full-dress
speech on the theme he had made his own—can stand beside the
best of its predecessors. With his old clear insight he seized on the
cardinal point. "The House must not conceal from itself," he said,
"what the grand principle—the practical point at issue—really is.
It is simply this—whether the slave-system is to be put an end to
by the imperial legislature or by the colonial Assemblies." And as
long as Parliament left it to the planters, the slaves would despair
of any real relief and in their despair they might take their cause
into their own hands and endeavour to effect their own liberation.

It is my daily and nightly prayer—it is the hope and desire I
feel from the very bottom of my soul—that so dreadful an event
may not occur. But it is a consequence which I cannot but
apprehend, and, as an honest man, it is my duty to state that
apprehension. Only consider what a terrible thing it is for men
who have long lived in a state of darkness, just when the bright
beams of day have begun to break in upon their gloom, to have
the boon suddenly withdrawn and to be consigned afresh to
darkness, uncertainty, nay, to absolute despair! Whatever
Parliament may think fit to do, I implore it to do it quickly
and firmly. Do not proceed with hesitating steps. Do not
tamper with the feelings you have yourselves excited. For hope
deferred maketh the heart sick.

But Canning was not to be shaken from his course. He declared
in his reply that he stood between two extremes. One side wanted
him to promise that no more should ever be done than was now
proposed. The other side wanted him to say what more he would
do and when he would do it.

I will not consent to be fettered by any engagements. I will
not be led by either side or in either sense to declarations from
which it may be impossible to advance and dangerous to retreat.
. . . The question is not—it cannot be made—a question of
right, of humanity, of morality merely. It is a question which
contemplates a change, great and difficult beyond example, one
almost beyond the power of man to accomplish—a change in

the conditions and circumstances of an entire class of our fellow-creatures—the recasting, as it were, of a whole generation of mankind. If this be not a question requiring deliberation, cautious and fearful deliberation, I know not what can be so.

It was hard to resist the force of this reasoning. Even Wilberforce must have recognised that the abolition of Slavery, which, as Canning had pointed out, had only been commended to Parliament for the first time nine months ago, was a far graver matter than the abolition of the Slave Trade which had lain before Parliament for nearly twenty years. And there was another point of difference. The men who had obstructed and procrastinated in those earlier days and pleaded for "gradual" abolition, had, most of them, desired in their hearts to do nothing at all. But as Wilberforce knew, Canning was sincere. He saw that Slavery in the end must follow the Trade. But Pitt's heir had inherited some of Pitt's encumbrances. Eldon, for instance, was back on the woolsack, obstructing and procrastinating. And Canning, for his own part, possibly because he had friends, and one intimate friend, George Ellis, among the West Indians, had not yet despaired of persuading the planters—despite what had happened in Jamaica, in Barbados, in Demerara, everywhere—to do what must be done themselves. For the time he had his way. The House was with him. There was no division.

Wilberforce's effort that night had overtaxed his strength. He was able to attend the debate, a few days later, on "Lord John Russell's motion about the French evacuating Spain"—"Canning invincibly comic," he notes—but then he collapsed with a severe attack of pneumonia. He weathered it, but it was more than two months before he could leave his room. On June 1, however, he was again in his place in the House. It was rash, no doubt; but indignation forced him there. The last entry he had made in his diary before his illness had mastered him was this: "Poor Smith, the missionary, died in prison at Demerara! The day of reckoning will come"; and, as he lay in bed, he had brooded long over this extraordinary affair. John Smith was a nonconformist missionary who had lived on an estate in Demerara since 1816. The exposition of Christianity to a slave or subject people is, as contemporary events in South Africa were showing, a delicate matter. It calls for discretion on the missionary's part, and John Smith may not have been discreet. His converts among the slaves were many and devoted to him; he sympathised with their resentment at the suppression of the orders from England; and on the Sunday preceding the "insurrection" of 1823 he chose an unfortunate text for his sermon: "If thou hadst known, even thou, at least in this thy day, the things which belong unto thy peace! But now they are hid from thine eyes." On the same day he had talked with a slave named Quamina. On Monday, on that very estate, the strike began. On the two following days, while the strike was at its worst, Quamina again visited Smith and was taken to task by him for threatening to use force. It would be un-Christian, he said, and also quite futile. Finally Quamina and his followers were persuaded by Smith to promise that no blood should be shed. Meantime Smith warned the manager of an adjacent estate that the trouble might spread. Those are the bare facts. They were enough for the military authorities. Two days after the declaration of martial law, Smith was arrested and confined in the colonial jail. "The upper chamber of the building . . . was exposed to the scorching fury of a tropical sun. The lower chamber had a damp mud floor." For nearly two months Smith was confined there, his wife voluntarily sharing his imprisonment. He had been arrested on August 21: on October 13 he was tried by court-martial—for martial law was still in force, although the "insurrection" had been completely suppressed in two or three days. The Colonial Fiscal conducted the prosecution. Smith had to defend himself. Slave-evidence was then admissible in Demerara, unlike most West Indian colonies, in accordance with the old Dutch custom; and the main evidence against Smith was given by some slaves. The chief of these witnesses afterwards confessed that his evidence, at a planter's instigation, had been falsified. Leading questions, moreover, were put to these witnesses, and the prompted answer was usually given. And much of the most damaging evidence was not evidence of fact such as would be admitted in an orthodox British court. The witnesses were allowed to repeat conversations they had listened to—to say what they had heard somebody say to some one else about Quamina or the prisoner. The President of the Court Martial made no objection, nor did the President of the colonial Civil Court, who, having been hastily appointed a colonel of militia, was one of the judges and the only lawyer among them. Smith, in his ignorance, made no objection either. But as soon as he testified himself, in his defence, to things that he had heard, the Court decided that no more hearsay evidence could be accepted. Smith, moreover, was compelled to testify against himself. His private journal, in which he had opened his heart in passionate resentment against the treatment of the slaves, was produced as evidence against him. The result was certain. Smith was convicted of fomenting discontent among the slaves with intent to excite revolt and on other more detailed charges, such as neglecting to arrest Quamina. He was sentenced to death, with a recommendation to mercy, which was promptly granted by the Home Government. Some months afterwards Smith died in prison. But his enemies' hatred was unappeased. They forbade the widow to attend the funeral. They tore up the railings which two negro members of his congregation set round his grave.

Such was the business which summoned Wilberforce from his sick-room to the House of Commons. He could not, of course, make the effort of speaking himself, but he had the satisfaction of hearing Brougham and Mackintosh say everything that needed saying. The Government had already gone so far as to reverse the proceedings of the court: but that was not enough for those who were determined to vindicate Smith's innocence beyond all question; and Brougham proposed a motion denouncing the whole trial as "a violation of law and justice." The debate was almost a re-trial. Brougham himself minutely reviewed the constitution of the court, the character of the witnesses, and the methods employed in their examination, with copious quotation from the *verbatim* reports. Wilmot Horton did his best, with counter-quotations, to state the other side, but he could not go farther than to ask the House to suspend its judgment. He was answered by Mackintosh who easily demonstrated the *prima facie* incredibility of much of the evidence against Smith, denounced the production of the journal as "precisely the iniquity perpetrated by Jeffries in the case of Sidney," and showed from the very statements made in court that Smith had done all he could to persuade the slaves to be patient. "He appeals to their prudence: the soldiers, says he, will overcome your vain revolt. He appeals to their sense of religion: as Christians you ought not to use violence. What argument remained, if both these failed?" All these were lengthy speeches, but the House was too keenly interested to allow the debate to close that night. It was adjourned till June 11; and in the interval Wilberforce rapidly gained strength. "I very much wish," he told Stephen, "if my voice should be strong enough, to bear my testimony." When the day came, he felt able to make the effort. Before the debate opened, he went to Stephen's house "to be quiet for three or four hours, and was so, and read papers and thought." Nevertheless his speech was not on the level of Brougham's or Mackintosh's, nor indeed of many of his own. "I quite forgot my topics," confesses the diary, "and made sad work of it." But those facts in the case which stood unquestioned scarcely needed eloquence to make them tell; it had been clear from the first that the House as a whole had been greatly shocked by them; and Ministers had not ventured to propose a decisive counter-motion. They simply moved the previous question; and even on this they were in some danger of defeat. But Canning had not yet spoken; and any one who questions that Canning was a great parliamentarian should read his speech. Once more he refused to be forced into one of two extremes—to say either that the proceedings of the court were entirely correct or that Smith was entirely innocent of any charge. On the second point, while clearly betraying his belief that the charges actually brought had not been sustained and that the sentence therefore was excessive, he argued that Smith had at least been guilty of withholding from the Governor his knowledge of impending trouble, not indeed because he desired to foment it but because he dreaded playing an informer's part. It was a clever point, not very strong, perhaps, but strong enough to make many of his listeners hesitate to pass a wholesale condemnation on the officials of a British colony. And the cold, impartial tone of the speech was in effective contrast— in that unemotional House—with the passion of Brougham's reply. It was enough, not to ensure the Government's customary majority, but to carry "the previous question" by 193 votes to 146.

"I greatly doubt," says the diary after this debate, "if I had not better give up taking part in the House of Commons." And certainly the doubt was justified by the increased feebleness of intellectual as well as physical power which his last illness had left behind it. But he had undertaken to present a petition for the abolition of Slavery from the town of Carlow and its neighbourhood; and he felt it to be an opportunity, perhaps the last, "of entering his solemn protest against the plan of Government as hopeless and dangerous." "It is nothing short of infatuation," he remarks, "to depend on the colonial assemblies for imitating a model to be set up in Trinidad." Accordingly he nerved himself for a short speech on June 15, and this time he did not fail. It was a clear and convincing assertion that the planters could not be expected, on any reasonable view whatever of their conduct and opinions, to extinguish Slavery or even to ameliorate it of their own motion.

I am disposed to think that my right honourable friend deceives himself as to the probable conduct of the West Indian Assemblies by insensibly admitting the persuasion that the West Indian proprietors in this country—many of whom are his own personal friends and men of the most humane and liberal minds—reflect the opinions and feelings of the colonists actually in the islands. Nothing, alas! could be more different. . . . The West Indians abhor alike the end we have in view and the means by which we hope to attain it. They frankly tell us that the emancipation of their slaves would be their inevitable destruction; and their prejudices make them disapprove of the various measures we recommend for the improvement of the negroes' condition. . . . When both means and end are alike obnoxious, it seems to me far too sanguine to look to their giving up their opposition and at length adopting the principles we recommend. . . . But only let the imperial legislature assume its proper tone and maintain its just authority, and all will go on quietly; you will soon witness with delight the accomplishment of your benevolent purpose. Hence it is that I have felt it my imperious duty to disavow the system of conduct which Government is now pursuing. It is with reluctance and pain I have come forward; but I believe it my absolute duty to protest against that policy. *Liberavi animam meam.* May it please God to disappoint my expectations and to render the result more favourable than I anticipate.

6

It was Wilberforce's last debate. Ten days later he was taken ill again on his way to pay a visit in the country; and on arriving at his destination, he was "but just able to be helped upstairs to bed." For a month he lay in a critical condition; and when, at last, he struggled back to health, it was clear that, for a long time to come,

no work of any kind was to be thought of. He retired to a small
house bordering on Uxbridge Common and lived there in complete
seclusion, "never visiting, scarcely receiving a single visitor." In
the autumn he moved, on the doctor's advice, to Bath, which he
found by no means so restful. "There is walking between the glasses
and after the glasses," he writes to his daughter, "and then in rolls
the tide of visitors as regularly as that of the ocean, and, like that,
this human influx makes its way through and over every obstacle.
. . . Continued knockings while I have been writing, and at last
one intruder has actually made a lodgement." It was a pleasure,
none the less, for Wilberforce to meet some of his older friends and
acquaintances again. "Venerable Rowland Hill dined with me—
aetat. 80," notes the diary, and again, "I talked with Mr. Nevill in
the Pump-room, whom I had met at Exton near fifty years ago:
he 82 aetat.—an astonishing man." And before he returned to
Uxbridge to spend Christmas with his family, he paid a visit to the
oldest and almost the closest of his spiritual comrades. "Sat with
Hannah More about an hour and a half, and she as animated as
ever I knew her, quoting authors, naming people, etc.—off about
one, after praying with her."

With the coming of the new year the question of retirement
could be postponed no longer. Doctors and friends were strongly
for it: to continue in Parliament, they said, might mean a fatal
seizure: but Wilberforce struggled hard against it. He confesses
to Macaulay that the idea is "very painful." "It is to me almost
like a change of nature to quit parliamentary life," he told his son.
And he had done so little! "I am filled with the deepest compunc-
tion," he writes to a friend, "from the consciousness of having made
so poor a use of the talents committed to my stewardship. The heart
knows its own bitterness." To be forced "to retire from public life
re infecta"—that is the burden of all his complaints. Indeed, he
could not bring himself at once to an instant and abrupt resignation. He would put it off just a very little. He would resign—quite
certainly—as soon as the present Parliament were dissolved. Then
his friends attempted, not very hopefully, an alternative plan. The
offer of a peerage was arranged. But Wilberforce courteously
declined the initial suggestion. "I have done nothing to make it
naturally come to me," he said. At last, however, he surrendered
to the inevitable. As was his wont, he noted down the reasons for
his decision—"I hope I may employ my pen to advantage if I retire

into private life; and my life just now is peculiarly valuable to my family.—I am not now much wanted in Parliament; our cause has powerful advocates who have now taken their stations.—The example of a man's retiring, when he feels his bodily and mental powers beginning to fail him, might probably be useful." Accordingly he requested Buxton to apply on his behalf for the Chiltern Hundreds—Buxton rather than Canning or Grant or Brougham, as sundry friends suggested, because he desired it to be a "testamentary designation and to hold him forth as a depositary of my principles on West Indian matters." "It is the first place that I ever asked for myself," he wrote, "and for near thirty years for any one else." Buxton finely quoted in his reply the inscription which the Carthaginians set on Hannibal's tomb—"We vehemently desired him in the day of battle."

It was a notable event in the life of the House of Commons when Wilberforce passed through its doors for the last time. He carried history away with him, this little, stooping, frail old man. Almost alone among living members of the House, he had stood among the giants, their contemporary and their equal, in the golden days of Pitt and Fox and Burke. And now for nearly twenty years, when all those others had gone, he had enjoyed the same kind of prestige; obtained from the House the same kind of respect, willing or unwilling; exercised over it, in many great matters, the same kind of power, as that which had been given to those others and to them alone. Like them, too, he had been a great figure in the country. The overthrow of the Slave Trade had given him something like the position in the public eye which Waterloo had given Wellington. Liverpool or Castlereagh, Grey or Brougham, Canning or Huskisson —none of them was famous in his generation quite as Wilberforce was famous. "When Mr. Wilberforce passes through the crowd," an Italian diplomat once remarked on the day of the opening of Parliament, "every one contemplates this little old man, worn with age and his head sunk upon his shoulders, as a sacred relic—as the Washington of humanity."

XIII

Rest

I

"WE have bought a house about ten miles north of London,"
wrote Wilberforce to Gisborne shortly after his retirement. "I shall be a little *zemindar* there: 140 acres of
land, cottages of my own, etc." Highwood Hill, as this estate was
called, lay about a mile from Mill Hill. "Late when got home,"
comments the diary on the day he took possession, "and had a too
hasty prayer for first settlement in a new house—all in confusion."
The confusion soon subsided into a regular routine of life. A systematic ordering of the day had been characteristic of Wilberforce
ever since his "conversion"; but now his abandonment of politics
and his seclusion from society and its sudden calls and interruptions
made it easier to keep strictly to the time-table. He rose soon after
seven o'clock and spent an hour and a half at his devotions. Three-
quarters of an hour were then allowed for dressing and listening,
as he dressed, to his reader. At half-past nine came family prayers
for half an hour, Wilberforce always reading and expounding a
passage from the Bible. Invariably after prayers, if the weather
permitted, he spent a few minutes in the garden. Breakfast was
late, usually about ten; and if friends were of the party, they often
sat talking round the table till midday. Then Wilberforce retired
to deal with the day's letters; but by three o'clock, when the post
had gone, he was out in the garden again, pacing up and down the
sunny path, preferably with a friend—"now in animated or even
playful conversation," one of them records, "and then drawing
from his copious pockets some favourite volume or other, a Psalter,
a Horace, a Shakespeare, or Cowper, and reading or reciting passages, and then catching at long-stored flower-leaves as the wind
blew them from the pages, or standing before a favourite gum
cistus to repair the loss." He liked to stay out of doors till dinner-
time which was never later than five. After dinner he went up to
his room, rested for an hour and a half, sometimes sleeping and

always coming down again as fresh and vigorous as if the day had just begun. And then came the "family reading." It was in these first years of his retirement that he indulged in so many of Scott's novels with that typical regret that their purpose was not more serious. "They remind me of a giant," he says, "spending his strength in cracking nuts. I would rather go to render my account on the last day, carrying up with me *The Shepherd of Salisbury Plain* than bearing the load of all those volumes, full as they are of genius." Naturally, therefore, novels were not by any means the only reading. History still holds its place—Clarendon, Orford, Pepys, Hallam. "Independent" to the last, he regularly subscribes to both the *Edinburgh* and the *Quarterly*. And of the poets, Shakespeare, at any rate, and Cowper are usually at his side or in his pocket; but not, one may guess, the most celebrated or notorious poet of his own day—not Byron. One wonders, indeed, if Wilberforce was ever aware of the doubtful compliment Byron paid him —if he ever read the three tributes to his name and fame in the pages of *Don Juan*. After reading, talk; and then evening prayers; and then more talk and more, usually till midnight if there were old friends in the house, and often beyond it. And so at last to a short and often broken night's rest.

For a casual visitor at Highwood Hill those evening talks were an unforgettable experience. They saw the old man at his best, pouring out the treasures of his long memory, arguing, criticising, orating on some favourite theme, and all with an astonishing facility and freshness and vivacity. "If he was lighted up," says an acquaintance, "and in a small circle where he was entirely at his ease, his powers of conversation were prodigious; a natural eloquence was poured out, strokes of gentle playfulness and satire fell on all sides, and the company were soon absorbed in admiration. It commonly took only one visit to gain over the most prejudiced stranger." The easy conquest of one such stranger is recorded. Some cynical friend had given her a thoroughly unpleasant idea of her host; but, after one night in the house, she dashes off a long dithyrambic letter to her sister, "Oh, he is a dear, good, admirable old man!" she exclaims. How could any one, indeed, regard this lively, indomitably youthful creature as a fanatic or a hypocrite? For he retained to the end his transcendent gift of youth. That dangerous talent for mimicry, for instance, had never been quite abandoned; and he would sometimes plunge the household into uproarious laughter by his imitation of some public man till, conscience pricking, he would "check himself and throw in some kind remark." "The close union between the most rigid principles and the most gay and playful disposition"—that was what still struck Lord Milton, his old rival of the hustings, as the most remarkable thing about him. And when his two sons came to write his biography, they were obliged to confess their inability to do justice to this "great and leading feature" of their father's character. Perhaps the younger Stephen is nearest it when, in a letter to Henry Taylor a few days after Wilberforce's death, he quotes a line of Coleridge as "expressing his nature to perfection as far as it goes"—"Delight in little things, the buoyant youth surviving in the man."

Time has thinned the company that used to gather for those great evening talks; but many of the old friends are still there—Stephen and Gisborne and Buxton and John Joseph Gurney and Macaulay, and, now he is of age, Macaulay's son. "Macaulay and Tom came to dinner, and night," says the diary in 1825. "Tom infinitely overflowing with matter on all subjects, and most good-humoured": and next day, "Macaulay off. Tom fertile and fluent to the last, and with unaffected good-nature." That fertility and fluency were soon to be famous. "I am much pleased with a review of Tom Macaulay's in the *Edinburgh*," notes Wilberforce a few years later: "it is not merely the very superior talent which it indicates, but (scarcely an "independent" judgment this!) its being on the right side." He keeps in touch, too, with allies, new and old, who are not of the inner circle. Sir Stamford Raffles and his wife are frequent guests. One day he pays a visit to the other survivor of the three who had talked of Abolition under the Holwood oak. "To Dropmore, where received very kindly; walked with Grenville for an hour before and after dinner; it grieved me to see him so feeble. Said he had profited more from Aristotle's *Rhetoric* than any other work." Another day, "Lord Harrowby rode over to see me . . . very clever and entertaining as always." But the inner circle itself was never now so constantly in session as it once had been; the brethren of the Clapham Sect no longer lived at each other's doors. And it had shrunk. Death had taken toll of its members and their families. John Venn the preacher had died in 1813, Henry Thornton and his wife in 1815, Mrs. Stephen, Wilberforce's only surviving sister, in the following year, and Isaac Milner in 1820.

In 1821 Wilberforce had lost one of his own children, his eldest daughter. But the family was growing; his two elder sons were married or on the point of marrying; and in his grandchildren Wilberforce was soon to discover one more proof of God's amazing mercy to an unprofitable servant. There were one or two friends, moreover, with whom, late as he had come to know them, he had quickly become intimate—foremost among them, Mackintosh. Wilberforce had naturally been drawn to him by his eloquent championship of humanitarian causes—"splendid" and "beautiful" are the diary's epithets for his speeches—but it was something more than that. There was something kindred, it seems, between those two; and certainly Mackintosh was as great a talker as Wilberforce himself. He had taken a house at Clapham; and "this extraordinary man," says Wilberforce, "spends, they tell me, much of his time in the circulating library-room at the end of the Common, and chats with the utmost freedom to all the passengers in the Clapham stage as he goes and comes from London." Two such talkers, indeed, could never have been friends if they had yielded to the besetting sin of their class. But both of them could also listen. Wilberforce spoke of Mackintosh as "full of information and sparkling like a firefly." "I drew the highest prize in the lottery," says the diary, of a big dinner-party; "I sat by Sir J. Mackintosh." Again, "Mackintosh came in and sat most kindly chatting with me during my dinner—what a paragon of a companion he is; quite unequalled!" "If I were called upon to describe Wilberforce in one word," said Mackintosh on his side, "I should say he was the most 'amusable' man I ever met with in my life. Instead of having to think what subjects will interest him, it is perfectly impossible to hit one that does not. I never saw any one who touched life at so many points; and this is the more remarkable in a man who is supposed to live absorbed in the contemplation of a future state. When he was in the House of Commons, he seemed to have the freshest mind of any man there. There was all the charm of youth about him. And he is quite as remarkable in this bright evening of his day as when I saw him in his glory many years ago."

And so, in regular routine, in prayer and correspondence and infinite talk, the quiet months went by. There was rarely any break, except the intermittent visits to Bath for the "potations" which the doctors ordered. Frequent or lengthy journeys soon become too great a strain. But in 1827 the old man set out on one last great tour. He wanted "to revisit the scenes of his childhood and early youth" before it was too late; and early in the summer he drove off for Yorkshire, stopping for a time on the way at his old haunt at Yoxall Lodge among the trees. "Much as I had admired it before, I never saw its riches displayed in such overflowing profusion." In Derbyshire he noticed how the country had been improved by the growth of woods on the bare hillsides of forty years ago. But it was in Yorkshire that the passing of time inevitably struck him most. At Huddersfield he met "a warm-hearted shopkeeper, originally from Hull—knew me when himself a boy—remembered the ox roasted whole"; but at Hull and elsewhere the answers to his inquiries after the companions of his youth were all too often the same: "Oh, he has been long gone" or "He died years ago." His "progress" round his native country was slow and thorough. Of his many visits to friends' houses, the last—to Wentworth House—was in a way the most moving of all. "The cordiality and kindness with which I have been received in this place," he wrote to Stephen, "has deeply affected me. Lord Fitzwilliam might well have been forgiven if he had conceived an unconquerable antipathy to me." And he recalls his famous first election as the member for Yorkshire in the teeth of Fitzwilliam's opposition, when he was only twenty-four, "a mere boy," without a single friend among the country magnates, and identified with Pitt against whom Fitzwilliam had "conceived a deadly hostility."

So back at last to Highwood Hill ("What cause for thankfulness after six months' absence and thirty-six visits"); back to the peaceful routine, the garden-path, the household devotions, the daily letters, the family reading, and the talk.

2

When Wilberforce left the House of Commons, he shut the door tight on politics. "I am now no politician," he declared, not without some secret satisfaction; for the party conflict had always jarred on him, and his excursions into other fields than the negro question had always seemed a matter of duty and rather an unpleasant duty, forced on him by his knowledge that so many people expected him to say something and were so strangely influenced by what he said.

So while England moved on into the sharpest political crisis in its history since the last ripple of the English Revolution had ebbed away in the alarms of "forty-five," the oracle was silent. That he was not indifferent, that he followed events in the newspapers and had his opinions on them is clear from his private letters. "In what a dreadful state the country now is," he writes to his son at the time of the "Swing Riots" in 1830. "Gisborne, I find, has stated his opinion that the present is the period of pouring out the 7th Vial, when there is to be general confusion, insubordination and misery. . . . Your mother suggests that a threshing-machine used to be kept in one of your barns. If so, I really think it should be removed. I should be very sorry to have it stated that a threshing-machine had been burnt on the premises of the Rev. Samuel Wilberforce; they take away one of the surest sources of occupation for farmers in frost and snow times." A week later, the old Tory observes with no dismay the long-delayed advent of the Whigs to power. "Assuredly," he writes, "this Government is greatly to be preferred before the last." But, as had always been his way, it is the men rather than their measures that he looks to, and their morals rather than their brains. "Brougham better than Copley," he says, "and several highly respectable besides, the Grants (Charley is in the Cabinet), Lord Althorp, Sir James Graham, Lord Grey himself, highly respectable as a family man; Denman a very honest fellow," and so forth. He expressed, as has been seen, a not unfavourable opinion on the first Reform Bill; and when both the first and the second Bills had been rejected by the Lords, he was given a chance of understanding, better perhaps than he had ever done, how fiercely the English people were bent upon Reform. Recluse as he was, he was brought into personal contact with the wildest of those outbreaks in the autumn of 1831, which showed how near now the country really was to the revolution he had dreaded in Pitt's day and in Sidmouth's. On the red Sunday of October 30 he was staying with his friend Harford at Blaize Castle, four miles from Bristol. News of rioting in the city reached him after church that morning, and at night he saw the sky lit up with the glare of its burning buildings. A few days later, when all was quiet again, he went with his host to inspect the damage. "It was dangerous to move forward," writes Harford, "for fear of the sudden crash of tottering walls; and it was appalling to stand still and contemplate the surrounding scene"; but nothing could daunt old Wilberforce's eager interest; he insisted that they must "examine and localise every principal feature of the recent outrages."

Only one cause—his own—could now drag Wilberforce before the public; and even to combat Slavery he was very loth to leave that quiet house and garden. "It seems like wishing to retain the reins when I can no longer hold them," he told Babington. And he positively declined to join in those deputations to Ministers which he had so often led. "I am a bee," he said, "which has lost its sting." But he yielded to repeated appeals that he should take the chair at a great meeting of the recently founded Anti-Slavery Society during the first winter of his retirement. "Above all, we feel the loss of you," Macaulay had written: "heart-stirring occasions are in prospect, when I should have been delighted to see you engaged *cominus ense.*" "Got to the meeting at twelve," the diary reports; "took the chair. Very kindly treated throughout, both by the very full room and the speakers." But the results of these new efforts of the Abolitionists were not very "heart-stirring." Canning's regulations had been duly applied in Trinidad, Demerara, Berbice and St. Lucia, and were about to be applied, in a modified form, in Cape Colony; and that was all. In vain Bathurst urged the authorities in Jamaica to take the example to heart and by their own legislation to anticipate the interference of Parliament. True, they passed an Act in 1826; but it was so meagre and on essential points so deliberately indefinite that Huskisson, who succeeded Bathurst, actually refused to sanction it. In 1830 Huskisson's untimely death brought Murray to the Colonial Office; and he lost no time in telling the planters that an amelioration of their slave-laws, which three successive Secretaries of State had urged on them, was "a matter of necessary policy." But another year passed and they had done nothing at all. Meanwhile the Abolitionists were chafing at the Government's inaction; in the spring of 1830 they appealed once more to public opinion with a monster meeting in Freemasons' Hall; and once more Wilberforce, over seventy now and rather shrunk and feeble, was prevailed on to attend. "All the old friends of the cause" were there, says the diary; and it was Clarkson who moved that "the great leader in our cause" should take the chair, to which Wilberforce responded with a tribute to his "friend and fellow-labourer" and a reference to the days "when we began our labours together, or rather when we worked together, for he began before me." So the patriarch sat enthroned above the crowd, while Joshua moved the resolution "for effecting at the earliest period the entire abolition of Slavery throughout the British dominions." It was Wilberforce's last public appearance in London. "The prohibition of my medical adviser is clear and strong," he wrote, when invited to a similar demonstration in the next year.

But the meeting of 1830 had given a greater impulse to the cause than the meeting of 1825, and the Abolitionists decided to join battle again in Parliament. Though Buxton, as has been seen, was Wilberforce's official heir in the conduct of the Abolition question in the House of Commons, it was Brougham who reopened the issue with his motion for the consideration of the state of the slaves "in order to the mitigation and final abolition of their slavery." He made a powerful speech; the subject was well suited to his lurid style; but the motion was lost by 56 votes to 27. Something, however, had been gained. Brougham was committed to the cause, and Brougham was certain of high place as soon as the Whigs came into office. Outside Parliament, meantime, the Abolitionist propaganda had been forcing the question to the front; and at the General Election which soon ensued, Slavery, though overshadowed, of course, by Reform, was for the first time an important electoral issue. Naturally it was nowhere more important than in Wilberforce's county. Brougham himself stood for one of his four seats which Yorkshire had possessed since 1821—almost certain of success with Wilberforce's name and the organised support of the Abolitionists to back him; and he and the other three members elected were all definitely pledged to Abolition. "The election," wrote Brougham to Wilberforce, "turned very much on Slavery, your name was in every mouth, and your health the most enthusiastically received."

3

Just at this time the evening calm of the life at Highwood Hill was rudely broken. Wilberforce suddenly lost the greater part of his wealth. All his life he had been a rich man; but his gifts of many thousands in public and still more in private charity had prevented him from adding to his capital. "I never intended to do more than not exceed my income," he once told his eldest son. "But believe me, there is a special blessing on being liberal to the

poor and on the family of those who have been so; and I doubt
not my children will fare better, even in this world, for real
happiness than if I had been saving £20,000 or £30,000 of what has
been given away." But since his retirement he had been involved
in unusual expenses. The return on the capital spent on the purchase of Highwood Hill was much reduced by his dropping all the
rents of his tenants between 30 and 40 per cent. At his first inspec-
tion of Highwood, moreover, he had been "most struck by its
distance from a church—three miles," and he had not been there
long before he resolved to build a chapel for the use of himself
and his tenants and the neighbouring hamlet of Mill Hill. After a
protracted and very irritating controversy with a local parson, he
carried out his project at a heavy initial cost. He was ill prepared,
therefore, for the disaster which overtook him in 1830. His eldest
son, William, had not received, like his three brothers, a call to
the Church. He had intended to practise at the bar; but it had soon
appeared that his health was not strong enough for it, and Wilberforce had set himself to find a career for him in agriculture. A
promising opportunity was presently forthcoming. A business-
man, in whom he had acquired a complete, but quite mistaken,
trust, was prepared to launch a farming enterprise. It was to be
on a large scale. William would take a remunerative part in it.
Only capital was needed. And Wilberforce produced the capital—
a very large sum—by selling out stock. Before long he had lost it
nearly all.

It was a blow, and the kind of blow which hits an old man
hardest. But Wilberforce took it with perfect calm. "A solitary
walk with the psalmist—evening quiet" is the entry, two days after
the full extent of his loss was known. "What gives me repose in
all things," said the Saint, and meant it, "is the thought of their
being His appointment." But of course the loss necessitated a great
change in his way of life. He was not left a pauper, but it was now
quite impossible to keep up Highwood. He must find, at seventy-
one, another home—unless, indeed, the man who had given so
much in charity were ready to receive in charity. Six of his countrymen, to their great credit, as soon as his change of fortune was
known, offered to make good the whole of the damage. One of
them was a "West Indian." Another was Lord Fitzwilliam. But
Wilberforce refused to accept anything for himself. Only towards
the completion of the unfinished chapel—it cost altogether about

£4000—would he allow his friends to help. So Highwood was abandoned; and he and his wife went to live, for alternate periods, with their second and third sons. Samuel was already installed in the vicarage of Brighstone (or Brixton) in the Isle of Wight, six miles from Newport; and Robert was shortly presented by Brougham to the living of East Farleigh, not far from Maidstone and almost within a mile of Barham Court with its memories of the Middletons and Ramsay and the first beginnings of the assault on the Slave Trade more than forty years ago.

The death of his second daughter in 1832 made Wilberforce more dependent than ever on the affection of those two sons and their families. They were intensely devoted to him, and he was intensely fond and proud of them. "You are able from experience to judge," he writes to Babington, "how a parent must feel in witnessing the pastoral labours of his own child." It did not trouble him that they had moved away from his own Evangelical stand-point. He had always been broadminded in those matters. But perhaps it was as well he could not know that, when they came to write his biography, they would be constrained to make excuses for his sympathy with Nonconformists; that Samuel would one day be an Anglo-Catholic prelate, suspected of Romanism; and that Robert—preceded by his youngest brother, Henry, and followed by his eldest brother, William—would one day even cross the frontier into Rome. No such clouds were visible about his sunset. The months at Brighstone or at Farleigh were as peaceful and as con-tented as the years at Highwood. "I can scarce understand," said the old man once, "why my life is spared so long except it be to show that a man can be as happy without a fortune as with one." So the days went on as before. He could do in his sons' homes exactly what he had done in his own. Those long evening talks were rarer; he was too far away from Mackintosh and the rest of the London circle. But there was still a garden; and at Farleigh, as of old, he would pace up and down the sunny gravel path, and at Brighstone he would venture out sometimes to the top of the downs or along by the sea below the cliff. In the spring of 1832 both sons were with their father for a time, Robert spending his holiday at Brighstone. "Like a first summer day," says the diary for April 4: "the air singularly mild and balmy, and not a leaf stirring. S engaged in a cottage reading. R. drove me out in the pony-chaise, which very pleasant." And for April 5: "Day, if possible, even sweeter than yesterday; as balmy and more air. Walked with my sons up the hill." Happily, almost to the end, Wilberforce was strong enough to enjoy these pleasures of the country; and his mind, if it began to move more slowly, was never clouded. "I thank God," he tells a friend, "my health is in about its ordinary state; though I am becoming yearly more and more stiff and crazy."

Of course he had quite abandoned work of any kind. When he first retired from Parliament he had meant to write. "I hope not to be idle in private life," he had remarked, "though less noisy." And the diary reveals what he had meant to write about: "Oh, that God would enable me to execute my long-formed purpose of writing another religious book. I have also a wish to write something political; my own life, and Pitt's too, coming into the discussion." Presently he began to plan out a work on the Epistles. But nothing came of it, nor of his political autobiography. Sometimes, indeed, he would take out from its drawer the sketch he had made of Pitt's character some years before, and read it over, and make a little correction here and there. For he had never forgotten the greatest of his friends; always he noted his birthday in his diary: "Poor Pitt dead above twenty-one years," it reads in 1827, "to-day he would have been sixty-eight." "I never knew so extraordinary a man," he used to say in these latter days. And so he would sit brooding, and sometimes talking to his sons, about Pitt and the far-off days of his own youth and prime. . . . the grammar school at Hull with the big robustious usher Milner . . . Putney . . . Pocklington . . . Cambridge . . . the plunge into London . . . Pitt in the gallery and at Goosetree's . . . that wintry day in the Castle Yard at York and the election for the county . . . Pitt at Wimbledon, in Paris; Pitt Prime Minister, fighting the Coalition . . . and all that gay London life and those gay London people . . . the Duchess of Gordon, Mrs. Siddons, Mrs. Crewe—No; he must not think of those days, except to thank God for the ten-thousandth time for his deliverance. . . . But after that, the wonderful gift of grace, the torments, and old Newton, and the new tranquil life that followed . . . and that long, strange talk with Pitt about it all . . . and so back, with a change of heart, to politics and the Hastings case . . . and presently the talk beneath the oak at Holwood and the beginning—how nearly it had been no more than a beginning!—of the long, long fight with the Slave

Trade . . . the quick success at first, the rousing of the country, Pitt's great speech; and then the Revolution . . . and those dreary, disappointing years, under the shadow of that endless war! . . . The cause of Abolition hopelessly shelved; and Pitt, still the incomparable patriot, but changing, ageing, drifting apart. . . . Years only brightened by his marriage, and by the growth of those new intimacies at Clapham, and by the success of the *Practical View* . . . and then at last the sudden revival of the cause. . . . Pitt's death and Fox's zeal . . . and the great night when Romilly (poor, noble Romilly) had praised him and the House had rung with cheers. . . . And the busy time that followed; the crowd of visitors at Kensington Gore; the efforts to enforce the British abolition of the Trade and to secure abolition abroad, at Paris and at Vienna. . . . And then the final phase of his political career— the Corn Law and the soldiers in the house, Peterloo and the Queen's Trial, Christophe and John Smith, and the opening of the anti-slavery campaign. . . .

A great life; but Wilberforce could not judge it as we judge it. "I am a sadly unprofitable servant" was all he could say. None the less—for humility can be sincere and yet not blind—Wilberforce must at least have hoped that his maintenance of Christian principles in public life had not been quite without effect; that if the tone of Parliament and politics was higher now than it had been forty years ago, it might perhaps be partly due to the influence of the "Saints." And, belittle it as he might, Wilberforce must have known how large a part he had played in the abolition of at least the British Slave Trade and how long a step that had been towards the abolition of Slavery itself at least within the British Colonies. But, humility apart, Wilberforce could never have guessed the full magnitude of his achievement. For it was not till the nineteenth century was growing old that Britain's dealings with tropical Africa extended appreciably beyond that fringe of trading-stations on the Western coast. But when one vast area and then another was brought, directly or indirectly, within the orbit of the Empire till at last the British Parliament and people had become responsible, in the last resort, for the peaceful and orderly government of a great part of Central Africa, then indeed it was evident how decisive and how timely the achievement of Wilberforce and his allies had been. If the conscience of Europe had not been roused in time, if Slavery and the Slave Trade had still been tolerated by a lax or fatalistic public opinion, the second phase in the relations between Africa and Europe would have been even blacker than the first. The plantation system of the West Indies and the Southern States would—one must suppose—have been reproduced on a gigantic scale wherever the teeming soil could be cleared and cultivated from Cape Verde to Mozambique; and not beyond the Atlantic only but in their native land, vast armies of negroes would have toiled in slavery beneath the white man's whip. Nor was it from that African nightmare only that Wilberforce, more than any other man, saved the world. He had done something positive. More than any other man, he had founded in the conscience of the British people a tradition of humanity and of responsibility towards the weak and backward black peoples whose fate lay in their hands. And that tradition has never died. Never since have cynics or fatalists dared to justify or palliate the old deliberate sacrifice of Africa to Europe and America. Selfish and cruel things have been done in Africa; now and again the morals of commercial exploitation have been indistinguishable from the morals of the slave system; but, within the frontiers of the British Empire, at any rate, such things could only be done in the dark and could not be done at all if British Ministers in far-off London or their officials on the spot were quick enough or strong enough to stop them. For, as the world's need for the produce of the tropics grew, there grew with it the conviction that the economic development of Africa need not, and must not, mean the subjection and degradation of the Africans. The dawn Pitt heralded may be broadening very slowly into day; but at least the civilisation of Africa is now something more than a theme for a peroration. British rule in Africa has not been pure altruism. Its standards have not always or in every quarter been the same. But on the whole—only ignorance or prejudice can question it—British rule in Africa has been true to the principle of trusteeship; it has striven to protect the moral and material interests of the natives; it has saved them from African and Asiatic as well as European slave-masters; it has given them stricter justice and truer freedom than they could have got for themselves; it has begun the long task of their education; it has tried to regard them as fellow members with Englishmen of a world-wide society, weak, ignorant, undisciplined as yet, their faculties for the most part cramped and stunted, but capable of a development to which only the centuries ahead can tell the end.

To contrast the principles and practice of British tropical administration in our own day with what was said in defence of the Slave Trade by leaders of British opinion in the eighteenth century and what was done in pursuit of the Trade by British traders is to measure the effects of what Wilberforce and his friends achieved. It was nothing less, indeed, than a moral revolution; and those who see the world's life as a whole, as an intricate, shifting complex not only of states and nations but of continents and races, discordant, yet interdependent, heterogeneous, yet all belonging to one human family, will give a high place in history to the Englishman who did so much to bring about that revolution, so much to transform the moral basis of the relations between Africa and Europe.

4

Meantime, the "Second Crusade" was once more on the move; and Wilberforce's friends began to wonder if indeed the victory might be won before he died. The return of the Whigs at the election of 1830, despite Brougham's committal, had led to no immediate step towards Abolition. Grey and his colleagues were naturally determined to subordinate all other issues to the great struggle for Reform; and, when Buxton again pressed his cause on Parliament, they were still unwilling to grasp the nettle. But a novel suggestion was put forward by Althorp. The planters, he pointed out, had not yielded to persuasion, but they might yield to a bribe. Why not lower the duties on the import of sugar from those islands which definitely undertook to improve the condition of their slaves? The Government clutched at this compromise, and Goderich issued a circular dispatch from the Colonial Office promising measures of fiscal relief to those colonies whose legislatures would adopt, in full and unaltered, the Order-in-Council already in force in Trinidad and the other colonies under Crown control. Meanwhile the immediate manumission of all slaves belonging to the Crown had been ordered. The result of these half-measures was the miserable result which had followed half-measures before. The slaves in Jamaica once more believed that the King of England had given them their freedom. Was not the manumission of the Crown slaves a proof of it? And in December they "struck," gathered into gangs, and began to destroy the plantations. As before they killed no white man. As before they were easily suppressed. As before the punishment was rigorous. And as before the Assembly ascribed the cause of the rebellion to the "unceasing and unconstitutional interference of his Majesty's Ministers with our local Legislature." But this time, Ministers, less masterful than Canning, acted as if the charge were true. They voted a considerable sum to make good the damage done to the planters' property. They agreed to a proposal for a committee of the Upper House to consider the interests of the West Indian trade. And, though the Reform issue was now out of their way and though Brougham, their own Lord Chancellor, presented a petition signed by 135,000 persons against any further delay in the enforcement of Abolition, they did nothing more. When Parliament met in 1833, no mention was made of Slavery in the Speech from the Throne. But Buxton was as irrepressible as Wilberforce. He at once gave notice of a motion on the question, and resisted all the subsequent efforts of the Government to induce him to postpone it. "Well," said Althorp at last, "if *you* will not yield *we must*," and he fixed a definite date, April 23, for a statement of the Government's views and a full debate. Ministerial changes gave them a little more breathing space. Goderich's promotion had brought Stanley to the Colonial Office, and Buxton agreed to give the new Minister three weeks' further grace.

May 14, then, was to be the first day of the decisive battle; and the Abolitionists, uncertain of the Government's intentions, set themselves to create an overwhelming demonstration of public opinion. An effective pamphlet, by a young clerk who had just returned from the West Indies, describing the scenes of suffering he had witnessed and showing from the official figures the terrible increase in regular floggings in the Crown colonies that had resulted from the disuse of the whip in the field, was hurriedly printed and nearly two hundred thousand copies were distributed. Meetings and lectures were organised all over the country. Petitions poured in—the total of their signatures fell not far short of a million and a half. Over three hundred delegates, appointed by Abolitionists in every considerable town in the British Isles, collected in London and marched in a body to 10 Downing Street to present an address to Lord Grey. The campaign of 1833, in short, was an even more impressive demonstration of public enthusiasm than the campaign of 1792. And Kent, like other counties, was caught up in it. A meeting was arranged at Maidstone for April 12 and a petition circulated for signatures in the neighbourhood. It came, of course, to Wilberforce, at East Farleigh; and Wilberforce, into whose eager ears Buxton and Stephen, on a short and a last visit to him, had poured all the details of the movement, was not content merely to sign it; against all his previous resolves and promises he actually agreed to attend the meeting and to propose its submission to Parliament himself.

His speech was not long, and there was only one controversial passage in it. Like all such movements, the anti-Slavery movement had its extremists, who regarded Buxton as half-hearted, watched jealously for any unwarrantable concessions to the enemy, and above all denounced the proposal to compensate the planters for the loss of their slaves. A fanatic of this type Wilberforce had never been; he had always declared not only that compensation was just in itself but that "smart money," as he called it, was owing by the British nation for its old encouragement of the Slave Trade. So he spoke out clearly for compensation. "I say, and I say honestly and fearlessly, that the same Being who commands us to love mercy, says also ' Do justice '; and therefore I have no objection to grant the colonists the relief that may be due to them for any real injuries they may prove themselves to have sustained." The speech was obviously an effort; his voice, feeble now and broken, could not fill the Town Hall as it had filled the House of Commons; but, at the very last, the audience caught an echo of what Wilberforce had been. "I trust," he said, "that we now approach the end of our career." And at that moment, by a strange coincidence, just such another beam of sunlight broke into the hall as had lit up the close of Pitt's greatest speech against the Slave Trade more than forty years before; and Wilberforce wove it, as Pitt had woven it, into his last words. "The object is bright before us," he exclaimed, with a new gleam in his eyes and a stronger ring in his voice; "the light of heaven beams on it and is an earnest of success."

A week later he moved from East Farleigh to Brighstone, and there he had an attack of influenza from which he seemed to make a poor recovery. It was hoped, however, that the waters of Bath would exert their usual influence on his general state of health; and to Bath accordingly he went on May 17, three days after Stanley had moved and carried the resolutions on which his Bill to abolish

Slavery was to be based. But Bath could no longer work its annual charm. A sort of languor settled on him and he suffered a good deal of pain. On July 6, while at dinner, he was suddenly taken very ill. "I ran for a medical man," records his youngest son, Henry, "and before I returned he was got to bed. He was suffering much from giddiness and sickness. . . . When his medical attendant came, 'Thank God,' he said, ' I am not losing my faculties.' ' Yes, but you could not easily go through a problem in arithmetic or geometry.' ' I think I could go through the Asses' Bridge,' he replied, and began, correcting himself if he omitted anything. . . ." Nothing but death itself could quench his youthful spirit; and indeed he seems to have felt that death was coming near. "What cause have I for thankfulness," he kept on saying. Once he began talking of the joy his married life had given him. "Think what I should have done, had I been left, as one hears of people quarrelling and separating. In sickness and in health was the burden, and well has it been kept." Just then Mrs. Wilberforce entered the room. "I was just praising you," he said. "I am a poor creature to-day," he confessed a little later. "I cannot help thinking if some of the people who saw me swaggering away on the hutsings at York could see me now, how much they would find me changed." But, after all, the end was not yet; he was presently able to get up; and on July 17 he could be moved a stage on the road to London —the road the dying Pitt had travelled in 1806. On the 19th he arrived at William Smith's house in Cadogan Place. "I am like a clock that is almost run down," he told one of the many friends who hastened to his side.

Within a mile of his lodging the House of Commons sat debating Stanley's Abolition Bill. The new Colonial Secretary had thrown himself at his task with the imperious vigour, the contempt of obstacles, and the dashing eloquence of "the Rupert of Debate." True to character, he had tried at first to frame his proposals without seeking the advice of the permanent officials of his department, at whose influence over transient Secretaries of State the newspapers had been grumbling for some time past. But he had been obliged, before long, to have recourse to the experts, and, chief among them, to James Stephen's son who was already winning a commanding position as an official at the Colonial Office. For more than ten years past the younger Stephen had given most of his time to the study of the Slave Question. "This task devolved on me by inheritance," he said; but there was more than that in it. His labours were inspired also by an almost reverent devotion to his father's famous friend. He once told his wife to see that their eldest boy "observed" Wilberforce. "Try to fix in the dear child's mind some recollection of him. He may live to be as old as Mr. W. himself without ever meeting any man whose image would be so worth retaining." To Stephen, therefore, no duty could have been more welcome than the duty of "coaching" the new Minister; and the final outcome of their collaboration was certainly at least as much Stephen's work as Stanley's.

The scheme, expounded by Stanley on May 14 in a long and moving speech, was drastic and direct. Once for all he rejected the plea that the colonial legislatures could be trusted to do their duty. His review of their past record was as damning as even Buxton could have desired. But his plan of emancipation was not quite the same as Buxton's. He objected to the enfranchisement of all children born after a fixed date, on the ground that a young generation of freed negroes could not live beside an old generation of slaves. He proposed instead an emancipation of all existing slaves in a year's time, to be followed by twelve years of apprentice-ship to their former masters. Refusal to work was not to be dealt with by the masters but by specially appointed magistrates only. The planters were to be mollified by a loan of fifteen million pounds. From both sides this scheme was attacked; but Stanley was ready to placate, if not altogether to satisfy, the Abolitionists, by reducing the period of apprenticeship to seven years for field-workers and four years for the rest, and to buy off the more dangerous opposi-tion of the West Indian interest by transforming the loan into a free gift of twenty millions. These modifications ensured his triumph. On July 22 the Bill—drafted by Stephen in two days at the cost of his Sabbatarian principles and his health besides—was read a second time. On the 24th the gift of twenty millions was approved in Committee by a narrow majority of 158 to 151. On the 25th the reduction of the period of apprenticeship was agreed to without a division. The final passage of the Bill was now secure.

As it carried the noblest measure in its history the House of Commons did not forget the man who had done most to educate his country up to it. "When Mr. Wilberforce hears of it," said

Stanley himself, in the course of these debates, "he may well exclaim, ' Lord now lettest Thou Thy servant depart in peace.' " And, of course, the news of the successive stages of the Bill was quickly carried to Cadogan Place. "Thank God," said the old crusader on the 25th, "that I should have lived to witness a day in which England is willing to give twenty millions sterling for the abolition of Slavery!" It was, in truth, his *Nunc Dimittis*. "Mr. Wilberforce is very poorly," reported the younger Stephen on the 26th. "I do not think he can last long." Next morning he seemed better. He read the family prayers with something like his usual fervency, and talked to the old servant, who wheeled him out in his invalid chair, with something like his usual animation. But he was taken ill again that night; and next day, Sunday, he had an alarming succession of fainting fits. In the evening, in an interval of consciousness, "I am in a very distressed state," he said to his son. "Yes," replied Henry, "but you have your feet on the Rock." "I do not venture to speak so positively, but I hope I have." He did not speak again. There was one deep sigh, and, about three o'clock on the Monday morning, he died.

On the news of his death a letter was addressed to his son, requesting that he might be buried in Westminster Abbey. "I am authorised to add," wrote Brougham, "that nearly all the members of both Houses of Parliament would have joined [in signing it] had the time allowed." The funeral was on August 5. The long train of mourners' carriages was accompanied from Cadogan Place to the Abbey "by immense crowds of people who flanked it, in moving columns, on either side." The body was laid near those of Pitt and Fox and Canning.

A year later, at midnight on July 31, 1834, eight hundred thousand slaves became free. It was more than a great event in African or in British history. It was one of the greatest events in the history of mankind.

REFERENCES

THE references to the *Life of Wilberforce* by his two sons, Robert and Samuel (2nd ed., 1839), are mostly references to quotations from Wilberforce's diary. The present writer was kindly allowed by the late Mr. H. W. W Wilberforce to read the portion of the diary in his possession, and he found that practically every item of interest or importance had been quoted in the *Life*. He is also indebted to the late Mrs. A. M. Wilberforce for permitting the full reproduction of a letter of Pitt's from her *Private Papers of William Wilberforce* (1897).

CHAPTER I

SECTION 1.—R. and S. Wilberforce, *Life of Wilberforce*, i., 53-63.

SECTION 2.—*Life*, i., 1-17. Holland Rose, *Life of William Pitt*, i. (London, 1912), chaps. iii.-iv.

SECTION 3.—MS. Diary, 1783-5. *Life* i., 13-79. *Private Papers of William Wilberforce* (ed. A. M. Wilberforce, London, 1897), 8-9. *Hansard*, xxii. (1781), 800, 1042 ; xxiii. (1782), 439-41, 1247; xxiv. (1783), 50, 312, 485-7, 702-5, 977, 1004; xxv. (1785), 462-3, 651-6. G. S. Veitch, *The Genesis of Parliamentary Reform* (London, 1913), chap. iv.

SECTION 4.—MS. Diary, 1783-5. *Life*, i., chaps. ii. and iii. J. S. Harford, *Recollections of Wilberforce* (London, 1865), 205, 210.

SECTION 5.—MS. Diary. *Life*, i., chap. ii. *Private Papers*, 3-6, 10-11. *The Correspondence of William Wilberforce* (ed. R. and S. Wilberforce, London, 1840), i. 1-2, 4-5. Harford, 202. Holland Rose, *Pitt*,.i, 95, 282.

CHAPTER II

SECTION 1.—MS. Diary, 1784-5. *Life*, i., chaps i.-iv ; v., 53. Harford, chap. iv. *D. N. B.* "Isaac Milner," "John Newton." Sir James Stephen, *Essays in Ecclesiastical Biography* (London, 1860), 400-13.

SECTION 2.—*Life*, i., chaps. v.-vii; iii., 4; iv., 154; v., 149-50. *Correspondence*, i., 50-1. Harford, 216. J. J. Gurney, *Familiar Sketch of the late William Wilberforce* (1838), 10. *D. N. B.* "Hannah More."

SECTION 3.—*Life*, i., 94-5, 113, 158-9, 191, 204, 210, etc. *Private Papers*, 12-15. Cf. Lord Rosebery's Preface to the privately printed edition of Pitt's letters.

CHAPTER III

SECTION 1.—*Life*, i., 78, 114, 130-8; ii., 9, 24, 446-7. *Hansard*, xxvi. (1786-8), 440-4. *Memoirs of Romilly* (London, 1840), i., 90, 334. S. Smith, *Works* (London, 1840), iv., 84-100.

SECTION 2.—*Life*, v., 340-1. *Hansard*, xxv. (1785-6) 1408-9; xxvi. (1786), 59-60, 101-13. *Warren Hastings' Papers* (ed. Forrest), vol. i. Gleig, *Life of Hastings*, vol. ii. C. C. Davies, *Warren Hastings and Oudh* (Oxford, 1939). Rose, *Pitt*, i., chap. x.

SECTION 3.—For the Slave-Trade, see *Report of the Lords of the Committee of Council . . . concerning the present state of the Trade to Africa and particularly the Trade in Slaves*, 1789 (see p. 100 above); Wilberforce's speeches and writings (cited above); T. Clarkson, *History of the Abolition of the Slave-Trade* (London, 1808); Bryan Edwards, *History of the British West Indies* (London, 1819); F. W. Pitman, *The Development of the British West Indies, 1700-1763* (Newhaven, U.S.A., 1917); C. S. Higham, *The Leeward Islands, 1660-1668* (Cambridge, 1921); F. J. Klingberg, *The Anti-Slavery Movement in England* (London, 1926); C. M. MacInnes, *England and Slavery* (London, 1936), etc.

SECTION 4.—Godwyn, *The Negro's and Indian's Advocate*, etc. (London, 1680). Clarkson, *op. cit.*, i., chaps. ii.-v. Prince Hoare, *Memoirs of Granville Sharp* (London, 1820), chaps. i.-iv. E. C. P. Lascelles, *Granville Sharp* (London, 1928), chaps. iii.-iv. W. E. B. Du Bois,

The Suppression of the African Slave-Trade to the United States of America (Cambridge, U.S.A., 1896), chaps. ii.-v. S. H. Swinny, "The Humanitarianism of the 18th Century" in *The Western Races and the World* (ed. Marvin, Oxford, 1922). Lecky, *History of England in the 18th Century* (Cabinet edition), vii., 357 ff.

SECTION 5.—*Life*, i., chap. vi. *Hansard*, xxiii. (1789-91), 41-67. Clarkson, i., chaps. vii.-x. E. L. Griggs, *Thomas Clarkson* (London, 1936), 1-36. *Memoirs of G. Sharp*, 229-39. Harford, 138-9. *D. N. B.* "T. Clarkson."

CHAPTER IV

SECTION 1.—*Life*, i., 151-66. Clarkson, i., chaps. xiv.-xxii. *Journal and Correspondence of Lord Auckland* (London, 1861), i., 266-7, 269, 277, 304-8. Holland Rose, *Pitt*, i., 459-60.

SECTION 2.—*Life*, 167-84.

SECTION 3.—*Life*, i., 171-3. Clarkson, i., 504-60. *Hansard*, xxvii. (1788-9), 495-506, 576-99, 638-52. *Memoirs of Sir N. W. Wraxall* (London, 1884), v., 146, 149.

SECTION 4.—*Life*, i., chaps. vii. and viii. Clarkson, ii. 12-20. *Report of the Lords of the Committee of Council, &c.* (1789).

SECTION 5.—*Hansard*, xxviii. (1789-91), 41-67.

SECTION 6.—*Life*, i., chap. vii. *Hansard*, xxviii. (1789-91), 68-101. Clarkson, ii., 40-118.

SECTION 7.—*Life*, i. 265-308. *Hansard*, xxviii. (1789-91), 311-15, 711-14; xxix. (1791-2), 250-359. Clarkson, ii. 212-338.

CHAPTER V

SECTION 1.—*Life*, i., 229-32. Clarkson, i., 446, 466, 492-3, 500; ii., 118-66. Griggs, chap. iii. Bryan Edwards, *History of the British West Indies* (London, 1819), vol. iii. T. Southey, *Chronological History of the West Indies* (London, 1827), iii. 33-7, 40-7. M. Rainsford, *The Black Empire of Hayti* (London, 1805), chap. iii. De Poyen, *Histoire Militaire de St. Domingue* (Paris, 1899), 1-15.

SECTION 2.—*Life*, i. 333-69. Clarkson, ii. 188-92, 346-55. Griggs, 71. G. M. Trevelyan, *British History in the 19th Century* (London, 1922), 51. T. Southey, *op. cit.*, iii. 50, 71.

SECTION 3.—*Life*, i., 326, 345-6. *Hansard* xxix. (1791-2), 1055-1158. Pitt's *Speeches* (1806 ed.), 50-82. Clarkson, ii., 355-448.

SECTION 4.—*Life*, i., 344-53. *Hansard*, xxix. (1792-3), 1204-93, 1349-55. Clarkson, ii. 451-60. Holland Rose, *Pitt*, i., 471-2.

CHAPTER VI

SECTION. 1.—*Life*, ii., 1-13. *Hansard*, xxx. (1793-4), 79-80.

SECTION 2.—*Life*, ii., 28-9, 45-7, 59-70, 391. *Hansard*, xxxi. (1794-5), 1016-27, 1230-8. Pitt's *War Speeches* (3rd ed. Oxford, 1940), 116-34. Fortescue, *British Statesmen of the Great War*, 94, 103-4. Rose, *Pitt*, ii., chap ix. Stanhope and Gooch, *Life of Stanhope*, chap. viii.

SECTION 3.—*Life*, ii. 72;80, 102, 434-7. *Farington Diary* (London, 1923), i. 85. Historical MSS. Commission, 15th Report, vii. 365.

SECTION 4.—*Life*, ii. 85-233. *Hansard*, xxxii. (1795-7), 1-36, 292-5, 304. Pitt's *War Speeches*, 137. Holland Rose, ii., chap. xiii.

SECTION 5.—*Life*, ii., 136-96, 211-20. *Hansard*, xxxii. (1795-7), 1252-6.

SECTION 6.—*Life*, i. 356-7; ii., 17-23, 48-55. Clarkson, ii., 462-71. *Hansard*, xxx. (1793-4), 513-20, 652-60, 948-9. Harford, 141. For the Clarkson controversy, see Clarkson's *Strictures on a Life of William Wilberforce* (London, 1838); Preface to the *Correspondence*, containing the biographers' reply to the *Strictures*; the editor's note in *Diary, Reminiscences, and Correspondence of Henry Crabb Robinson* (3rd ed.), ii., 209-10 and Griggs, chap. xii.

SECTION 7.—*Life*, ii., 48-51, 82-5, 133-47, 195-6, 225, 234-8. Clarkson, ii., 472-5. *Hansard*, xxx. (1793-4), 1439-49; xxxi. (1794-5), 467-70, 1321-45; xxxii. (1795-7), 737-63, 862-902; xxxiii. (1797-8), 251-94, 569-76. Holland Rose, i. 472-9; ii. 299-320.

CHAPTER VII

SECTION 1.—*Life*, i. 290, 316-17; ii., 23, 97, 165-6, 187, 315, 338, 424; iii., 97, 151; iv., 340; v., 66, 132, 135, 143. Harford, 4-7.

SECTION 2.—*Life*, ii., 33, 104, 183, 190, 198-209, 405-6. Harford, 2, 9. *Autobiography of Arthur Young* (London, 1898), 287-8. Bishop Wilson's *Introduction* to *Practical View* (6th edition, 1837).

SECTION 3.—*Life*, i., 276, 286, 315, 359; ii., 28-9, 56, 86, 99, 137, 190; iv. 277-8; v., 16, and *passim*. Byron's *Works* (1834 ed.), iii., 138 (Letter dated Oct. 31, 1815).

SECTION 4.—*Life*, i., 31-2, 279, 312, 327; ii., 143; iii., 63, 70, 191, 237, 457, 461, 467; iv., 92, 277, 390; v., 133, 199, 254, 268, 270, 285, 287, 291, 298, and *passim*. Harford, 8, 168. Sir J. Stephen, "The Clapham Sect" in *Studies in Ecclesiastical Biography*, 521-82. *Letters of the First Sir James Stephen* (privately printed, 1906), 87. J. C. Colquhoun, *William Wilberforce, his friends and his times* (London, 1866). *D. N. B. sub nom.*

SECTION 5.—*Life*, ii., 214-5, 220. Southey, *Life and Correspondence* (London, 1849-50), iv. 316-7. *Letters of William and Dorothy Wordsworth : The Middle Years* (London, 1937), 823-8; *The Later Years* (1939), 55.

CHAPTER VIII

SECTION 1.—*Life*, ii., 220-50. *Hansard*, xxxiii. (1797-8), 1089, 1203-4, 1218-26. Holland Rose, ii., chap. xv.

SECTION 2.—*Life*, ii., 358-60, 384-7; iii., 4-6; v. 36. J. L. and B. Hammond, *The Town Labourer* (London, 1925), 115-29.

SECTION 3.—*Life*, ii., 222-3, 278, 292, 297, 315-18, 324-5; iii., 2-3. *Hansard*, xxxiii (1797-8), 1507-11.

SECTION 4.—*Life*, ii., 257-65, 277-8, 329-38. *Hansard*, xxxiii. (1797-8), 1376-1415; xxxiv. (1798-1800), 518-66, 1092-1140. Clarkson, ii., 475-88.

SECTION 5.—*Life*, i., 305-7; ii., 157, 173, 233, 344. *Memoirs of Granville Sharp*, ii., 1-180. Lascelles, chap. xi. Lucas, *Historical Geography of the British Colonies*, iii., 284-91. Sir G. O. Trevelyan, *Life and Letters of Lord Macaulay*, chap. i. Lady Knutsford, *Life and Letters of Zachary Macaulay* (London, 1900), chaps. iii.-vii.

SECTION 6.—*Life*, ii., 312, 355-6, 373; iii., 16-19. *Pitt's War Speeches*, 303. *Hansard*, xxxvi. (1801-3), 140-4.

SECTION 7.—*Life*, iii., 89, 97-101, 141-61. *Hansard*, xxxvi. (1801-3), 1398-1408. *Creevey Papers* (1903 ed.), i. 15.

CHAPTER IX

SECTION 1.—*Life*, i., 369; ii., 270, 280-4, 334-5; iii., 19-21, 113, 131, 142.

SECTION 2.—*Life*, iii., 218-30. *Hansard*, iv. (1805), 255-322. *Lord Malmesbury's Diaries, etc.* (London, 1844), iv., 338, 347. *Diary and Correspondence of Charles Abbot* (London, 1861), i., 548. *Tenth Report of the Commissioners of Naval Enquiry* (in *Hansard*, iii., 1147-1212). Earl Stanhope, *Life of Pitt* (London, 1862), iv., 270-84.

SECTION 3.—*Life*, iii., 162-83; Clarkson, ii., 490-4. *Hansard*, ii. (1804), 440-75, 543-58, 613, 649-62, 779, 848, 863-75, 926-33.

SECTION 4.—*Life*, iii., 210-16. Clarkson, ii., 494-500. *Hansard*, iii. (1805), 521-2, 641-74.

SECTION 5.—*Life*, iii., 183-5, 216-17, 230-4. Rose, *op. cit.*, chap. xxiii.

SECTION 6.—*Life*, iii., 238-54. *Correspondence*, ii. 71. Holland Rose, ii., 557. The "Sketch of Pitt" is printed in *Private Papers*.

SECTION 7.—*Life*, iii., 255-74. Clarkson, ii., 501-68. Rogers, *Table Talk*, 82. *Hansard*, vi. (1806), 597-9, 805, 917-19, 1021-5; vii. (1806), 31-4, 227-36, 580-603, 801-9, 1143-5.

SECTION 8.—*Life*, iii., 272-305. Clarkson, ii., 569-80. *Hansard*, viii. (1806-7), 257-9, 431-2, 468-9, 601, 613-18, 657-72, 677-83, 691-3, 701-3, 717-22, 829-38, 940-95, 1040-53; ix. (1807), 59-66, 114-40, 146. *Statutes*, 47 Geo. III., cap. xxxvi.

CHAPTER X

Section 1.—*Life*, iii., 315-35, 372, 458, 486-7, 526-7; iv., 158-67, 265; v., 232. Harford, 47. *Diary and Letters of Mme. d'Arblay* (1905 ed.), vi., 93-4.

Section 2.—*Life*, ii., 57; iii., 307, 344-8, 426-8, 433, 458, 518; iv., 5-9, 17, 23-7, 37-40, 184-5. *Correspondence*, i, 241-2. *Hansard*, xxi. (1812), 788-91, 1150-1; xxvii. (1813-14), 834-64.

Section 3.—*Life*, iii., 300, 307-11, 362, 408, 444-53; iv., 94-9. *Hansard*, xi. (1803), 602-4; xiv. (1804), 734-6, 979; xvii. (1810), 776-7; xxiv. (1812-13), 1238-41. *Report of Committee on Woollen Manufacture*, July 4, 1806.

Section 4.—*Life*, iii., 469-78, 529-44; iv., 53-70, 83, 91-2, 138-9, 205, 363.

Section 5.—*Life*, i., 257-60; ii., 251, 360-5; iii., 91-2, 407, 510-12, 536, 553; iv., 128-9. E. A. Walker, *History of South Africa* (London, 1940), 154-6. Sir G. Cory, *The Rise of South Africa* (London, 1910), i., chap. 7, etc.

Section 6.—*Life*, ii., 24-8; iii., 350-3, 359; iv., 11-22, 101-26. Harford, 26-30. *Hansard*, xxvi. (1813), 831-72, 1054-79. Ilbert, *The Government of India* (Oxford, 1922), 73-9. A. Mayhew, *Christianity and the Government of India* (London, 1929), chap. vii.

Section 7.—*Life* iii., 360, 374, 382-5, 434, 459, 483, 505, 514, 546-7; iv., 3, 19, 75, 132-7, 173-92. *Correspondence*, ii., 284-6, 295. *Hansard*, xxvii. (1813-14), 1078-82. *Memoirs of G. Sharp*, ii. W. E. B. Du Bois, *The Suppression of the African Slave Trade* (Cambridge, U.S.A., 1896), chap. viii.

Section 8.—*Life*, iv., 192-267. *Hansard*, xxviii. (1814), 267-97, 438-42. C. K. Webster, *British Diplomacy, 1813-15* (London, 1921), Nos. cxx., cxxix., cliii.

CHAPTER XI

Section 1.—*Life*, iv., 244-9, 277, 308, 319-29, 373. *Hansard*, xxx. (1815), 116-18; xxxvi. (1817), 1109-43, 1246-9; xxxvii. (1818), 363-6, 375, 850-61. J. L. and B. Hammond, *The Skilled Labourer* (London, 1920), 372-4.

Section 2.—*Life*, v., 34-46. *Hansard*, xli. (1819-20), 135-6, 319-22, 800-2. H. A. Bruton, *Story of Peterloo* (John Rylands Library Bulletin, October, 1919, and separately printed).

Section 3.—*Hansard*, xxxviii. (1818), 709-14. Hazlitt, *The Spirit of the Age* (London, 1825). Wallas, *Life of Francis Place* (1918), 147. Melville, *Life and Letters of Cobbett* (1913), i., 154-68; ii., 106-7. J. L. and B. Hammond, *The Town Labourer* (1925), 127-9, 221-46. Mathieson, *England in Transition* (1920), 153-5.

Section 4.—*Life*, i., 131; ii., 171-2; iii., 44-5, 440; iv., 256, 368-70, 376; v., 12-15, 48. *Hansard*, xxxv. (1817), 346; xxxvi. (1817), 925, 1157; xxxviii. (1818), 171; xxxix. (1819), 396, 452, 484, 828, 977, 1079; xl., (1819), 379; v. (N. S., 1821), 964. *Greville Memoirs* (London, 1896), i., 17. Mathieson, *England in Transition*, 117-19, 181-2, 213-14, 267-9. Hammond, *The Town Labourer*, chap. vii.

Section 5.—*Life*, v., 54-88. *Correspondence*, ii., 435. *Hansard*, i. (1820), 1390-2. Melville, *Life and Letters of William Cobbett*, ii., 148-57. *Diary and Letters of Mme. d'Arblay*, vi., 386-7. Spencer-Walpole, *History of England from 1815* (1914 ed.), ii., chap. vi.

Section 6.—*Life*, iv., 315, 349; v. 16, 73, 95-6. *Private Papers*, 264-6. *Hansard*, xli. (1819), 913; i. (1820), 1062-3; iv. (1821), 883-5, 1290-2; v. (1821), 356-8; vii. (1822), 1651-2. Hazlitt, *Spirit of the Age* (1825), 359. Stuart Reid, *Life and Letters of Lord Durham* (1906), i., 129-31. G. M. Trevelyan, *Lord Grey of the Reform Bill* (1920), 188.

CHAPTER XII

Section 1.—*Life*, iv., 284-5, 320, 330; v., 1-10, 121, 136-7, 152-3. *Hansard*, xxxvii. (1818), 67-80, 232-60; v. (1821), 1331-2. T. F. Buxton, *The African Slave Trade and its Remedy* (London, 1840), chap. ii. W. E. B. Du Bois, *The Suppression of the African Slave Trade to the United States of America* (Cambridge, U.S.A., 1896), chaps. ix. and xi. W. L. Mathieson, *Great Britain and the Slave Trade* (London, 1929), 1-74.

Section 2.—*Life*, iv., 239-63, 283-8, 304-7. *Hansard*, xxxi. (1815), 772-85, 1132-3; xxxiv. (1816), 722, 1151-68; xxxvi. (1817), 1321-36; xxxviii. (1818), 294-323, 1201-7; xl. (1819), 1542-7; v. (1821), 1325-34. *Life and Letters of Sir Gilbert Elliot* (London, 1874), i. 401.

Bryan Edwards, *History of the British West Indies* (London, 1819), v. 102-7; see also v. 96-201 for an abstract of the laws respecting slaves passed by the West Indian legislatures from 1788 to 1817. W. L. Mathieson, *British Slavery and its Abolition* (London, 1926), 26.

SECTION 3.—*Life*, iv., 352-61; v., 1-5, 31, 42, 82-4. Bryan Edwards, *op. cit.* v., 129-207. J. W. Vandercook, *Black Majesty* (New York, 1928). The philanthropists' high opinion of Christophe's ability and character is confirmed by an account of him by J. Clarke, written for Castlereagh and based on personal acquaintance. It is printed in Historical MSS. Commission, *Bathurst MSS.*, 58 ff.

SECTION 4.—*Life*, v., 128-31, 154-80. Wilberforce's *An Appeal, &c.* (London, 1823). *Memoirs of Sir T. F. Buxton* (London, 1849), 125-7. *Hansard*, vii. (1822), 1783-95; viii. (1823), 624-30; ix. (1823), 257-360. Mathieson, *British Slavery, etc.*, chap. ii.

SECTION 5.—*Life*, v., 200-23. *Hansard*, x. (1824), 1046-1198; xi. (1824), 961-1076, 1206-1313, 1406-27. Mathieson, *British Slavery, etc.*, chap. ii. The authorities confirm the accuracy of Spencer Walpole's account of John Smith's case, *History of England since 1815*, iii., 398-402.

SECTION 6.—*Life*, iv., 373; v., 223-47.

CHAPTER XIII

SECTION 1.—*Life*, iv., 229, 272, 299; v. 27, 50, 109, 248-53, 272-98, 314-15. *Letters of the First Sir James Stephen* (privately printed, 1906), 33-4.

SECTION 2.—*Life*, v., 249, 262-3, 317-18. *Private Papers*, 258-9, 271-3. *Hansard*, xxv. (1830), 1171-92. Harford, 230-2. *Greville Memoirs*, ii., 128. Colquhoun, *Wilberforce and his Friends*, 375.

SECTION 3.—*Life*, v., chaps. xxxviii., xxxix.

SECTION 4.—*Life*, v., 352-78. *Hansard*, xvii. (1833), 1193-1262; xviii. (1833), 112-66, 204-36, 308-60, 458-509, 515-53, 573-98; xix. (1833), 1056-69, 1184-1220, 1234-42, 1252-70. Harford, 241, 248. *Buxton Memoirs*, 329-43. *Autobiography of Henry Taylor* (London, 1885), i. 130-7. *Letters of the First Sir J. Stephen*, 16-17, 28, 31. *Annual Register*, 1833, Chronicle, 114-15. Walpole, *History of England since 1815*, iii., 410-13.

INDEX

123